The Wild Wild West, the Series

First Edition
Copyright 1988, Arnett Press
ISBN #0-929360-00-1 (1988)

eBook .pdf Edition
Copyright 2008, Arnett Press & Susan E. Kesler
ISBN # 978-0-929360-02-7

POD 2nd Edition
Copyright 2018, Arnett Press & Susan E. Kesler
ISBN # 97801984030436

Published by
Arnett Press (1988) Downey, CA 90241
Marketing Agent and Editor (1988): Judith F. Donner

Originally Printed in the United States of America
by California Offset Printing, Glendale, California (1988)
Color separations and preparation by Graphic Depot, Santa Fe Springs, California (1988)
Assisted by Tracy Castle, Orange, California (1988)

Cover design modified from original artwork provided by CBS
Entertainment and Viacom International (1988 & 2008)

Original text layout and design by Judith F. Donner (1988)
Assisted by Micro Solutions, Inc. Los Angeles, California (1988)

Text layout, redesign, editing by Jude Bradley (2008 & 2018)
Special appreciation to Terry Flores and Glenda Tamblyn (2008 & 2018)

THE WILD WILD WEST — THE SERIES

by Susan E. Kesler

Dedication

With his warm smile, he touched our hearts.
With his inimitable grin, he made us laugh.
His love for life, family and friends showed us
a man of unselfish nobility.

For all that he was,
I dedicate this book to the memory of Ross Martin.

Thanks, Artie

Foreword
By Bruce Lansbury

Here, in Los Angeles, a sorely-needed rainstorm blew into my neighborhood at 3:00 a.m. The lashing wind and water with the accompanying thunder and lightening left me wide awake, haunted by nocturnal anxieties, nagging duties left undone… like this foreword.

Twenty years, after all, is a substantial hiatus from an experience that only just lingers sweetly in my memory. How do I do justice to that memory… and what the hell is a foreword, anyway?

But then, in the tumult of the storm it occurred to me that while it was certainly a night unfit for man nor beast, there was one person who would be found abroad in all that muck. Wind-whipped, sopping wet, lashed by stinging branches and astride his skittering, magnificent black stallion, James West would indeed be squinting, slit-eyes under that flat-brimmed hat into this demonical night on his way to rescue a beautiful woman from some abhorrent fate.

As I pen these florid words, I realize that when James did rescue the girl, in all likelihood, she would accept his embrace and then, with a carnivorous smile, reach into her reticule and produce a lady's derringer and level it at him. "Love aside, now to business, Mister West." Nothing and nobody were ever quite what they appeared to be.

I think it was story editor Henry Sharpe – with a small debt to Longfellow – who first put the words into Jim West's mouth, while in the varnish car, mulling the problems of a particularly complex case: "Things, Artemus, are not always what they appear to be." This admonition was quickly embroidered and framed by set decorator Raymond Molyneaux and forevermore hung over the desk at story conferences so that we would not soon forget to do the unexpected.

Thus Jim's world was one of two-faced villainy, male and female, countless Mickey Finns and needle-tipped Baroque pinkie rings that put him to sleep even as he embraced their dispensers. There were the inevitable trap doors; hotel walls that ground their victims to dust or revolved into lush Aubrey Beardsley settings next door; lethal chairs that tossed their occupants skyward or alternatively dumped them into dank sewer systems that subterraneously crisscrossed countless cow towns of the period. And then there was the old Dutch sea captain, leaning on the corner of the swill-hole of a bar, who inexplicably winked at him as he entered… Artemus, of course, in one of his thousand disguises. What a joy and privilege to work on such a series!

It was initially sold to the network as "James Bond in the West," describing an undercover operative of the 1880s who carried an arsenal of lethal weapons in his hat, up his sleeve, in the heel of his boot and elsewhere. It was called a gimmick show, and while the notion of a Bondian Western was certainly a useful handle, it quickly became much more than that. Grounded in the West of myth and lore, and always reliant on imaginative stunts and violent action, it was also a series of imagination, fantasy, Jules Verne sci-fi and romance. It was truly an artful comic strip.

Classics of literature, film and contemporary science were shamelessly commandeered as their elements were submerged and made over in a style that was, and still is, unique to television. We sought words and images to convey that style… baroque, rococo, outré. Tiffany hues, rich crimson and forest green, all lit in the mystery of chiaroscuro. Hence, it was no accident that the episode titles all began with "The Night of…"

The series' life was too brief. With a share of audience in the mid-thirties, contrary to what anybody else will tell you it was taken off the air ostensibly for being too violent. In truth it was a sacrificial lamb to certain Capitol Hill powers that were making political hay out of the "sex and violence on television" issue. No matter. The series stands by itself, and I welcome this book as a record of a very fulfilling and enjoyable personal career period; and for the fact that it serves as a salute to the many talents who contributed to the fun and games that made, "The Wild Wild West" the memorable series that it was, and is today.

Bruce Lansbury

5

Table of Contents

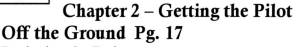

Oh, My Aching…
Ross, the Not So Stuntman
After Hours – The Backstage Bar
Better, Better, Perfect
Boxing vs. Kung Fu
Acts of Violence
End of an Era

From the Author's Collection

CBS Photos

CBS Photo

CBS Photos

CBS Photo

CBS Photo

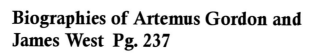
Photo Courtesy Dick Cangey

Editor's Note: Although every effort has been made to present an accurate depiction of the CBS Television Network's corporate structure during the period between 1963 and 1970, obviously there have been substantial changes over the past 20 (now 40) years. Positions have been created and/or eliminated and the ownership of the network itself has changed. Therefore, any errors or omissions with regards to the network structure and conditions of CBS during this period are completely unintentional.

CBS Photo

Introduction
By Susan E. Kesler

In 1966 I fell in love with two very special men. Although I was only seven years old at the time, from the moment they caught my eye, my Friday nights were booked. Since then, they have both been a very big part of my life. It has been a wonderful relationship that has lasted more than 20 (now 40) years.

It all started on a particular Friday evening in 1966 when I met my two soon-to-be favorite heroes, James T. West and his partner Artemus Gordon. Although they had already made their television debut one year earlier, it took time for me to discover their charms. As it turned out, they were beyond my wildest dreams: handsome, dapper, suave, and yet, amusing. Skilled in the arts of adventure and romance, the two swept me away with wild enthusiasm. And why not, since they were the integral part of "The Wild Wild West."

James Bond of the 1870s was the concept that placed James T. West on his private railroad car, The Wanderer, traveling with his associate, Artemus Gordon, across the plains of the rural West, combining spy intrigue with a Western flair, a dash of comedy and, of course, adventure and romance.

And "wild" it was, as every deranged villain and wicked madman ever to stalk the earth rose from the imaginations of the series' creators. Appropriately accompanying the excitement were the most bizarre devices and gadgetry ever invented, most well ahead of their time. West and Gordon were Washington's two finest Secret Service agents under special assignment to President Ulysses S. Grant: Between them they kept the world safe from potential evil.

Some of my favorite episodes featured Dr. Miguelito Loveless (Michael Dunn) as a dwarf-sized madman with a gigantic rage against the world and, most particularly, James West. The evil doctor delighted in creating new and fiendishly diabolical ways to destroying Jim, Artie and society. Loveless failed every time, but not until after a fair match with the pair, leading to his invariable escape, and eventual return in some future episode.

Part of what made the show special for me was the great friendship between Jim and Artie. They were a team in every sense of the word. Combining their talents and respecting each other's capabilities made them able to depend on one another, even in the most desperate situations, and against the greatest criminal minds of all time. Together, they created small-screen magic that lasted four years. Even today the magic continues as "West" still plays in reruns and has recently been released on DVD.

Photo by Jeanne Kesler

Susan Kesler and her "Wild Wild West" birthday cake.

People like me who watched the show in its first run are now considerably older and, also like me, are enjoying the show even more, along with a new generation who is having the pleasure of meeting Jim and Artie for the first time.

So sit back in the saddle and hang on to the reins because you're in for the wildest ride that the "West" has ever had to offer.

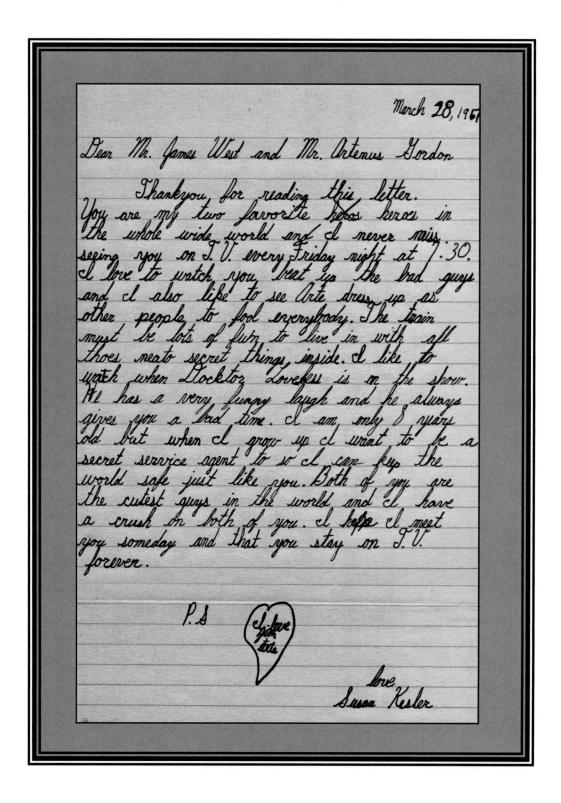

March 28, 1967

Dear Mr. James West and Mr. Artemus Gordon

Thankyou, for reading this, letter.
You are my two favorite ~~heros~~ heroes in the whole wide world and I never miss seeing you on T.V. every Friday night at 7:30. I love to watch you beat up the bad guys and I also like to see Arte dress up as other people, to fool everybody. The train must be lots of fun, to live in with all thoes neato secret things, inside. I like to watch when Dlocktoz Loveless is on the show. He has a very funny laugh and he always gives you a bad time. I am, only 8 years old but when I grow up I want to be a secret service agent to so I can keep the world safe just like you. Both of you are the cutest guys in the world and I have a crush on both of you. I hope I meet you someday and that you stay on T.V. forever.

P.S

I love you Arte

love
Susan Kesler

Chapter 1
How the West Was Won by CBS

The Idea for the Pilot

In 1965, television took a new turn in programming, intending to cash in on the current James Bond craze. What developed was a sudden trend of secret agent and spy shows that literally controlled the prime-time airwaves. The Western format that was so prominent in the 1950s and early 1960s was virtually being pushed aside, making way for intrigue, espionage and adventure.

One of the earliest catalyst shows in the James Bond syndrome was "The Man from U.N.C.L.E." Debuting in 1964, "U.N.C.L.E." was true to the concept of spy adventure and hence became extremely popular with the television viewing audience. The popularity of "U.N.C.L.E.'s" suave Napoleon Solo (Robert Vaughn) and his charming European partner Illya Kuryakin (David McCallum) prompted television producers to continue to develop the evident spy trend. The fall lineup started to look like a call sheet from international espionage featuring NBC's "I Spy" with Robert Culp and Bill Cosby. For crime fighting with a feminine twist ABC formulated "Honey West," starring Anne Francis. An ideal illustration of the '65-'66 spy trend was "Amos Burke, Secret Agent." The program originated in 1963 as "Burke's

Law" and starred Gene Barry as the Los Angeles police chief. Anxious to take part of the hot spy trend in the making, and bucking NBC's popular "I Spy," ABC completely altered the format of the show, re-imagining the character Burke (Barry) as a secret agent and cleaning house of all the series' regulars except for the star. One of television's most successful situation comedies of the era was NBC's "Get Smart," starring Don Adams, which took a more amusing look at the spy world.

Michael Garrison started his Hollywood career as an actor, but later became an associate producer working on several hit motion pictures such as "Peyton Place, The Long Hot Summer," and "An Affair to Remember." Garrison went on to produce such popular feature films as "Dark at the Top of the Stairs," and "The Crowded Sky." Although a seasoned producer, Garrison's first television venture came with the creation of "The Wild Wild West." In 1956, 10 years prior to the origination of the concept behind "West," Garrison and his then- partner, Gregory Ratoff, entered into a joint venture by purchasing the rights to Ian Flemming's first James Bond book, *Casino Royale*. The two intended the story as feature film material but, at the time, 20th Century Fox rejected the project, deemed as "too ahead of its time." With the project back-burnered [sic], Ratoff died suddenly and his widow, in need of finances, sold her husband's interest in the project. Garrison soon followed by relinquishing his half to the new owners, but evidently his interest in "Bondian intrigue" remained.

The Proposal

After acquiring several producer credits, Garrison saw the excitement behind television's new Bond Craze and decided to try a little trend mixing. Bringing together the already popular Western with the rapidly becoming popular spy trend, Garrison had the groundwork for James Bond set in the Wild West. Conveniently at the same time, Garrison's close friend, Hunt Stromberg, Jr., was head of programming at CBS. Garrison presented Stromberg with the idea of doing James Bond on a horse and Stromberg liked the concept: It had that certain flair about it, followed the current trend and yet maintained originality. One evening,

Michael Garrison

while Stromberg was having dinner with CBS's associate director of program development, Ethel Winant, he told her about this innovative concept which he'd been presented.

"Hunt wanted to do a show about James Bond in the West," she said. "He told me that when I got back to California he wanted me to write out a couple of pages of a proposal." Winant admitted that at first she wasn't sure what Stromberg was talking about and she thought he'd forget about this silly notion. But he didn't forget. "When I got back to California, Peter Robinson, my boss, who was head of program development, called me and said that Hunt told me to do something on James Bond in the West. I said, 'Yeah, that's about it.' So he said, 'We'll do it... just write it out!' I made up this sort of thing about President Grant and after the Civil War there were these terrible international spies. So we had these secret agents like Jim West, Tom East, Sam South and Hal North. Anyway, all the others got lost very soon, but Jim West remained. He would report only to the president. He worked with the classy Secret Service and used all these secret devices. So I wrote this thing up and I thought it was okay. Hunt Stromberg wanted to do it, and he could do anything he wanted to because he was head of programming."

The Writer

The proposal was enough to show Jim Aubrey, president of the CBS Television Network, that the project was worthwhile. He gave the authorization for the development of the pilot and gave Garrison the go-ahead as producer. Originally entitled "The Wild West," the pilot, "The Night of the Inferno," was written by noted television writer Gil Ralston.

Ethel Winant

"I was one of the busiest characters in the business. I was doing "Ben Casey" and half a dozen other shows at the same time. The only person who approached me was my agent who said, 'You'd better do it.' I wrote the pilot film in Mendocino where I had a house. There was nothing unusual about it. It was just a pilot film," Ralston remembered.

Ethel Winant recalled how difficult it was to get the pilot written. "It was hard because nobody knew what the show was meant to be. Was it a spoof? Well, James Bond is a spoof. Was it a Western? No, but it was in the West. It was going to be bigger than life with big villains."

In the original proposal James West did not have a partner per se.

"In the James Bond stories, Bond goes to town and sees the guy that runs this lab who makes his de-

---

'I made up this thing about President Grant and after the Civil War there were these terrible international spies. So we had these secret agents like Jim West, Tom East, Sam South and Hal North.'

— Ethel Winant

---

vices. Well, he couldn't have that if he was out in the middle of nowhere in the West. Where was he going to go? So Artemus was the traveling peddler who would make West's devices. That is what he was in the beginning: a peddler with a bag full of tricks who brought West messages and devices. That's how the Gordon character was created. But that didn't seem very sensible in the long run. You just couldn't have a wagon drive up. That was okay once, but not for a weekly series," Winant said.

It was Ralston who developed the idea to give James West the full-time partner. "We need a foil for him because James West is pretty square. We needed somebody that was pretty far out to work with. So over a period of time we developed a partner that traveled with West and could do different characters and invent devices. As I recall, Artemus came out of an early book on Greece that I owned," he said. "It was a character named 'Artemicio.' I thought it was fun."

Most of the fascinating gadgets and devices created for James West were the result of Ralston's experiences in the armed forces. "I had spent a number of years in three survival groups for the Navy, the Army and the Marines. I went to booby-trap school for a while. That was fun, really fun. A lot of those gimmicks I created for 'The Wild West' pilot came out of booby-trap school."

Meet Secret Agents West and Gordon

With the pilot script close to completion, the process of casting the lead character James West soon began.

"We cast [sic] about 400 people for Bob's part. CBS wanted a star; we couldn't get a star. If Hunt (Stromberg) had his way, we would have had Paul Newman. He wanted a major Western star. We tested actor after actor and it was hard," Ethel Winant recalled.

At the time, a new, young actor named Robert Conrad was in the midst of a film called "Young Dillinger" with up-and-coming actor Nick Adams. Conrad's agent called him about a big project at CBS, "The Wild West."

Conrad remembered, "So I rushed over at lunch and had to wait because they were auditioning 18 other actors. I was the 17th. The 18th was an actor named Skip Ward who later produced 'The Dukes of Hazzard.' John Derek, who was really worried about it, didn't show up at all. They had some good actors; people who had a lot more experience than I certainly had. Then I was waiting for my opportunity to do the scene with the actor who was playing the Artemus Gordon part and I knew that the role had already been cast."

According to Conrad, Rory Calhoun had been lined up for the part, since a friend of his was already reading the Gordon character. Calhoun did a screen test to give his friend every opportunity, but... "When they

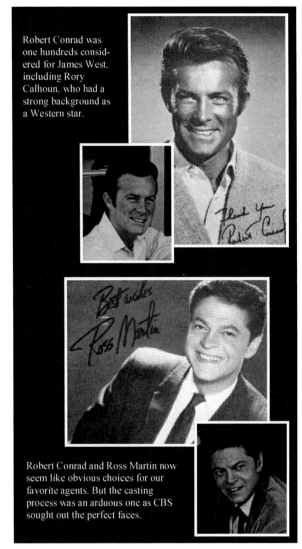

Robert Conrad was one hundreds considered for James West, including Rory Calhoun, who had a strong background as a Western star.

Robert Conrad and Ross Martin now seem like obvious choices for our favorite agents. But the casting process was an arduous one as CBS sought out the perfect faces.

saw Rory (they had hired him before they had seen him) *recently*, and (CBS) didn't think he was right for that role, so he was fired," Conrad said, and pointed out that the network chiefs changed their minds even though the costumes had already been designed to Calhoun's specifications.

Even though Conrad personified James West in many ways, CBS was faced with the slight problem of his height, coming in at just around 5 ft. 7 in., which posed a few logistical problems. Before casting could send any tests back to New York, they had to be revised. Bruce Lansbury, head of programming at CBS in New York and later became producer of the series, wrote the test before returning to New York.

A unidentified camera crew prepares a shot as Bob Conrad looks on.

Ethel Winant said, "We shot this crazy scene with a pool table. We always put Bobby in the foreground and the other actors in the background. We always used the same set, which forced perspective, and we would test people so we could have short people around. Bobby would wear a hat and have boots and lifts, and we made these very elaborate chaps to make him look taller in the tests. We figured we could probably get away with it in the show because he'd be on horse, but it was hard to do on the test."

Conrad recalled, "They made me wear these shoes that I had gotten from Warner Bros. – Alan Ladd's elevator shoes – to make me look taller. I have wider feet than Alan's so I was in a lot of pain and I felt silly in those things. I kept complaining about it and I was making network slurs, you know, 'What do these guys know?' and 'Why do I have to stand up on this stuff,' and 'Why don't they buy me as I am instead of making me two and a half inches taller than I really am?' All that was going right back on a direct feed. Then I did the scene and I probably did a real average job, but I think it was the attitude that I had prior to the opportunity to act that got me the role."

Casting did very elaborate tests to dazzle Jim Aubrey and to convince him that Conrad was taller than he actually was because Aubrey had been at ABC when Conrad did "Hawaiian Eye." The tests were

successful.

"I remember Jim (Aubrey) called me and asked, 'How tall is Bob Conrad, really?' I said, 'He's tall enough,' and Jim laughed and Bob got the part," Ethel Winant recalled.

For the rest of the series they had they had to cast around Conrad. According to Winant, they couldn't have 6 ft. 2 in. guys playing opposite him. "If he was supposed to be this great hero, he couldn't look like a child," she said.

The next character cast was Artemus Gordon. While CBS tested hundreds of actors for the James West role, there was no question as to who would play Artemus. "Ross Martin was always the choice for the role," said Winant. "CBS wanted him for the part and he wanted the part. We never had a chance to cast anyone else."

At one point, there had been some talk about using actor Pat Hinkle for the Gordon part, but CBS was impressed with Martin's ability to do dialects and different characters – exactly what the role required. Among Martin's previous experiences was the CBS-TV game show "Stump the Stars," a pantomime program that was a perfect vehicle for the actor to show off his diversity. His appearance in 1959's "Mr. Lucky," a short-lived CBS series, showed Martin as *Andamo*, the right-hand man to the owner of a plush floating casino, and further showcased his versatility. Although Martin had refused the role of Artemus Gordon four times, the actor explained in a 1965 interview that there were certain changes in the character and in his co-starring status that needed to be made before he would accept it. CBS complied, and Martin was appropriately cast as the irrepressible and unpredictable Artemus Gordon.

In that same interview, Martin illustrated his view of the newly-acquired role of Artemus Gordon. He called Gordon… "An absolute rogue; self-educated; a spellbinder; 'The Music Man' and 'The Rainmaker' rolled into one; he hates to fight, is completely amoral; has two major weaknesses – booze and women, not necessarily in that order; his aversion to fighting is not from cowardice, it's because he's a complete conman; if he can't talk a man out of it, he's failed."

14

The Director

Originally there was another director (whose identity could not be recalled) prepared to do "The Wild West" pilot. He was dismissed one day prior to filming as the result of a communication problem between him and Garrison. Richard Sarafian, one of the hottest directors in town at the time, stepped in. Sarafian had a reputation for taking shows that had script problems and turning them into nice product.

"I had worked on a series called 'The Great Adventure,' and I believe I was going to do the pilot for that. But because I was going over to 'Ben Casey' at the time, I couldn't make it. It was really sad because I wanted to do it very much. By the time I came in to do 'The Great Adventure' for CBS, the series was in trouble, but the episode that I did got good grades. I think it was a D script, but I gave it an A treatment and it came off really well," Sarafian said.

As a result, Sarafian believed, he was chosen because he was held in high esteem at CBS. "I always stood in a kind of awe or fear of the CBS people, and the networks, when I didn't know who they were. I was just an embryo director at the time, juggling things the best I could. So I don't know why or how anything was done. I just knew that people were asking for me and, after working two years at Warner Bros., they suddenly wanted me."

Garrison took an immediate liking to Sarafian and, without any preparation at all, chose him to direct the pilot. On December 16, 1964, shooting began. Sarafian recollected, "I was told to report the next day to Sonora. I was to take a plane to Sonora where we would have one day of preparation and then shoot the following day. That evening, when I told my agent that I was going to Sonora to direct the pilot, he told me I couldn't because they hadn't made a deal. So I ignored it. The next morning when I woke up everybody was yelling at me. The producers had a private plane waiting to take me to Sonora. My agent said, 'Mr. Sarafian will not leave the ground until we have a deal set.' I was told that if I didn't go to Sonora I would never work in Hollywood again. Nevertheless, a deal was made and I was able to go. The next day we started shooting."

Sarafian remember Michael Garrison as "a really creative guy." He said that Garrison was truly the *creator* of the show whether anyone was willing to admit it or not. "He (Garrison) was friends with Hunt Stromberg and Jim Aubrey, and amongst the three of them they saw this as a takeoff on the James Bond genre of filmmaking set in the Wild West. It was an ambitious pilot with a lot of detail and special effects.

"Bob Conrad was still an embryo actor. He had some experience at Warner Bros. where I first worked with him. Though he was talented in some ways, he was not as focused as he is now in his work. He's sort of grown with it and is much more settled now. In those days, he was wild. He wasn't a disciplined actor. I would have to arrive at five o'clock in the morning to go over lines together. Whether or not he liked me, I think he respected me," Sarafian said.

The pilot took 11½ days to shoot, according to Sarafian, and for three days he was "a tremendous hero."

"The film was great. They loved the stuff. I was working in the cold rain. I was getting it done and film had a great texture, feature look. It was big and moody. Then came the time, for whatever reason, they started to nitpick. Bob Conrad's belt buckle was not right, or the ashtray was wrong... something."

The director said the situation became so stressful that he would have to unwind at The Backstage Bar before returning home at the end of the day. "In one instance, I went across the street (to the bar) and sat there like a taut rubber band. I couldn't move I was so upset

Director Richard Sarafian and Robert Conrad on the set.

15

with all of these absurd things that were coming down on me. Here I was trying to do my best with no preparation. It was one o'clock in the morning and there was nobody in The Backstage. The bartender was looking at me and being very charitable in keeping the place open; very sympathetic. He just sort of leaned against the cash register as I gripped my drink.

"Suddenly, the phone rang and it was for me. It was Ethel Winant and she said, 'What's the matter, Richard? Is anything wrong?' She spoke in a soothing voice, and I couldn't understand how she knew I was there; but she knew. All I could say was, 'Ethel, if you could please keep them off my back, I'll make you a good movie.' I think that's what she did, in her own way. She was pretty strong and good woman and a good producer. I liked working with her. I could feel her strength and her support and she knew how to tap dance with the network."

Sarafian said that the following day when Stromberg and Aubrey came onto the set, he threw them off. "It wasn't that I was being mean, but I was doing a setup and they were walking right in front of me. Apparently, they took it good-naturedly [sic] because it was the next day that the network wanted to sign a long-term contract."

Sarafian said that, for unknown reasons, he was only asked to return for one more "Wild Wild West" episode, "The Night of the Thousand Eyes." He claimed that he had heard that Conrad didn't want to work with him and, when Garrison was bumped up to executive producer and restricted to watching dailies in another room, Sarafian wasn't asked to return.

"Actually, I think a lot of it had to do with the fact that Aubrey was replaced. There was a new head at CBS and he wanted his producers. It may have been something to do with Bob Conrad. It was several months later that I got a call from the network; would I come back? Would I do several more shows? The series was going off track. It didn't have the style, the format, I initially set up; and would I agree to do more? I said I would."

Richard Sarafian said he would like to have taken some of the credit for being one of the creative forces that set up the series' style. "Ross Martin was terrific and the whole concept was fun. Early on there was some competition going on between Martin and Conrad. You could sense the tension. Martin wanted to work with Conrad as an equal and not as a stooge. It was Conrad who wanted to be the boss. I think, eventually, they understood that there was a symbiotic relationship."

CBS Photo

Actor James Gregory (top) ably portrayed President Ulysses S. Grant in the pilot episode, "The Night of the Inferno."

Roy Engel (below) was later chosen for the role in the series — continuing as one of the semi-regulars.

CBS Photo   TNOT Colonel's Ghost

16

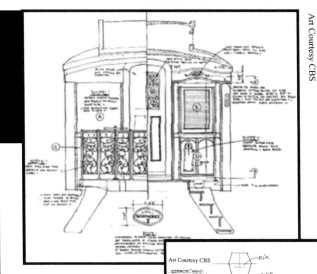

Chapter 2
Getting the Pilot off the Ground

The Train

As James Bond had his 1963 Aston Martin DB5 brimming with hidden weaponry, so, too, would James West have his preferred mode of transportation. Since the automobile was yet to debut for more than 30 years, West and his trusted associate Gordon toured the country in a specially equipped private railroad car. Like Bond, West would need his regulation array of impressive gadgets, many of which would be concocted by Gordon on board *The Wanderer*. With the proposal accepted, script written, costumes designed and casting completed, it was time for art director Al Heschong to get to work designing this very special railroad car.

The interiors were comprised of a specially constructed set at CBS Studio Center in Studio City, California. They included a coach car, kitchen, gun room and a laboratory. The combined cost of the set was $35,000 – one of the earliest indications that the uniqueness of this program would be accompanied by an equally unique price tag.

The task of designing the set was not an easy one. Among the challenges was designing a billiard table small enough to fit in the middle of a coach car.

"The train was one of the trickiest design problems on the series. They had the script written with a billiard table in there and we soon put a couple of lines on paper and realized that if you put a billiard table in a normal-sized train car you haven't got elbow room to get around. So we had to cheat on the size of the billiard table and also on the width of the car; which we made 11 feet wide instead of the normal nine," said Heschong.

The coach car was supported so that the various walls could be removed for certain angle shots and the entire structure would remain standing. The train was also put on a platform for occasions when West and Gordon would be horse-chased alongside the car.

The secret weapons soon came into play, such as two mounted pistols that could be fired by a hidden foot pedal. At the other end of the car, a panel inconspicuously hid the duo's vast gun and knife collection. The billiard table also had an ulterior purpose complete with cues that cleverly disguised a rifle and a rapier, and billiard balls that were actually bombs that either emit-

A crew member works with the train's elaborate rigging.

ted smoke or exploded.

On another table, a rack of books was actually a box that hid the frequently used telegraph the agents used to report case results and receive presidential orders. If telegraphing was not possible, the two had other means of communication via carrier pigeons Anabella, Arrabella and Henrietta. All of the train's exterior shots were those of a stock train located in Jamestown, California, which was frequently used by movie studios.

Al Heschong's film and television career began in 1955 with "The Climax Mystery Theater," (AKA "Climax!") and he worked as both production designer and art director on numerous shows. Heschong died of a cerebral hemorrhage at the age of 82 on March 1, 2001 [imdb.com].

Detail of the train interior.

The Theme Music

With the filming of the pilot finished and the first cut of the film completed, the next step was establishing the theme music for the show. CBS hired Academy Award-winner Dimitri Tiomkin and Paul Frances Webster to come up with a song for the opening of the show. What emerged from these great minds was "The Ballad of Big Jim West." The score was originally accompanied by lyrics and appeared to

be very similar to Tiomkin's other works. There proved to be a problem with the material, however, when the creative staff attempted to modernize it. After three attempts, Garrison hated it and refused to accept it. Shortly thereafter a young composer named Richard Markowitz was hired at the last minute by Garrison to come up with a theme song.

Markowitz remembered, "I was an unknown, practically, and here they had this top-of-the-line expensive talent. I had done a series, my first TV series, called 'The Rebel,' and had written a song Johnny Cash sang called 'Johnny Yuma Was a Rebel.' I guess I was hired on the basis of that being a Western, even though my background was jazz; I grew up a jazz musician. Garrison liked what he heard and hired me."

Composer Richard Markowitz during an unknown recording session.

Unfortunately, CBS did not see eye-to-eye with Garrison regarding his choice of Markowtiz and ended up paying Markowitz very little for his score.

"They didn't want to give me screen credit. Now I don't know if that was a secret deal with Tiomkin, 'cause Tiomkin was threatening to sue them. They (CBS) finally had to pay Tiomkin off and the money they paid him off with [sic] *not* to use his theme was about 10 times what they paid me just to write the score." According to Jon Burlingame of the Film Music Society, Tiomkin was paid a whopping $7,500, a significant amount at the time. Burlingame's research uncovered the original lyrics to "The Ballad of Jim West" (see page 19), which had been safely tucked away in Tiomkin's private papers.

But Markowitz didn't seem to mind. Being young and with very few credits behind him, he was happy to get the project. The Markowitz theme did not have lyrics, unlike the Tiomkin score, but it did have the tongue

Composer Richard Shores did the score for 13 "West" episodes throughout '67, '68 and '69 and was instrumental in retaining the uniqueness of the music.

-in-cheek feeling of the original. "What I did was essentially write two themes, one which had a rhythmic little contemporary feeling and, at the time, was a new sound – I used an electric bass, brushes and a vamp sound for the cartoon effects for when West was getting out of trouble; and a heraldic kind of Western/outdoor theme over that, so that the two worked together – a kind of A -B formula." Markowitz said that he tried combining jazz with Americana. "That's what nailed it. That took it away from the pseudo-serioso [sic] kind of thing that Tiomkin was trying to do. It just didn't fit the concept and I thought that the concept was, on the surface, taking itself seriously." Markowitz softened and lightened the theme in his version, added a little more imagination and made it not as serious as Tiomkin's rendition.

With Markowitz's score written and the orchestra hired, everything was ready to go in the morning. Then the head of CBS network told the head of the music department that he wanted to pass judgment on what the composer had written.

Markowitz remembered, "I went over to the head of the music department, who was then Lude Gluskin, and I sat in his office to cool my heels. Two hours of waiting for the big executive to come down and I had nothing to show him except to play the theme on this little upright piano. I had already written it and it was too late to change anyway. He finally came and so I was really sweating it out. He was followed by four underlings who all sat down and said, 'Let's hear it,' like they were in a hurry. They made me feel like nothing. So I said, 'Here is the concept. I feel that it's not a traditional Western. Not only do we want to get some

sort of Americana feeling, but we also want to get a spoofy [sic] kind of feeling, which is my B theme and then my A theme is this.' I played the B theme first, which is the rhythmic pattern for his (West's) schtick; whenever he goes to do his tricks; escape things and all that. Then the main theme is the American type thing. Now the two can work together and I'm playing and doing rather poorly on the piano.

"I stopped finally, going through it two times, and there was deadly silence. I said, 'Of course I can play it this way for a love scene,' and I played it a different way. I just kept faking it and all these guys were waiting for him (Gluskin) to say something and finally he said, 'Yeah, I like it,' and immediately after he said that everybody else chimes in, 'Yes, it has a very expansive… etc.' and all echoing this guy like kissing his ass. I think that the whole exercise was meaningless, but I was scared to death. Garrison was very pleased. After the pilot I got involved in other shows later on, but didn't do as many as I'd liked to have done. 'The Wild Wild West' is my favorite of all the themes I've written."

For the first season, Richard Markowitz came up with some very creative ideas for music for each

The Ballad of Jim West
Sing me a song of the good companions
Tell me a tale of the tall, tall men,
Riding the wind on the snow-white stallions.
When will we see their like again?
Sing me a song of the distant canyons,
Men who could climb to the eagle's nest,
Men with their eyes on the far, far horizons.
Such was the man they called Jim West.
— *Dimitri Tiomkin*

Photo and lyrics courtesy of Jon Burlingame and The Film Music Society

character. The Artemus Gordon character also had a theme. "When the audience knows he is in disguise and he's hanging around or snooping; that's when I used his theme. We knew it was Artie, but I would disguise his theme in character, so if he was playing a Chinese guy I'd play it Oriental; a lot of creative fun."

Markowitz particularly liked the episodes with Michael Dunn, "… because of the type of character he played. I had a lot of different sounds to work with a certain evilness and childlike attitudes; special Loveless traits. A lot of music was involved with him."

Markowitz felt that "The Wild Wild West" boosted his career, but a personal problem that started in 1965 kept him from working for the show beyond the middle of 1966. He also had some problems finishing his assignment. It was then that Morton Stevens, the new head of the CBS music department, took over and the theme music morphed into a more fully orchestrated version.

"Morton Stevens decided he wanted to change things and didn't consult me. A lot of times, when composers are writing, they would do variations on it in order not to pay me my share; they would do their own approach on the show. It got changed more and more as it went on. Plus nobody used my character themes very much after I left," Markowitz recalled. Although Markowtiz's career started in 1958, he does credit much of his success to Michael Garrison and recognizes his good fortune to be picked for "The Wild Wild West" project. He went on to work on such notable programs as "Mission Impossible," "The F.B.I.," "Mannix," "Quincy, M.E." and "Murder, She Wrote," among dozens of others. He passed on December 6, 1994.

The Costuming

With casting complete, the director selected and music in the making, the development of the wardrobe and costuming for the unusual protagonists had to be considered. Since the series was not an ordinary Western, CBS felt the costumes needed a different look – something totally unique to the characters. Conrad

The Main Title sequence was as innovative as the rest of the "West," illustrating a mini-drama with every show opening.

Art Courtesy of CBS

remembered, "They bought out Rory Calhoun and then I walked in after getting the role and they had all of Calhoun's clothes. He was considerably taller than I, and considerably larger. It was sort of funny and the clothes were more Western and the wardrobe woman said, 'No, I think for this man we'll go a different way.' That's how the clothes were designed." Editor's Note: According to the various sources, Calhoun was 6'3" and Conrad 5'7", a obvious and notable difference.

Along with a new look Conrad felt that the West costume reflected his own personal style. He said he had always been involved in the arts of bull fighting and Flamenco dancing. "When the designer put those clothes on me; the high-tailored vest and the tight pants; she was responsible for creating an extension of what I was going to do, 'cause I'd walk around and I'd make passes at women and I'd ride high on my horse (which was an extraordinary animal), and pretend that I was a Portuguese matador. I studied Flamenco dancing before I did "The Wild West," and I lived in Spain. So I said, 'Now here's character! They've given me a Flamenco costume so why don't I embellish it?' I did and it worked."

The Main Title Animation

CBS decided to take an equally unique approach to the pilot's main title. The main title is an entertaining series of short film clips showing the audience what the show has to offer, listing who the stars are and often listing the producer. The question was whether to take the live action or animated approach. Only a few television programs, such as

"Bewitched," "I Dream of Jeannie," "Batman" and "The Flintstones" used an animated title. So now CBS decided to go with an animated format. The animation company chosen to do the animation work was DePatie-Freleng. Owned by David DePatie and Friz Freleng of the Warner Bros. cartoon fame, together they were best known for animation of the "Pink Panther" films.

The concept involved four sections with one oblong box in the middle. Each section had its own figure inside: a bandit that had just robbed a bank, a card cheat attempting to lift an ace from his boot, a hand reaching for a gun, and a not-so-innocent looking woman that pulls a knife on our

> Only a few television programs, such as "Bewitched," "I Dream of Jeannie," "Batman" and "The Flintstones" used an animated title.

hero. The lone cowboy/agent occupies the center box and with each turn defeats his opponents. The animation itself is very rough but moves quickly as our hero exits for a quick zoom in on "The Wild Wild West" title, which then scans down to a train caboose displaying the starring roles. Richard Markowtiz's theme throughout the animated sequence made for to be a quick-paced, toe-tapping entertaining main title.

The Commercial Break Artwork

The accepted procedure for commercial breaks in television at the time was to cut or fade to black and go to the commercial. But like many other aspects of the series, "The Wild Wild West" pilot went for a very different approach. At the end of an act, instead of a quick cut to a commercial, a freeze frame of the scene was taken and transformed into a rough sketch. The sketch was then dissolved into one of the four squares already established in the main title. At each commercial break, for a total of four times, a new freeze frame sketch would be placed in each square until all squares were filled; similar to putting together pieces of a puzzle.

In the pilot, Ross' credit appeared on the back of a wagon signifying his *roving peddler* status while his character was still being formulated. Note the missing "Wild."

At the close of the episode, the closing credits would run over the completed art. The company responsible for this unusual style of segueing into a commercial break was Consolidated Film Industries in Hollywood. Each year, as the show progressed, the process was modified, creating a slightly different look for each season.

21

The Night of the
Inferno

In this, the pilot episode of the series, Washington's finest Secret Service agent, Captain James T. West, is requested to go undercover as an Army deserter in order to attend a secret meeting with President Grant. There, he is told that a Mexican revolutionary named Juan Manolo (Persoff) has been looting and burning several towns in the Southwest Territory. It is up to West to stop the raids and establish peace, once again, in the region.

West travels as the dandiest dude that ever crossed the Mississippi in his private railroad car and arrives in Quemada, New Mexico, the town from where the raids seem to originate. However, upon entering his private car, complete with pool table, West is greeted by Artemus Gordon who, West soon discovers, is his partner.

After arriving in Quemada, it becomes evident that this town, too, has been recently raided by Manolo. West and Gordon decide to split up. The story follows West as he enters the only building not destroyed by fire — a store owned by a large Chinese man named Wing Fat (Buono). West soon makes his business known – that he is seeking information. Fat, always eager for business, hands him a calling card and, for a price, directs him to a woman named Lydia Monteran (Pleshette) who, coincidentally, was previously sent to prison by West.

West makes contact with Monteran, who is actually an innocent partner with Manolo in a swank gambling casino. She claims not to have any information to offer our handsome agent. Later that evening West and Gordon meet at their train. West says that he had noticed several covered wagons entering the town's cemetery. A short wagon ride and quick search leads the agents to a crypt where several wagon tracks dead end. After sliding the crypt wall aside, they discover an arsenal that Manolo and his men have been stockpiling and using against the surrounding towns. They soon realize that the crypt, which harbors enough munitions to launch a full-scale war, is hidden beneath the house where Lydia Monteran lives. They also dis-

The Pilot Episode — "The Night of the Inferno" with Robert Conrad as James T. West and Suzanne Pleshette

CBS #6501 Shooting Order 01   CBS Photos
First Air Date: 9/17/65

Directed by Richard Sarafian
Written by Gilbert Ralston

Wing Fat: Victor Buono
Juan Manolo: Nehemiah Persoff
Lydia Monteran: Suzanne Pleshette
Colonel Shear: Walter Woolf King
President Grant: James Gregory
Mei Mei: Bebe Louis
Major Dome: Alberto Morin
Bedford: Chet Stratton

Victor Buono and Nehemiah Persoff in "TNOT Inferno"

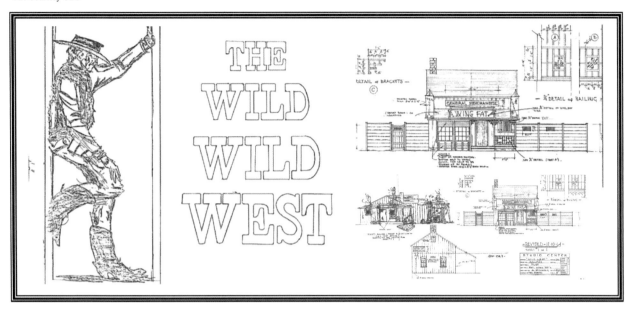

cover several tunnels leading into the hillside.

Traveling through one of these tunnels and other secret doors, West and Gordon find themselves in Lydia's living room. West proclaims, "This one's mine, Artie. I'll meet you at the wagon." Not long after Gordon's exit, Lydia appears and demands and explanation from West. West accuses her of being involved with Manolo and shows her the tunnels as evidence.

Lydia still denies any involvement and is proven innocent when they are surprised by Manolo and his men, quickly disarmed and thrown into a cell. This is the moment we discover why James West is called the best agent alive. He quickly assembles a gun that was hidden in the heels of his boots and loads it with bullets from a compartment in his belt buckle. Taking a pick from his lapel, he begins to work on the cell door. His work is postponed, however, when another of Manolo's men arrives. The man hands Manolo a calling card and glances toward the two prisoners. Manolo announces that he must attend to some business. But before Manolo has the chance to leave, West takes a small ball from the bottom of his holster and throws it through the cell bars. The ball explodes into billows of smoke, giving the deft Captain West ample cover to unlock the cell door.

West frees himself and, with the help of Gordon, triumphs over Manolo's men. "You take care of the girl, I'm going to the train," West proclaims and takes Manolo with him. West and Manolo enter the railroad car and are met by Wing Fat and some of Manolo's men. An unsurprised West exposes Wing Fat as the real Manolo. West realized that the only person powerful enough to call "Manolo" away for business with a calling card would have to be the real Manolo and Wing Fat was known for distributing calling cards.

Fat, now revealed as Manolo, complements West and orders his men to take the fake Manolo out and kill him. Now alone, West asks Manolo if he would consider hiring him now that his army is a man short. Manolo agrees but insists that Artemus and Lydia be killed. Appealing to Manolo's competitiveness, West proposes that a friendly game of pool decide the outcome. Again, Manolo agrees. Pushing an unseen switch, West turns on a light outside the train. The train engineer takes the cue, blasts a curtain of steam into the faces of Manolo's men. Inside the car, West throws the cue ball at the floor and moves quickly behind the wall of smoke the ball emits. Grabbing a pool cue West exposes a rapier from within and throws it across the room impaling Manolo in the chest. As Manolo dies he proclaims, "No one would ever suspect a fat Chinese of being a revolutionary."

Ross Martin in his first disguise as Artemus Gordon.

23

Michael Garrison was such an unusual character that many felt it was the infusion of his personality that gave "The Wild Wild West" its bizarre, exotic and fascinating essence. It was *his* show in every way.

Chapter 3—First Season: The Night of the Terrible Spring

Editor's Note: Upon the first publishing of this book in 1988, references to "20 years ago" were accurate. Things have changed, however, and in the blink of an eye another 20 years have passed. It's amazing to all of us who worked on the original book that another lifetime has slipped away so quickly. The following text has been modified accordingly.

Forty-plus years ago, while CBS was changing producers for the eighth time on "The Wild Wild West" television series, little did the upper echelons of the network realize that they were creating an enigma not easily solved by an author in the year 2008 attempting to "revisit" 40 years into the past. "Sources indicate," and "*Daily Variety* reports," have woefully failed to provide all the necessary pieces. One fact remained evident, though, regardless of conflicting views: The shakeup at CBS-TV in 1965 could have been appropriately entitled "The Night of the Terrible Spring."

Ethel Winant said, "Michael Garrison was so stylish, he was bigger than life; a very colorful and quite bizarre character; wonderful, bright and very,

very smart. He had a sense of the show but he had no sense of production costs or value, or how to make it work. And things cost thousands of dollars." While Garrison did have a sense of the size of the show, and how bizarre it could potentially be, CBS stepped in and wanted to tighten it up and make it into much more of a conventional program. And yet, despite all the problems, the network made the pilot and kept on producing the show. "We made it endlessly [sic], because we'd look at the dailies and if they didn't like something they would re-shoot it or they would add things. It was bizarre. We sort of muddled through that pilot and the show went into the schedule," Winant said.

"The Wild West" pilot turned out to be up to CBS standards, which was made obvious by the fact that then-president of CBS (Television Network,) Jim Aubrey, supported it, even though, as a rule, he would generally support the projects and concepts of his good friend, Hunt Stromberg. Once the pilot passed approval from William S. Paley, the founder and CEO of CBS, Frank Stanton, president of CBS, and Aubrey, "The Wild West" was comfortably secured into the 1965 Fall schedule.

With the "Wild West" well on its way and

shooting scheduled to begin in June the bottom suddenly dropped out of the CBS-TV regime and in March of 1965 CBS announced the firing of top management. Among the first to be ousted was president of the CBS Television Network Jim Aubrey, who was replaced by Jack Schneider. Michael H. Mann became top man on the program totem pole. Mann quickly announced the resignation of Hunt Stromberg Jr. who was replaced by Perry Lafferty.

On March 5, 1965, *Daily Variety* reported:

> *"Stromberg ouster is tied to that of Aubrey by insiders. Mann, it's known, has long resented what he considered undermining of his authority by Stromberg because the latter's recommendation had considerable weight with Aubrey. Just how far the personnel shakeup may go isn't known, and there was a great deal of trepidation among execs as CBS.*

Ethel Winant, one of the few survivors of the swinging axe, remembered, "We put a lot of attention into 'The Wild West.' The show got picked up, then the whole management of CBS changed. Most of the people on the team that put the show together got fired. They all got swept out when Aubrey was fired on that terrible spring."

At the same time it was making the key management changes, CBS reshuffled drastically the 1965-66 program schedule arranged by Aubrey, axing some series he had set and restoring some he had gotten rid of. Some of the programs returned to the schedule after being ousted by Aubrey's administration were, "Rawhide," "Hazel," "Sally & Sam," "Password" and "The Loner." One of Aubrey's keepers that CBS immediately attempted to axe was "The Wild West."

Robert Conrad recalled, "I got my cancellation notice in spring of '65, when the new regime took over. I was singing in a nightclub in Mexico and my agency called and said, 'Guess what? They're not going forward with the "Wild West" because the regime said it's not a standard show. It's not a Western. They don't know what

Temporary "Wild West" producer Gene Coon. Coon was one of eight producers for the series' turbulent first season.

Photo courtesy Ken Kolb

the hell it is.' I said, 'Win a few; lose a few.'"

For unexplained reasons, CBS reevaluated the show and reinstated "The Wild West" into the 65-66 schedule. All these years later, it's hard to imagine how close we came to never getting to know the characters of James T. West and Artemus Gordon and, of course, the eccentric and wickedly endearing Miguelito Loveless, now all of whom are so wonderfully emblazoned into our media psyches and pop culture history. With the management changes, CBS had an expensive, non-Western, special effects-laden, crazy show that no one knew quite how to categorize. Winant said, "Michael (Garrison) had no track record. He never produced a television show; only a few movies that he worked on with producer Jerry Wahl."

The new management wanted no part of anything (or anyone) connected to Stromberg, and that included Michael Garrison, but the fact remained that Garrison did own a large part of the show. As a solution, CBS upped him to executive producer, which took away some of his creative input. CBS felt that they could not afford to have Garrison as a producer because of the exorbitant cost of the "Wild West" pilot, coupled with the fact that CBS was terrified of this elaborate show that nobody understood. There also remained a certain mystery as to who in the upper echelons of CBS knew that Garrison had struck such an advantageous deal with Stromberg and that he (Garrison) literally owned the show.

"CBS thought it would be better to have a Western and they decided they were going to get rid of Michael, but all in due time," Winant said. "So there was this big to-do about it really not being his show; that it was CBS's show and they sort of pushed him aside." The search for a producer of CBS's choice lead to a long line of candidates, the first of whom was Jack Arnold, a well-know director of several science fiction films. Although Arnold was the first choice, he only lasted for a brief time and never had the opportunity to

COLLIER YOUNG EPISODES:
The Night of the Double-Edged Knife (AKA Greatest Train Robbery)
The Night of the Casual Killer (AKA Tug-o-War)
The Night of the Fatal Trap (AKA Oh, What a Tangled Web We Weave)

produce a single episode. Arnold left the position for unknown reasons, later going on to other CBS projects such as directing "Gilligan's Island" episodes.

Once again, CBS executives resumed their search for the ideal "Wild West" producer. The second choice was Ben Brady, best known for producing "The Outer Limits" (ABC-TV), "Perry Mason" and "The Red Skelton Show" (CBS). Prior to his producing experience, Brady was Coast Program Chief for ABC. Brady was at the time a professor at California State University, Northridge, in the television and film department. The choice of Brady as producer was announced in March of 1965, but CBS was obviously unsatisfied with their choice because in less than two months he was replaced by Collier Young. Brady, like Arnold, was never given the opportunity to produce a single episode. When contacted for a statement with regards to his unusually brief status with the series, the former TV executive declined to comment on the incident.

It appeared that Young would be the final choice for the series, but the show had a reputation to uphold. Now becoming notorious for producer shifts, "The Wild West" concept was again proving elusive to the executives. After Young had produced only three episodes the search continued. Young had worked on the tongue-in-cheek adventure comedy "The Rogues" for NBC-TV and tried to apply the same concepts to "The Wild West." His first change in the series was the title. Young thought that "The Wild West" sounded too much like a typical Western, which the show obviously was not. The title –meant as a pun – highlighted the show's contrast to the more traditional Westerns, worked better with the addition of a second "Wild." Production began in June of 1965, on the first episode of "The Wild Wild West," entitled "The Greatest Train Robbery," guest-starring Leslie Nielsen. In an unplanned effort to not stray from the show's usual epidemic of changes and alterations, the episode was renamed "The Night of the Double-Edged Knife."

"The Night of the Double-Edged Knife" was not what Garrison expected his show to be, but he had very little control over the producer and over CBS. The same feeling went for the two other shows that Young produced. Young saw "The Wild Wild West" as a tongue-in-cheek Western with minimized gimmicks, more humor and less action. Young felt that the show was going to be a kind of "The Rogues" of the West. It was never intended to be. In July of 1965 Young was summarily replaced. The reason cited for his dismissal

was, "…a difference in concept between the network and Young." His exit was by mutual agreement and on positive terms. Young stayed on with CBS to help develop new properties.

The Night of the
Double-Edged Knife
AKA Greatest Train Robbery

Cheyenne Indians are believed responsible for the deaths of five laborers every day who are working at *Rails End* constructing the railroad line. West and Gordon are assigned to investigate. General Harrison Ball (Leslie Nielsen) tells them that the Indians are demanding to be paid $500,000 in gold railroad spikes or each day five more laborers will to die. West meets up with Sheila Parnell (Katherine Ross) and discovers that her father, one of the dead workers, had been threatened by an educated-sounding gentleman the day before his demise. Suspicion mounts as West tries to figure out how Indians could have devised such a complex plan.

After Artie, (disguised as an old railroad worker) has his horse shot out from under him during an alleged Indian raid, West pursues the attackers. West kills one of the attackers and is captured by the real Cheyenne, who have taken the fallen Artemus to their camp. The agents are shown the true identity of the killed attacker: a white man. The agents are now inclined to believe American Knife (John Drew Barrymore), the college-educated Cheyenne chief who has been trying to prove that his people are being unjustly blamed. Before being released, however, West is tortured at the Indian camp – for the sake of tradition.

Artie poses as the dead attacker's body and, when his comrades come to pick him up, the agents force them to divulge the location of the campsite where the *Jayhawkers* –white guerillas still fighting the Civil War – are hiding.

West and Gordon seek out the leader of the Jayhawkers. Overhearing their plans, they plot an ambush at the next raid. The agents, however, are set up

James West confronts the crazed General Ball, played by Leslie Nielsen in "Double-Edged Knife."

CBS #6509 Shooting Order 02
First Air Date: 11/12/65

Produced by Collier Young
Directed by Don Taylor
Written by Stephen Kandel

General Ball: Leslie Nielsen
American Knife: John Drew Barrymore
Sheila Parnell: Katherine Ross
Mike McGreavy: Elisha Cook
Penrose: Harry Townes
Adamson: Vaughn Taylor
Parnell: Tyler McVey
Merritt: Ed Peck
Farrell: Harry Lauter
Tennyson:
Charles Davis

The general (Nielsen) contemplates his missing hand in "Knife."

by General Ball, who we discover is passionately opposed to General Grant and is actually the head of the gang. Ball's vengeance comes from losing his commission as a result of his missing hand. He now plans to ambush the ambush. West is aware of the plan that Ball has play-acted for his benefit and plots to ambush the ambushed ambush. Our heroes are intentionally captured and Farrell (Lauter), one of the Ball's men, relieves West of his hidden devices, since the General is well aware of the Agent's tactics.

As part of his plan, West had recommended that the gold be turned over to the attackers, and the captive heroes free themselves from their bonds in time to foil the ambushed ambush. West and Ball engage in a fight to the death, but American Knife steps in and kills the General for West, knowing how hard it would have been for him to kill a man who was once a friend. The episode closes with West being enticed by two very different dishes: Irish stew and Buffalo Tongue.

Author's Notes:

After the series pilot, producer Collier Young did the first show of the season called "The Greatest Train Robbery" (later re-titled "The Night of the Double-Edged Knife.") The simple fact that its original title involved a train robbery gives some indication as to how Western Young was trying to make the show. Young's approach to the series was definitely more traditional, complete with cowboys and Indians, and dramatically strayed from the original concept of James Bond in the West. An added character was the agents' personal manservant, a displaced Englishman named Tennyson, played by actor Charles Davis. The manservant was added to serve as part of James West's wealthy businessman masquerade that was supposed to explain his high living. Tennyson only lasted the duration of Young's stint as producer.

Leslie Nielsen does a nice job as the corrupt Indian-hating General Ball. Katherine Ross, who went on to become a motion picture star, appears as Sheila Parnell, a West conquest. Joining the crew at this time was Director of Photography Ted Voigtlander, replacing Frank Phillips, who had originally worked on the pilot but passed on the series.

Statistically speaking: Four *very Western* fights and four *very Western* opponents.

The Night of the
Casual Killer
AKA Tug-O-War

A man from the Attorney General's office in Washington is killed while attempting to take the wanted John Avery (Dehner), a corrupt politician-tuned-outlaw, into custody. West is assigned the task of recapturing Avery, and is refused military help because of the impenetrable fortress that protects the outlaw. Even U.S. Marshall Kirby (Williams) refused to cooperate. West and his aide, Artemus Gordon, pose as touring Shakespearean actors and allow themselves to be captured. Avery, suspicious, tests West by having his men engage him in a fight, during which West purposely offers no defense. Then he gives West the chance to shoot him, which he refuses to do. Now even more convinced that West can be trusted, Avery introduces him to his girlfriend Laurie (Lee). This proves to be Avery's first mistake, because Laurie takes an immediate liking (surprise, surprise) to the secret agent. At show time, West leaves with Laurie. Enter, Marshal Kirby (Williams), who betrays the agent and identifies him as James West.

After the performance, Avery tells Laurie to invite her new friend, West, to dinner. She invites him but warns him about the lawman who visited Avery and identified him. Artie is also alerted. West attends the dinner and Avery divulges his newfound information, of which West is already aware. Artie, playing a drunkard, knocks out the guard at the door and hears Avery summoning the guard to help with his prisoner. Artie nabs Avery and the quartet — Artie, Avery, West and Laurie — leave through a secret tunnel. West then seals the end of the tunnel using his explosive pocket watch. Unfortunately, more of Avery's men are waiting at the tunnel's exit. Trapped in a gun battle, Artemus impersonates Avery's voice and demands his men surrender. West tries to eliminate Avery's men by explosives. In a quick escape, our heroes climb into a coal cart and speed to safety.

We find Avery and Laurie at the train, where Avery awaits officials to take him into custody. Laurie would like to travel with them, but she decides to enter show business instead. Artie quips, "James, my boy, you just can't win them all." A comical violin accents the moment.

West and Tennyson flank corrupt politician John Avery (John Dehner) in "Casual Killer."

CBS #6505 Shooting Order 03   CBS Photo
First Air Date: 10/15/65

Produced by Collier Young
Directed by Don Taylor
Written by Bob Barash

Laurie Morgan: Ruta Lee
John Avery: John Dehner
Marshal Kirby: Bill Williams
Tennyson: Charles Davis
Mason: Len Lesser
Harper: Mort Mills
Hendriz: Ed Gilbert
Captain Davis: Curtis Taylor

Author's Notes:

The second of Collier Young's episodes proved to be another Western with West and Gordon going after a corrupt politician-turned-outlaw. There is nothing bizarre, strange or even unique about the character John Avery. What did prove to be an interesting switch was the fact that *both* Jim and Artie went undercover, as actors yet, with West using the name of Conroy Whitney and Gordon, appropriately, using his own name. Overall, the story lacks the luster and punch found in later episodes. A note of interest, though, involves the scene where Artie plays the violin. It's a little known fact that Ross Martin was actually a concert violinist in his youth.

The Night of the
Fatal Trap
AKA Oh, What a Tangled Web We Weave

West disguises as a notorious gunman in order to team with Mexican bandit Colonel Vasquez (Randell) in "Fatal Trap."

Agent James West dons a mustache while posing as the notorious desperado Frank Slade, in a plan to arrest a Mexican bandit, Colonel Vasquez (Randell). Vasquez and his men have been robbing banks in American border towns and then fleeing to the sanctuary of Mexico, always escaping the sheriff's pursuit just in time. West's partner, Artemus Gordon, disguises himself as Mojave Mike, an old gold prospector, and goes to Mexico to contact Vasquez through his lieutenant, Viper (Ruskin). Mojave Mike informs Vasquez that the notorious Frank Slade is coming to town. Meanwhile, West accidentally leaks to Vasquez information about a U.S. shipment of $1 million in gold bullion.

West, as Slade, arrives in Mexico to help Vasquez steal the bullion. The ruse will bring Vasquez into U.S. territory and make it easy to arrest him. Vasquez's beautiful girlfriend, Linda Medford (Moore) recognizes West from a news clipping in her earlier days in Washington D.C., but she opts to keep West's identity a secret. Vasquez, not trusting Slade, locks West in to the back of the wagon that will be picking up the gold. Dressed as guards, Vasquez and Viper, drive the wagon to the bank to pick up the gold. Vasquez spots a wanted poster of the real Frank Slade and realizes he's been duped. Vasquez makes a fast exit out of town.

West escapes the wagon by using a vial of sleeping gas released from the heel of his boot. West shoots the door open and fights with Vasquez atop the speeding wagon that is rapidly approaching a cliff. West dives off just in time, but Vasquez is caught by his wrist band and plummets to his death.

Author's Notes:

This is definitely not the best "Wild Wild West" ever made, not to mention the last for producer Collier Young. "Fatal Trap" served as a swan song for Young and the agents' manservant Tennyson, both of whom had been seriously misplaced in the "West." At the hands of Young, Jim West couldn't seem to stay out of disguises, donning a mustache and the alias of outlaw Frank Slade. This episode missed the mark by being placed squarely in the West, and leaving little room for any bizarre elements, whatsoever. Artemus Gordon, as the boisterous Mojave Mike, is probably the most popular of Artie's characters among fans, and justifiably so. It gave Ross Martin a real opportunity to show off his skills as an actor. Director Richard Whorf came from a long history of Western TV shows including "Gunsmoke" and "Rawhide," and a few 1940s screwball comedies. His heavy Western style is evident throughout the episode.

CBS #6515 Shooting Order 04
First Air Date: 12/24/65

Produced by Collier Young
Directed by Richard Whorf
Written by Jack Marlowe and Robert V. Barron

Charlie: Walker Edmiston
Colonel Vasquez: Ron Randell
Mark Dawson: Christian Anderson
Linda Medfore: Joanna Moore
Mat Dawson: Alan Sues
Viper: Joe Ruskin
Tennyson: Charles Davis
Luke: Dal Jenkins
Sheriff Cantrell: Don Briggs
Police Chief: Rodolfo Reyes

New Blood

CBS tried yet again to draw from the producer mill by assigning the show its fourth producer, Fred Freiberger, who earlier had produced MGM-TV's "A Man Called Shenandoah." Freiberger's assignment was clear: Bring the show back to its original concept.

"I got a call from Stan Schpetner from CBS and he asked me if I wanted to do 'The Wild Wild West.' I was still under contract at Metro at the time, but I was very interested and wanted to get away from MGM," Freiberger said. The producer went to talk to Schpetner, who filled him in about the show and its problems. CBS had only one script and an impossible air-date in just four weeks, but Freiberger felt that his situation at Metro was wearing thin due to a personality clash with Bob Horton, the star of "Shenandoah." So Freiberger quickly got out of his contract at Metro and started with CBS the following Monday.

By then CBS was terrified of a new NBC comedy called "Camp Runamuck," starring Dave Madden. It was fair competition opposite "The Wild Wild West," especially after Young's less-than-perfect attempts. The consensus was that "Runamuck" would kill them in the time slot. CBS was in *delightful shock*, according to Freiberger, when "The Wild Wild West" killed "Runamuck" in the ratings, and the competition was cancelled after one season.

Freiberger continued, "Schpetner told me, 'The reason I wanted you instead of anybody else is that they tell me you love Vegas and I want to gamble.' I said okay, you've got the right guy." Freiberger later returned to CBS with the one "Wild Wild West" script warning Schpetner that it was going to be murder to do. Schpetner agreed and tossed the script into the trash telling Frieberger, "We don't like it either." At that point, Freiberger brought in George Schenck and his partner, Bill Marks, to write a new script. Freiberger said that he had also met with both Conrad and Martin and, at the same time, CBS briefed him on the previously shot episodes.

"It's not that the shows weren't any good but the shows were Westerns. Now they were doing this way out combination/association of two guys, James West and Artemus Gordon." Freiberger observed a contradiction in styles in the program, decided to avoid dealing with the geography as much as with the period and to reach for a more bizarre approach. According to Freiberger, Schpetner had told him to… "Do anything you want to do." The first episode produced by Freiberger with his new approach was "The Night of the Deadly Bed," AKA "The Night of the Lethal Bed." This was the only "West" episode penned by Schenck who went on to write and produce numerous series, most recently "Navy NCIS."

Immediately the morale of the show picked up. Freiberger said that he had heard stories of Bob Conrad's notoriety as being hard to handle, yet he admitted that he had never come across a more cooperative actor. "He worked until midnight. He really wanted that show to succeed." Because of the tight schedule for air dates, everyone on the crew also worked very late. In order to help writers keep on schedule with scripts, Freiberger, along with story editor Richard Landau, drew up an amusing list of 10 Commandments of "The Wild Wild West." The top three rang clear in his mind:

1. Have a gorgeous woman.
2. Have a strong adversary.
3. Have something very bizarre.

"The ideal thing was to have a writer place Conrad or Martin, or both, in a situation at the end of the second act where even the writer, at the time, didn't know how to have it end. It had to be absolutely impossible. That's what we wanted. If we had that, somehow we'd figure them out. But we made the story so impossible that even we couldn't figure out how to get them out of it," Freiberger said. So he had 10 Commandments – or rather, guidelines – that he always checked to make sure were a part of each script.

Fred Freiberger

FRED FREIBERGER'S EPISODES:
The Night of the Deadly Bed (AKA TNOT Lethal Bed)
The Night the Wizard
　　　Shook the Earth
The Night of the Sudden Death (AKA TNOT Circus)
The Night of the
　　　Thousand Eyes
The Night of the Glowing Corpse
The Night of the Dancing Death
The Night that Terror Stalked the Town
The Night of the Red-Eyed Madman
The Night of the Human Trigger
The Night of the Torture Chamber

Dr. Loveless, I Presume

CBS Photo

Michael Dunn's dynamic personality made him a natural for the quintessential "West" villain, a recurring, indestructible and formidable adversary to the agents.

Fred Freiberger knew he was on the right track with "Deadly Bed." He felt it worked well with the key concept of "The Wild Wild West," to keep it *bizarre*. Writer John Kneubuhl recalled one afternoon sitting with Freiberger in his office as they were both trying to think up a great gimmick for the show. "While we had no idea of what kind of script to write, I was flipping through a *TIME* magazine and came across a picture of an actor named Michael Dunn. I point the picture out to Fred and said, 'Can you get Michael Dunn? He'd make a wonderful villain,'" Kneubuhl recalled.

Dunn suffered from hypochondroplasia, a genetic form of dwarfism, leaving him with some unique health challenges. He had already become a successful performer on Broadway, having been nominated for a Tony Award in 1964 as Best Supporting or Featured Actor (Dramatic) for "The Ballad of the Sad Cafe." Freiberger knew that type of unusual villain was exactly what the show needed and immediately called Dunn's agent.

While Freiberger got hold of Dunn in New York, Kneubuhl began to write the first show for the new villain. The script, "The Night the Wizard Shook the Earth," was written within two days with very little rewrite. In the meantime, Michael Garrison, still with the power to hire –subject to the network's approval that is – was off to New York to meet Dunn at his nightclub act.

Phoebe Dorin, Dunn's performance partner, was cast opposite Dunn as Dr. Miguelito Loveless' female companion, Antoinette. Dorin recalled, "After our act, Garrison came backstage to meet with Michael and to tell him he was very pleased to have him on the show. I told Michael (Dunn) that I thought it was a fantastic opportunity to do the show. Then Garrison said, 'I want Michael to be on the show as a continuing character, as a nemesis; a wild villain. I like the singing. Let's use it on the show. We can use old songs from the 1800s, and every time you do the show we'll do a lead-in on a song.' Garrison then turned to me and said, 'You can be his little... henchwoman. We'll find some reason why you're there.'"

Dorin met Dunn while working in New York designing sets. The two worked on the same play and quickly became close. Each evening after the play they would go with friends and sing outside by a giant fountain next to the theater. Later they formed the nightclub act.

While John Kneubuhl was writing the script for Dunn, the first consideration was to make Dunn's character *wild* and *crazy*; someone totally out of the ordinary. Kneubuhl remembered, "How I came to think of the name that would go with a dwarf, something [sic] less than three feet tall, was a kind of set of historical jokes on my part; partly on myself. I'm half Samoan and I thought it would be funny if I teased myself, a no-account half-cast, and made Michael Dunn half Mexican and half, what; European? White, anyway. That's why the first name was Miguelito, for Michael; Michael Dunn and Michael Garrison.

"So the Miguelito part was easy enough. Loveless? If you're going to make as colossal a villain as I hoped to write, what name better than Loveless – completely devoid of Love. So it was Miguelito Loveless; and I wrote out a little character sketch. I think it was spelled out in that first script. His mother was a landed patrician lady –Californian, I guess, Spanish extraction, and the father, the exploiter, the plunderer, the colonialist, the imperialist, the whatever; *(Although*

31

Phobe Dorin and Michael Dunn pre- "West."

it isn't quite spelled out that way – ed.) robbed Miguelito of all his lands, his heritage and his culture. Therefore, he hates everybody. But the real joke about Miguelito Loveless is that his real enemy and target of his Miltonic wrath is God himself for having made him such a monstrosity."

Kneubuhl said that he liked to write silly stories. "I do it well because I'm partly silly myself, I think. I like the illogical discontinuities, the illogicality of silliness. In brief, that's how Loveless came to be. I would like to emphasize, however, that as silly as the whole thing was, it was *seriously* silly. I had hoped that anybody who would write the character afterwards *(Nobody did for quite a long time-ed.)* that some of that very adult serious silliness would be kept throughout the series."

A special magic was instantly created on "The Wild Wild West" with the introduction of Dr. Miguelito Loveless, and the character was a tremendous hit with audiences. At first, however, Freiberger admitted that CBS was afraid the Loveless character would not be well received. "They were a little leery of the situation, but after seeing him, Mr. Paley and the network flipped over Dunn and

James West stands beside 7' 2" Voltaire (Richard Kiel) in "Whirring Death."

wanted to get him on multiples (*several episodes – ed.*). So we kept signing Michael Dunn, and he became a big man on 'The Wild Wild West.'" Dunn was immediately contracted to do four Dr. Loveless roles each season. Michael Dunn died in 1973 at the age of 38, as a result of complications from his condition.

Another character incorporated into the Loveless team was a seven-foot-two-inch giant named Voltaire, played by actor Richard Kiel. According to Kneubuhl, Voltaire went well with the smallness of Miguelito Loveless. As much as he said he would like to, Kneubuhl could not claim credit for the creation of the character.

"Naming a seven-foot-tall man Voltaire doesn't sound like me. That's a little bit too stylish. I have a dull kind of imagination. I probably would have called him Shorty. I have a feeling that the Voltaire character had been thought up before I started writing that first script and just incorporated him. (He was probably thought up) by Fred Freiberger. It sounds like Fred," Kneubuhl said.

Prior to his becoming an actor, Richard Kiel was a high school teacher. Like Dunn, Kiel suffered from a rare disease. In contrast, the actor was afflicted with acromegaly, otherwise known as gigantism, a pituitary disorder that causes abnormal and unstoppable growth. Dorin recalled that Kiel and Dunn did not get along very well. "They liked each other and worked well together, but they weren't close," she said.

The Night of the
Deadly Bed
AKA TNOT Lethal Bed

While waiting for Captain Jackson (Herron), an important contact, James West is attacked by an unknown assailant. Jackson appears, but before West can get to him, the Captain is blown up. With his dying breath, Jackson whispers the name, "Flory." West follows a trail to a tiny Mexican village where he asks too many questions. After being drugged and almost killed by a spiked bed, he notices peons carrying baskets of coal into an old mission on a warm day.

CBS Photo

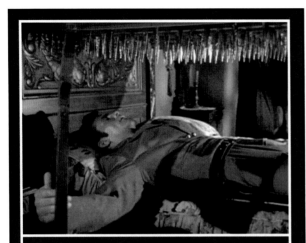

James West narrowly escapes a permanent nap in "The Night of the Deadly Bed."

CBS #6502 Shooting Order 05
First Air Date: 9/24/65

Produced by Fred Freiberger
Directed by William Witney
Written by George V. Schenck and William Marks

Gatilla: Barbara Luna
Flory: J.D. Cannon
Roxanne: Danica D'Hondt
Margarita: Anna Shin
Captain Jackson: Bob Herron
Angelo: Bill Catching
Bartender: Don Diamond
Guitar Players: Jose Gallege and Dale Van Sickel

J.D. Cannon (right) plays Flory, a Napoleonic despot intent on taking over Mexico.

At the train, West shows the coal to Gordon, who promptly makes his own special coal out of dynamite. West returns to the mission and discovers a huge underground complex containing a steel plant. The agent is captured and brought before the mastermind of the project, Flory (Cannon), whose plan includes reclaiming Mexico and re-establishing Napoleonic rule. Since Napoleon failed to claim Mexico, Flory calls himself Napoleon the Fourth and is ready to take over. Flory has created a special armored train with secret railroad lines to the trunk line of the United States. This train will prevent the U.S. from interfering with his aim to take over the country.

West is to be exterminated until Gordon, disguised as a Mexican peon, appears and uses a special knockout gas to help them escape. Flory tries to stop their escape by shooting a hole in Gordon's gas bag. The agents are knocked out also and are thrown in with the underground workers to shovel coal. Gordon quickly rallies the workers into a revolt. West frees himself using a special ring that can cut through his shackles. The workers revolt and overpower the guards. West throws his explosive coal into the furnace. Everyone except West and Flory get clear of the plant. Flory tries to hold West captive, but the agent defeats him and escapes just in time before the plant to explodes.

Author's Notes:

Fred Freiberger does a nice job of covering up for Collier Young's misjudgment. The first of Freiberger's episodes starts with all the qualities of a Bond movie. The villain, General Flory, is a bit crazy having created a fantastic armored train that breathes fire and sports a battering ram on the front. In this episode Gordon claims to have invented knockout gas, but it was Sir Humphry Davy, some 80 years earlier, who first discovered the medical applications of nitrous oxide, commonly known as laughing gas.

Director Bill Witney reminisced about the shot where James West was laying on the *deadly bed.* Witney didn't want Bob Conrad to do the stunt, seeing incredible danger in the heavy spikes that were rigged to fall onto the victim. Witney was adamant about Conrad not doing the stunt himself, but Conrad was equally adamant about doing it. The set was actually closed down for several hours as a result of the ensuing argument. As you might guess, Conrad won.

The Night the
Wizard Shook the Earth

A persistent Dr. Miguelito Loveless shows James West his many marvelous inventions in "The Night the Wizard Shook the Earth," Loveless' first "West" appearance.

CBS Photos

CBS #6503 Shooting Order 06
First Air Date: 10/01/65

Produced by Fred Freiberger
Directed by Bernie Kowalski
Written by John Kneubuhl

Dr. Miguelito Loveless: Michael Dunn
Greta: Leslie Parrish
Voltaire: Richard Kiel
Miss Piecemeal: Sigrid Valdis
Wrestler: Mike Masters
Professor Neilsen:
    Harry Bartell
Governor: William Mims
Antoinette:
    Phoebe Dorin

Richard Kiel as Voltaire

D r. Miguelito Loveless (Dunn), a dwarf, watches his giant assistant Voltaire (Kiel) subdue a dock guard as Loveless prepares to kill disembarking Professor Neilsen (Bartell), who is arriving to present his formula for a new explosive to the U.S. government. Secret agent James West uses a pair of spectacles to disguise himself as Neilsen and foil any attempts on the professor's life. Unbeknownst to West, Loveless worked with the professor and immediately recognizes the ruse. He succeeds in blowing up Neilsen with a pea shooter and a glass pill made from the very explosive they together perfected. West, and the professor's secretary, Greta (Parrish), manage to avoid the explosion.

Later at the hotel, West fears for Greta's life, unaware that she is involved with Loveless. While Greta prepares to join West for dinner, Voltaire delivers the message that she is to lead West out of the hotel in order to expedite his demise. Greta entices West to go for a walk and an unsuccessful attempt is made on his life. Gordon arrives in a specially designed coach brimming with secret weaponry. West returns to the hotel and tells Greta that the professor was not the only person with the formula and he intends to use the formula for his own financial gain. He tells her that he is willing to sell the formula to the highest bidder and would like to meet with whoever killed the professor. Greta leads West to Dr. Loveless, who is suspicious of West and tests his honesty by sending him to the governor of California to deliver his demand that an area of the state that once belonged to Loveless' ancestors be returned to him. If West fails, Loveless intends to blow up the entire area where 5,000 people now reside.

West meets with the governor who, at first, doesn't believe his story, but he soon realizes that West is sincere and gives the agent extra men to watch over Loveless. The governor tells his secretary, Miss Piecemeal (Valdis), to make the arrangements, not realizing that she, too, is an ally to Loveless. She gives the signal to capture West when he leaves. West invites his captors to join him in his special coach, after which he quickly disposes of them through various hidden devices, including an ejector seat. But he is eventually subdued by Voltaire, who takes him back to Loveless where he is held in a hanging cage, or gibbet, unable to move while Loveless prepares to set off the explosives that will end 5,000 lives.

Greta arrives to offer West some supper and he charms her into aiding his escape. Greta tells West that the bomb is hidden in the clock tower by the governor's mansion. West finds Loveless in the tower, where the explosives are attached to the clock mechanism. At exactly midnight the bomb will explode. Using Loveless' cane, West manages to jam the clock, but Loveless jumps on the pendulum and forces the mechanism to snap the cane. With Loveless occupied West is able to climb to the bomb and unplug the detonator.

Back at the train Gordon informs West, and his guest, Greta, that Loveless is behind bars. Gordon tells them that Loveless brought a strange invention to jail with him; a glass tube that could catch pictures and send them through the air. They all share a laugh in disbelief.

Author's Notes:

In this, the first of a series of 10 Loveless episodes, the doctor is introduced in all demented splendor alongside his evil giant, Voltaire. Later becoming known for his chemical explosives, Loveless was one of the most appealing villains of all time. Writer John Kneubuhl spoke of the impact of his new "Wild Wild West" villain, stating that they

Michael Dunn: A Little Man With a Big Talent

Michael Dunn, the 3'10" actor, made a successful career out of portraying villains and intellectuals. Born Gary Neil Miller on October 20, 1934, in Shattuck, Oklahoma, Dunn was a prodigious child blessed with an IQ of 178. His parents, Fred and Jewell Miller, had much to be proud of as Michael attended the University Michigan before he was 16 years old. At 15 he became a concert pianist until he was stricken with complications to his chondrodystrophy, a congenital and progressive disease that permanently crippled his elbows and abruptly ended his career as a pianist.

CBS Photo

Bob Conrad and Michael Dunn in a behind-the-scenes shot from "Wizard"

Enamored by music, he took to singing, which eventually led to his meeting Michael Garrison. In an interview, writer John Kneubuhl recalled, "There is a wonderful play by Philip Barry called 'Here Come the Clowns.' There's a tag, I think, at the end of the second act. A dwarf looks up at a rather satanic magician figure and he cries out in anguish, 'If there is a God why did he make people like me?' The satanic figure looks down and grins and says, 'Would you deny him a sense of humor?' That was such a shattering line that I always remembered it and I think that line was going through my mind when I was thinking up Miguelito Loveless. At any rate, he is an existential figure of colossal evil and, at heart, a thoroughly contradictory little boy. That is his glory, his humor and his silliness."

According to Dorin, Dunn was very excited about his newfound role and the popularity it brought him. In a 1966 *New York Times* interview Dunn talked about his unique role as Dr. Loveless.

"Miguelito Loveless' ambition is to destroy the world and, in particular, 'bug' the main characters played by Robert Conrad and Ross Martin. Secretly, all Miguelito wants are some chocolate creams and a pretty woman; oh, and a chance to sing. Singing gave Miguelito an added dimension. He may be nuts, but that doesn't stop him from singing beautifully."

Eventually the actor's physical frustrations and personal problems caught up with him. According to Dorin, Dunn realized that most of his problems would still be present no matter how successful and rich he became. For Dunn, she said, "…that was a killer. It destroyed Michael."

Best known for his portrayal of Dr. Carl Glocken in the motion picture adaptation of Katherine Anne Porter's "Ship of Fools," Dunn's career ended too soon with his death in August of 1973 in London.

all waited for some response after Loveless debuted with "Wizard;" and response they received. Soon after the first one, they started work on the second Loveless episode, "The Night the Terror Stalked the Town," which Kneubuhl didn't write but rather simplified the story for writer Rich Landau. Actually, "Terror" received an even stronger favorable response than "Wizard," not just for the series, but for the Loveless character in particular.

West shows noticeable shades of James Bond with his new, weapon-filled carriage which was clearly reminiscent of Bond's Aston Martin. During the scene in the coach, West is held at gunpoint by three men. By pulling a secret lever, one man is held by a metal clamp around his neck while the other is ejected from the top of the coach. The third man, the driver, is tossed from the coach by his seat. The ejected man, Hal Needham, who went on to direct features, ("Cannonball Run," "Smokey and the Bandit," "Hooper") remembered that the stunt didn't go off as planned; as the attached wires broke, he fell back into the coach and onto Bob Conrad.

Another character introduced in this episode was Miss Piecemeal, in the tradition of Bond's Miss Moneypenny, Piecemeal is the governor's secretary and is basically a bitch. She will return in more episodes.

Cameraman Ted Voightlander found working with Michael Dunn a complete joy, with the only problems arising were from the actor's diminutive stature. "Michael was 3'10" tall and when we put the average person beside him we would have to put him up on a box or something high to get a decent shot."

Loveless discusses his inventions in this episode including his flying machine, a sound recording machine, penicillin and the automobile. At the end of this show, we witness the only time that Loveless gets captured and sent to jail.

There are several special "spy" connections in classic 1960s television, one includes actor Michael Dunn, who served as the devilish Mr. Big in the pilot episode of "Get Smart." Only then he meets with a more permanent demise, with no chance of returning as the resident villain.

The Night of the
Sudden Death

James West contends with circus owner/counterfeiter Warren Trevor (Robert Loggia) in "Sudden Death."

CBS #6504 Shooting Order 07   CBS Photo
First Air Date: 10/08/65

Produced by Fred Freiberger
Directed by William Witney
Written by Oliver Crawford

Warren Trevor: Robert Loggia
Corinne Foxx: Julie Payne
Foxx: Harlan Warde
Cosette: Elisa Ingram
Boone: Henry Hunter
Hotel Clerk: Don Gazzaniga
Janet Coburn: Antoinette Bower
Hugo: Sandy Kenyon
Sterling: Bill Cassady
Chief Vanoma: Joel Fluellen

Two men, aided by an unscrupulous guard named Foxx (Warde), gain entrance to the U.S. Mint in Carson City and connect hoses to a street gaslight in order to asphyxiate three workers. They also knock out Foxx, substitute counterfeit engraving plates for the real ones, and cover their crime by setting off an explosion. Agents West and Gordon are assigned to investigate.

West is attacked in his hotel by a hooded stranger who tries to crush him with inordinately powerful legs. Corinne Foxx (Payne), daughter of the wounded guard, goes to West and tells him that her father can help. Unfortunately, West finds him dying in the hospital having been crushed by West's apparent attacker. Before dying he warns the agents, "Find Corinne and find death." With no leads West and Gordon meet in a bar and are nearly poisoned. They run out of the bar to catch the culprit and notice a banner from a circus where Corinne works.

West goes to the circus and meets with the owner, Warren Trevor (Loggia). Later, West is almost killed by a crocodile after the platform he is walking on collapses. He defeats the beast and while walking through the forest hears in the distance what sounds like presses, possibly printing money. He returns to the village and attends a dinner for Chief Vanoma (Fluellen) from whom Trevor wants to purchase a piece of Africa. Artie shows up dressed as a clown and creates a diversion, but soon all are captured.

West, Gordon and Corinne are sewn into raw, wet skins that are meant to dry in the sun and imminently crush our heroes to death. West manages to roll over the side of the platform on which they are placed and tear his skins. West follows his earlier lead and retrieves the missing engraving plates. Artie stays behind and destroys the printed money. Artie is captured once again and Trevor goes hunting after West. After the two battle it out, Trevor falls into the crocodile waters and is eaten (chomp, burp). West gets Janet (Bower), Trevor's assistant, out of a cage, but leaves Artie all locked up. When West goes to change out of his circus costume, Artie uses a hairpin to pick the lock then merrily leaves with both Janet and Corinne, leaving nothing for West when he returns.

Author's Notes:
This is the first episode in which West and Gordon deal with what the Secret Service is actually known for, investigating counterfeiting. Not only does West fight off the bad guys, but he gets a few licks in with a crocodile. Guest star Robert Loggia went on to become one of Hollywood's most noted character actors.

Nice tag as West tries to pull a fast one on Artie, leaving him locked in the cage as he goes to change. The resourceful Gordon doesn't take it lying down, however, as he expeditiously picks the lock and exits with the girls. This episode is a lot of fun and full of bizarre characters, guaranteeing a good time for true "Wild Wild West" fans.

The Night of a
Thousand Eyes

A temporarily blinded James West faces off with Captain Coffin (Jeff Corey), a blind man with a penchant for sinking ships.

CBS Photo

CBS #6506 Shooting Order 08
First Air Date: 10/22/65

Produced by Fred Freiberger
Directed by Richard Sarafian
Written by Preston Wood

Captain Coffin: Jeff Corey
Jennifer Wingate: Diane McBain
Peavey: Donald O'Kelly
Captain Tenney: Barney Phillips
Oriana: Linda Ho
Crystal: Janine Gray
Glory: Jeanne Vaughn
Pilot: Jack Searl
Arnold: Victor French
Miss Purviance: Celeste Yarnell

Traffic on the Mississippi River has come to a virtual standstill because of the marauding tactics of an evil pirate. When the marauders smash another victim by using false landmarks to lure the riverboat aground, destroy the craft, carry off its contents and cause the boat to disappear without a trace, West and Gordon are called in to investigate. The only clue left behind is a single poker chip inscribed *The Pot of Gold Gambling Palace*. West investigates while Gordon searches for clues.

At the Palace, West meets Crystal (Gray), a croupier. West is alone in the Palace as he keeps playing and winning at the roulette table. Adversaries appear from nowhere and a fight breaks out. It seems West is asking too many questions. West defeats the attackers and asks Crystal for an explanation. He follows her to a room where she is shot by a painting. With her dying breath she tells West the name Coffin.

Meanwhile, Coffin (Corey), a blind ex-riverboat captain who now leads a cutthroat gang, scolds his men for not eliminating West. He then recruits the talents of a highly specialized killer – a beautiful woman named Jennifer Wingate (McBain.)

Later, West and Gordon hear a scream from a hotel room. They discover Wingate in the bathtub, so West invites her to dinner. That night, Artemus disguises himself as a riverboat gambler and tries to get information. West and Wingate have dinner and Wingate falls under the notorious West charm and is unable to carry out her deadly duty. She tells West everything she knows about Coffin and takes him to Coffin, where they are ambushed. The agent is captured and tied up in an underground office. Coffin explains that he was blinded by a freak explosion which robbed him of his status as the best captain on the Mississippi. He felt that he'd been unjustly treated after the accident. Now he plans on becoming the richest riverboat captain in history. He receives a telegram from one of his one thousand agents that a flatboat is on its way down the river. West is locked in a suspended cage that has been attached to a lightening rod that, when struck, promises to electrocute the agent.

Meanwhile, Artie is looking for West. He encounters two men who know he is looking for West and they try to detain him. A slippery escape and a quick bribe send Artie off in the right direction. West escapes the cage by using a wire lock pick, and he pursues Coffin. A rigged explosive blinds West, matching the odds against the captain. The two fight as best as they can, but when Coffin attempts to kill West he accidentally kills his Asian wife, Oriana (Ho). The upset Coffin shouts at West, who suddenly regains his sight and quickly escapes, being closely followed by Coffin. They end up back in the underground hideout when the cage that originally held West falls onto Coffin, is struck by lightening and kills the vengeful captain.

The tag finds West being seduced by Jennifer Wingate as she attempts to get her sentence reduced. Artie has his doubts, so she redirects her charm his way. The agents eventually give in stating, "I guess we can figure something out."

Author's Notes:

The only thing really going for this episode is the twist in the plot where a blind ex-captain is the mastermind behind such mammoth disasters. The chiaroscuro feel of this episode offers a nice effect. The skillful direction of Richard Sarafian (the pilot director) adds to the ambiance that was to become a signature of "The Wild Wild West."

Artie dons a Clark Gable-type costume for that riverboat gambler look. Olavee Martin, Ross' widow, recalled that this type of character was how Ross Martin always saw himself; more dashing and debonair than Artie was usually allowed to be.

The Night of the
Glowing Corpse

West is assigned to guard a scientific conference when a large man and a woman break into the locked area. The man kicks in the door where the powerfully radiant substance, *franconium*, which is owned by France, is being kept. West tries to stop the thieves, but is rendered unconscious after tightly grabbing the woman's ankle. West is castigated by French Lt. General Renard (Pine), but stoutly defended by Renard's niece, Cluny Ormon (Hamilton). He is later blamed for an impending international crisis due to the missing *franconium*. With France at war with Prussia, possession of the powerful material by the Prussian enemy is now looming as a frightening possibility. West's only help is in the substance itself; it has the ability to make inanimate objects glow when in its

Amelie (Marion Thomspson), is stunned by what she sees as the agents look on in "Glowing Corpse."

CBS# 6507 Shooting Order 09
First Air Date: 10/29/65

Produced by Fred Freiberger
Directed by Irving J. Moore
Written by Henry Sharp

Cluny Ormont: Kipp Hamilton
Lt. General Renard: Phil Pine
Ironfoot: Charles Horvath
Amelie : Marion Thompson
Consul-General Potez : Ron Whelan
Dr. Ormont : Oscar Beregi
Senator Hastings : Ralph Roberts
Cecile: Jayne Massey
Barker: Frank Delfino
Blonde: Louise Lawson

presence. Another clue is a set of fingerprints he discovers on the ankle of a pretty French secretary, Amelie (Thompson), after he identifies her as the woman who stole the substance. He corners the Amelie, but she shoots him. She exits as he casually stands up and reveals his bulletproof vest. Actually, he was hoping Amelie would lead him to the real culprit.

Meanwhile, Artie has devised a chemical leech that is capable of suspending a man's weight for 10 seconds. He demonstrates for West just as a tele-graph comes in indicating that Amelie was followed to the Hannibal Amusement Park. West investigates and follows Amelie into the Fun House. Amelie meets Renard's niece, Cluny, who is also a woman botanist. She tells Amelie that the scheme was botched and West is still alive. Cluny kills Amelie and leaves. West finds the body along with a clue; an orchid in her hand.

West meets Cluny and Lt. General Renard in a restaurant, unaware that she is Amelie's murderer. He becomes suspicious when he notices the lieutenant has the same orchid on his lapel as was found on Amelie's body.

Back at the hotel West finds Artie testing out an artificial lung that can keep a man alive underwater for five minutes. The hotel valet arrives with Artie's suit that has been planted with a bomb. Discovering it just in time, the agents avoid disaster.

West then scours the embassy botany room with a radioactive counter. He discovers the body of Lt. General Renard in a box. West is discovered by Cluny and Ironfoot (Horvath), the man who had kicked in the door. When West attempts to escape, he is locked in a giant metal box used to fumigate orchids. He uses his handy artificial lung to survive while he rigs his escape using an explosive device. Artie appears as an Express Man called to pick up a trunk. Just when Artie meets up with Ironfoot, West detonates his explosives and escapes from the box. A fight ensues and West uses his shoe knife to kick Ironfoot only to break the knife on his legs which are made of steel. Artie is knocked unconscious while West fights. West is tossed over the side of a balcony, but is saved by the chemical leech. Ironfoot looks over the side and West grabs him and pulls him over and into a vat of boiling oil. Artie awakens and stops Cluny from leaving, thus saving the *franconium* from the hands of the Prussians.

The tag finds West meeting the lovely new secretary to the consulate. The French government thanks the agents for returning the *franconium* to them. Instead of attending the presentation, however, the agents opt to skip out to a play with the new secretary and her friend.

Author's Notes:

This was the first episode directed by Irving Moore and the network was so pleased with the results that he was signed on to direct numerous others. By the series end, he had put his signature on 25 "West" episodes, and went on to accumulate even more, equally as impressive, credits, including work on "Dallas" and "Dynasty." According to Moore, Bob Conrad, who had worked with him on "Hawaiian Eye," insisted that Moore come aboard.

This is one of the few episodes that actually shows the inside ceiling of the train when Artie is suspended as he demonstrates his chemical leech.

This is another of the author's favorites, even though West still appears a little hard on Artie at times, there is definitely a little more of Artie as a friend instead of merely as an associate.

The Night of the
Dancing Death

Secret agents West and Gordon are sent by the government to protect the Princess of Albania (Brander). While the agents are waiting at the docks, they meet with a princess, who is later revealed as an imposter and assassinated, while the real princess is kidnapped. The agents are then left the sad task of telling her brother, Prince Gio (Richman), of her disappearance. The prince is outraged and demands her return. The prince's secretary tells West that she has vital information for him and requests the agent meet her for dinner at the hotel. When West arrives, he is nearly blown to bits by a rigged doorknob. Finding the secretary, he forces information from her and notices that she has a mark on her hand that signifies the Kamora, a secret society of criminals in Albania. West suspects that the princess was kidnapped and replaced before her ship arrived in the United States. The secretary tells West to look for the missing princess at a riding academy.

West discovers the location of the Kamora hideout and is promptly captured. He soon to realizes that it is actually Prince Gio who heads the secret society. After escaping his captors, West meets with Gordon and devises a plan to rescue the princess from her brother. They are invited to attend a party given by the prince. Gordon attends disguised as the Grand Electro of Saxony. He creates a disturbance that enables West to sneak in and look for the princess. West finds Her Highness in the dungeon behind a hidden wall. She explains to West that she was sent by her

The *stakes* are high for James T. West in "Dancing Death."

CBS#6508 Shooting Order 10   CBS Photo
First Air Date: 11/05/65

Produced by Fred Freiberger
Directed by Harvey Hart
Written by Fred Freiberger and William Tunberg

Prince Gio: Mark Richman
Marianna: Ilze Taurins
Princess: Leslie Brander
Major-Domo: Byron Murron
Nola: Francoise Ruggieri
Marius Ascoli: Arthur Batanides
Perkins: Booth Colman
Gina: Lynn Carey
Landgrave: Wolfe Barzell
Baroness: Eva Soreny

father the king to disband the Kamora. Prince Gio finds West with his sister and challenges him to a fight to the death. In a room above the party, they engage in hand-to-hand combat with West delivering the final kick and sending Gio falling to his death.

At the train West and Gordon are trying to spark some interest from Gio's pretty secretary, but she is too busy trying to learn to type to pay any attention to the frustrated agents.

The Night the
Terror Stalked the Town

James West confronts his increasingly familiar adversary, Dr. Miguelito Loveless, in "TNT Terror Stalked the Town."

CBS #6510 Shooting Order 11

CBS Photo

Directed by Alvin Ganzer
Written by John Kneubuhl and Richard Landau

Marie Pincher: Jean Hale
Janus: Chuck O'Brien
Dr. Loveless: Michael Dunn
Antoinette: Phoebe Dorin
Voltaire: Richard Kiel
Baron Colinelcy : Jordan Shelley
Mr. Abernathy : Joe Hooker

Agent West is kidnapped by a beautiful blond woman named Marie (Hale), and is sent to a deserted ghost town. When he awakens, he encounters his increasingly more familiar nemesis, Dr. Miguelito Loveless (Dunn), and his seven-foot-tall assistant, Voltaire (Kiel). Loveless has big plans for the agent, but West is kept in suspense until the annoying doctor chooses to tell him more. West is taken to a room and held captive as Loveless performs an operation changing the face of one of his henchmen, Janus (O'Brien), to resemble West. His plan is to infiltrate the Secret Service and recover the priceless atomic explosive formula that he claims West stole from him. The operation is a success and Loveless sends his West facsimile to see if he can fool Artemus Gordon.

The fake West pretends there is nothing wrong as Gordon questions him about his whereabouts. The phony West claims he was on another assignment, but Gordon knows better and is careful not to give away any of his suspicions. The pseudo-West returns to Loveless and gives him the go-ahead for his plan, not realizing that Gordon is hot on his trail. Loveless prepares to kill the real West, but becomes confused as to which one is the fake West, when the two stand side-by-side. Loveless instructs Marie to kiss the real West. The charmed female switches Wests, but Loveless thinks he's being outsmarted. Marie manages to outsmart the doctor and the real West is left unharmed. The pseudo-West, Janus, escapes, and West and Marie manage to blow up the lab while fleeing. Loveless and Voltaire are trapped in the lab, but manage to crawl into a large glass box that protects them. The two Wests meet and are forced to try each other skills, but the truth triumphs. When Gordon holds West at gunpoint, not knowing for sure which one is the real West, the problem is solved, yet again, by West kissing Marie.

At the train West pulls a gun on Gordon and tells him to turn around and reach for the sky. Gordon momentarily believes that the fake West has triumphed, but as he awaits his fate he slowly turns around to find West, once again, kissing Marie. With all of his doubts assuaged, Gordon replies, "You're the real James West, alright."

Author's Notes:

This marks the second appearance of Dr. Miguelito Loveless, whose popularity was rapidly growing. This is also the first episode where audiences hear about Artemus Gordon's Great Aunt Maude, who becomes a staple reference for the agent in upcoming episodes.

The Night of the
Red-Eyed Madman

Martin Landau (second from right) plays the appropriately named General Grimm in "Red-Eyed Madman."

CBS #6511 Shooting Order 12
First Air Date: 11/26/65

Produced by Fred Freiberger
Directed by Irving Moore
Written by Stanford Whitmore

Lola Bracer: Toian Matchinga
Cloris: Mariana Case
General Grimm: Martin Landau
Jack Talbot: Ted Markland
Sgt. Must: Joan Huntington
Trooper: Don Rizzan
Jenny: Shary Marshall
Sen. Rawls: Nelson Olmsted
Otto: Gregg Martell
Cavalry Officer: Ray Kellogg

Agent James West is visited by Lola Bracer (Matchinga) who tells him that she has received a troubling letter from her fiancé, Jack Talbot (Markland), just before his disappearance. The letter tells her that he has joined a secret army of fanatics that plans to overthrow the United States Army units stationed in the southwest. West tracks the letter to Mars, Nevada.

Inside the military camp, Talbot is being tortured for revealing the existence of the camp to his fiancée in the letter. West arrives and pretends to join their perverted forces. He is introduced to the commander of the army, General Grimm (Landau), who boasts of his radical plan of using both men and women in his army. After dinner, West is stopped by a woman soldier named Jenny (Marshall) who wants to help him crush Grimm's plans. She is assigned to go to town to help blow up an ammunition depot. West tells her to contact his partner, Artemus Gordon, while she's in town and he will know what to do. Afterward, West tries to help Talbot escape from his torture, but it appears that Talbot is too devoted to the cause and he betrays West. The agent is then recognized by an earlier assailant and exposed.

Gordon is contacted by the woman soldier and heads off to find West. Gordon arrives at the fort disguised as Colonel Cross, a German military expert and instructor who would like to join the renegades. The charade doesn't last too long before the agents are captured. Gordon manages to escape, but West is scheduled for execution in the morning. West escapes momentarily, only to find himself trapped in a cage with General Grimm. West fights Grimm and defeats him. With their leader vanquished, the soldiers throw down their arms.

At the train West and Gordon talk to the two former women soldiers. One announces to the boys that she was an equal at the academy, but Jim and Artie both scoff at the outrageous idea of female equality.

The Night of the
Human Trigger

While waiting at a bar, West and Gordon experience a huge earthquake that destroys the bar. The agents conclude that all areas struck by the quake were on a fault line. The next city to be destroyed is Ellenville, Wyoming. The oddity is that the town had been informed by distributed flyers that an earthquake is about to strike. Everyone is leaving town just as the agents arrive. At the hotel they

Burgess Meredith steals the show as Professor Cadwallader, a geologist with cataclysmic plans in "Human Trigger."

CBS Photo

CBS #6512 Shooting Order 13
First Air Date: 12/03/65

Produced by Fred Freiberger
Directed by Justus Addiss
Written by Norman Katlove

Sam: Robert Phillips
Harry: James Jeter
Professor Orkney Cadwallader: Burgess Meredith
Sidney: Robert I. McCord
Faith Cadwallader: Kathie Browne
Sheriff: William Henry
Thaddeus Cadwallader: Gress Palmer
Bartender: Lindsay Workman
Hercules Cadwallader: Mike Masters
Piano Player: Dick Winslow

sends the brothers back to find them.

We soon discover that Professor Cadwallader is a demented geologist who is systematically devastating the state of Wyoming with man-made earthquakes. The professor precisely positions dynamite on fault line to trigger the quakes, with an ultimate aim to turn Wyoming into an independent nation over which he shall preside. As the agents stop for a break and Gordon seeks out water, West is confronted by the brothers. During a gunfight, West kills both adversaries, but he and Gordon are soon confronted by two more henchmen, Sam and Harry. The agents are brought to the professor where they're tied up an a vial of nitroglycerine is placed at their feet. West deduces that it couldn't really be the explosive liquid or the professor wouldn't be hanging around so long.

While bragging to the agents the professor reveals the next target on his destructive schedule: Sawtooth. Planning to kill the agents, he has them placed in a coal bin, sent into a mine and toward a crusher. They rock themselves free and West returns to stop the professor while Gordon goes on to Sawtooth to warn of the imminent quake. When returning to the hideout, West shoots arrows at the henchmen, fooling them into believing Indians are attacking. Fearing for their lives, they leave. West is, yet again, captured by the professor who then decides to use the agent as the detonator for his next quake explosion. West is rigged accordingly, but Gordon intervenes dressed as a fellow geologist and distracts the professor. West breaks free just as the professor figures out the ruse and attempts to trigger the explosion. His calculations are not accurate and Sawtooth remains unharmed. The professor, surprised and annoyed by his error, is carted off to jail.

Author's Notes:
An excellent show and definitely worth watching even if just for guest star Burgess Meredith as the delightfully wacky geologist. He is so nutty and believable that you almost hate to see him get caught. Actor Bob Phillips, who portrays Sam, recalled that the character of Cadwallader was not too far removed from Meredith's own personality. "On the set we used to call him Bugs, 'cause he was buggy. You could have a 10 minute conversation with him and then, a few minutes later, talk to him again and he wouldn't remember who you were."

Regardless of his idiosyncrasies, Meredith steals the show, upstaging everyone, including Ross as fellow geologist, Professor Neinkindorf of Austria.

meet Faith Cadwallader (Browne) who holds them at gunpoint. Her father, Professor Cadwallader (Meredith), has instructed his daughter to eliminate the interfering duo. Her two brothers, Thaddeus (Palmer) and Hercules (Masters) are assigned to kill the agents, but their attempt fails and West and Gordon escape. The agents follow their attackers to their hideout. Faith tells her father that the agents are still alive and he

The Night of the
Torture Chamber

The agents must face another case of dangerous look-alikes in "Torture Chamber." guest starring H.M. Wynant.

CBS #6513 Shooting Order 14
First Air Date; 12/10/65

Produced by Fred Freiberger
Directed by Alan Crosland, Jr.
Written by Philip Saltzman and Jason Wingreen

Miss Piecemeal: Sigrid Valdis
Durand: H.M. Wynant
Governor Bradford: Henry Beckman
Angelique:
Viviane Ventura
Prof. Horatio
Bolt:
  Alfred Ryder

West appears to ponder the universe as Sigrid Valdis looks on.

Governor Bradford (Beckman) and his secretary, Miss Piecemeal (Valdis), watch as the governor's statue is unveiled at the Bolt Museum. Suddenly, the statue blinks and Bradford is immobilized by an injection and taken prisoner. The statue is, in reality, an actor named Sam Jamison who looks just like Bradford and assumes the post of governor. Both Jamison and Miss Piecemeal are flunkies of the evil Professor Bolt (Ryder), the owner of the museum. Bolt aspires to assemble the world's most valuable art collection, which he is determined will include the Mona Lisa. "Governor" Jamison's role in the plot is to obtain the necessary funds by draining the state's treasury of millions of dollars. He must first contend with West and Gordon, however, both of whom were sent for by Bradford before the statue incident.

The agents arrive and are greeted by the fake governor, who tells them his life is in danger and instructs them to find the culprits. West catches the impersonator, who is right handed, while the real governor is left handed, and arrests him. When the agent attempts to locate the real governor, he is captured. Gordon disguises himself as a French art collector, Gaston Larousse, and visits the suspicious Professor Bolt. Gordon proceeds to tell Bolt that all of his priceless art pieces are forgeries. Holding Bolt at gunpoint, Gordon asks where West and the real governor are being held. When Gordon finds his partner, he is also captured and thrown into a giant wine press. They escape by using magnesium strips and burning through the wall. Bold is quickly caught and sent to prison.

Another interesting tidbit of information regarding the secret *spy connection* between two of CBS' top shows of the 1960s — "Get Smart" and "The Wild Wild West." Twice did shades of "West" appear in "Smart" episodes. The first time is where Maxwell Smart is pretending to be a traveling dignitary and finds Jim and Artie's elegant railcar to be perfect accommodations. We see a little "West" again in a later episode when the dragon used in "The Night of the Watery Death," appears in the Tunnel of Love and breathes smoke on Max and 99.

Whole Lotta Shakin' Going On

Fred Freiberger's successful reign as the show's producer continued for a total of 10 (including two Loveless) episodes. Praised for helping to get the show back "on the right track," Freiberger's departure was laced with controversy. According to sources, the show was doing very well in the ratings and the NBC-TV opposition, "Hank" and "Camp Runamuck," were both in the bottom 15 of the Nielsens. Both "Hank," starring Dick Kallman, and "Runamuck," starring Arch Johnson and Dave Madden, lasted only one season.

> Garrison knew nothing about the impending change until he was contacted for comment by *Daily Variety*. It came as a complete surprise...

On November 4, 1965, in an evident power play, CBS fired Fred Freiberger, executive producer Michael Garrison and most of "The Wild Wild West" crew. One source claimed the show was going downhill and that Garrison was having a difficult time staying within the show's budget. It was also suggested that the reason for the move involved the series' star, Robert Conrad. Apparently, CBS felt that Conrad was getting too much control and that the crew would only listen to him. There were also rumors that the actor had a habit of participating in an array of unacceptable after-hour activities. One source claimed that CBS was attempting to "slap Bob's hands" by firing everyone close to him; Freiberger included.

The situation with Garrison was entirely different. Garrison knew nothing about the impending change until he was contacted for comment by *Daily Variety*. It came as a complete surprise to the show's creator, who quickly contacted his attorney Bertram Fields, from Shearer Fields. Immediately, a wire was sent to the network questioning their contractual right to make such a unilateral move.

Freiberger's replacement was the former associate producer of "Gunsmoke," John Mantley. Accompanying Mantley as executive producer would be Philip Leacock, who had served as producer on the same show.

Mantley recalled his situation with Freiberger. "I walked in and said, 'I'm John Mantley,' and Fred said, 'Oh, yes, I've heard of you. What can I do for you?' I said, 'Well, I don't know what to say.' Fred replied, 'Am I being replaced?' I told him yes."

The situation was different for Garrison, however, as sources revealed that he was furious and would not let Leacock into his office or allow him to read any scripts. Even though Leacock was credited as "The Wild Wild West" executive producer, he was actually allowed to do very little during this brief period with the show and eventually returned to "Gunsmoke."

CBS told *Daily Variety* in a November 4, article announcing the changes that Freiberger would be devoting his time to producing a pilot property for the network. Freiberger blatantly replied that he'd been fired for accomplishing what he had been hired to do. "I was hired to pull the show together when it was in chaos. We are now 13th in average share and tied for third at the last national Nielsens. I have no pilot plans. That was just a face-saving thing," Freiberger said.

Conrad told *Daily Variety* his view of the shake-up. "I was totally shocked by the producer switch. I think Fred Freiberger is totally correct in his concept of the show. It's an administration change, for what reason, I don't know. I don't think Mr. Freiberger knows. I was delighted at the way the show was going. My relationship with Mr. Freiberger is such that I thought he was going to keep us on the air four or five years. Now a change has been made without my knowledge. I accept it because I'm an employee of CBS, which is aware of my feelings regarding Freiberger. He is the same producer who started 'Shenandoah' and got it into the top 10. He's done a great job on this show. I would be a hypocrite because he is no longer producer of the show to say he has not done well."

JOHN MANTLEY EPISODES:
The Night of the Howling Light
The Night of the Steel Assassin
The Night the Dragon Screamed
The Night of the Flaming Ghost (The Ghost Who Would Not Die)
The Night of theGrand Emir
The Night of the Whirring Death
The Night of the Puppeteer

After CBS attempted to fire Garrison they discovered they had made a sizable error in judgment. During the earlier negotiations between Hunt Stromberg, representing CBS, and Garrison, sources indicated that Garrison had secured 40% of the show and neglected to inform the entire administration. In addition to his 40%, Garrison also retained certain rights involving personnel changes.

Bertram Fields, representing Garrison, said, "As far as I'm concerned CBS' announcement was premature. I don't think they have the right to move him without permission. They have approval rights, but it doesn't give them the right to make lateral changes without consulting him. The contract provides Garrison Productions, who produces the show and hires personnel, subject to network approval. It doesn't provide the network will hire and fire as they please without consulting the company which owns the show. The title of the show belongs to Garrison Productions, who is responsible for it. This has been a premature release and I'm writing CBS saying we haven't been consulted and haven't approved. The position is CBS doesn't have the right to act unilaterally in this matter. Aside from the control it's a matter of courtesy to let Garrison know the changes."

> After CBS attempted to fire Garrison they discovered they had made a sizable error in judgment.

Another observer suggested that the reason there hadn't been any problems with Garrison and CBS prior to the shakeup was because Garrison had his executive producer credit and CBS had three or four line producers (*associate or assistant producers — ed.*) ready to take over duties in a pinch. They claimed that Garrison didn't care as long as his name was on the screen and he was making $5,000 a week.

Overall, it became evident that CBS was waiting for an opportune time to oust Garrison for several reasons. There was the situation with Conrad's abundance of control and some sources speculated that Garrison may have fallen prey to forces in the upper echelons who questioned his lifestyle.

Story editor Bill Koenig remembered, "About all Mike was doing was stewing, and going through whatever legal processes to get his show back."

Meanwhile, back at the ranch, the show must go on regardless of the administrative and legal rumblings. Air dates were rapidly approaching; Mantley was in, Freiberger was out, and Mantley had walked into a problem. On one Friday afternoon as they finished shooting one show they needed to begin preparation for the new shoot the following Monday.

"We didn't have any outlines, there was no writer anywhere writing or working on a script, and no possibility of even having a preemption," Mantley recalled. He was frantic so he called some friends, went through the files and found outlines that had long been discarded. "I found an interesting one that had to do with a man whose body was loaded with steel and extremely strong. That was 'Steel Assassin' (starring John Dehner)," he said. "I called writer Cal Clements and told him he had to do a script for me this weekend. We got together and in less than two hours blocked out the story, and by Monday we had a script."

After that, Mantley called art director Al Heschong and instructed him as to what was required. By Monday they were ready to shoot and, from that moment on, Mantley was in control. He gave out six or seven outlines to hired writers and told them to do the scripts.

Joe Ruskin, who appeared in dozens of classic TV shows throughout the 1960s and 70s, and continues his successful career today, appeared in two "West" episodes, "The Night of the Fatal Trap" and "The Night of the Falcon." I asked Joe about his experiences when working on "West," and he said that he immediately noticed the high level of professionalism when he walked on the set.

"Of course, I always played the usual Western heavy. I believe I was blown up one time. But I know when I got on the set I was truly impressed by the level of professionalism, especially with the directors. I was so impressed by Richard Whorf. I remember how he would choose a shot. I looked at Whorf's script and he had this incredibly detailed sketch of the entire set on it. The cinematographer said, 'I wish everyone was like that.' The professionalism and care by everyone they hired was very, very high." Born in Massachusetts, like Ruskin, Whorf also came from a theatrical background, which would explain his extreme attention to detail. Whorf died in 1966 at the age of 60, just one year after his "West" experience.

The Night of the
Howling Light

Agent James West must endure agonizing mental conditioning that leads him to murder in "TNOT Howling Light."

CBS Photo

CBS #6514 Shooting Order 15
First Air Date: 12/17/65

Produced by John Mantley
Directed by Paul Wendkos
Written by Henry Sharp

Superintendent: E.J. Endre
Hag: Ottola Nesmith
Dr. Arcularis: Sam Wanamaker
Trowbridge: Clancy Cooper
Ahkeema: Scott Marlowe
Siles: Roy Bancroft
Indra: Linda Marsh
Caged Man: Kay E. Kuter
Ho-Tami: Ralph Moody
Coast Guard Officer: Dan Riss

Secret agent Jim West and Ahkeema (Marlowe), a college educated Indian, are awaiting the U.S. President's reply to Ahkeema's father, Ho-Tami (Moody), who has persuaded 100,000 Indians from various tribes to sign a peace treaty. West is lured into a hospital where he believes he will find his friend and partner, Artemus Gordon. In the hospital, West is gassed and carried out in a coffin by the weird, zombie-like aides of Dr. Arcularis (Wanamaker).

West finds himself the prisoner of the evil doctor in an old lighthouse. Through mental conditioning Arcularis dominates his weird aides. When he demonstrates that they are impervious to pain by brutally twisting the arm of the pretty Indra (Marsh), West protests. The agent is immediately bound to a chair and made ready to begin his own conditioning process. It soon becomes apparent that Ahkeema has hired Arcularis to program West to kill his father and sabotage the peace treaty.

After a week of conditioning, it appears that West is ready to carry out the evil deed and kill Ho-Tami. Gordon goes to the hospital where West was and finds out, from an old lady patient who had kept a diary, where he was taken. Ahkeema is told by Arcularis that West is prepared to kill Ho-Tami. While under a trance, the agent is attracted by a tie pin on Ahkeema. West arrives at the peace conference and the brilliant tie pin brings the agent out of his trance before he is able to shoot Ho-Tami.

West shoots Ahkeema instead of Ho-Tami and tells everyone that Ahkeema was behind the plot. West returns to Dr. Arcularis and discovers that Gordon, too, has been conditioned. When free, Gordon tries to kill his partner, but West triumphs, leaving Gordon unconscious. West tells the doctor's aides to take their lighthouse back and fight to break the trance. Gordon awakens, is snapped out of the trance and the agents watch as the aides reclaim their lighthouse. As they watch the doctor's demise they can't seem to think of a reason to rush to his assistance, until Gordon thinks that he might be useful conditioning women to be only sweet and kind and never nag or complain. They proceed to rescue Arcularis.

Author's Notes:

This episode brought Director of Photography Ted Voightlander an Emmy Award nomination. He lost out to Winston Hotch for his work on the popular series, "Voyage to the Bottom of the Sea."

The Night of the
Steel Assassin

John Dehner plays Colonel Torres, a man who takes the idea of a steely stare to a whole new level in "Steel Assassin."

CBS Photo

CBS #6516 Shooting Order 16
First Air Date: 01/07/66

Produced by John Mantley
Directed by Lee H. Katzin
Written by Calvin Clements

Maria: Sara Taft
R.L. Gilbert: John Pickard
Colonel Torres: John Dehner
Dr. Meyer: Arthur Malet
Nina Gilbert: Sue Ane Langdon
President Grant: Roy Engel
Guthrie: Allen Jaffe
Bartender: Bruno Vesota

Agent Jim West happens upon Colonel "Iron Man" Torres (Dehner) as he strangles a shop owner named Gilbert (Pickard). Attempting to thwart the attack, West soon discovers his efforts are fruitless as even bullets glance harmlessly off Torres' body. West finally drives him off with a smoke pellet. Gilbert is Torres' sixth victim as he seeks revenge against seven U.S. Army officers he served with during the Civil War. He believes that they cheated him in a drawing for a night of guard duty which resulted in his being badly mangled in an explosion. Now his hand and most of his body are made of steel. When Nina (Langdon), Gilbert's niece, produces a photograph of the eight officers in her uncle's regiment, West recognizes President Grant as one of the two men still alive. Torres is the other.

Grant is scheduled to speak at a nearby town and West and Gordon must act fast. Nina goes to warn Torres that someone might be out to get him, not knowing that he is the culprit. Torres hypnotizes her and instructs her to ignore the situation. He tells her to banish all serious thought. West and Gordon later see Nina as a showgirl in the saloon under Torres' hypnotic suggestion, and rescue her. Later the agents are told that Grant refuses to protect himself and is going to speak at the festivities anyway.

Gordon is captured by Torres and he, too, is hypnotized into knowing the location of Torres hideout, hoping the agents will return so that he may eliminate them. They go to Torres' hideout with Nina and are captured. Gordon manages to escape but West and Nina are caught. Torres has set up a deadly display of fireworks, one remote control rocket set and aimed for President Grant and the other aimed at the control room where West is tied up. Grant comes to town, but is actually Gordon in disguise.

Torres leaves before the rocket is launched. West gets his foot loose, knocks the controls out of range, breaks free and pursues Torres. West confronts Torres and knocks the "Iron Man" into his own underground river, sealing his fate. Nina is dehypnotized and, when she realizes she is running around half naked in a dance hall costume, she promptly begins shouting and hurling objects at the innocent West and Gordon.

Besides "Steel Assassin," writer Cal Clements went on to write three more episodes of "The Wild Wild West:" "Juggernaut," "Undead" and "Brain."

Garrison's attorney Bertram Fields has maintained a highly successful and long career representing dozens of major names in Hollywood.

48

The Night the
Dragon Screamed

James west shares tea as he figures out the whereabouts of a Chinese princess in "TNT Dragon Screamed."

CBS Photo

CBS #6517 Shooting Order 17
First Air Date: 01/14/66

Produced by John Mantley
Directed by Irving J. Moore
Written by Kevin De Courcey

Mo Ti: Benson Fong
Wang Chung: Richard Loo
Princess Ching Ling: Pilar Seurat
Tsu His: Nancy Hsueh
Allenby-Smythe: Ben Wright
Lieutenant: Vince Eder
May Li: Beulah Quo
Oriental: Paul Hing

Agents West and Gordon set out to crack a thriving opium/alien smuggling operation in San Francisco and become involved in a struggle for control of the Hunan Province, China. West learns that the opium and aliens are being used to finance and man an invasion army with which ex-British soldier, Clive Allenby-Smythe (Wright), plans to seize the Hunan throne. Before he can succeed, he must locate the Princess Ching Ling (Seurat) and make her his puppet empress.

A loyal Thong leader, Wang Chung (Loo), who has been hiding the princess, decides she would be safer back in China. Gordon poses as an armaments salesman, Captain Sumatra, but is held captive only to be rescued by Smythe who employs him.

Chung orders West to see that the princess remains unharmed as she embarks on her voyage home. West comes to rescue the Princess and gets caught by Smythe, who takes West to his munitions dump to prove that the province is his. Gordon is then discovered by Smythe and he and West are locked up. West uses his vest buttons to burn through the door and the agents race to set the timing devices that will blow up the munitions dump. With the dump destroyed, along with Smythe, the Princess is safe to return to her homeland.

Author's Notes:
Mysteries of the Orient set off this interesting tale that has all the makings of a 1940's spy movie. An interesting note: West finds a message in a fortune cookie, which were not introduced in the United States until 1918.

The Night of the
Flaming Ghost
AKA The Ghost Who Would Not Die

Agent Jim West is investigating the loss of government supplies of kerosene and copper when his stagecoach is halted by a sheet of flames. West resists the attack but fails as a band of hooded men kidnap passengers Barbara Bosley (Sharpe) and Carma Vasquez (Loring). The leader of the hooded men takes the women to a secret fort where they meet his superior, a man named John Brown (Doucette).

Brown orders Carma, an artist, to sketch his likeness for posterity as he progressively garners the wealth and power never attained by his uncle, the original John Brown. His second captive, Barbara, a dress designer, is ordered to create a fire-resistant suit so that Brown may be protected as he operates his secret

A fireproof suit and a deadly flame-thrower cause problems for Agents West and Gordon in "TNOT Flaming Ghost."

CBS #6519 Shooting Order 18
First Air Date: 01/21/66

Produced by John Mantley
Directed by Lou Katzman
Written by Robert Hamner and Preston Wood

Carma Vasquez: Lynn Loring
Luis Vasquez: Robert Ellenstein
John Brown : John Doucette
Will Gover : Harry Bartell
Barbara Bosley: Karen Sharpe
Shukie Summers: Charles Wagenheim

weapon; a giant flame-thrower. Barbara is placed in the suit and used in an experiment as to its effectiveness. When she escapes, she is wounded, but is able to tell the agents about Brown's elaborate plan. They quickly spring into action. West heads for the fort, but is captured by Brown's men. Gordon also sets out, but this time as R.P. McGuffy, a whiskey peddler/smuggler.

Meanwhile, back at the fort, Carma is diligently working on the commissioned portrait. She sees Gordon but foils his disguise by recognizing his ears, claiming that a person can alter almost any aspect of their appearance, except their ears. With West and

Gordon under lock and key, Brown is ready to test his new cannon. The agents manage to escape and Gordon leaves to warn the Cavalry while West is, again, captured. Our dynamic agent again gets free, this time defeating Brown and his deadly scheme.

The Night of the
Grand Emir

West and Gordon are assigned to protect Middle-Eastern despot Emir El Emid (Middleton) from assassination, but find their task complicated by the attitude of the tyrant who has survived so many attempts on his life that he no longer concerns himself with such annoyances. The agents accompany the Emir to a café to watch a Can-Can dancer named Ecstacy La Joie (Craig), who has repeatedly tried to kill the despot. When the Emir demands a garter from Ecstacy, she obliges, but West intercepts and disposes of the garter just before it explodes. Ecstasy runs to her employer, Dr. Mohammed Bey (Lanphier), who wants the Emir dead. West pursues the dancer but is scratched by her drugged ring and taken to Dr. Bey. When he awakens, West is immobilized by a straightjacket. Bey gives Ecstasy a tambourine that has been sharpened into a deadly weapon and sends her back out to attack the Emir.

Cable (Jaeckel), one of the Bey's henchmen, decides it's time he took control. He kills Bey and places himself as the head of the operation. At another banquet for the Emir, Ecstasy dances with her deadly tambourine. West manages to escape in time to stop Ecstasy's assassination attempt but the Emir decides he likes the dancer very much and refuses to press charges. West leaves for a change of clothes, a toast is proposed and soon everyone in the room, except Gordon, is overcome by a drug. Ecstasy tries to stab the Emir, Gordon intervenes but is knocked unconscious by Cable.

Cable and Ecstasy decide to take the Emir with them. When West returns to the room, he finds everyone unconscious and the Emir missing. The agents begin to suspect a snoopy upper crust by the name of T. Wigget Jones (Francks), and take him along on the pursuit. Gordon, thinking ahead, had placed a luminescent tape on the wheel of the Emir's coach so they would be

A pompous Emir cavalierly resists the agents' efforts to guard his life in "The Night of the Grand Emir."

CBS #6518 Shooting Order 19
First Air Date: 01/28/66

Produced by John Mantley
Directed by Irving J. Moore
Written by Donn Mullally

Dr. Mohammed Bey: James Lanphier
No. 1 Girl: Arlene Charles
Ecstasy La Joie: Yvonne Craig
No 2. Girl: Phyllis Davis
Emir El Emid: Robert Middleton
Willard Drapeu: Tom Palmer
T. Wiggett Jones: Don Francks
Clay: Ralph Gard
Christopher Cable: Richard Jaeckel
George: Arthur E. Gould-Porter

able to follow the trail aided by special glasses.

West discovers that Jones is behind the kidnapping and murder attempts. It is discovered that he is a part of an assassins club that has been trying to use the Emir as a ploy in their negotiations to purchase the land located at the isthmus of Suez, where the canal is scheduled to be built. Jones wants West to join them, but the agent refuses and is put into a glass cage affixed with canisters of poison. Gordon appears as one of the

Emir's sheiks, Hussain Bin Hokar, but the arrogant Emir believes he doesn't need to be saved and reveals Gordon's identity.

By now the old West charm has taken its toll on Ecstasy and she rescues the agent from his cage. In the ensuing battle Jones proves to be a fair match for West, but the agent eventually catches him off guard, trapping Jones in his own device, the glass booth. When the cage locks, the poison automatically dispenses, killing Jones. The Emir is, once again, safe and West and Ecstasy dance the night away.

Author's Notes:

"Grand Emir" was written by Don Mullally who said that the concept actually came to him through friendly ties. "I had a friend that was a shirttail relative to the King of Libya. He had this crazy, mixed-up Libyan connection going, and it gave me the idea for the story."

The Night of the
Whirring Death

Secret agents West and Gordon help Governor Lewis (White) keep the state of California solvent by seeing that a pledged $5 million from each of three wealthy, but disreputable, people is received in exchange for state bonds and respectable positions. Jeremiah Ratch (Fell), a money lender; John Crane (Avery), a builder; and Bessie Bowen (Nichols), a gambling hall owner, have all pledged the sizable sum. West and Gordon first arrive at Ratch's business to collect the funds. Outside they meet Miss Ames (Austin) and a group of children trying to make money by selling toys. West buys the toys, but one little boy gives his toy to Ratch, and the toy explodes. Ratch is presumed killed, Gordon escapes the explosion, but West is injured. Gordon sees the small boy run with the money and gives chase. During the pursuit, Gordon runs right into the giant Voltaire (Kiel), who speaks briefly, then knocks him out .

West awakens in Miss Ames' home. Soon the agents realize that the diminutive Dr. Miguelito Loveless (Dunn) has positioned himself as their adversary once again. His current determination is to keep the money from the governor. The agents must protect the

Dr. Loveless and Voltaire return to have some fun and games with agents West and Gordon in "Whirring Death," the third Loveless episode.

CBS Photo

CBS #6520 Shooting Order 20
First Air Date: 02/18/66

Produced by John Mantley
Directed by Mark Rydell
Written by Jackson Gillis

Voltaire: Richard Kiel
Governor Lewis: Jesse White
Dr. Miguelito Loveless: Michael Dunn
Bessie Bowen: Barbara Nichols
Priscilla Ames: Pamela Austin
John Crane : Val Avery
Jeremiah Ratch : Norman Fell
Antoinette: Phoebe Dorin

whereabouts of the evil doctor. Bowen knows, but fears for her life and is reluctant to tell.

West finds Loveless' hideout, a toy company, and is captured. Loveless explains his scheme, or rather, dream, of making California his private nation and a paradise for little children. West is placed in a giant clown. Loveless reveals that he plans to kill the governor upon his arrival, using a note from the agent.

Gordon eventually persuades Bessie to reveal the doctor's hideout. When they arrive, it is dark but they are still able to locate West and rescue him. When the governor arrives, West and Gordon save the day, defeating Loveless who, as always, manages to slip through their fingers and escape. It is also discovered that Ratch and Crane were only wounded by their explosions and are able to pay the promised money to the state.

Author's Notes:
By this third episode featuring the tiny Dr. Loveless, Michael Dunn's popularity had elevated him into being a semi-regular for the show. He had also earned the prestigious rank of being the agents' favorite nemesis, always posing an unusually bizarre challenge.

The Night of the
Puppeteer

Two U.S. Supreme Court Justices have died mysteriously. Secret agent James West expresses concern for the life of Justice Chayne (Hoyt), who summarily dismisses his him. Chayne must admit, however, that there may be a danger since he has received a mysterious miniature casket similar to those received by the other two justices prior to their murders. In his home, Chayne enters an adjoining room where a puppet show is taking place for his grandson's birthday. The puppets are depicting a court trial with the judge, and exact duplicate of Chayne, is being threatened by the puppet defendant. When Mrs. Chayne (Taft) mentions that she had been wondering who was responsible for such a treat for the children, West grows suspicious. A gun is suddenly aimed at Chayne from beyond the puppeteer's drape, but West shoves the justice aside just in time and shoots the assassin puppet. West is drugged by a poison dart and falls unconscious.

Later, after the assailant has escaped and

other two millionaires.

West goes to the home of John Crane, who has chosen to disregard any of the agent's warnings. Crane is too busy playing with his new toy train set, a surprise gift from an admirer. West deduces the danger, but before he can act, the train explodes, killing Crane.

Meanwhile, Gordon has gone to see Bessie Bowen, the third benefactor. Gordon is disguised as the Italian opera singer, Artoro Caruso del Artemo, who manages to save her from her explosion, and seeks the

Lloyd Bochner dons a bald cap to portray the severely crippled and vengeful Zachariah Skull in "Puppeteer."

CBS #6521 Shooting
Order 21
First Air Date: 02/25/66

Produced by John Mantley
Directed by Irving J.
Moore
Written by Henry Sharpe

CBS Photos

Zachariah Skull: Lloyd Bochner
Vivid: Imelda de Martin
Dr. Lake: Nelson Olmsted
Mrs. Chayne: Sara Taft
Sandwich Man: Len Rogel
Butler: Jack Tygett
Justice Chayne: John Hoyt
Caveman: Walter Painter
Waitress: Janis Hansen
Harlequin: Wayne Albritton

West is revived, the agent notices that each of the puppets is deformed in some way: missing fingers, eyes, etc. with the exception of Vivid, a beautiful ballerina puppet. Vivid wears a talisman that leads West to a trap at Triton's Locker, a waterfront saloon. Upon his arrival, a fight ensues and West attempts to escape through an elevator that descends, then plummets, to a

place deep beneath the surface. The elevator slows to a stop and West finds himself in a dark and mysterious cavern. He is confronted by the brilliant sculptor Zachariah Skull (Bochner), who was unjustly sentenced some years prior and is seeking revenge on the justices. Long ago Skull managed to escape his imprisonment and impending death sentence by diving off a speeding prison train, only to be faced with a sentence far worse than death.

West must face a mock trial for murder of the marionette he shot at the birthday party. He meets a life-size Vivid (de Martin) along with an array of surly criminal puppets seated as the jury. They quickly find him guilty as charged. Skull presides over the hearing and sentences West to death.

West's expeditious execution is interrupted by the arrival of Gordon, who has traced his partner's whereabouts using the same clues that lead West to Skull. The two agents defeat their puppet adversaries and go after Skull. They are amazed to discover that Skull is also a puppet.

They soon learn the only one who isn't a puppet is Vivid, Skull's protégé. West happens upon a steam shut-off valve and deduces that the puppets are all steam operated. Shutting off the supply stifles all the puppets, then the agents follow Vivid to the main works of the puppet kingdom where they meet the real Zachariah Skull; a grossly deformed figure severely crippled by his dive from the speeding train. His twisted form huddles in the center of an elaborate web-like mechanism that operates his kingdom of life-size marionettes.

The agents try to stop the madman, but he had long since chosen death before submission. A shot is fired that pierces one of the highly pressurized steam pipes. The agents must make a fast exit before the entire cavern explodes. West, Gordon and Vivid escape in the nick of time.

Later, at another children's puppet show Gordon watches the entertainment with Judge Chayne. Gordon notices the puppets acting strangely and investigates. The new puppeteer, Vivid, is distracted by kissing her rescuer, Jim West.

Author's Notes:
Of all the "West" episodes, "Puppeteer" is a favorite of the producer Mantley, the director Moore and the art director, Al Heschong. When Mantley received the script he loved it, but CBS demanded that it be under budget going in. Moore and Heschong brainstormed to come up with an interesting, but inexpen-

sive, concept. The resulting set was completely the director's idea.

"The sets were built, lit and shot by my design," Moore said. "Ethel Winant came to me and said that of all the television shows she had seen, this was the first time she'd ever seen a director's concept of a script." Moore worked with Heschong to create the mysterious set and Heschong's background in theater was effectively applied, using backdrops and solitary pieces of furniture.

Heschong explained how the puppeteer's elaborate *web* was designed. "Basically, it was like a dome sitting on a stage floor melded into the darkness. This whole system was supposed to be operated by steam, our usual mode of energy. Above the dome suspended a platform where the villain had levers to activate the steam and ropes to activate the puppets. We tried to make a web with lines going up and down. There was a circular console of levers and a ramp, too, so it seemed suspended, and looking down, you could see the steam pipes going off in different directions."

At the time the episode ran in black and white, but everyone working on the show remembered the vivid colors against the black background. "It's hard to watch the show today and think it was shown in black and white, because the colors in the costumes and sets are still etched in my mind," Mantley said.

CBS Photo

Actor John Hoyt faces troublesome puppets *again* in "TNOT Puppeteer."

An interesting aside to this episode is that it featured actor John Hoyt as Justice Chayne. By the mid-1960s, Hoyt was a well-known character actor who had appeared in hundreds of movies and television series. He had also managed to establish a minor reputation for himself as a star of a few notable B-grade horror films, not the least of which was Bert I. Gordon's 1958 thriller, "Attack of the Puppet People." Hoyt played the demented Dr. Franz, a lonely scientist who had perfected a machine that could be used to shrink people to doll size. I can't imagine that there wasn't an intentional irony to his being cast as the man targeted by marionettes seeking justice.

Garrison Returns

Daily Variety, *December 30, 1965*

Mike Garrison, yesterday, was restored to his post as executive producer of CBS-TV's "The Wild Wild West" series, a job from which he was evicted about six weeks ago. Philip Leacock, who had taken over the function of executive producer on the series, returns to full time producership of the network's "Gunsmoke," and in addition will work on a 90-minute format of that vet oater for next fall, it is disclosed by Perry Lafferty, coast program VP of the web. As for John Mantley, who was moved from associate producer of "Gunsmoke" to producer of "WWW" at the same time Leacock joined the show, he will remain with "WWW" for the period still to be determined, (Perry) Lafferty said. Garrison created "WWW" and at the time he was removed from the series, asserted his pact with the web that did not permit unilateral personnel changes on the show by CBS-TV, stating he owns 40 percent of the series.

After six weeks of a legal battle, Michael Garrison trapped CBS on a legal technicality. If the network tried to place anyone else in as executive producer of the series Garrison would reclaim the show.

Freiberger commented on Garrison's reinstatement. "Now he had them, so he took the show over and became executive producer once again. They asked him who he wanted as producer and he said, 'Fred Freiberger.' Well, by then my situation with CBS was very tenuous. I had given out an interview that they probably didn't enjoy at the time. Anyway, Leacock had to be dumped and they kept John Mantley to finish up."

Mantley stayed on for only two more episodes. Then in January of 1966, yet again, another producer graced the notorious series. Gene Coon, who became better known for his work on NBC-TV's "Star Trek," stepped in as the seventh producer of "The Wild Wild West" while Mantley returned to Dodge City.

On March 10, 1966, *The Night of the Terrible Spring* continued when the series had an unexpected switch. A complete reversal of the saga of juggling producers occurred when Coon suddenly quit. He had taken on a screenwriting assignment from Warner Brothers on the film "Tell It to the Marines." As a result, Michael Garrison began playing a dual role for the network as *both* producer and executive producer.

The Night of the
Bars of Hell

Arthur O'Connell plays a weakling warden with a brand new electric chair in "Bars of Hell."

CBS Photo

CBS #6522 Shooting Order 22
First Air Date: 03/04/66

Produced by Gene L. Coon
Directed by Richard Donner
Written by Bob Wright

Gideon McCoy: Elisha Cook
Executioner: Milton Parsons
Warden Ragan: Arthur O'Connell
Kitten: Jeni Jackson
Jennifer McCoy: Indus Arthur
Borg: Bob Herron
Kross: Paul George
Driscoll: Roy Sickner
Adams: Chet Stratton
Convict Painter: Shawn Michaels

Agents West and Gordon are assigned to halt an organized outbreak of terror that has paralyzed a Western community. Jennifer McCoy (Arthur), whose uncle is schedule to die, goes to West,

hoping for help in retrieving money from her criminal uncle. West poses as Federal Prison Inspector Charles Lane to investigate strange goings-on at the local prison that may be related to the crime problem. Warden Ragan (O'Connell), a gentle law officer who greatly opposes capital punishment, greets West and shows him around the prison. He proudly exhibits the new electric chair, the first of its kind, that is scheduled to be broken in by notorious prisoner Gideon McCoy (Cook), Jennifer's uncle.

When West meets McCoy the agent immediately notices that he doesn't look like a condemned man: He sports a healthy tan, manicured nails and fails to convince the agent that he has the thoughts and demeanor of a man who is about to die. West discovers that all of Ragan's prisoners have been receiving luxury treatment and are recruited to utilize their best talents, be it murder, robbery, or whatever is needed by the warden.

West is recognized by a prisoner and an angry Ragan places the agent in the fighting ring with Kross (George), a giant man who Ragan thinks is sure to triumph over West. When West wins, Ragan decides to schedule him to be the first man to die in the electric chair in place of McCoy.

Meanwhile, Gordon poses as a preacher to get information from the townspeople. Later, he dresses as the *electrocutioner* and infiltrates the prison as the man assigned to operate the chair for the McCoy execution. Artie sees that West has been substituted for the *real McCoy*. Artie pulls the electrical wires out of the wall and uses them to threaten the warden and get West freed. A guard sees the commotion and shuts off the generator, leaving the agents to fend for themselves. A fight ensues and the agents escape. They discover that the warden is doing a little escaping of his own along with the funds he has accumulated from the crime ring. They leave the prison with the warden and get the money to Jennifer McCoy, who is justifiably unmoved by the fact that her uncle is really scheduled for execution.

Author's Notes:

"Bars of Hell" was the first of four "West" episodes from director Richard Donner. After minor involvement with the series' pilot while at CBS, Donner had built a good relationship with Mike Garrison, so for Garrison's first show as the returning executive producer he chose Donner to direct.

The director remembered that "West" was a

very well received show and anyone involved with it was also well received in the industry. "Garrison was one of the most outgoing, crazy, wonderfully funny men I had ever met. Back then directors had little input on the episodes they worked on, but with Garrison I had free-rein. I was involved with everything; editing, music and effects," Donner said. Today Richard Donner is one of Hollywood's most successful feature directors with such credits as the "The Omen," the "Lethal Weapon" series of films and "Superman" (1978)." He continues to leave his mark on Hollywood with upcoming productions.

We see an interesting performance by veteran actor Arthur O'Connell, who does well as the feeble, but diabolical warden Ragan. This episode is a little different than what Garrison usually aimed for, but the end result is a nice production with that Donner touch.

The Night of the
Two-Legged Buffalo

Agents West and Gordon are assigned to protect a stubborn and carefree South Sea Coral Islands prince (Adams) who insists on going to an exclusive health resort where ceremonies are to be held (and assassins are waiting to kill him.) Murder of the prince would mean the loss of an important treaty he is to sign with the United States, and would precipitate the massacre of missionaries living on his islands. West pretends that the Prince is kidnapped from the train and, as not to endanger the treaty, Gordon attempts to pose as the prince. The ruse fails and serves only to convince the conspirators that West must die before the assassination can be carried out. The assassins are led by Lady Beatrice (Wynter), a demure Englishwoman whom West first meets when she brings flowers to the prince's suite.

Her first attempt at ridding the world of West is to arrange for him to drown in one of the resort's mud baths. The attempt fails. Meanwhile, Gordon is kidnapped by Lady Beatrice and taken to a hideout, where he is persuaded to tell where the real prince is being hidden. West, the prince and

Popular actor, Nick Adams takes an unusual approach to his role as a Hawaiian Prince in "The Night of the Two-Legged Buffalo."

CBS Photo

CBS #6523 Shooting Order 23
First Air Date: 03/11/66

Produced by Gene L. Coon
Directed by Edward Dein
Written by John Kneubuhl

Prince: Nick Adams
Lady Beatrice: Dana Wynter
Claude Duchamps: Robert Emhardt
Vittorie Pellagrini: Paul Comi
Bandit: Clint Ritchie
Manager: Lindsay Workman
Coach Driver: Al Wyatt

some backup go to rescue Gordon from his failed ruse. When the agents meet, West tells Gordon that the kidnapping attempt was a fake designed to keep the prince away from the spa until the potential assassins could be identified. The prince suddenly turns a gun on the agents and reveals that he is connected to Lady Beatrice and her scheme. The prince wishes to go buffalo hunting, using the two agents as his "Two-Legged Buffalo." West's skills shine through as he overpowers the prince. Lady Beatrice suddenly aims a rifle at the prince, who is aghast by her change of heart. She tells him that she got the jewels she wanted and no longer needs him. West announces that the jewels are phony and Gordon and the prince join in to catch her off guard and relieve her of the rifle. Lady Beatrice is placed behind bars, leaving the world safe for princes.

Back at the train, the agents tell the prince how lucky he is not to be in jail. He only scoffs at their warnings, telling them they're lucky that his savage instincts don't provoke him to cook and eat them as well as kill them. He announces that both agents should visit his country and they will go hunting together. West asks what they would be hunting, and the prince replies, "I wouldn't dream of telling you. I do adore surprise endings. Don't you?"

Author's Notes:

"Two-Legged Buffalo" is a very entertaining "West" episode written by one of my favorite "West" writers, John Kneubuhl. I asked Kneubuhl if the story came out of his Samoan roots. "It was actually the first thing I did for Mike Garrison on his return as executive producer. I thought of a Hawaiian friend of mine who was very famous on the islands. He was a con man, a check forger and was into just about everything. His name was Sam Amado and I thought it would be funny if I spoofed that kind of tradition by spoofing Sam in an episode. Red Buttons, I think, was considered for the part. So I revised it for Red and the evening before shooting started he came down with pneumonia, so they cast Nick Adams, who I thought did very well. But the story isn't taken from my roots, it's taken from the posed public appearance of that friend of mine in Hawaii."

Actor Nick Adams, who was close friends with Bob Conrad, is excellent as the prince and at making West and Gordon's job very frustrating. This episode also guest stars Dana Wynter, better known for her role in the universally creepy 1956 sci-fi thriller, "Invasion of the Body Snatchers," opposite another "West" alumnus, Kevin McCarthy ("Doomsday Formula").

Don Rickles guest starred in dozens of shows throughout the 1960s including: "Twilight Zone," "The Addams Family," "The Munsters," "Get Smart," I Dream of Jeannie" and "Gilligan's Island," to name a few.

The Night of the
Druid's Blood

"Druid's Blood" finds comedian Don Rickles (foreground) trying his hand at magic, mysticism and murder.

CBS #6524 Shooting Order 24
First Air Date: 03/25/66

CBS Photo

Produced by Gene L. Coon
Directed by Ralph Senensky
Written by Henry Sharp

Dr. Tristam: Rhys Williams
Asmodeus: Don Rickles
Astarte: Ann Elder
Perry: Sam Wade
Colonel Fairchild: Simon Scott
Professor Robey: Don Beddoe
Butler: Emanuel Thomas
Senator Waterford: Bartlett Robinson

While Agent James West is probing the murder by fire of one of his former professors, Dr. Robey (Beddoe), a distinguished archaeologist, he is ordered off the case by special request of U.S. Senator Waterford (Robinson). West discovers that the action by Waterford was prompted by his beautiful young bride, Astarte (Elder), the same girl with whom the ill-fated Dr. Robey was smitten before he was killed. Despite elaborate attempts to discredit him, West sees Robey's murder as part of a pattern in which a number of scientists have met with violent death, each after falling in love with Astarte. In each case a sinister magician names Asmodeus (Don Rickles) was nearby.

The agents investigate the graves of the murdered scientists to confirm they are actually dead. They discover the affirmative, but West hears a humming noise coming from a mausoleum at the cemetery. They discover a room full of black-hooded mannequins and the magician, Asmodeus. He holds them at gunpoint until West kills the evil magician with his own saber. A panel slides aside and Dr. Tristam (Williams) steps out. The physician has developed a way to keep the brains of the murdered scientists alive and use them for evil doings. West gives the brains a pep talk, convincing them to join together as one force to destroy the doctor. The imprisoned brains manage to create enough energy to burn down the lab, thus ending Tristam's reign of terror.

West and Gordon attend a party that Senator Waterford is giving. West warns the senator that his young bride is part of Tristam's gang. Taking a mysterious cape from Waterford's shoulder, West places it onto Astarte who quickly confesses her involvement before the cape ignites. The Senator is obviously convinced.

The Night of the
Freebooters

James West, posing as a notorious gunman, and his partner, Artemus Gordon, disguised as the corrupt Colonel Sandoval, infiltrate the forces of the Freebooters, a renegade army lead by Thorald Wolfe (Wynn), who has been recruiting men for the military conquest and occupation of Mexico's Baja Peninsula. Wolfe is an ex-army major and top ordinance man who was discharged from the army for taking bribes. He immediately tests West's ability with a gun and finds him capable of serving his cause. Gordon, as the Colonel, is also accepted when he offers his complete cooperation in the planned invasion. Wolfe shows the two agents his amazing arsenal, which includes an X-P rifle

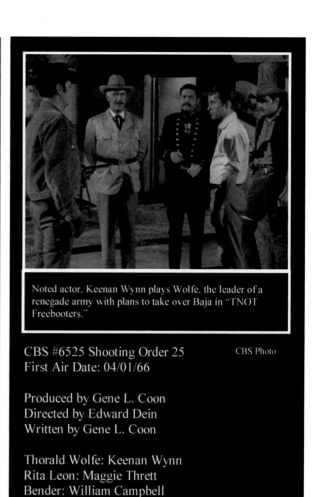

Noted actor, Keenan Wynn plays Wolfe, the leader of a renegade army with plans to take over Baja in "TNOT Freebooters."

CBS #6525 Shooting Order 25   CBS Photo
First Air Date: 04/01/66

Produced by Gene L. Coon
Directed by Edward Dein
Written by Gene L. Coon

Thorald Wolfe: Keenan Wynn
Rita Leon: Maggie Thrett
Bender: William Campbell
Enrique Leon: Andre Philippe
Oldfield: Robert Matek
Egan: James Gammon
Richard Henry: James Connell
Worker: John Sterling

that fires explosive bullets, and a revolutionary vehicle that appears to be the forerunner of today's tank. After the display both West and Gordon think they have won Wolfe's full confidence until a man appears and recognizes West as a government agent.

The agent is arrested and locked up with Enrique (Philippe), the member of the Freebooters gang who originally warned the agents of Wolfe's plan. Gordon comes by the cell and hands West an explosive to facilitate his escape. The next morning Gordon shows up as an old lady, accompanied by other women who are offering wine to the thirsty military men. This creates enough of a diversion to give West the opportunity to set off the explosives. West escapes and seizes the tank, quickly finishing off Wolfe and his men.

Back at the train, West and Gordon have dinner with Enrique and his wife. West proposes a toast to Gordon, calling him the "grand old lady of the Secret Service." Artie knows that this is one he's never going to live down.

The Night of the
Burning Diamond

Robert Drivas plays Midas, a man with a passion for speed and power in "The Night of the Burning Diamond."

CBS Photo

CBS #6526 Shooting Order 26
First Air Date: 04/08/66

Produced by Gene L. Coon
Directed by Irving J. Moore
Written by Ken Kolb

Morgan Midas: Robert Drivas
Lucretia: Christiane Schmidtmer
Baines: Dan Tobin
Serbian Minister: Vito Carbonara
Clive: Calvin Brown
Rudd: Whitey Hughes
Serbian Guard: Chuck O'Brien

Agent Jim West asks the Serbian Minister (Carbonara) to place his country's fabulous Kara Diamond in federal custody until the International Jewel Exhibit opens. As he stresses the importance of protection, the glass case holding the diamond suddenly explodes and the jewel disappears. The minister thinks it is an unusual persuasion tactic by West to show the weaknesses in the security measures presently in force. West denies that he had any such motives, but the minister still believes him responsible and attempts to detain him until the jewel is safely returned. West must fight off the Serbian guards in order to escape. Now the agent is wanted for suspicion in the theft even as he must find the missing diamond.

West pays a visit to a woman named Lady Margaret whom Gordon had attempted to visit with earlier, but to no avail. Lady Margaret is the owner of a collection of British diamonds scheduled for exhibit. She knows the agents and would surely have met with them had she been in town. Instead, the Lady's nephew, Morgan Midas (Drivas), greets the agent and insists that his aunt is out of town on an extended vacation and knows nothing of the impending exhibit. West observes that Sultan, Lady Margaret's cat, is still at home and he knows that she never goes anywhere without her cat. The agent asks to check the safe for the diamonds and discovers that they, too, are missing.

Midas behaves suspiciously, excusing himself as he leaves his lady friend, Lucretia (Schmidtmer), to entertain West. After questioning Lucretia, West is suddenly knocked unconscious by an invisible force. He awakens later in Midas' laboratory where it is explained that Midas has been stealing diamonds to melt them down as the prime ingredient in a potion that speeds up the metabolic composition of a man. When the resulting potion is ingested it allows a man to move so fast that he becomes invisible. Midas wants West to help him work toward his goal of becoming the most powerful man in the world.

Meanwhile, Artie is concerned about West's disappearance and pays a visit to the house disguised as Baron Felix von Schlesweig und Holtzegergen, an aged friend of Lady Margaret's. Upon arrival, he is told that the lady is out of town but he insists on waiting. With Artie upstairs, West escapes from the laboratory, causing a commotion that quickly involves his partner. Both agents are subdued by the invisible Midas.

The exhibition is taking place complete with

several foolproof security methods devised by Artie for each display. Government official Baines (Tobin), who is present at the exhibition, had his doubts about the agents' abilities throughout the case, and has even expressed suspicions about their credibility. Midas has slipped the agents a sample of the potion and travels with them to the exhibit so they can watch him in action. He warns them not to move too quickly or their accelerated state would cause them to singe. Midas quickly foils all the security measures taken by Artie and walks away with the diamonds.

The potion given to the agents intentionally wears off too soon for them to leave and they are captured by a security cage after Midas planted some stolen diamonds on them. Baines believes he has caught the criminals.

The agents are imprisoned, but not for long. A cigar-turned-blowtorch aids in their escape and they return to Midas' home. Artie causes a diversion in the kitchen while West locates Midas, who is quickly drinking his potion. West drinks some also so the two are well-matched as they engage in a little high-speed hand-to-hand. West gets the better of Midas and pushes him into his laboratory bench causing alcohol to spill onto the criminal. The friction causes him to ignite and disappear. As West returns to normal speed he tells Lucretia that the small flickering flame is all that remains of the evil Midas.

The tag involves West checking on Gordon's kitchen diversion to see how he is faring with the servants. He enters to find Artie and two bound and gagged servants. West inquires, "How did you do it?" Artie quips, while stabbing a giant butcher knife into the table, "I used force."

Author's Notes:

This episode was the first of many for writer Ken Kolb. He admitted that the idea was prompted by a popular H.G. Wells story. "It is a Wells story, but I can't think of the name. It has to do with a scientist who discovers this elixir that enables him to move so swiftly that everyone else seems to be motionless. He invites his friends over and they each take a couple of drops of this, then he simply releases his hold on the vial and the vial appears to stand in midair. That's because it takes that long for it to begin to fall. That's what we started with; then I had to devise a conflict. Well, I thought, 'what's the most expensive thing available that could make this elixir?' I came up with a

process of melting diamonds, which means you'd have to pull off the greatest diamond heist in history to get enough diamonds to make the elixir. That's how the stories were put together, the one idea that either Mike (Garrison), or one of us, would come up with. Sometimes we'd switch ideas. I'd get an idea and Garrison would say, 'Johnny could write that,' or 'Gene should write that.' At the same time it was the three of us that were doing most of them."

Actor Robert Drivas, who portrayed Midas, had a problem on the set remembering his lines. Director Irving Moore said that Drivas used to write his lines all over the set, on props, or whatever.

This is another of my favorite, totally fantastic "West" episodes. The concept was interesting; a man moving faster than sound by drinking melted diamonds; and why not? The script spells out any and all questions the viewers may have with logical answers. Can you disprove the theory and stay within your budget? The concept was also used in a 1968 "Star Trek" episode "Wink of an Eye," written by Gene Coon, with a teleplay by Arthur Heinemann.

For those of you who are wondering about the H.G. Wells story; it was called "The New Accelerator," written in 1943, just three years before Wells' death in 1946 at the age of 79.

The Night of the
Murderous Spring

A tall, powerfully built woman named Kitten Twitty (Jackson) registers at the same hotel as James West. West helps her carry her trunk to her room unaware that it contains his arch enemy, Dr. Miguelito Loveless (Dunn). Loveless soon sneaks into West's room to pour a powerful new drug into the agent's shaving water. After shaving, West develops a horrible headache and starts hallucinating. Loveless appears at West's window and shoots at the agent. West fires back and Loveless falls dead on the street below. West goes down to the street to investigate, but finds no body and no one in town seems to know what has happened. The stagecoach arrives with his partner, Artemus Gordon, who senses that something is wrong with West and suggests that he "take it easy." West angrily turns on Artie, giving cause for even more concern.

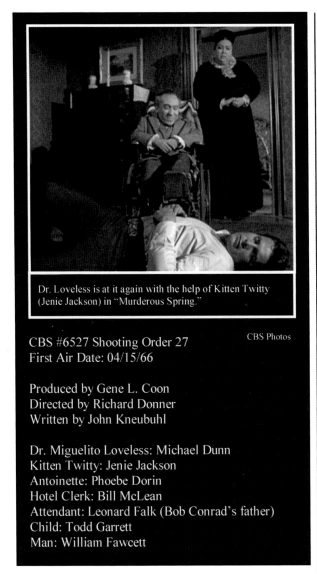

Dr. Loveless is at it again with the help of Kitten Twitty (Jenie Jackson) in "Murderous Spring."

CBS #6527 Shooting Order 27   CBS Photos
First Air Date: 04/15/66

Produced by Gene L. Coon
Directed by Richard Donner
Written by John Kneubuhl

Dr. Miguelito Loveless: Michael Dunn
Kitten Twitty: Jenie Jackson
Antoinette: Phoebe Dorin
Hotel Clerk: Bill McLean
Attendant: Leonard Falk (Bob Conrad's father)
Child: Todd Garrett
Man: William Fawcett

That night the agents receive a note from the doctor instructing them to meet him at a shed. West keeps seeing Loveless and Artie keeps insisting that he's not there. Arties then tell West to go back to the hotel, but West gets mad and yells at him. Arties doesn't understand his actions, but neither does West. He confesses to Artie, "It was almost like I hated you."

West returns to his room and wipes his face with more of the drug-laced water. Later, West hears Loveless laugh in his head and returns to the shed. Artie is already there and tells West that he is in no condition to be there. West starts and argument, then

shoots and kills his partner in cold blood.

West quickly realizes what he's done and goes back to the hotel to turn himself over to the hotel manager (McLean) for arrest. The manager claims that Gordon's stage is due to arrive tomorrow. West is perplexed as he returns to his room and collapses.

Artie arrives in town the next day and is told that West was taken away to a hospital because he's gone mad. At the hospital, Loveless tells West his experiment worked on him and he plans to control the world with his new powder. When Artie arrives, West realizes that he had hallucinated the entire scenario. Both agents find it hard to believe that Loveless can control the whole world, so the good doctor must, once again, prove his point. Loveless puts the powder in the hospital staff's wine at dinner and West and Gordon witness the murder of the entire staff. Convinced, they proceed with the escape plan.

Loveless intends to fill pellets with the powder and attach them to the feet of ducks. When the ducks fly freely to the lakes and ponds all over America the powder will be released into the water supply, resulting in mass hysteria, death and destruction. Loveless sees this as the rebirth of the world. The agents escape and chase Loveless to the barn where the ducks are being kept. As they secure the ducks, Loveless, and his attractive assistant, Antoinette

West is kept under the watchful eye of attendant Leonard Falk, Conrad's real-life father.

(Dorin), make their escape in a small boat. They cast off but West quickly catches up to them and shoots holes in the boat. It sinks, taking Loveless and Antoinette with it. When no survivors are located everyone agrees that Loveless must be dead. Unnoticed bubbles mysteriously appear at the lake surface, hinting that Loveless has likely survived to continue to torment James West.

Author's Notes:

"The Night of the Murderous Spring" was the fourth in the ongoing saga of Dr. Miguelito Loveless v. James T. West. The story showed Loveless at his nastiest, as he drives our hero to the brink of insanity with an evil drug that could also be used to kill everyone and everything in the world.

Writer John Kneubuhl remembered "Murderous Spring" as one of his favorite episodes. "It captured beautifully the crazy, childish, existential, nutty kind of murderousness of the character of Miguelito Loveless. I'm rather naïve about drugs and maybe I knew about LSD at the time, but I wouldn't be surprised if I didn't. The powder was just one of those mysterious Loveless inventions. I thought of a powder simply because it carries well in capsules on ducks' feet when they fly back and land in all the rivers and ponds and lakes of the world. The drug mixes with the water and kills everybody in the height of spring."

And what better way to test the drug's effectiveness than to use it on West as he imagines that he shoots and kills his best friend and partner, Artemus Gordon. West's cold and unemotional expressions say it all, as does Gordon's look of bewilderment at the idea that West has shot him. Conrad's great performance in this episode proves the he is certainly capable of doing more than just stunts.

Loveless' mute attendant assigned to keep a watchful eye on West and Gordon is played by Leonard Falk, Bob Conrad's real-life father.

The opening scene showed Loveless in a wheelchair because of a leg injury that happened while shooting. Director Richard Donner said, "We were shooting the scene with Michael Dunn in the chicken coop first, which was the last scene in the show. Michael ran out the door and, being very fragile, fell and hurt himself. So when we shot the first part of the show we rewrote it to have him in a wheelchair."

The lake assigned to the evil duty of releasing the ducks for Dr. Loveless is actually the cement, man-made lake used as the lagoon in "Gilligan's Island." There are no great stunts or disguises to report in this episode, just excellent acting, a fantastic story and wonderful directing. All this made "Murderous Spring" my personal favorite "West."

The Night of the
Sudden Plague

Theo Marcuse (left) plays Dr. Kirby, a demented physician with a talent for paralyzing and eventually poisoning the townspeople. M.M. Wynant (right) plays his cohort, Rodman.

CBS #6528 Shooting Order 28   CBS Photo
First Air Date: 04/22/66

Produced by Michael Garrison
Directed by Irving J. Moore
Written by Ken Kolb

Dr. Kirby: Theo Marcuse
Coley Rodman: M.M. Wynant
Anna: Nobu McCarthy
Governor Hawthorne: Elliott Reid

Agents West and Gordon ride into the town of Willow Springs and find it mysteriously quiet. They notice that all of the townspeople are frozen; still alive, but immobilized. They also discover that the bank has been robbed. West goes to the governor (Hawthorne) with the news, but the governor thinks there's not too much to worry about. They receive word that a telegraph transmission from Sand Hills was cut suspiciously short. West is on his way while Gordon goes to the morgue to investigate one man who died from being frozen. There he meets Dr. Kirby (Marcuse), who is performing the autopsy. Suddenly, Kirby fakes an attack of paralysis and when the agent tries to help, he is knocked unconscious.

West goes to Sand Hills and finds a gang of men looting stores and robbing banks while the entire township is paralyzed. West follows the robbers to their hideout but is soon captured. He manages to escape and meets a woman, Anna (McCarthy), who willingly hides him from his captors. It is Anna's professor/father who has developed a powerful bacterial based serum that is capable of complete temporary paralysis. He has been breeding the bacteria and intends to poison the water supply with it. His next target is San Francisco.

West is making his way out of the fort, but is seen. Gordon, who is outside snooping around, is mistaken for West and is captured in his place. Gordon recognizes Dr. Kirby from the morgue as the professor who has devised this diabolical scheme. It is discovered that Kirby staged the autopsy when he got word of the inquiry. West still gets no help from the stubborn governor and chooses to return to the fort himself to stop the mad doctor and rescue his partner. West is captured again, and he and Gordon are injected with the serum by Anna. It is revealed that she only pretends to inject them and they are able to move freely once alone in the locked room. After a fight, the agents defeat Kirby's henchmen and Kirby is shot. The lab, along with Kirby's work, is destroyed by fire.

At the train, Anna tells West that there is no more worry of his work being used for evil and that the bacteria could, someday, be used as an anesthetic.

Author's Notes:

"Sudden Plague" is the last black and white "West" shot. In Season Two the best was yet to come; in color. This was Garrison's first show as reinstated producer. In a February 15, 1966, Daily Variety interview Garrison asserted, "Never before in the history of TV has a new show caught its audience at 7:30 p.m. as has 'The Wild Wild West.'"

Garrison was so satisfied with joining in with the James Bond trend that he added, "I don't think you could really transpose Bond to a 7:30 p.m. timeslot, such as we have, because of all the sex, but you don't need it when you have Conrad, with sex appeal."

He explained that he found people exceptionally interested in the espionage trend at that time. But, as to the future, he insightfully predicted an upcoming science fiction trend. CBS had already okayed scripts for the next season of "West," an obvious indication that the series would be renewed. When the show returned for its second season it would join the ranks of the color tinted programs rapidly becoming popular with network audiences.

B ob Conrad was, by nature, very spur of the moment. Once he had his mind set on something it was difficult to change. If a stunt appeared too dangerous, Bob went for it.

It was well known on the set that Dick Cangey was deathly afraid of heights. In "Night of the Tycoons," one scene called for Jimmy George, doubling for Conrad, to grab Cangey and fall from the top deck of an outside stairway and land on the padding below.

During the run-through Cangey and George accidentally knocked loose the railing at the top of the stairway. Cangey searched for an excuse to not do the stunt, threatening to *chicken out*. Bob's response, "No, you won't. I promise you that you won't chicken out."

When the director shouted ACTION! Bob took on five villains in the street. Defeating his adversaries he proceeded to chase his target villain, who had disappeared up the outside stairway. Bob dashed up the stairs and Cangey grabbed him, as planned. Cangey struggled with Bob and they knocked against the loose railing while George waited inside an open doorway to take Bob's place. Instead, Bob pushed George back, beyond camera view, and did the stunt himself. Grabbing Cangey by the shirt, Bob literally pulled him, head first, over the side. Cangey reflected that director Mike Moder and stunt coordinator, Whitey Hughes nearly had heart attacks. They were under strict order, "No stunts for Bob!"

Cangey not chickening out.

After the stunt, Bob casually brushed himself off and quipped to Cangey, "I told you that you wouldn't chicken out."

CBS Photo

Chapter 4
Bob & Ross Alias Jim & Artie

In a television series where actors play off of one another there needs to be a certain chemistry that works between the performers. The audience must be made to believe in the characters being portrayed.

Ross Martin said, in an earlier interview, "If it's properly established by interplay between the co-stars, it humanizes the hero. It rounds out what might be just two-dimensional, basic character."

By establishing loyalty and warmth between two co-stars, it can give the audience insight into more than just the action. They can be made to feel that there is more to the show than just one man following another into victory. If the relationship does not work between the characters on screen then it will not work for the audience. This was the case for the James West and Artemus Gordon characters during the first season of "The Wild Wild West."

In the beginning of the first season the two

characters seemed distant, even though they were written as a team. They were simply two secret agents doing a job, fighting crime, and only requiring each other's presence occasionally with very little interaction. Like most TV shows, the characters needed to evolve. The friendship between the two men was implied, but limited. West always got the girl while Gordon was left to admire from afar. If Gordon commented on something with his usual wry humor, he was cut short by West and his penchant for "getting back to business."

Although Ross Martin had an agreement with the network prior to accepting the part of Artemus Gordon, he was still limited to what he could do with the role. "Principally, the network and I did not see eye-to-eye on the character I played. I wanted to play each character Gordon disguised himself as with complete conviction. But, CBS said, 'We want the audience to know that it is you; so that's the way it is.'" Martin continued, "Every time I walked through a door, I was knocked unconscious and Bob was left to fight it out alone with 14 guys. The scripts didn't let me look at a girl, win a fight or even think for myself." Martin believed that the problem was with all the changes in producers. "Just as things got organized, a producer was fired and the show got a new one along with new writers," he said.

When Michael Garrison was reinstated at the reins, Martin's character slowly started to emerge and return back to the original concept with Artemus Gordon as the *assistant hero* with humor. Throughout the second season, Martin's talents and abilities shined through. He was able to develop his characters to his liking and his role as assistant hero improved.

In "TNOT Casual Killer" Jim and Artie really show off their special camaraderie as they both go undercover as actors.

"Every disguise was slanted toward my sense of humor. I'd changed lines to put my own character to it so I retained my key characteristics, whatever I would do," Martin said.

The James West character also experienced some changes. The West role was not nearly as diverse as the Gordon character so the changes were minimal, but evident. In the second season West softened his seriousness, adopted a lighter view and became noticeably more warm and caring about his partner's well-being. Additionally, West developed a more realistic charm toward women by not winning over as many as in the first season. His *kissing ratio* was also considerably lower.

Another issue that plagued Martin was in his desire to become the romantic leading man. That honor fell to Robert Conrad and Martin had to settle for second banana. As in the first season, Artemus Gordon was only allowed to look, but never touch, the opposite sex.

"Conrad was interested in doing his thing and he didn't want Martin to intrude in this area. See, Bobby had the girls at the end of the show. He would be in the (railroad) car and there would be a short love scene," said producer Fred Freiberger.

But again, as Martin's assistant hero image improved, so did his romantic appeal. At the start of the second season in "The Night of the Big Blast," writer Ken Kolb developed a storyline especially for the Artemus Gordon character. Gordon not only gets the girl, Mala Powers, who was his real girlfriend at the time, but keeps her throughout the episode. This pleased Martin and "Big Blast" became one of his favorite episodes.

Ken Kolb remembered, "Ross never did understand why he was the second banana in that show because, in his eyes, he was as handsome as, or better looking than, Bob Conrad. He liked 'The Big Blast' because, at last, the show was switching around to the way it should be. Martin would say, 'It's about me and my pal the stuntman.' But he never did understand the situation. 'Why the hell does Bobby always get the lead? We're supposed to be in this together, right? How come I'm never the lead?' You didn't want to say, 'Well, cause you're kinda funny looking, Ross.' He'd have really gone bananas."

Ross' widow, Olavee Martin, remembered, "Ross was not the handsome leading man and, invariably, he was in competition with the leading man because of his age; because of his unbelievable talent. He could do anything. But when it got down to the final decision it was always the handsome leading actor that

The dapper gentlemen look their best in "TNOT Brain" as they prepare to go out on the town with a couple of lovely ladies.

got the part. So his career was a constant struggle. That was one reason why it was so easy for him to go into all of those characters. He spoke seven languages with 52 dialects, fluently. He could also design his own makeup. Whatever they wanted he could become, so his career was successful and busy. His talent was what he built his career on; not his looks."

During the second, third and fourth seasons, the West and Gordon characters developed into a working relationship, with each getting their fair share of the female companionship and facing danger side by side.

Occasionally, West and Gordon were known for playing dirty tricks on one another. In the second season episode, "The Night of the Returning Dead," West and Gordon are trapped in an alley by three gunmen. They see West, but not Gordon. When they close in on the vulnerable West, Gordon appears behind them and orders them to drop their guns. After they're disarmed Gordon holsters his gun and motions them to West, telling the adversaries, "All right, gentlemen, he's all yours." With the playing field leveled, West looks at Gordon with a 'thanks a lot' expression and proceeds to neutralize the three attackers in his usual fashion. Afterward, West asks his partner why he didn't help. Gordon replies, "Fighting on the Sabbath? Never on Sunday." Gordon knew that West was of capable of handling the situation, and we knew, as the audience, that had he thought otherwise he surely would have joined in the fight. This was the way the true friendship of the characters eventually evolved.

> **Although Jim and Artie maintained a close friendship on-screen, the bonding was not so intent for Bob and Ross.**

One of the first problems that developed with Martin as a "Wild" Westerner was in his inability to ride a horse. First assistant director, Rowe Wallerstein, remembered, "During the first few shows we'd shoot Ross already up on the horse, but never getting on, because Ross had difficulty getting up on the horse."

Martin recalled a scene when his horse decided to go into a full gallop. "I hung onto the saddle horn and prayed," he said. "I dislocated a thumb and it took weeks to heal. Finally, the crew got the shot, but without sound because I kept yelling, 'Whoa! Whoa!' out of sheer terror. It would have been most unbecoming for a TV hero."

Artie and Jim spent a great deal of time together on screen, but after hours, Ross and Bob went their separate ways.

Although Jim and Artie maintained a close friendship onscreen, the bonding was not so intense for Bob and Ross. When "The Wild Wild West" first went into production Martin had real difficulty accepting his co-starring role. He loved his role as the inimitable Gordon, but felt his character should have been equal to that of James West, and this strained the relationship off camera. Also, the fact remained that Martin and Conrad had two drastically different personalities and chose not to socialize after hours.

It appeared, though, that it was this difference in personalities that made the chemistry between the two men work so well on the screen. The fact that they were diametrically opposed helped balance their characters' need for one another while fighting villains. It was as if the two men combined made the perfect super crime fighting equation; one clever and inventive, the other strong and fearless.

Conrad and Martin may have had little in common off screen, but their private relationship proved to be an interesting one. "They were *so* different that it wasn't a love-hate situation; they didn't hate each other," Olavee Martin remembered. "They really admired one another. Ross really respected Bob for his ability to do stunts, while Bob really admired Ross' acting ability. I'm sure, secretly, Ross would have liked to have swung from a chandelier occasionally, and perhaps Bob would have liked to have done a scene and have the crew burst into applause because of the fine acting job. That's why it worked; the chemistry showed on the film."

Chapter 5
Stunts: Falling for CBS

Introduction

A typical scene in a 1960s action-adventure television series: The starring actor, resourceful and debonair, attempts to cleverly elude an angry mob. Suddenly, our hero discovers he is cornered on an isolated rooftop and is edged closer and closer to imminent doom, as the mob scowls, growls and closes in on him. His only chance for escape is to jump from the top of the three-story building into a large haystack conveniently situated below. He perches himself, braces his stance and, just before he jumps, a commanding voice echoes from the blackness: "CUT!" The director signals the stunt double to take his place as the star casually walks away.

Webster defines the word *stunt* as a notable feat of strength, skill or daring, especially when done as part of a challenge or as part of an entertainment. Definitely a challenge and invariably entertaining, a stuntman is hired to risk life and limb to make a star appear brave, daring, infallible and sometimes, indestructible. The television hero's image is at stake so the transition must be inconspicuous.

For a majority of principals — starring actors — this occurred several times during the daily shooting schedule as a mandatory practice, since a star performing his owns stunts was risking much more than self-injury. Losing the main character of a show to injury and lengthy recuperation meant, at best, production would shut down and the company would lose thousands of dollars a day; at worst, the future of the series would be at stake.

There were a remaining few, however, a minute percentage of daring actors who knew no fear and loved the thrill of every stunt performed or attempted. One of the select few starring actors who fit this category was Robert Conrad, AKA James T. West.

Jim tackles a trio of henchmen: Fred Stromsoe, Whitey Hughes and Bob Herron.

CBS Photo

In "Spanish Curse" Jim and Artie team up to toss away their troubles.

CBS Photo

CBS Photos

67

In the Beginning

In the beginning of "The Wild Wild West," Robert Conrad did some basic stunts, but he, too, fell into the stunt double syndrome. Originally, Bill Catching was the series' stunt coordinator and old pros like Jerry Summers, Chuck O'Brien, Bill Couch and Lou Elias doubled for Conrad since CBS did not want their prime star doing stunts. But the show chronically pressed too close to deadline and time became a deciding factor. It became evident that it required less time to complete a shot using no stunt double for the star.

"Dancing Death"

According to Whitey Hughes, one of the earliest members of the stunt team, "Bob didn't like too many doubles, and he could do just about everything they could do. CBS warned me when I first came on the show, 'We don't want him two feet off the floor.' I kept pushing, telling Bob he couldn't do this and Bob kept saying, 'I can do this.' 'I'm not doubting you,' I'd say, 'but you got me the job and I don't want you to have CBS march me out before I even get started for getting careless with you.' I'd figure things out and let him do it instead of putting in a double. We got away with a lot."

"This was a bastard show; the show that the network didn't understand. There was action, action, action," said Conrad. He explained that Perry Lafferty had taken over for Hunt Stromberg, CBS's vice-president in charge of development, and later programming. Lafferty was more inclined to identify with "Gunsmoke," a traditional Western.

"They were having an awful time getting this thing done and I was sitting on the sidelines hearing rumbling that the stunt budget was exorbitant and that the show was in jeopardy because they couldn't make it. So I said that I have a simple solution to that. I'll do it." Conrad snapped his finger for added emphasis.

Conrad told the camera crew to put two or three cameras into place, "We'll have the principle. It'll save you a ton of production time. I got on a horse, a guy was supposed to bulldog me, knock me off, and I did it." This was the start of the television series that was to become famous, and infamous, for its exciting stunt action.

The Team

Conrad felt for the first time he was in control, but was faced with the added problem that the complement of stuntmen never seemed to be available. "They'd get a major feature, like 'Major Dundee' and disappear," he said. So his first order of business was to hire stuntmen who would stick with the show. During the second season, he gradually developed a team of stunt regulars. This proved a great advantage as time went on. Having a group of regulars virtually eliminated the second guessing that comes with stunt preparation. With the stunt players regularly working as a team, they became like a well-oiled machine, knowing each others' moves and understanding the production goals and standards of the show, something that day players have a difficult time doing.

Whitey Hughes

Hughes was one of the first to join the team. Catching, who had worked with Hughes on Sam Peckinpah's 1965 picture "Major Dundee," called him for a

"Vicious Valentine"

Whitey Hughes brought a special enthusiasm to the "West" stunt team.

stunt assignment when Jerry Sommers was not available. Hughes first appeared in "The Night of the Torture Chamber" doing a gag involving a wine press. According to Hughes, Conrad was so impressed with his performance that he later pushed Eddie Denault, the head of CBS programming, to allow Hughes to gaff the show in place of Catching.

"Eddie said, 'You want him, you got him,'" quipped Hughes. "It was four of the greatest years of my life. We loved what we did. That's what made the show a hit. Bob and I would dream up stunts together and we'd try to figure out some of the ungodliest things that would ever happen on a TV show. We became a team; a kind of brotherhood."

Hughes was known as a *flyer* because of his small frame and light weight. At 5'6" and 135 lbs., he was extremely agile and could often double for female performers. Because of his experience he was able to perform some of the most dangerous stunts. Hughes has since appeared as either an actor or stunt performer in more than 100 television programs and films.

According to Conrad, Hughes had gotten into some trouble while working on "Dundee." Hughes admitted, "I'm a little man with a big mouth." He said he did some off-camera activity that wasn't acceptable. Nevertheless, Conrad was impressed enough to bring Hughes onboard as one of the first of the stunt team. Later, after replacing Catching as the stunt coordinator, Hughes helped develop the remainder of the team.

Dick Cangey

The second to join the entourage of stuntmen was former fighter Dick Cangey. His bulky stature made him ideal as a *catcher*, a stuntman specifically assigned to break falls or catch other stuntmen. Cangey said that he had to have all his costumes made special because he was only 5'7" tall and had a 53" chest. Previously, Cangey was stuntman and assistant to Peter Breck who played Nick Barkley on "The Big Valley," but he was fired after an argument with the star.

Dick Cangey's imposing stature made him a perfect *catcher*.

Conrad remembered, "One night I had a little confrontation with Mr. Breck and Mr. Cangey, in his role of protectorate, I guess. Chuck Bale, who's a director now, came out to protect the star. It didn't mean a hoot to me. Mike Moder, who was the first assistant on our show, said that Dick would like to leave the employ of, (etc.), so I hired Dick Cangey. He became a resident stuntman."

At first printing (1988) of this book Mike Moder had moved on to serve as vice president in charge of programming at Viacom International. Now he may be better known as the father of Daniel Moder and Julia Roberts' father-in-law.

Tom Huff

During Conrad's recuperation from a stunt accident, he met Tommy Huff. At the time Huff was well on his way to becoming a world-class fighter, but was suffering from bone chips and calcium deposits that were inhibiting his career. Conrad recalled, "We were sitting in a place called The Tahitian, which is a shopping mall now, and I said, 'Shit! Why don't you become a stuntman?' So we added Tommy Huff."

Cangey remembered Huff as a man who used to love to drink. Recalling a particular evening, he said, "One time Tommy put a dime in the payphone and called the operator and said, 'Operator, trace this call. I want to know where I am.'"

Tommy Huff was a former fighter when Conrad recruited him.

Hughes remembered Huff's appearance on the show with Jack Williams. He said that Williams was known as "Fallin' Horse Jack," famous for doing a series of John Wayne films. "We wanted a horse fall and we had just gotten Tommy into the group. We were out in the woods in Calabasas and Tommy was riding an English saddle and was supposed to trail behind Jack. The director called 'Action!' and here comes Jack with Tommy right behind him. You could've bounced a basketball between Tommy's ass and the saddle on every jump. It was 'Cut! Do it again!' and he was still bouncing up and down. We had to pay Jack Williams for four horse falls cause we couldn't get Tommy's ass in the saddle."

Tommy Huff went on to become one of the most noted stunt coordinators in the business. He worked up until 2005, having made his mark on more than 150 films before his death in 2006.

Jerry Laveroni

For a brief time, stuntman Jerry Laveroni was a part of the group. Not quite a member of the team, Conrad recalled his first meeting Laveroni at The Backstage Bar, a hangout frequented by the cast and crew across the street from the studio. "We went to The

Jerry Laveroni went on to work for the U.S. Drug Enforcement Administration.

Backstage across the street. Jerry Laveroni was there and he seemed to fit into our company because he was big, about 6'2" tall and 240 lbs." Laveroni appeared in a total of nine "Wests" during his brief tenure, later becoming a law enforcement officer and joining the United States Drug Enforcement Administration (DEA) during its formation in the early 1970s. He was later featured in the 1975 Radfilms documentary "Who is the American Connection," as an agent disillusioned by the system. He moved on to work in private security.

Red West

Red West soon joined the ranks. Because of his imposing frame he teamed with Cangey as a resident catcher. Later, West developed his acting career and has been a starring performer in several of Conrad's projects, including "Baa Baa Blacksheep" and several TV movies.

Cangey said, "Red was a tough son-of-a-bitch." He remembered his co-worker sitting in Charlie Brown's restaurant one evening before the fights. "Red asked the band to play something from

Red West has had a long film and television career.

Memphis. A group of businessmen, who had been drinking, said that Memphis was the asshole of the

Jimmy George takes a big chance rescuing *damsel in distress* Whitey Hughes in "Doomsday Formula."

United States. Red slowly walked over to their table. They took one swing at Red. Red threw five punches and all three of them ended up in the hospital. When it went to court, the judge all but laughed and it was thrown out. It has something to do with 'present ability;' how could one man do so much damage?"

Formerly a bodyguard for Elvis Presley, Red was one of the first to know the singer and reportedly stopped a group of kids from cutting Elvis' hair in high school. West reminisced about how he first became involved with "The Wild Wild West." "I was working with Elvis Presley at the time and met Bob (Conrad) when playing on Elvis' football team (against the "WWW" crew). We became good friends and when I left Elvis I went on 'The Wild Wild West' set doing stunts. Being very athletic I *fell* right into it," he said.

Since the 1988 printing of this book, Red West has continued to stay active in the business.

Jimmy George

It wasn't until after an accident sidelined Robert Conrad and the network insisted on a stunt double that Jimmy George was initiated as a member of the team. He had already been serving the series in the wardrobe department, and Conrad had insisted that if he was going to be doubled, "Double me with a guy we can at least get real close to. By this time we had cho-

A difficult stunt for Bob Conrad is prepared and executed without a hitch in "TNOT Bubbling Death."

reographed and directed these things and I'm satisfied that they were classic action sequences." George was an enthusiastic addition and Conrad said you could put a camera extremely close to him (George) and not tell them apart. Additionally, Conrad had started to do rodeos and personal appearances and had to seriously curb all of his stunt activities. During his time with the show, George suffered a broken leg and a dislocated shoulder. He has since retired from show business.

Slowly "The Wild Wild West" developed a reputation for being the only show in Hollywood that used the same stuntmen in every episode.

Oh My Aching...

Part of the excitement of stunts for both the viewer and the performer is the ever-present element of risk involved. The risk factor enhances the thrill and the adventure, it also greatly enhances the possibility of injury. Spending 14-16 hours a day being knocked off horses, falling from balconies, dodging flying fists and encountering furious mobs gives rise to an inevitable array of potential mishaps.

According to Conrad, a usual stuntman initiation rite involved some type of injury. He remembered how each member became part of the team. "The first shot that Huff was in I opened my eye like a watermelon because he didn't know to step back and he didn't understand

(Top) Jimmy George (right) and Bob Conrad. (Below) Cangey and Tommy Huff in beards and costumes.

71

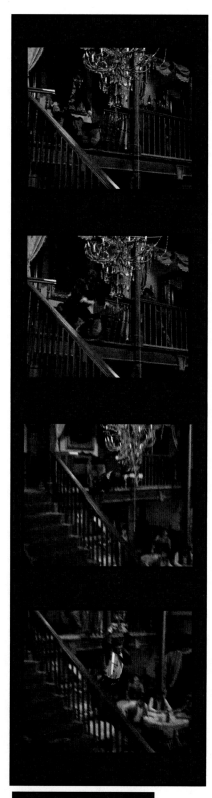

make-believe. So I put these big paws on his head and opened him up. Then he was one of the team." He added that the fights got out of control on the average of once a week.

In one instance, a Fiberglass brace was devised to cover Red West's whole back. The stunt involved cannon shells going off and, without the necessary protection, a fragment could have gone right through the stuntman.

Conrad said that the team wore standard hip, elbow and knee pads and the only place they couldn't pad up were their heads, the same place where most of them would get hurt.

According to Hughes, "We had a lot of crashes. We used to say, 'Roll the cameras and call the ambulances.'" He recalled an incident that occurred during a scene with polo ponies. "Bob was supposed to jerk a polo mallet out of my hand and knock me off the horse. I had a cable from the back of my neck to the saddle, and when I did the backflip off the horse it would hold me until I got straightened out and keep me away from it. It would get me parallel with the horse and then let me loose. Somehow I got hung up too long and went behind the horse's heels. His foot caught me in the head and knocked me colder than a well-digger's backend. I was out cold."

By comparison "The Wild Wild West" stunt team suffered relatively few mishaps considering the number and the caliber of the stunts performed on a daily basis.

The short-lived stunt career of John Stelly was another casualty of "The Wild Wild West." Conrad said, "I met him (Stelly) down in Louisiana. I was flirting with this

After his serious injury, Bob Conrad resumed filming 12 weeks later. The script called for him to show some reaction to the fall, though in reality he'd been knocked cold and hospitalized.

woman and I found out that her boyfriend had been incarcerated and had just been released. I walked outside and was going to have a problem from the blind side. Stelly got involved in this. So I said, 'Stelly look, if I can ever do you a favor give me a call.' That's how Stelly got to be cast."

Hughes remembered, however, that Stelly only lasted with the show for one stunt. It was a scene from "The Night of Miguelito's Revenge" that placed Stelly atop a 12-foot wall. "Cangey and Red West had a hold of Bob and as they crashed into the wall Stelly was supposed to come down and land on top of them." Hughes said that he warned Stelly that he wouldn't hit them unless he started the jump early. When he saw the fighters coming toward the wall Stelly was supposed to anticipate the crash and start coming down to land on top of them. But Stelly, being inexperienced, couldn't think fast enough for flawless execution. When the men hit the wall, Stelly fell straight onto the ground and broke his arm. "That was the end of his career and he didn't come back," said Hughes.

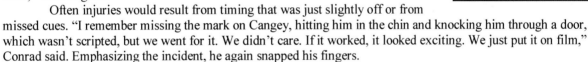

Often injuries would result from timing that was just slightly off or from missed cues. "I remember missing the mark on Cangey, hitting him in the chin and knocking him through a door, which wasn't scripted, but we went for it. We didn't care. If it worked, it looked exciting. We just put it on film," Conrad said. Emphasizing the incident, he again snapped his fingers.

Other injuries included Cangey's broken nose; Red West's six stitches in his head and a concussion; Hughes' concussion and lacerations of the cranium; Stelly's broken arm and, of course, Ross' broken leg.

Near the end of the third season, on January 24, 1968, Conrad sustained a major injury while filming "The Night of the Fugitives." A missed cue by Laveroni and no time to grip-tape the chandelier found Conrad landing head-first on a concrete floor that had been painted to resemble wood. Production was shut down the following day and Conrad was released from the hospital one week later. His daughter, Christy, was born that same week. According to Cangey, the crew returned to work 12 weeks later on April 16, and started shooting with that fateful scene. Cangey also said that this was the same scene where Tommy Huff was injured and the same day Jimmy George took over as double for Conrad.

Remembering the occurrence, Conrad explained, "I had a bad injury in '68, a very serious injury. I had a

high-temporal concussion and a six-inch lineal fracture to my skull. The last two episodes (of that season) were cancelled."

Hughes remembered the day of the accident. He said he was off the set because he went to do a commercial and was reticent to leave on the day of such a big stunt. Conrad had insisted he take the commercial job. He said that Jerry Laveroni was new at the time and, although they had rehearsed the scene the day before, the stunt in-

73

volved Conrad swinging from a chandelier and kicking Laveroni, thus helping break his swing and guide the ensuing fall. Before leaving, Hughes insisted Laveroni not anticipate Conrad's kick. "When you see Bob swinging through the air, you stay there until he gets to you. He won't kick you. When you see him fake the kick, take off and go through the window."

Laveroni did step back too soon, Conrad over-extended and jerked himself loose from the chandelier, "And the first thing that hit the floor was his head. The next day I found out that Bob got hurt and was in the hospital and I felt bad that I wasn't there to make sure everything went right. So I asked the guys, 'Did you tape the bar?' and they said, 'No.' Then I asked Tim Smyth, the special effects supervisor, why the bar wasn't taped. He said, 'Well, Bob always knows so much about everything, I just thought I'd let him do it himself.' If I'd been there, it never would have happened," Hughes said. The remainder of that show was shot 12 weeks later.

Not only were missed cues and over-enthusiasm causes for accidents, but some-

Bob Conrad's acumen as a stunt performer is unquestionable, though after his accident he was forced to frequently use a double. Still, rarely did the actor turn away from an opportunity to execute a complicated *gag*.
In the top photo, Bob Conrad overtakes the fleeing Whitey Hughes. The bottom photo shows Conrad's double, Jimmy George, leaping off a building to tackle Red West and Dick Cangey. The resemblance is uncanny.

times it was a result of the elaborate costuming. In "The Night of the Wolf," stuntman Cangey started a fight with Conrad in the train. Cangey wore a large flowing cape that eventually became wrapped around his head, "But he (Conrad) was so involved in the stunt that he didn't realize that I couldn't see. As he threw me out the door, I missed the opening and hit the door jamb with the bulk of my weight. I knocked the train nearly a foot," said Cangey.

Sometimes Bob would get so caught up in a stunt that even more stuntmen would suffer. Occasionally expensive antiques would be the victims. Cangey remembered, "We had a fight down a stairway and then someone hit Bob with a 2x4. He crashed through a showcase made of round glass and smashed it to bits."

All Photos Courtesy CBS

74

Ross, the No-So-Stuntman – Enter Bob Herron

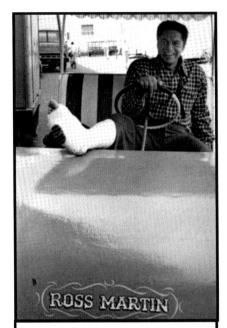

Ross Martin earned his stripes while filming "Avaricious Actuary." A mishap with a rifle caused a broken leg, a troublesome cast and several weeks recovery.

Bob Herron

Stuntman Bob Herron, who had originally worked with Conrad on "Hawaiian Eye," eventually started doubling for Ross Martin who was not so inclined to do his own stunts. Herron said that he doubled for Conrad in "Eye" and in only one episode of "The Wild Wild West."

"Since I was too big to double for Bob, he suggested I double for Ross. I doubled for Ross in 95% of all the shows." According to Herron, Bob Miles or J.R. Reynolds, two earlier stuntmen, doubled Ross before he came along. Hughes said Herron was the perfect double for Ross. "You could photograph fairly close and didn't need makeup. They had pretty much the same features."

Although Herron was the same build and height as Martin, a problem would occasionally arise. "Ross was right handed and I am left. If a scene required that I throw a bomb through a window, I had a difficult time doing it," Herron said. At times Martin tried to become a part of the stunt "gang." Conrad said that Martin wanted to be as physical as possible. An exceptional tennis player, Martin wanted to become more involved inn the physical aspect of the show. "Up to a point, Ross participated. But there were certain athletic limitations. That's when Bobby Herron would be there," Conrad said.

Herron recalls frequently standing in for Martin during fight scenes until Conrad didn't want him getting the added attention. Apparently Herron, a former boxer, added a little too much flair to Artie's prowess. On June 26, 1968, Ross broke his leg in a freak accident. In "The Night of the Avaricious Actuary," Artemus Gordon, in costume as an aged gas meter reader, tripped over his rifle. This resulted in his injury and a place of honor (sort of) with the stunt team. Conrad said, "Ross made certain he participated. In fact, Ross broke his leg during one sequence. So he got his medal; the dubious medal award. Ross was a very theatrical guy, but he didn't have to be in that situation when he broke his leg."

After Hours

The craziness went beyond a regular day's work on the set for Conrad and his stuntmen. The Backstage Bar, their local watering hole across the street from CBS, was visited by the stunt crew almost every

TNOT Undead

TNOT Eccentrics

Stuntman Bob Herron stepped in for Ross Martin in 95% of the shows. Herron had similar features and was able to take on difficult stunts. A consummate professional, Herron was usually undetectable while standing in.

night. Mike Moder, one of the show's directors, recalled, "The crew was a family back then. We also had a football team that met every Saturday. It branched off to a flag football team. We made it to second place in the city's play-offs two years in a row."

At times the wild goings-on went beyond The Backstage Bar. "After work, all the stunt guys piled into my car and went to a bar called the Out of Sight," Cangey recalled. Red West and a couple others tried to put Cangey up on the stage with the dancers. "They tried, but they couldn't get me off the ground. Then we did a fake stunt fight. Even the bouncers decided to stay out of it."

Tom Huff, Red West, Bob Conrad, Dick Cangey and Jimmy George — circa 1968

Tom Huff, Red West, Bob Conrad, Dick Cangey and Jimmy George — circa 1986

Right after the escapades they all walked out and went back to the studio. All this happened within 10 minutes. At the studio, Conrad went upstairs to his dressing room, took the window out and said, "Hey fellas, catch!" and he threw them the window. It shattered into ten thousand pieces.

The next day the owner of the Out of Sight came to the studio. Cangey recalled, "We thought he was going to make a big fuss and complain about what happened at the bar. He told us that the people in the bar loved the excitement and what he really wanted was to hire us to come back and do it all again."

Other reminiscences of the stunt team were: driving off the CBS lot in the studio golf carts, hiding co-worker's cars in parking spaces other than their own, and the occasional brawl at The Backstage Bar, which resulted in the firing of some of "The Wild Wild West" personnel.

Better, Better, Perfect

A key element in what made the stunts work was the timing. A majority of the time Conrad and his company of stuntmen carefully laid out the choreography for each stunt. According to Conrad, each stunt had to be fast-paced to be consistent with the show. Sec-

ondly, the stunts had to have an aura of danger. "Not only did it look good on film, but there was an adrenaline pump going," added Conrad.

Cangey admitted that, although Hughes was the stunt coordinator, it was Conrad who really gaffed, that is, set up, the stunts for the show. "Whitey would set up where and what it was going to be, then when Bob got there Bob did everything. We only had one or two things we had to remember, three or four different moves, but Bob had to remember maybe six times that; and he remembered them. Ninety-nine percent of those fights were one takes," said Cangey. Between the efforts of Hughes and Conrad, the directors were saved a notable amount of time and money.

Director Charles Rondeau said that Hughes would lay out the action and then take main action from Conrad. After they blocked out the moves, the director would come in. He said things were made very easy from the director's standpoint, because it had already been blocked out. Cangey remembered, "If we were running behind, Bob would grab the script and say, 'That's ok!' He'd take three or four pages, tear them out and say, 'We'll do it right here.'"

Co-workers remembered Conrad's attitude toward performing stunts. "Conrad loved it, adored it and lived for it," Jimmy George said. Writer Ken Kolb recalled, "The whole idea of jumping off a stairway, grabbing a chandelier and swinging across the room was his idea of good work."

Jack Muhs, formerly of "Wild Wild West" wardrobe, said, "Bob knew what he was doing; was comfortable in it and loved to fight. The character was him; he loved to be challenged. Each little boy dreams that six guys attack and he beats the hell out of them. Every boy grows up with that kind of a dream and here was Bob living that kind of a dream."

According to Ethel Winant, assistant program director, "He does his stunts and he plays and he kids, but he's a hard-working actor. He's always there. He's a kidder and he runs around with his stuntmen, but he's good hearted and he works hard. He was never difficult about scripts, but was more concerned with doing what he had to do. He was never sick or decided to stay home or threatened to quit. He was wild, fun and crazy!"

Conrad's spur of the moment nature led him to give nonprofessional stuntmen and actors a shot at doing stunts. Frank Cappiello, a greensman on the set, got a chance to give it a try. Even a visiting insurance salesman Jerry Spicer, had the opportunity to try a bit part. Later, according to Cangey, Spicer became and important part of the group. Jimmy George recalled that Conrad always kept his stuntmen working and added that Conrad always stood up for his friends and would not back down if he believed in something.

Conrad made sure that the stunts looked right by frequently visiting the editing room. Bob Blake, the assistant editor, said, "Bob (Conrad) came to our cutting room fairly often because there were so many stunts involved. He would come to look at stunts to see what they did the day before or see how a stunt was going to work. He'd line it up through what Alan Jaggs, the editor, had cut, up to a certain point, then go to the stunt, do the inserts and everything to make it work. We had more contact with Bob in the cutting room than a star normally does."

Cangey recalled an anecdote about seasoned motion picture director James Clark, shooting his first television stunt scene for "The Night of Miguelito's Revenge." Clark expected several takes for a complex fight scene. "The fight was completed, first time around, flawlessly. Clark was impressed at the ease and execution. He was awestruck, watching the fight come off perfectly." Cangey said that's what made the essence of the *team*.

Boxing vs. Kung Fu

During the first season, the stunts usually incorporated a noticeable amount of martial arts. Cangey recalled that Conrad was really into the art of Kung Fu, but when Cangey came onto the set, he convinced Conrad to use a boxing style of fighting. Conrad explained the situation in a late 1960s article from *Boxing Illustrated* magazine.

"Dick was a pretty good light-heavyweight boxer. He used to clown around with some of the stuntmen at CBS during breaks in filming. He could plant his feet, stand in one spot and defend himself. The other guys couldn't touch him. I saw Cangey do that several times and, while I admired the way he handled himself, I though, his sparring partners weren't trying very hard. So one day I put the gloves on with him and I couldn't hit him either. That's when I decided that there really was something to the game of boxing and I wanted to master it, or at least become proficient at it."

At Conrad's direction, CBS' Stage 14 on the Studio City lot was converted into a fully-equipped boxing gym. Conrad became so interested in boxing that he decided to try a professional bout, but his injury, along with the fact that CBS ex-

Bob Conrad became interested in boxing later in the show and shifted his fighting style accordingly. He was so fascinated with the art that he bought in on a featherweight prizefighter named Frankie Crawford. Conrad was also instrumental in bringing in known fighters as guest stars on "West," including Floyd Patterson and Wilhelm Von Homburg.

Photos From the Author's Collection

pressly forbade it, crushed any plans of a boxing career. He even bought a featherweight fighter named Frankie Crawford. After a well-fought bout with Pete Gonzalez in 1968, and on the advice of resident boxer Cangey, each member of the stunt team bought in on the fighter's contract with Conrad.

Hughes, the only stuntman who didn't want to buy in on the contract, said, "Every Thursday night we'd go to the Olympic Auditorium when Bob had a great yen to do a fight. He would have had to do middle-weight, but he was too old. That's when he bought Crawford. But he and Frankie had a personality clash like you wouldn't believe. I don't think Frankie wanted to fight Bob."

This didn't discourage Conrad from boxing. He had gotten so involved in boxing that, even though CBS allowed him only to train and do no real fighting, even for exhibition, he wanted to have boxing incorporated into "The Wild Wild West" to demonstrate he could fight. He was also instrumental in bringing in fighters as guest stars or bit players in the show. Heavyweight champion Floyd Patterson guest starred on "The Night of the Juggernaut," and fighter Wilhelm Von Homburg appeared in three episodes including as Hess, the ruthless henchman, in "The Night of the Big Blackmail." Heavyweight Roland LaStarza, better known for his starring role as Lucavich in ABC-TV's war drama "The Gallant Men," also guest starred in two episodes.

Cangey reflected on the outcome of the Crawford/Conrad relationship. He said that, although Conrad no longer owned the fighter, a questionable debt between them lead to their eventual falling out. The former stuntman read the headline from a January 24, 1974, article in the *Long Beach Press Telegram*:

Actor Conrad Called Hired Thug Target. Conrad had suspicions that Crawford intended to resort to less than legal methods of collecting a debt. Crawford was arraigned in connection with a standing threat against the actor but was eventually acquitted.

Several years later Crawford's boxing career came to an abrupt end. In a Las Vegas casino in December of 1977, Frankie Crawford was shot. The bullet shattered his spine and left him permanently confined to a wheelchair. Five years later, he took his own life.

End of an Era

After the demise of "The Wild Wild West," Bob Conrad and his entourage of stuntmen went their separate ways. The "WWW" years proved to be a valuable asset to Conrad, who continued his career with an array of television series and increasing his steadfast popularity. His stunt team was not so lucky. Cangey recalled, "Since "The Wild Wild West" used the same stuntmen all the time, the industry frowned on the show for not using different people. Anyone that worked regular on the show couldn't get a job for a long time afterward. We were all a very tight group. The industry blackballed everyone from that show."

Conrad reminisced about the break-up of the team. "We had a relationship off camera: a football team called The Heart of the Lion Club. On Friday nights we'd all go to my dressing room and gamble. On Saturdays we'd play football all day and Saturday nights we'd usually end up at Jimmy George's house listening to John Davidson records. It was pretty crazy and I'm glad it's part of my past and not a part of my future. I wouldn't ever do it again for money, but I'm glad to have had that opportunity to be a part of those crazy four years."

Acts of Violence

In "Bogus Bandits" Bob Conrad takes a bullet point blank from a bank robber.

The show suffered a dramatic change in stunts near the end of the fourth season. In 1968, just five days after the assassination of Robert F. Kennedy, President Lyndon Johnson appointed the National Commission on the Causes and Prevention of Violence. The urgency of the issue was enhanced by the assassination of Martin Luther King Jr. In just seven months, the remainder of Johnson's term of office, the Commission was asked to pinpoint the potential causes of what was seen as a trend toward criminal acts, disrespect for law enforcement and escalating violence in society. With so little time, the Commission relied heavily on existing, often erroneous, data. The report offered no real recommendations, claiming that no single cause could be cited. The report did, however, offer a blanket warning to the entertainment industry to be more judicious regarding its portrayals of violence, and encouraged parents to take a more proactive role in monitoring their children's viewing habits.

Regardless of its inconclusive nature, the ball was rolling on the issue of violence on television, and everyone from the Senate to the Surgeon General's office climbed aboard the bandwagon. It wasn't until 1972, when the Surgeon General's office released a study that directly linked aggressive behavior with viewing violence, under certain conditions. The five-volume report found a distinct correlation between the increases of blatantly violent acts portrayed on television, the increased amount of television viewing time spent by the average viewer, and the likelihood of violent behavior as a result. It became the "cause of the week" for politicians and an impetus for the government to step in with a call for tighter controls on the medium.

As a result, CBS came down with the list of rules and restrictions for stunts:

NOTE TO DIRECTORS: The producers respectfully ask that no violent acts be shown which are not depicted in the script or discussed beforehand with the producer or the associate producer. Most particularly, stay away from gratuitous ad-libs like slaps, pointing of firearms or other weapons at characters, especially in close quarters, kicks and use of furniture and other objects in fight scenes. We will be most grateful for your caution in these matters.

Mike Moder, director of the episode "The Night of the Cossacks," explained: "During the 'Cossack' show, on the last day I had to do one of the earlier sequences where Bob had to antagonize the head of the Cossacks. Bob was supposed to cold-cock the Cossack and the other Cossacks were to step in and get Bob. Lenny Katzman, the associate producer, was down in a flash because someone had called him. At that time you were only allowed so many acts of violence. A fight was an act of violence. So was a saddle fall. I had used up my acts of violence. Now I was not allowed to let Bob hit this guy. So we had to have Bob motion to hit the guy, hesitate long enough for the other Cossacks to grab his arm, and that's what was supposed to make the guy angry, the fact that Bob would even attempt to take a punch at him. He should've hit the guy, but Lenny would not let me."

Even after restrictions were placed on the *Acts of Violence* allowed in shows, the sincerity and the pain of each stunt were still evident. In one of the final fight scenes of the "Cossack" episode, Conrad barreled Cossack Red West through a window. Apparently both Conrad's heart and knee were in it. Conrad misjudged the position of the edge of the window and crashed his knee against the sill. Being the trouper that he was, he attempted to hide his anguish, and resulting limp, until the end of the shot.

Regardless of all their efforts, stuntman Dick Cangey observed, "Near the end of the show, the fights started to look like a ballet."

Part of the good times on and off the set involved a running joke about the treatment of stuntmen. The team put together the following list of demands that was presented to Bob Conrad and the "West" producers.

TO WHOM IT MAY CONCERN (Bob Conrad):
We, the undersigned, do hereby demand (PLEASE) that upon the commencement of the new season of "The Wild Wild West" we have the following:

ARTICLE I
1. No beards
2. Less masks
3. Neat wardrobe
4. Doubles when doing parts
5. Stuntmen hereafter referred to as stunt artists
6. All calls will begin when camera rolls*

ARTICLE II – Extra Curricular Activities
All activities on off hours to be paid for accordingly:
a. Ego boosters rate -- $25 per day
b. Laughing at jokes that are unnecessary -- $10 per joke -- $15 for big laughs -- $1.50 for courtesy smiles
c. Sparring partners who can't hit back $20 per round
d. Sparring partners who hit back softly $5 per round
Equipment handler 5¢ per day

ARTICLE II
a. Mr. Katzman will not upset stunt artists by kicking boxes
b. Unit Manager's appearances and ideas not to be tolerated.
c. Producer announces all appearances prior to coming to set.
D. All production personnel will not recognize stunt artists in drag.

a. Stunt artists will not be bothered before needed
b. No (absolutely) standing in for Charlie Scott
c. Dressing rooms to be furnished for each stunt artist
a. Heated on cold days – air conditioning when hot
b. With a wet bar (stocked)
c. Own personal makeup artists
d. More respect to be shown stunt artists by Charlie Scott
a. Personal chairs to be monogrammed and handled by Jack Benjamin
b. Green men admitted to association (WILD WEST) by request of members only.
c. Pads for Laveroni's slow dismounts
d. Guidelines and larger windows for Cappiello
e. More rehearsals for Cangey
f. More close-ups for Whitey
g. Crash helmets for Red West
h. Shorter horses for saddle falls
i. Safety belts for saddles
j. Pad to be furnished for foot falls
k. Repertory guest spots for all stunt artists
l. Individual close-ups for group shots (masters)
m. The name "Cangey" to be stricken from Mr. Conrad's vocabulary
***

The above demands, being fair and reasonable, to be accepted without explanation or question.

Michael Dunn & Phoebe Dorin
— Unexpected Stunt Performers

Michael Dunn and Phoebe Dorin in one of the last scenes of "Murderous Spring." Were it not for Dunn's quick thinking, this could have been Dorin's *final* scene.

Stunt coordinator Whitey Hughes said that Michael Dunn always did his own stunts. Even in his first episode, "The Night the Wizard Shook the Earth," Dr. Miguelito Loveless was pursued by James West into a clock tower of a sleepy town. The fiendish Doctor had rigged the tower to explode at the stroke of midnight. Although West jammed the explosive mechanism, Loveless jumped on the pendulum to force it to start again. West foiled the plan by disconnecting the explosives while Loveless was occupied. Nevertheless, jumping onto the swinging pendulum was a risky stunt aptly executive by the diminutive performer.

Phoebe Dorin, Loveless' usual accomplice, said that when their agent heard about them performing their own stunts for "West" he was furious. "He yelled at us, 'What are you doing stunts for!' and 'You should have been paid for the stunt!' Michael and I didn't realize it was a stunt. We thought that's how the script was."

Dorin explained, "We did stunts that were so dangerous we were almost killed. In 'Night of the Murderous Spring,' we were in a boat and the boat sank. I was in a big, flowing dress and they were taking a long shot to get the right shot of the boat going down. Just sit, they said, and the boat, equipped with a pulley, was wired to sink the right way. They would bring us to the bottom of the lake and we were to hold our breath until we got the signal, and then we would surface. It was a one-shot scene, since once we were wet we couldn't do the shot again."

She said that she and Dunn didn't think about getting stunt doubles. In fact, she thought it would be fun to do the stunts themselves. "I asked Michael, 'What if we don't get the signal?' He said, 'What are they going to do, let us die? They'll give us the signal.'" Near tragedy occurred when Dorin's flowing dress became entangled in the boat's sinking mechanism. "It (the dress) didn't have a zipper, but instead had 300 buttons," she said facetiously. "I couldn't get up and nobody knew I was trapped down there."

Fortunately, Dunn was very proficient in the water. Upon surfacing, he noticed right away that Dorin had not yet surfaced. He immediately dived back down to assist her. By the time he reached her she was turning blue and Dunn saved her life by literally tearing her free of her confining dress and helping her to the surface of the lake.

In "Green Terror," Dorin and Dunn found themselves awaiting rescue from a burning set, part of another *one-take* scene for which "West" became known.

Another foiled stunt nearly cost the duo their lives in "Night of the Green Terror." Once again, Loveless found himself creatively escaping James West. The villains crawled through a log with a trapped door in the back to aid in their escape. Dorin said this was another one-take scene since the set was to be torched and burned down around them. Again, awaiting the signal, they found themselves trapped in the log until the sprinkler system doused the flames and free them.

All Photos Courtesy CBS

Chapter 6
Second Season — A Change of Season

Michael Garrison was on top of the world in 1966. Not only did he get control of his show back, but he had a hit show on his hands, and for the 1966 fall season, "The Wild Wild West" was to be shot in color. Along with color, a few more improvements were being made. The first involved the train.

"The first thing that came off was the huge metal structure to hold the lights. That was developed so that when the train was jiggling, the interior lighting wouldn't go with it. Without the structure, the lighting would have been changing all the time. Then the train came off the wheels and got set down on the stage floor because being up on the platform meant that the camera had to be on a platform, the grips had to have a platform for lights, etc. There was a problem getting the camera up and down all the time and, for a weekly series, they wanted to go fast. So the lighting structure was removed, the train came off the platform and it never got jiggled again," remembered art director Al Heschong.

This restructuring of the train set caused a problem. How could West and Gordon travel in a train that showed no movement? Special effects man Tim Smyth came up with a creative solution. "I rigged up fishing line to the curtains. The train appeared to be moving when I juggled the line. I'd get the wobbling effect of the train in motion," he said.

The main title would now be in color.

The train was also redesigned in the beginning of the second season. Upcoming scripts called for inventive escape routes, definitely not through a window or door. "We came up with a fireplace that opened up when a secret button was pushed; this enabled West and Gordon to get out and climb up through a space in the roof, "Heschong said.

"The Wild Wild West" had a great look, especially in the rich colors of fabrics and costumes as appropriately illustrated in this book's foreword by Bruce Lansbury. Lush crimsons, forest greens and the Victorian ambiance all appropriately accented the 1870s setting.

Another change developed in the main title animation. The characters were now to be in full color with two action changes. The woman, who had previously wielded a knife at the unsuspecting James West, was no longer overcome by his kiss and allowed to turn and walk away. The *image of justice* lets her have it with a punch that leaves her aghast and innocuously planted on the ground. Also, the animated action was redesigned to take place with a backdrop of the American flag.

For the black and white episodes of the first season, the commercial break artwork used a freeze-frame photo of the action dissolved into a textured screen of the photo. The second season would use the same process, but in a colored sepia tone and, later,

The backdrop of an American flag was added to the main title sequence.

One of the first changes in operations was to simplify the train function.

into a painted animation cell.

With the new season, and all its improvements, Garrison wanted to feature major guest stars. Ethel Winant, who was directly involved in the program's casting at the time, said part of the fun of the show was in having fun guests. "He got Sammy Davis Jr. and others. He went after them because the show was so campy and the guests were part of the camp aspect. It was wonderful to have all those movie stars. It was part of the cache of the show. Later, people started doing the show because it was fun and everyone had a fun time, because Michael made it fun. He made it crazy and alive."

CBS did not approve of all the stars that Garrison had in mind for the show. One idea for a guest star came from writer John Kneubuhl. "One of the ideas that I suggested that he (Garrison) absolutely adored was to have Liberace (on the show.) I asked him, 'How would you like me to write a "Wild Wild West" for Liberace?' He said, 'Liberace what? The fastest gun in the West?' I said, 'No his Aunt Patsy Kelly

> With the new season, and all its improvements, Garrison wanted to feature major guest stars.

is.' (That's an old timer joke.) That sent him off into other gales of laughter. He asked me what the teaser was. I thought of a Western saloon and in walks Liberace with chaps and a vest and such, with a kerosene lantern in one hand, and he comes and places it on top of the piano; a player piano. And he sits down and turns it on and controls the loud and soft keys while it plays.

"By this time Michael was ready to give me the Pulitzer Prize, the Nobel Prize and three quarters of his shares in the series. I wrote out the teaser and an outline for the first act only and he immediately sent it down to CBS. Liberace wanted to do it very much. He called him immediately, but CBS killed it right then and there. I found out later that Michael was not only a dedicated homosexual; he was an impassioned, dedicated homosexual. I think CBS was very nervous about Michael playing around with any material that would bring that association up in the front office. So they killed that story immediately."

The writers loved working with Garrison. Several attested that he had good sense and put faith in his writers. Kneubuhl recalled, "He would agree on the first big step and then leave (the writer) alone; but

he was very supportive. As I said, Mike's laugh, his merriment, his spontaneous sense of fun, were remarkable incentives to me anyway, for coming up with ideas right on the spot in his presence. He could somehow make me do that. He knew exactly how to react, where to react, and exactly where to shut up. It's a very rare gift. He was a gifted, sensitive man; far more gifted than television would have ever allowed him to be."

A Slightly New Look -- Costuming by Jack Muhs

The second season also brought in a new costume designer, Jack Muhs. Muhs made a few changes and brought his own special touch to the James West wardrobe. Previously, the character wore primarily a short bolero-style jacket along with a variety of other styles. Muhs felt that, since West was an action oriented individual, always reaching for his gun and using fast movements, that the short bolero-style jacket worked much better. After several costume changes, the bolero jacket remained.

"Let's be honest about it. The tight pants showed off his butt. I got many letters and they were always positive, and Bob was comfortable in them," Muhs said.

He put Conrad in mostly blues and greens, noting that it brought out his coloring. Total cost for his costumes ran $400— $300 for the jacket and $75 for the trousers. "I made the pants out of a blend. It was relatively thin as opposed to bulky, heavy fabric, something that would wear better. What we needed was strength because the pants were so tight that when he fought he was always

TNOT Underground Terror

TNOT Pistoleros

Because of his unique costume and the unusual demands of his character, Bob Conrad frequently suffered wardrobe malfunctions.

CBS Photo

83

splitting the butt out of them," Muhs said. Bob's wardrobe malfunctions were evident in several episodes including: "The Night of the Pistoleros" and "The Night of the Underground Terror."

As a designer, naturally Muhs would try to make the individual look as good as possible. More importantly, he would try to use something unique about them, the character and the player, and produce a costume that *was* that individual. "The correct coat for the period was a frock coat, which was more like what Artemus Gordon wore. No one ever told me to be authentic on the show. Mike (Garrison) would tell me to have fun with it and try to do something with the clothes to keep the feeling of fun and adventure."

Muhs also created a trail outfit for Conrad that consisted of a blue, bolero-length corduroy jacket with leather lapels and cuffs and black leather chaps. For Ross, Muhs designed a buckskin coast. These costumes were seen primarily in the third and fourth seasons.

Muhs said that he had a great deal of freedom as a costume designer for the show. "No one saw the costumes until the day the scenes were shot. We were working on such a tight schedule that I did the show in two days." It was the last two days before shooting when everyone was firmly cast; then Muhs got the go-ahead. The costume people worked all day and into the night to get everyone costumed and on stage. "I was on the set for the first day of shooting. This was the first time directors and actors saw the costumes. No one knew what anyone was wearing until that time."

Muhs admitted that the most difficult actor to

James West's new look kept the bolero jacket and was tailored to his *action-oriented* character.

fit was Ross Martin because of all the different disguises involved. "Because of the time factor, I was the same size as Ross at the time, I used to dress up in his costumes at Western Costume to check out how they would look. Ross always liked what he wore."

A problem arose, however, with a tinge of jealousy between the starring actors. "Ross had a slight weight problem and Bob was all muscle. Ross was more fleshy, but he didn't want to play second fiddle. If Bob had tight pants, he wanted tight pants, and he didn't see himself looking bad. I made him a cut-away with a tail because his butt would have looked bigger if they were in light colored pants and not covered. Each season when I designed something for Bob I'd make a sketch for Ross. Ross wanted to look good and elegant. There was a little jealousy because it was Bob's show and Ross wanted to be treated the same way; certainly in clothes. I tried to keep them happy."

Partly because of Muhs outstanding design talents, Ross Martin was awarded the *1967 Best Dressed Men's Award* by the *Men and Boy's Apparel Club of America* for being the best dressed star of a television series.

Many of James West's coats were trick costumes with special places for his devices. In production meetings, Muhs would note which scenes West would use certain devices in and get the proper coat to the set so that time wouldn't be wasted waiting for costuming. "One example would be the sleeve gun.

Ross Martin's costume was sophisticated Western; he wanted to look elegant.

84

The sleeves on the trick coat would be shorter as to show the gun coming down into his hand," Muhs explained.

Returning guest stars Michael Dunn and Victor Buono proved to be challenges for the designer, considering the lack of time allotted for costume preparation. "For Michael Dunn everything had to be made to his size because the period of style did not exist in stock for his size. For Victor Buono, because of his large size, if we made something it took days."

Overall, people were pleased with the costuming. They were so pleased that even up to the 1988 printing of this book Muhs was receiving calls from people wanting to know how to get a pattern to make the James West costume. After "The Wild Wild West," Muhs continued to make full use of his creativity as costume designer for Disneyland and Disney Productions.

Introducing the Count

Victor Buono was introduced as the hopefully recurring villain Count Carlos Manzeppi.

With the outstanding popularity of Dr. Loveless, another unique villain was introduced on "The Wild Wild West." A debonair, but intrinsically evil magician by the name of Count Carlos Mario Vincenzo Robespierre Manzeppi was flamboyantly portrayed by character actor Victor Buono. CBS was intrigued by villains, but not the traditional comic book villain as seen in the "Batman" series. "West" dealt with villains that were international spies with super powers, as opposed to your ordinary Western villain such as masked bandits and bank robbers.

Ethel Winant remembered the series' unique approach to villains. "They were either magicians, or they were plugged into things, or they had international contacts, so that defeating them, their mysterious forces and exotic powers, was different. The hard part of 'The Wild Wild West' was to keep it from being a Western and try to keep it within budget and to give it style. The writers were constantly creating these super-villains that made it different from being a Western. If they worked, we brought them back. It's like Sherlock Holmes and Moriarty. You have the ongoing threat that is always lurking around the corner, and this guy is going to turn up again for a duel to the death. You hope to hit the magic formula with villains."

The magical Manzeppi character first appeared in "The Night of the Eccentrics," an episode produced by Michael Garrison. Although sixth in shooting order the episode was scheduled as the opener for the series' second season hoping to make an abundant impression on audiences.

Bruce Lansbury

On July 12, 1066, *Daily Variety* printed:
Lansbury returns to CBS as ninth producer of The Wild Wild West!

Bruce Lansbury has been named producer of CBS-TV's The Wild Wild West series by Mike Garrison. Garrison explained he made the move so that he will be able to work on new projects as well as WWW, which has been renewed for next season. Until now, Garrison has been functioning both as exec producer and producer on the series, which stars Bob Conrad and Ross Martin. Lansbury formerly produced The Great Adventure series for CBS and was an exec producer with the network.

With the success of "The Wild Wild West" behind him, Garrison ventured out to develop other projects, including two half-hour situation comedies called "Kelley's Country" and "Happy Valley."

Ethel Winant explained that upcoming projects weren't the only reason for hiring another producer to watch over "West." "Michael had a vision of the series.

TNOT Cutthroats

Bruce Lansbury (left) discusses a scene with Robert Conrad.

He thought up very extravagant things and the shows were way over budget and out of control. But he did have a feeling for the show so it began to take shape. Now CBS was terrified because he was in control and they were millions of dollars over budget. Michael couldn't control himself because he didn't know about budgets. I think, had he allowed himself to be concerned about the bottom line (budget wise), he couldn't have had the ideas that he had. That's why he didn't care. Now the show was going to be successful and they had to keep it on the air. But it was disorganized."

When "West" was first being developed, Bruce Lansbury was part of the Jim Aubrey regime, but

> **Lansbury and Garrison had been close friends for many years and Lansbury had much more producing experience than Garrison.**

when the axe fell on the administration, Lansbury, too, felt the blade. "After I left CBS, I produced a Broadway show which was a total failure. When I moved out to California, I got a call from Boris Caplin, director of programming for the network. He had seen three one acts that I had written and directed that were produced out here. In fact, I had a kind of kinky approach to it that would work for 'The Wild Wild West.' I came out because Boris thought I could handle the show, and I had been with CBS for many years," he said.

Lansbury and Garrison had been close friends for many years and Lansbury had much more producing experience than Garrison. Ethel Winant remem-

bered that, initially, Lansbury was not well liked by management because he was part of that old team. "CBS could see the possibility of bringing Bruce in, but the fact that he was part of old management, and that he was close friends with Michael Garrison, created certain reservations by the network. But he could control the show physically. He (Lansbury) would be able to take all those ideas and make them work so they wouldn't be totally out of control."

The first episode produced by Lansbury was "The Night of the Bottomless Pit," a story that finds James West at the mercy of a deranged commandant in charge of a prison known as Devil's Island.

Season 2 – Episode Listings

The Night of the
Golden Cobra

Territorial Indian Commissioner Colonel Mayo (Scott) recruits the services of agent James West to investigate strange happenings in the Pawnee Indian reservation area. West is attacked by a band of horsemen and defeats his adversaries. From the distance, the agent hears enticing music when he is suddenly confronted by a cobra which bites him and renders him unconscious.

West awakens in the palace of the Maharajah of Ramapor, more affectionately known as Mr. Singh (Karloff), who has heard of West's fighting expertise. Singh wants West to instruct his sons in the art of hand-to-hand combat. The agent battles his abductors but, when the sons resort to weaponry, West pretends that a simple box of matches is actually a secret weapon known as Rosebud X51. The frightened captors allow his escape. West runs up a staircase and meets up with Veda (Dalton), Singh's beautiful daughter. West discovers Colonel Mayo tied up in an upstairs bedroom. He wonders why they're holding the Mayo. Veda knocks West unconscious with a dart and he asks her, "Why did you shoot me with a dart, Veda?" Veda explains she drugged the agent to save him from her brothers.

Iconic actor Boris Karloff plays Mr. Singh, a Maharajah seeking James West's expertise in "Golden Cobra."

CBS #6602 Shooting Order 29
First Air Date: 09/23/66

CBS Photo

Produced by Michael Garrison
Directed by Irving J. Moore
Written by Henry Sharp

Mr. Singh: Boris Karloff
Veda Singh: Audrey Dalton
Colonel Mayo: Simon Scott
Chandra: James Westmoreland
Gupta: Michael York
Sarrkan: John Alonzo
Dancers: Sujata and Asoka
John Jose De Vega
Mudjaz: Morgan Farley

Artemus Gordon has been at the Pawnee reservation awaiting word from West and Mayo. His Indian friends tell him about the mysterious palace. Concerned, he goes to the palace where he meets Veda outside. She tells him that West is in danger. Again, West meets with Singh who tries to persuade him to stay on and train his sons. Artemus appears disguised as an East Indian rope trick artist. He demonstrates the Indian rope trick to Singh and the two agents use it to escape. Jim and Artie split up. West tells Artie to look after Veda while he looks for some answers. West is quickly recaptured when he falls through a trapdoor.

West soon discovers that Colonel Mayo is actually working with Singh to frighten the Pawnee Indians off their oil-rich land. The two men want to recruit West and Gordon, who are trusted by the Pawnee, to help persuade them to move. By now Mayo has captured Artemus and Veda and threatens to kills them if West does not cooperate. Singh did not anticipate Veda's involvement and he quickly turns on Mayo.

As the Colonel shows West a murky pool of black gold, Singh hurls a saber at Mayo who shoots Singh. Mayo falls into the pool of oil and drowns before the agents can save him.

Back at the parlor car, the agents receive an unusual package from which a leopard cub emerges. While Artie holds the cub, Jim leaves to get a saucer of milk for their new pet. Suddenly a fierce growl emanates from the supposedly empty box. A surprised Artie quips, "Better make that a large saucer of milk."

Author's Notes:

This very vibrant episode was the first shot in color and, although the sets were dramatic and the theme lent itself perfectly to an amazing array of hues, CBS probably felt the storyline and characters were not as appealing as those of "The Eccentrics," so this was

passed over as the season opener. Veteran actor Boris Karloff, better known for his portrayal of Frankenstein's monster in the 1931 classic film, was excellent as the mysterious East Indian Mr. Singh. Garrison, who was known for getting big names for the series, signed Karloff. Director Irving Moore remembered that working with Karloff was a great joy, although the actor hated animals and children.

Moore also recalled an incident on the set that was a good example of Garrison's flamboyant tendencies. He said that an elephant had been rented for the background. An actor stood with the elephant feeding it grapes, which was supposed to add to the East Indian ambiance, but the shot was too tight and half the elephant was cut out of the scene. Garrison was furious. He said that he had paid for a whole elephant and he wanted to see a whole elephant. It was impossible to get a good shot of the entire beast. Moore believes that Garrison never forgave him for not showing the whole elephant.

The Night of the
Big Blast

The fanatical Dr. Faustina (Lupino) and her mute servant, Miklos (Manning), convert a corpse made into a duplicate of agent James West, into a robot. Lightening charges life back into the body and it is sent on a mission to kill four members of the U.S. President's cabinet at a meeting in New Orleans during Mardi Gras. The duplicate West is instructed to personally deliver a message to the group. The pseudo-West is rigged with a bomb that will blow itself up and at the same time kill the officials.

Artemus is on vacation and meets an old classmate, Lily Fortune (Powers), who he quickly sweeps off her feet and into his private railroad car. The West double works his way through the Mardi Gras crowd observed by Faustina and Miklos. The convincing facsimile is lead into the room where the Secretary of the Interior, Secretary of War and the Secretary of State meet. The ensuing explosion claims the lives of everyone including the West double. Everyone is lead to believe that the real West died in the explosion, but when Artemus is notified, he is sure that West must still be alive.

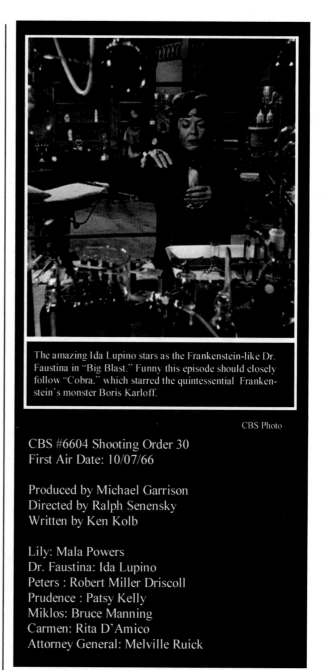

The amazing Ida Lupino stars as the Frankenstein-like Dr. Faustina in "Big Blast." Funny this episode should closely follow "Cobra," which starred the quintessential Frankenstein's monster Boris Karloff.

CBS Photo

CBS #6604 Shooting Order 30
First Air Date: 10/07/66

Produced by Michael Garrison
Directed by Ralph Senensky
Written by Ken Kolb

Lily: Mala Powers
Dr. Faustina: Ida Lupino
Peters : Robert Miller Driscoll
Prudence : Patsy Kelly
Miklos: Bruce Manning
Carmen: Rita D'Amico
Attorney General: Melville Ruick

Back at Dr. Faustina's lab, Miklos has just returned with another body for whom the good doctor will alter the facial characteristics. It is explained that Faustina is bent on revenge against government officials who refused her request for $1 million to aid her in her electrical experiments. Artemus and Lily set out to find West. They attend a masquerade ball where they are met by three less than merry musketeers. Artie subdues the men and coerces one into talking. Artie is told to seek out the carriage driver on St. Peters Street. Artie locates the carriage and, at gunpoint, tells the driver to take him to West. A switch has been played as his companion, the supposed Lily, is suddenly Dr. Faustina wielding a pistol.

At the laboratory, Faustina designs a robot of Gordon, who has been tied up with ropes. The doctor plans on sending the Gordon double to kill President Grant. West escapes from the cell he has been in this whole time and frees Artie. The two go directly to the lab just in time to watch the pseudo-Artie come to life. After a fight, the robot, Faustina and Miklos escape.

The robot Artie makes his way to the government building where the President is and the two agents arrive just in time to lasso the robot and drag him away as he explodes. The episode closes with Artemus asking for Lily's hand in marriage. Although Artie cannot speak the words Jim helps him out and asks Lily for him. She refuses because of Artie's *explosive* profession. West pops a champagne cork loudly in the background. "Thanks a lot, Jim!" quips Artie.

Author's Notes:

This is probably my second favorite episode because we see Artemus Gordon in an entirely different light. This is one of the few episodes with Artemus as the featured hero and the romantic lead. I was impressed by the fact that Ross Martin, who was an excellent fencer, did most of his own fencing during the masquerade ball scene. He was doubled by stuntman and expert fencer Dave Sharp for the more physical stunt work involved in the wide-angle shots. Dave Sharp also doubled Ross in the 1965 film "The Great Race," where Martin played Rolfe Von Stuppe opposite Jack Lemmon and Tony Curtis.

Writer Ken Kolb remembered his unique approach to the Artemus Gordon character in this episode. "I tended to (put a lot of Gordon in it) because Ross Martin was so much better an actor than Bob. If you had something that required a lot of plotline, then Ross ended up with the lines because you knew people would be able to follow the story; whereas, Bob was not really into plot. I doubt if he knew what the plot was most of the time because he was, essentially, a great stuntman. He could do quick reactions and nobody ever asked him, 'Why don't you try to carry the

story,' because he would throw the line away. We ended up writing most of it for Ross when we had somewhat of a complicated plot."

Of the many considerations put into the concept, one was definitely the budget. Kolb felt that the idea came about because there were standing sets available. Kolb said that when he saw a castle in one of CBS' back lots he came up with the idea. He presented the teaser, using the sheet-covered body twitching back to life during a mood-setting lightening storm: The monster – James West! The switch was in making Dr. Frankenstein a woman. Crediting Garrison, Kolb said, "I don't want to take credit for all the inventiveness that went into the show because Garrison was really helpful in those things. He was very engaging character and I've never had anyone treat me as well."

Film great Ida Lupino appears as the wicked Dr. Faustina. A trail blazer for women in Hollywood, Lupino was one of the first women to direct and the second woman to be admitted into The Directors Guild. She broke free of the studio system and in the 1950s and repeatedly proved her talents in front of and behind the lens. She appeared in more than 100 roles since the start of her career in 1931. She died in 1995 at the age of 81.

Oddly, you'll find no disguises and very little gadgetry for Artie in this episode. Just loads of quality acting.

The Night of the
Infernal Machine

Agents West and Gordon have been assigned to welcome and protect a convention of federal judges arriving for a judges convention to be held at a hotel in Denver. Gordon is disguised as the hotel's German pastry chef, Herr Osterpolyer, in order to keep an eye on the proceedings. Both agents are searching for a box of stolen dynamite hidden somewhere in the hotel. After Judge M'Guigan's (Begley) billiard opponent is blown to bits by an exploding cue ball, M'Guigan, who is chairman of the convention, is warned by the agents this he, too, was in danger. West finds a piece of the bomb and traces it back to Zeno Baroda (Kuluva), a known expert in *infernal machines*. Baroda was previously sentenced by M'Guigan and the

Ed Begley stars as Judge M'Guigan, a marked official in need of protection in "The Night of the Infernal Machine."

CBS Photo

CBS #6613 Shooting Order 31
First Air Date: 12/23/66

Produced by Michael Garrison
Directed by Sherman Marks
Written by Shimon Wincelberg

Judge M'Guigan: Ed Begley
Zeno Baroda: Will Kuluva
Cefalu: Vito Scotti
Inspector Bulvon: Bill Zuckert
Vashti: Elaine Dunn
Bledsoe: Michael Pate
Moody: John Harmon
Vickerman: John Lormer

agents think he may be seeking vengeance.

West visits the recently paroled Baroda in the convict's clock shop. The agent tries to get him to confess to killing the judge, but to no avail. While returning to the hotel West is accosted by a man named Bledsoe (Pate) and, after unsuccessfully trying to kill West, is forced to reveal who is gunning for M'Guigan. Before talking, Bledsoe is shot and killed by an unseen assailant.

M'Guigan is taken to the agent's train for protection, but the judge is soon swayed by the charms of one of the girl dancers from the opening ceremony of the convention. He leaves with her to hide out until the convention begins. M'Guigan requests that Gordon bake a large Statue of Liberty cake for the convention and Gordon obliges. M'Guigan specifically requests a special sparkler in the torch of the cake that a lady on a flying trapeze will dramatically light.

When West returns to the hotel, the kitchen help tells him that the pastry chef (Gordon) had and accident and was badly burned. West investigates their story and finds Artemus laying face down on the ground, his face covered in bandages and a wire attached to him. West assumes that the wire is an explosive device. He follows the wire which leads him to the freezer locker. When the agent enters the freezer, the door slams and locks behind him. Then West discovers Gordon tied up in the locker. The burned Gordon was actually impersonated by M'Guigan, who has been behind the deadly pranks in order to eliminate judges and blaze the path for his own appointment to the Supreme Court. The cake that he has requested is actually a bomb and the sparkler the fuse.

The agents escape the freezer locker by blowing through the door with explosive putty. The agents race to the convention hall where the cake has just been lit. West climbs onto the trapeze with a seltzer bottle and douses the fuse. M'Guigan, infuriated by his failed attempt at the killing, randomly shoots at the judges and tries to escape. West pursues the fleeing judge, leaps onto him and the two tumble into the giant Liberty cake. Gordon asks, "did you have to ruin my cake." West replies, "It was either your cake or my reputation."

Author's Notes:

This was not an exciting episode. CBS apparently agreed, which is likely why it was pushed up from third on the shooting list to fourteenth in air date. I guess West and Gordon can't have all the exciting jobs from Washington and need to take a break from the crazy, wild villains to deal with the occasional corrupt government officials. Small potatoes and any secret agent could have done it. The German cook, Herr Osterpolyer, was one of Martin's favorite roles.

The Night of the
Raven

Michael Dunn and Phoebe Dorin return as Dr. Loveless and Antoinette in a fantastic tale of miniaturization in "TNOT Raven."

CBS Photo

CBS#6603 Shooting Order 32
First Air Date: 09/30/66

Produced by Michael Garrison
Directed by Irving J. Moore
Written by Ed Di Lorenzo

Wanakee: Phyllis Newman
Antoinette: Phoebe Dorin
Dr. Miguelito Loveless: Michael Dunn
War Eagle: Howard Hoffman
Chawtaw: Santy Josol

An Indian uprising is threatened if secret agents West and Gordon do not produce a chief's abducted daughter, Wanakee (Newman), within three days. Lead to Gravetown by a telegram ruse, the agents find themselves confronted by their arch rival, the diminutive Dr. Miguelito Loveless (Dunn). Loveless; scheme this time is to rule a world of *little people*.

West gains entrance to Loveless' home to find himself first in a room that resounds with the inimitable laughter of the good doctor, and later with Wanakee and Gordon as prisoners. The three are placed in shackles, but West is able to burn through the metal with an acetylene pencil and, with Gordon's help, subdues the two guards.

It appears that Princess Wanakee was kidnapped only to lure the two agents to Loveless. Loveless is also trying to prevent a peace treaty from being signed. This will result in more bloodshed and priming his target area for a takeover. In a private room West fights two more guards and is knocked against a wall that spins him around and lands him face to face with Loveless who gives West a doped cigar. West wakes up later to find he has been reduced to six inches in height. He tries to escape but is cornered by Loveless and his pet cat. West is placed in a doll house with a miniaturized Wanakee. West admits, "The little man can do *anything*."

For the first time Loveless can actually look down on West. Wanakee and West are seated at a miniature table while Loveless and Antoinette (Dorin) sing "Sloop John B." Artemus, who is still normal size, is brought to the room and is astounded by what he sees. Loveless proceeds to detail his plan to shrink the human world so that animals can play in the sun and

James West finds himself contending with the *big cheese* in "The Night of the Raven."

man will recapture the Garden of Eden. Artie sarcastically adds, "I recall a certain snake in the last garden." His comments enrage Loveless, who *insists* that his plan will restore the balance of nature.

West points out that all of the doctor's plans have failed in the past. The agent attempts another escape, this time through a mouse hole. He encounters a giant web, a spider and a mousetrap before eventually finding himself in a giant arena facing his new worst enemy; a cat. Wanakee is bound to a post and forced to witness the slaughter of her would-be rescuer. Artie's quick thinking saves West as he tossed his pen lock pick to the pint-sized agent, who then stabs the cat. Arties was also able to grab the restoring solution, which he throws to West enlarging him in time to subdue more guards.

Again, Loveless and Antoinette escape via miniaturization and a speedy exit on the wings of a raven. The exit is accented by the doctor's recognizable laughter. Wanakee is returned to her betrothed in time for their wedding.

Author's Notes:

This is one of my personal favorites. This episode was a technical achievement. "The Incredible Shrinking Man," based on the Richard Matheson novel, was made into a film in 1957 with quite a few of the same elements, but is was unusual for a television show to venture into these types of effects. When I first saw this episode I said, "This is 'The Wild Wild West.'" If any episode were to epitomize the essence of the program, this was it. It was way out there in the complete and utter fantasy realm. Leave it to Dr. Loveless to come up with a powder that could shrink people. It was a lot of fun for everyone involved and wildly imaginative.

Garrison wanted to get two big names for the roles of Princess Wanakee and Chawtaw. Quoting Irving Moore, "We needed a couple to play the Indian maiden and her boyfriend. Mike (Garrison) came to me and said, 'What would you think if I could get Sonny and Cher to play the Indian boy and girl?' I said, 'Mike, you're kidding. You've got to be out of your mind. How are you gonna get Sonny and Cher to do a six day shoot television show?' Garrison replied, 'You ask them, that's how.' He was wild. There was nothing that detoured Mike Garrison. He would do anything and did anything."

One of the set stories involved the raven. According to Moore, the bird was not very cooperative. He said that the bird wouldn't do anything. They could-

n't get it to budge. So they tied a string to the bird's leg and, when the SPCA man wasn't looking, they'd pull the string. The bird would take off and fall to the ground, but at least they got a couple of feet of flight on film.

Moore admitted that the use of special effects was a new experience for Lenny Katzman and him. They used blue screen, split screens and it took some serious planning and equally as much guessing to keep the size proportions accurate.

The Night of the
Man-Eating House

West and Gordon are sent to transport prisoner Liston Day (Hatfield) an elderly but dangerous man dying of swamp fever, to a hospital. Day has spent the last 30 years in solitary confinement for treason of his native state, Texas, during its fight for independence. That night they prepare to bed down at a seemingly deserted mansion. As they approach the house, the door mysteriously opens. Once they enter, it closes behind them, trapping the agents, Day and the Sheriff (Talman) accompanying them.

The agents hear a woman crying, but can find no one in the house. Day's condition is rapidly deteriorating as more strange things happen. West and Gordon discover that the mansion has a life, and mind, of its own, possessed by Day's long-dead mother. When Day, suddenly full of energy, tries to escape, he dashes upstairs and the Sheriff follows. The agents follow the Sheriff but soon discover a grisly sight: The Sheriff is dead in the hallway with every ounce of blood drained from his body. Meanwhile, Day is observing from behind a doorway suddenly appearing 30 years younger and bearing a striking resemblance to Dorian Gray.

The next morning, Jim and Artie find that the house is holding them captive and has restored itself to the exact condition of the night before. Day's ghostly mother reveals her diary to the agents, showing that Day has actually paid for a crime that had been committed by his father. When West and Gordon confront Day, they realize that all of his reasoning is gone: He is obviously mad. He plans to return Texas to Spanish

Hurd Hatfield is Liston Day, a man heading back to a strange home full of mystical powers in "The Night of the Man-Eating House."

CBS Photo

CBS #6612 Shooting Order 33
First Air Date: 12/02/66

Produced by Michael Garrison
Directed by Alan Crosland
Written by John Kneubuhl

Liston Day: Hurd Hatfield
Sheriff: William Talman

Author's Notes:

Although CBS made their aversion to fantasy stories quite evident, occasionally writers and producers could slip one in by toning it down on paper. Writer John Kneubuhl remembered that he never had to sell a story to the network. "When it came to writing 'House' I just thought it would be good fun for a change of pace. I was usually given carte blanche, but when I wanted to do a ghost story my agent called and said CBS wanted to pay me off. They didn't want children scared. I had my agent call CBS back and tell them, 'Don't worry, there won't be a ghost in the house.' I was being facetious. But later my agent called back and said they bought the idea. So I wrote a haunted house story where the house itself is the ghost. It turned out to be three times more frightening than a ghost story with a nice, conservative, Republican ghost. They wanted me to soften it even more. So I made it a dream. I don't know what was saved in horror by casting it as a dream."

Kneubuhl strikes again as one of the most creative and imaginative writers on the "West" staff. Along with Garrison's input, and occasional influence from fellow scribe Ken Kolb, Kneubuhl had a special talent for creating episodes in a class by themselves.

Hurd Hatfield is placed in a role blatantly reminiscent of his memorable portrayal of Dorian Gray in the 1945 film, "The Picture of Dorian Gray," where a man's evil deeds age his portrait rather than the man. While aging vicariously is not a new concept, it is well handled in this eerie mansion in our "Wild West" setting.

The Night of the
Eccentrics

Agents West and Gordon go to a deserted warehouse after being contacted by a fellow agent about a group of assassins that are plotting to kill President Juarez of Mexico. The two gain entrance using a miniature blowtorch only to find the agent has been murdered. The seated victim has an advertising flyer firmly placed in his back with a knife. The flyer says, *For a Happy Time Go to the Echo Amusement Park.* Suddenly a floating ball of fire spins around the room and the lights go out. When the lights come up, Artemus is hanging by his neck. West shoots the rope

rule and infest the state with plague-carrying rats. He has similar plans for the agents, but they stop the clock on his plan and convince the spirit of Day's mother to open the house and let her son go free to die in peace.

The doors swing open and the three men exit, but Day has other plans. He grabs a gun and holds the agents at bay. Preparing to shoot West and Gordon he suddenly finds himself rapidly aging and trembling from disease. He falls to the ground and succumbs to swamp fever.

Sleeping out in the wild, Gordon suddenly snaps awake from a bizarre dream. The agents begin their day's journey, ending up at a house that looks remarkably similar to the one in Artie's dream. The door opens by itself and the agents enter cautiously.

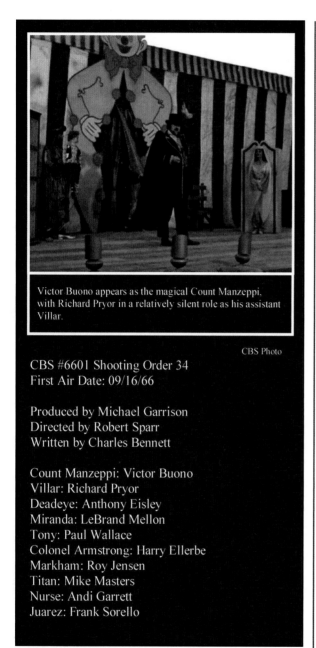

Victor Buono appears as the magical Count Manzeppi, with Richard Pryor in a relatively silent role as his assistant Villar.

CBS Photo

CBS #6601 Shooting Order 34
First Air Date: 09/16/66

Produced by Michael Garrison
Directed by Robert Sparr
Written by Charles Bennett

Count Manzeppi: Victor Buono
Villar: Richard Pryor
Deadeye: Anthony Eisley
Miranda: LeBrand Mellon
Tony: Paul Wallace
Colonel Armstrong: Harry Ellerbe
Markham: Roy Jensen
Titan: Mike Masters
Nurse: Andi Garrett
Juarez: Frank Sorello

and Gordon falls to the floor, spraining his ankle.

Agent West, now going it alone, is lead to the deserted Echo Amusement Park where he finds the Eccentrics' magical leader, Count Carlos Mario Vincenzo Robespierre Manzeppi (Buono), adventurer, poet and lover of all that is corrupt, forbidden and blasphemous. Manzeppi and his helpers force West to fight their strongman, Titan (Masters). When West wins, the count's sharpshooter, Deadeye (Eisley) kills Titan. West then subdues Deadeye and Tony (Wallace), an expert knife-thrower, only to fall into a huge elaborate room where Manzeppi outlines his plans to assassinate the Mexican President Juarez in return for $1 million from Juarez' successor, the Archduke Charles Lewis of Austria. The group wants West to help, but he must first prove his loyalty by killing his best friend and partner, Artemus Gordon.

When the agent refuses, Manzeppi decides to frame West as Juarez' killer. Using a magic lantern show, a futuristic projection screen, Manzeppi shows West his murderous scheme. West escapes with the help of lady Eccentric Miranda (Mellon), but Manzeppi is watching the escape through a magical closed circuit television.

Back at the train, Artie is greeted by West and Miranda, who fill him in on the plan. The count appears and we discover that Miranda was a ruse for getting West and Gordon together and at the mercy of Manzeppi, who will now blame both of them for Juarez' imminent assassination. West offers the Eccentric $2 million to not kill the Mexican President. Doubtful, Manzeppi and his cohorts are surprised by a diversion as the agents douse the lights and Artie escapes through the fireplace.

West is brought back to the Eccentrics' hideout and placed in the feminine arms of *Amorous Amanda*, a clenching device that suspends the agent above a circle of electricity. In 14 minutes the frayed rope will plummet West to his shocking death. Miranda appears to help his escape motivated by the $2 million offer. Using her prowess with a whip, she severs the electrical wires and releases our hero. They rush to President Juarez's office and must scale the walls, only to be stopped by an old Mexican military guard who is actually Artemus. They discover that Juarez is actually a disguised Deadeye waiting for the real Juarez to meet his fate. Manzeppi is always one step ahead of the agents. The agents are captured and now Miranda is at the mercy of the Count. West vexes Tony, the knife expert, into demonstrating his skills, thus cutting the agent's bonds. West is held by Deadeye. When Manzeppi enters the room, Deadeye shoots Tony for helping the agent escape. West, seeing an ideal opportunity, entices Deadeye into a shootout. West wins. With his team of Eccentrics depleted, Manzeppi vanishes behind a secret passage and the real President Juarez arrives on time to demand an explanation.

The episode ends with government men confirming the absence of an escape passage and Colonel Armstrong (Ellerbe), a supervisor, suggesting the two agents need a vacation. An unnoticed hand appears mysteriously out of the wall in the president's office, grabs a flower from a vase and transforms a photograph of Juarez into one of Count Manzeppi.

Author's Notes:

The sixth episode in shooting order, the network probably felt it made the most dramatic use of the color and it was slated as the season opener. The changes in the train, including the fireplace escape route, and the colorful costumes and sets enhanced the new tinting of the series. With the success of the Dr. Loveless character, CBS decided that a new villain, Count Manzeppi, the prince of black magic, might bring as much success. The storyline conformed to the bizarre fantasy approach that they had been trying to achieve for "The West."

"The Night of the Eccentrics," written by noted Hitchcock writer Charles Bennett, was reviewed by *Daily Variety*. "The opening episode of 'The Wild Wild West' was so loaded with tricks that CBS might just trick itself out of an audience." *Variety* found the entire episode unappealing, satanic and sadistic. "West's" newly created villain relied so heavily on tricks and gadgetry that it left much to be desired. According to *Variety,* there was no comparing Manzeppi to the inventiveness and appeal of Dr. Miguelito Loveless, evil doing aside.

The reviewer gave no mention of the colorful appeal of the traditionally ornate sets. I found this episode very enjoyable because of the element of sheer fantasy alone. Victor Buono's portrayal of Count Manzeppi was fun, but he appeared to be a very bored villain and, as he was known to do, noticeably underplayed the character.

Manzeppi fared well overall with fans, but not so with critics. It was unfortunate that Richard Pryor, who went on to have a hugely successful career, had little to say or do in this episode. One of the *guest stars*, The Amorous Amanda, didn't disappoint audiences, who watched attentively as West escaped from her captivating stage presence and shocking appeal.

The Night of the
Returning Dead

"Returning Dead" pits legends Sammy Davis Jr. and Peter Lawford against each other in John Kneubuhl's tale of psychism and revenge.

CBS Photo

CBS #6605 Shooting Order 35
First Air Date: 10/14/66

Produced by Michael Garrison
Directed by Richard Donner
Written by John Kneubuhl

Elizabeth: Hazel Court
Tom Kellogg: Ken Lynch
Jeremiah: Sammy Davis Jr.
Ned Briggs: Alan Baxter
Carl Jackson: Peter Lawford
Bill Mott: Frank Wilcox

Agents West and Gordon meet with wealthy ranch owner, Carl Jackson (Lawford) and Sheriff Ned Briggs (Baxter) to investigate the appearance of a mysterious, bullet-immune Confederate night rider. The two were sent an anonymous letter summoning their help to find *the truth*. They are suddenly charged at by the ethereal equestrian who quickly vanishes.

Jeremiah (Davis), a local stable boy, is questioned and West accuses him of guiding the rider with his eerie flute music. He is also blessed with the special ability to hypnotize animals into following his commands. West rigs an explosive saddle horn to stop the ghostly thief on his next attempt to mount his horse. Artie attempts to lure the night rider out of his cave dwelling by playing Jeremiahs' flute. The rider appears again and West tangles with the apparition and exposes the skull face of the ghoul. West is astonished and the rider mounts West's steed, detonates the charge and remains unharmed as he rides away, but he loses his hat.

The rider's hat bears the inscription of Colonel Beaumont Carson who suffered a fiery death 13 years ago. It was Jackson who set fire to the shack that claimed the Colonel's life. Jackson and his accomplices, Tom Kellogg (Lynch) and Judge Bill Mott (Wilcox) decide that the agents must be killed before they uncover *the truth*. West and Gordon find out that it was Jeremiah who sent the anonymous note asking for their help. He was trying to compel Jackson to reveal *the truth* about the Colonel's death. Jeremiah had witnessed the crime as a small boy and had been living with *the truth* for several years.

West and Gordon are attacked, but Jeremiah uses his power over animals to entice the attackers' horses to throw them. West subdues three more attackers as Artie exits – after all, he never fights on Sundays. Jeremiah informs everyone that the ghost will speak at the courthouse that night. The criminal accomplices think it's time to get rid of Jeremiah and the agents all at once while together at the courthouse.

At the courthouse that night, Jeremiah enters a trance and speaks for the ghostly Colonel. He elaborates on the cause of the fire that claimed his life and the lives of his family and servants. Suddenly, the horses that were earlier driven away by Jeremiah's special talent return to destroy the courthouse exterior: a demonstration of the dead Colonel's rage. The spirit warns of the animals' imminent return for complete destruction unless *the truth* is revealed by Carl Jackson.

Enter Jackson's fiancé, Elizabeth (Court), who ends up held captive in Jackson's basement along with Jeremiah and the agents. West and Gordon devise a makeshift cannon loaded with Powder Potpourri Surprise and explode pepper into the gang of thugs who are quickly overcome by sneezing. Three mock shots are fired leading Jackson to believe the heroic trio has been killed. Jackson returns to the stable to find the ghost of Colonel Carson walking toward him. After

Jackson empties his six-gun into the apparition, Jeremiah shoots the gun out of Jackson's hand just as West arrives. Jackson confesses to torching the house and killing the Colonel and the truth is finally revealed. The mysterious rider is exposed as a string puppet rigged by Jeremiah to frighten Jackson into confessing.

Jeremiah saddles his horse to ride off into the sunset. West asks him to work with them but the former stable boy declines stating, "I'm still looking for my place."

Author's Notes:

Writer John Kneubuhl outdoes himself with this exciting view of the historical and the supernatural. Guaranteed to please even devout skeptics, Kneubuhl's talents for making the unbelievable believable are evident in this star-studded "West."

Kneubuhl recalled how they brought Sammy Davis Jr. to the set of "The Wild Wild West." "Mike (Garrison) asked if I would write a show for Sammy Davis, Jr. who was up in Las Vegas. I thought it was impossible. How is the man going to do the show if he's up in Vegas until two in the morning?"

The schedule was grueling, but not impossible. Davis would finish his morning show at 2:00 a.m. An ambulance would transport him to the studio while he would sleep in the ambulance gurney. Upon arrival at the studio at 6:30 a.m. he had had a good rest (the actor could apparently sleep anywhere), he'd go into makeup, have coffee and breakfast and walk onto the set. Finished by three or four he'd be driven to the airport and fly back to Vegas in time for his dinner show. For seven to 10 days, he performed this routine. Now, that's a trooper.

> "What I liked best about the 'Returning Dead' was that I wanted to make a civil rights comment..."
>
> — John Kneubuhl

Richard Donner

Kneubuhl talked about the concept for "Returning Dead," one of his favorite shows. "What I liked best about the 'Returning Dead' was that I wanted to make a civil rights comment. That was, you remember, during the days of all the marches, the protests and young men being killed in the south. I could not physically be involved, but I was very active raising money, bail money, for the young people down south. Sons of some neighbors of mine were incarcerated so I was terribly involved that way."

The writer said that when he was approached with the idea, he felt he couldn't blatantly write *that* kind of a show. "Sammy is, how shall I say, politic. He circumvents everything tactfully. He did then. I thought I'd do a fantasy, so I invented a black stable boy who could talk to animals and birds. They were his allies against the evil southern colonel and the evil that is in the world. I wanted to suggest a kind of character so full of tenderness and attached to the mystery of life. I wouldn't have to make an outwardly political statement of any kind. It's a funny kind of show that has an undercurrent of muscle running through it all the time."

Director Richard Donner said that "Returning Dead" got him his first motion picture job. Garrison had recruited Donner as director, asking him if he'd like to do a show with Sammy Davis, Jr. and Peter Lawford. Davis and Donner became friends and, at the end of the show, the two actors wanted to do a movie together called "Salt and Pepper" and they wanted Donner as the director. Donner said, "It changed my life."

The Night of the
Bottomless Pit

West has been assigned to find a fellow agent unjustly imprisoned on Devil's Island under the identity of prisoner Henri Couteau (O'Brien). The prison commandant, Gustave Mauvais (Marcuse), with an evident dirt phobia and his aid Le Cochon (Carson), who sports a powerful iron right leg, try to crush West. West learns the location of Vincent Reed (Drake), the agent he was sent to free. For bad behavior, West is sentenced to 20 lashes and a prolonged visit to the pit, where he finds Reed, who tells him that he has only 10 hours until he is to be executed. A third prisoner in the pit, the assumed harmless Le Fou (Franken), appears insane.

Enter Pierre Gespard, AKA Artemus Gordon, dressed as an unscrupulous prison guard applying for work at the Island. Gespard's outrageous record precedes him having been discharged from the Foreign Legion for the good of the service. He gets the job.

Theo Marcuse (center), already a "West" alumnus, appears as a brutal prison commandant. Joan Huntington plays his unhappy wife hoping for West's assistance in "TNOT Bottomless Pit."

CBS # 6608 Shooting Order 36   CBS Photo
First Air Date: 11/04/66

Produced by Bruce Lansbury
Directed by Robert Sparr
Written by Ken Kolb

Gustave Mauvais: Theo Marcuse
Camille Mauvais: Joan Huntington
Vincent Reed: Tom Drake
Mrs. Grimes: Mabel Albertson
LeFou: Steve Franken
Lime: Seymour Green
Le Cochon: Fred Carson
Couteau: Chuck O'Brien
Guard : Ernie Misko
Guard : Gregg Martell

One night Artie walks by the pit and drops an egg to his partner. West finds a key in the egg and climbs out only to be recaptured. This time he is taken to Mauvais' wife, Camille's (Huntington), room where she asks him to help her escape. Mauvais overhears the conversation and has West staked to the ground in the expected pathway of ants. Artie strolls outside the prison gates to go into town and meet with fellow agent Mrs. Grimes (Albertson). She tells Artie about West's predicament and knows the whereabouts of a boat that will get them off the island. Artie frees Jim and they head back to the prison. Artie pretends to have West under guard, accusing him of having attempted to escape. At the pit, our heroes help Reed escape. Having been informed by the *not so mad* Le Fou, the Commandant stops them.

West is subjected to Le Cochon's *foot of doom*. A battle ensues and West is victorious. Quick-thinking Artie sets off a smoke bomb that he had planted in his walking stick and the agents escape with Camille, who steers them through her bedroom and out her back window.

It is discovered that Le Cochon has killed Mrs. Grimes, but not before he tortured her into revealing the whereabouts of the boat. Mauvais has been waiting in the bushes for their arrival. He steps forward to shoot his pistol and stumbles into quicksand. He calls to Le Cochon, but the iron-footed man walks by and refuses to help him. Mauvais fires numerous shots into Le Cochon's back but he keeps walking into the water. He continues walking until a shark appears and he is devoured. Our heroes are saved by a waiting ship.

Author's Notes:
Bruce Lansbury had a tough act to follow after relieving Michael Garrison, who had been acting as producer over the last eight episodes, and taking over the budgetary reins of the series. Garrison resumed his position as full-time executive producer and went on to develop other projects.

Speaking of islands – you may notice, as our heroes paddle away from Devil's Island on the boat, that the lagoon looks suspiciously familiar; bearing a not-so-coincidental resemblance to the lagoon used on "Gilligan's Island."

Overall, Bruce Lansbury's first attempt at being "Wild" has some nice results: The villains are suitably insane, there was just the right amount of humor, and the duties between our partners/heroes were appropriately balanced.

The Night of the
Ready-Made Corpse

The inimitable Carroll O'Connor is frighteningly diabolical as funeral director Fabian Lavendor, a man with unusual ways of drumming up business.

CBS Photos

CBS #6611 Shooting Order 37
First Air Date: 11/26/66

Produced by Bruce Lansbury
Directed by Irving J. Moore
Written by Ken Kolb and
      Bob Wood

Fabian Lavendor: Carroll
    O'Connor
Antille: Alan Bergmann
Rose Murphy: Karen Sharpe
Leda Pellargo: Patricia Huston
Pellargo: Daniel Ades
Barmaid: Andi Garrett
Finley: Gene Tybum
Golo: Jack Perkins

Ross Martin is at his best as the criminal Link in "Corpse."

Agents West and Gordon are assigned to welcome and protect the controversial and unpopular Latin dictator Colonel Pellargo (Ades) when he arrives in Whitmanburg. Pellargo has come to have his portrait done at a photo studio. The photographer turns out to be hired assassin Claudio Antille (Bergmann), who murders the Colonel using poisonous gas emitted from the flash of the camera. Antille is shot and wounded by the agents but escapes, outfoxing our heroes by ducking into a secret *back door* of a funeral parlor through an advertising poster. Gordon finds a single cufflink as a clue to Antille's whereabouts.

Inside the funeral parlor Antille is greeted by Fabian Lavendor (O'Connor), a neat, non-law-abiding citizen who specialized in granting new identities to wanted men. Lavendor and his assistants seek out John Does whose characteristics match the assassins and murder them, creating a ruse for the authorities as he verifies the death of the criminals. After facial surgery, the bad guys go free under new identities.

Enter Senora Pellargo (Huston), the grieving widow. She appears angry with West for not effectively protecting her husband from the assassin. When word is received that Antille is dead, the agent and Senora Pellargo go to Lavendor's funeral parlor to see for themselves. West is somewhat convinced that Antille is dead after checking for identifying scars and noticing the missing cufflink.

Still a little suspicious, West and Gordon go to a bar to meet Rose (Sharpe), a waitress who had reported her father missing just three days prior. She is convinced that something terrible has befallen her father, a burley Irishman. After Rose gives the agents a description of her father, West and Gordon notice the evident similarities between him and the dead Antille. Rose explains that there would be one significantly noticeable difference, her father was missing the little toe on his right foot. The agents visit the crypt and find themselves trapped inside while poisonous gas pours in through a lion's head. Artie uses an explosive putty to blow the lock and they escape.

Later, Rose helps the agents as they investigate Lavendor's parlor, she playing the grieving widow/sister, and Gordon pretending to be a client for Lavendor. West sneaks in through the recently-discovered advertising poster in the alley and quickly searches the premises while Rose occupies Lavendor. When Gordon's disguise is found out, he is locked in the cooler. West uncovers files of evidence against Lavendor, revealing the names and locations of his clients, all of whom he blackmails after his services are completed.

Rose is hustled out the door by Lavendor. West helps Gordon escape Lavendor's deadly grasp by leaping from a coffin (Ah! The element of surprise.) They get the drop on Lavendor and his men but, alas, in walks Antille with, you guessed it, Senora Pellargo. The two having plotted to eliminate her dictator husband so that she may rule in his place. The agents are held at gunpoint by Antille who turns on the devious funeral director and shoots him. West quickly douses the assassin with a handy bottle of alcohol and gets the better of Senora Pellargo.

The ending finds the agents back at the bar planning a Christian burial for Rose's father. They mutually inquire about Rose's romantic interests, but she states that she already has a boyfriend. A typical Western sheriff enters the saloon and she leans back proudly stating, "Now that's a lawman." (I know there's a point in there somewhere, but this one eludes me.)

Author's Notes:
During the making of "The Ready-Made Corpse," there was another unfortunate and far more devastating change in the series: word of Michael Garrison's tragic death came during shooting. Director Irving Moore remembered the day he was told of Garrison's untimely death. "We were just about to shoot the

O'Connor has an axe to grind with agent Gordon.

scene where West and Senora Pellargo enter the funeral parlor to look at the body in the casket. Lenny Katzman and Eddie Denault came on the set and announced that Michael Garrison died last night. Now we had to shoot this funeral scene. It made everyone uncomfortable. It was a very eerie feeling."

Producer Bruce Lansbury took complete control of the series and CBS did not hire a new executive producer to replace Garrison.

Carroll O'Connor, best known for his role as Archie Bunker in the 1971-1979 sitcom "All in the Family," is wonderfully cast as the diabolical Lavendor, complete with his signature purple gloves. Writer Ken Kolb recalled how Bob Conrad felt that every time he and O'Connor appeared on screen together O'Connor would steal the scene. O'Connor was already known as a great performer and had dozens of character appearances to his credit.

When Ross Martin appears as Lavendor's potential client, he did a masterful job of creating a morbid and despicable character through makeup and facial expression, and easily shifts into a British accent and then into Artemus Gordon when his disguise is discovered. I can't help but wonder what a treat it must've been to have seen these two great actors play off one another during that scene.

Kolb recalled, "That was my first exposure to Carroll O'Connor... who was a fine actor even then. As a matter of fact we were watching a rough cut of the show and Mike, Ross and Bobby were there. We were watching a scene with Bob and O'Connor together and you could feel Bob getting upset about something. Finally, Garrison asked, 'What's the matter, Bob?' and Bob said, 'That son-of-a-bitch upstages me, even with his back to the camera. How does he do that? How does he get everybody to look at him when I'm looking at the camera and he's looking the other way?'"

Many people involved with "The Wild Wild West" felt that the "West" was never the same without Mike Garrison. While I'm sure everyone missed Garrison's famously elaborate and creative personality and the loss was undoubtedly a profound one, I have always felt that Bruce Lansbury carried on the "West" tradition with integrity, flair and as close as he could to the way that Garrison would have intended. He accomplished his charge for two more successful seasons.

The Death of Michael Garrison – A Man Sadly Missed

In 1966, Michael Garrison celebrated his success with the purchase of a fabulous mansion in the elite Bel Air district of Los Angeles, California. It wasn't long thereafter that he threw a party to demonstrate his accomplishments. While at the party, guests Richard Donner and his girlfriend were sitting on the richly carpeted stairway that lead to the mansion's second floor, when they noticed a small section of carpet

Michael Garrison

that had been worked loose. Curiosity getting the better of the two, they lifted the corner of the carpet, and revealed a gorgeous marble floor beneath. Donner called the hidden marble to Garrison's attention and both agreed that the floor was just too beautiful to keep hidden. A few days later the carpeting was removed.

> It is a poignant and unfortunate irony that Garrison's taste for the elaborate eventually contributed to his demise.

In the late evening of August 17, 1966, Garrison was at the top of his stairway, lost his footing and tumbled to his death, having fractured his skull on the marble floor that only days before had been cushioned with carpeting. It is a poignant unfortunate irony that Garrison's taste for the elaborate eventually contributed to his demise.

Among the various conflicting accounts of Garrison's death was the possibility that foul play occurred, spurred by the producer's notoriety in the industry. While some questions can never be answered, one thing remains certain, the untimely death of the much-loved Michael Garrison was a shock to the cast and crew of "The Wild Wild West," and many have said that the true essence of the show died on that same fateful night in August.

More Changes and the Show Must Go On

Even after his death, Garrison remained listed on the show's ending credits as the series' creator. Producer Bruce Lansbury was faced with a tough act to follow and, although he now had total control of the show, he would work in the shadow of Michael Garrison.

Many felt that Lansbury and CBS could not grasp what Garrison had struggled for all this time to produce. Writer John Kneubuhl said, "Working with Lansbury, well, he wasn't any Mike Garrison and he wasn't any Fred Freiberger. Even though he was a gentleman, he was kind and he was good, in his hand I thought that 'The Wild Wild West' had become just a funny paper. I didn't stop writing 'Wild Wild West' (episodes) because of him. I stopped writing because Michael Garrison died, tragically. From then on I was a little bit turned off and I didn't last much longer with Lansbury, who's a nice fellow, but he just does an entirely different kind of thing from what I do."

Ken Kolb remembered, "I got along fine with Bruce Lansbury, who's a nice guy, but whose talents are very different from Mike's. Bruce is a diplomat. He knew how to make the network happy. He knew how to preserve certain aspects of the show."

Although the feeling had now drastically changed, Lansbury quickly got things under control. He figured out how to accomplish the task at hand so it was possible to renew the series and maintain good ratings. "Bruce did a good job keeping the show alive over the years it was on. It's hard to come up with new gimmicks, special effects, gags and devices and still make it seem like it could take place in the West," Ethel Winant said.

Because of the number of producers and the problems between the producers and the stars of the network, there was no continuity in the series. "I came in with a point of view about the show that was fairly obvious. The only difference in my point of view and the network's was fantasy. I liked to do fantasy and the network wanted it to be more like James Bond in the

"They (the stories) had to be considerably more credible. We got away from time travel, magic and other dimensions. That tended to taper off."

— Ken Kolb

West. I think (William) Paley had a particular point of view about that. We got away with some, like 'Flying Pie Plate,' which we had to make into a hoax, and 'Green Terror,' both, of course, sheer fantasy, along with 'Lord of Limbo.' 'The Night of the Man-Eating House' had to be turned into a dream. But there were a couple that we got away with like 'The Night of the Surreal McCoy,' Lansbury said.

CBS would have liked it to be a Western, not so much because they didn't believe in fantasy, but because it was so expensive to do the show. Winant commented, "Once Bruce came on the show, it was a kind of glossy Western with tricks, but it became more of a Western every year, physically. And the more it did the more we could control the budget, because horses, Western streets and locations are easy; more so than palaces, caves and all those gadgets, special effects and glitz."

Ken Kolb recalled the change in the approach to the scripts. "Those (fantasies) were the kinds of stories that they wouldn't let us write anymore. There were plenty of normal Westerns around. Our ratings were good, but the ratings were good on most Westerns. (i.e. "Wagon Train," "Rawhide," "Have Gun Will Travel") And there were no fantasy shows that were getting good ratings. So network thinking is, 'Fantasy is dead; we're doing a Western. Don't let anybody get the idea it's a fantasy because people don't like fantasies.'"

Although Lansbury enjoyed doing fantasy

shows he had to use caution when picking a script concerning Dr. Loveless. "We really had to be careful with Loveless stories because of the sanctions from CBS not to do fantasy, even though we had to break the rule just to find the right script," the producer said.

Kneubuhl, whose writing was on an unusual and fantasy-oriented level, felt, "It's really got to work on a real level or all the fantasy becomes nonsense. And when that was removed, when the existential basis, for instance for the dwarf, was removed all you get is a funny, silly little man. When you remove a certain amount of intelligence from fantasy, what you get is funny paper, cartoon trash. I'm afraid toward the end that's what 'The Wild Wild West' was becoming."

Part of the *comic book* look was the result of a joint effort between Lansbury, Henry Sharp and Lenny Katzman. Sharp started on "The Wild Wild West" as a writer and when Lansbury took over the reigns, he was promoted to story editor. Lansbury said, "Henry wrote a fair number of stories. His background was illustrative art and cartooning. As a writer he was a visualizer [sic]. So whatever he did he had his style and fanciful look to it." Katzman, who had been promoted from first assistant director to associate producer, also played a key role in the *comic book collaboration*. At the first printing of this book, Katzman had worked on numerous series throughout the 60s and 70s. His last gigs included serving as executive producer of the television series "Dallas" and "Walker, Texas Ranger." Katzman died of a heart attack in September of 1996.

Story editor Sharp was not popular among the many "West" script writers. John Kneubuhl expressed negative feelings toward the editor, claiming that Sharp would not allow the writers to express their ideas about something they wrote, but would rather jump in with his own concepts. Kneubuhl attempted to work with Sharp but recalled that the two butted heads almost constantly. Kneubuhl quit after writing "The Night of the Surreal McCoy."

Ken Kolb said that his time for writing for the series was limited because of the shift from fantasy to reality. "They (the stories) had to be considerably more credible. We got away from time travel, magic and other dimensions. That tended to taper off."

Kolb felt that he was *written out* with the show and noticed Sharp doing more and more rewriting of the scripts he would turn in, for no particular reason. "It was a struggle with CBS because there would be more changes and then Henry Sharp would tend to rewrite

more than I thought necessary. I always got along fine with Henry, but he thought that was part of his job; to rewrite everything to give it a certain look. Then you'd find that the script, when it was shot, was a lot different than when you had turned it in."

Kolb compared his days with Garrison to the new regime. "With Mike Garrison, to give you an example, I had waited around home for a week after I had mailed the script in and I hadn't heard a word, which is always bad news. So I called up the office and said, 'So what's wrong, Mike?' He'd ask, 'With what?' I'd say, 'Well, you know, the script. What am I gonna have to redo?' He'd say, 'Christ! We're shooting it. Didn't anybody tell you?' I got along with Bruce alright and he put together a pretty decent staff, but I was *written out* on the show. I had done as many scripts as I had good ideas for and it wasn't the same kind of fun."

"The Wild Wild West" used a variety of writers, some on staff, but many were freelancers. Lansbury tried to use many older writers claiming that the type, or form, of show required a certain amount of plotting and appreciation of the kind of humor from their youth, a kind of appreciation of their era.

The ongoing character development of West and Gordon didn't change once it was established that they were equal partners. "The only thing was Bob (Conrad) wanted action and not a lot of dialog; so he got action. Ross wanted meaty characters. That was what made the show unique. Beyond that the characters rarely changed," Lansbury said.

The second season marked the series' first television academy recognition with the 1966-1967 Emmy Award going to actress Agnes Moorehead for her supporting performance as the devious Emma Valentine in "The Night of the Vicious Valentine." "West" had only been acknowledged once before with Director of Photography Ted Voightlander's 1965 nomination.

The second season proved to be an interesting (but comic) approach to "The Wild Wild West," and the show slowly and systematically drifted away from Michael Garrison's original concept of fabulous fantasy.

 The Wanderer, the train used in "The Wild Wild West" was actually the same train used for the Hooterville Cannonball in the popular program "Petticoat Junction," (1963) starring Bea Benaderet and Edgar Buchanan.

The Night of the
Flying Pie Plate

The agents encounter supposedly intergalactic females in need of gold as fuel in "The Night of the Flying Pie Plate."

CBS # 6606 Shooting Order 38
First Air Date: 10/21/66

Produced by Bruce Lansbury
Directed by Robert Sparr
Written by Daniel Ullman

Ben Victor: William Windom
Simon: Ford Rainey
Morn: Leslie Parrish
Alna: Arlene Charles
Pan: Cindy Taylor
Wingo: Woodrow Chambliss
Byron Pettigrew: Pitt Herbert

CBS Photo

West accompanies a government gold shipment to Morning Glory, Arizona, and contacts an assayer named Ben Victor (Windom). He meets Victor at the local saloon in time for the town preacher, Hellfire Simon (Rainey), to burst in and spout warnings of approaching evil. Suddenly, a loud crash echoes throughout the town and everyone witnesses a glowing flame about to hit earth. Again, Simon warns of impending evil.

West and the townspeople go to the landing site and are amazed when they see a metal spaceship. As Simon approaches the ship, a tremendous force hurls him back. The ship doors open and the frightened people are greeted by three green women resembling Martians. They introduce themselves as Morn (Parrish) and her two sisters, Alna (Charles) and Pan (Taylor). They claim to be from Venus and have crash landed on Earth.

With their fuel in short supply they request the township to supply them with *mildum*, a substance better known to earthlings as *gold*. The Venusians need 400 pounds of the precious metal to fuel their way home to Venus where they claim there are mountains of it. To further tempt the Earth people, the aliens' clothing is adorned with stones resembling precious jewels. They give a sample to the townspeople and claim that these, too, are in abundant supply on their planet.

Back in town where the shipment of gold is being stored in a vault, West and Victor go to verify the authenticity of the jewel given to them by the alien women. West and the jeweler test the stone and it proves to be genuine. Gordon arrives in town posing as expert jeweler Dirk DeJohn. He, too, verifies the authenticity of the gem. As the two agents leave, Victor talks to the townspeople about getting more jewels and West and Gordon soon figure out

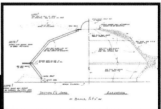

Art Courtesy CBS

The ingenuity of art director Al Heschong is evident in his design of the "Pie Plate" spaceship.

that it is all a scam. West is attacked in the bar and is taken to the spaceship, but quickly executes an escape with the usual West resourcefulness. He manages to talk to one of the space women before leaving.

During this time, Victor has managed to convince the naïve townspeople to give up their gold shipment in exchange for the jewels. West returns to the town and quickly douses the idea, telling Gordon to watch the vault as he returns to the spaceship.

Gordon and two other men stand guard outside the bank until two of the space women appear and feign fainting. The guard goes to their aid and brings them into the bank, but the ploy is revealed when everyone is rendered unconscious by gas. Gordon fakes being knocked out (after protecting himself with a handy oxygen mask). Victor enters and proceeds to clean out the vault with his alien friends. They head back to the ship. Gordon follows, but when he arrives at the ship, he is knocked unconscious.

West shows up at the landing site soon after, along with his favorite *Martian*. He hears his partner's moans coming from inside the craft and discovers a green Gordon. Victor is now holding both West and Gordon at gunpoint, but the actual ringleader is revealed as Hellfire Simon himself.

Victor and Simon plan to escape with the gold and blow up the pie plate with West and Gordon trapped inside. Simon says that he will leave with the gold and no one will ever suspect a preacher. He continues to explain that the pie plate's landing was no more than balloons, flares and a noise box. Simon's dramatic thrust away from the ship was a simple wire attached to his pants. As the bad guys prepare their getaway, West and Gordon get free via shoe knife and Gordon takes on Victor while West is struck by Hellfire. After the fight, Victor is knocked out, but Simon falls back into the spaceship and is locked inside. The agents take the girls to the wagon full of gold and clear the area in time for the ship to explode.

The tag finds West back at the train and back to business with Artie, still green and very red. It turns out that the dye will fade in about three days. West says, "Think of the good side. You'll be a sensation at all the dinner parties." A noise erupts from outside, similar to that of the spaceship landing and the two agent investigate only to witness a shooting star. West thinks they should alert Washington, but Gordon doesn't agree, telling Jim, "If *you* want to, go right ahead."

104

Author's Notes:

This episode begins totally unbelievably, but is tempered by a nice twist when it is revealed as a scam. The costumes for the green space women look like something out of a 1960s peace march, but that's what makes this episode so fun to watch. The art department outdoes itself by combining the futuristic concept of a spacecraft with a Victorian style essence, complete with enough flashing lights to convince anyone from Morning Glory, Arizona, circa 1880, that they are real travelers from space. This was the first episode without Garrison's creative input but Lansbury pulls it off with style. A noticeable change occurs in the commercial break art. The color sepia photos that were previously placed in each square at each break had been replaced by a painted line drawing. This new look continued until the end of the series.

The Night of the
Poisonous Posey

Jim and Artie are given an unusual welcome while passing through Justice, Nevada, on vacation. After being roped on their horses and accused of robbery, they find themselves the guests of honor at a hanging.

Their impending demise turns out to be a joke orchestrated by the town. They're awarded the key to the city for being their first visitors during their Law and Order Week celebration. As they're entering their hotel Jim encounters a well-dressed Latin man who seems oddly familiar. The gentleman's identity becomes known when a tarantula is discovered on the pillow on Artie bed. Jim shoots the poisonous spider and deduces that the fancy stranger is actually Gallito (Iglesias), a notorious killer whose trademark is to neutralize his victims by spider bite.

Jim and Artie begin to notice that this small town is full of noted criminals from all over the world. The agents watch as a strange funeral procession marches through town. Jim follows them to the funeral parlor and discovers a coffin brimming with champagne and ice for the criminals' meeting. A brawl ensues and Jim is subdued and taken to a boardroom where he meets Lucrece Posey (Lawrence).

A town of killers and a strange funeral procession awaits the agents when they arrive in the ironically named Justice, Nevada.

CBS # 6607 Shooting Order 39   CBS Photo
First Air Date: 10/28/66

Produced by Bruce Lansbury
Directed by Leigh Chapman
Written by Don Mullally
Teleplay by Alan Crosland Jr.

Lucrece Posey: Delphi Lawrence
Gallito: Eugene Iglesias
Brutus: Percy Rodrigues
Snakes: Christopher Cary
Pinto: H.M. Wynant
Sergei: George Keyman
Sheriff Cord: Shug Fisher
Cyril: Mike Masters
Ascot Sam: Andre Philippe

Dressed in men's clothing she has a passion for poison and has gathered a small army of masterful murderers: Gallito, the tarantula expert; Brutus (Rodrigues), a giant known as the bone-breaker and scourge of the Caribbean; Cyril (Masters), the firebug; Snakes (Cary), the explosives expert; Pinto (Wynant), the sadistic gunslinger with a penchant for pain; and Sergei (Keymas), a knife expert.

At the meeting, Posey is given a gavel as a gift from Snakes. She suspects it is an explosive device and

vengefully retaliates by scraping Snake's face with a toxic ring, killing him instantly.

Artemus appears on cue as the dapper criminal Ascot Sam, a predictable addition to the clan. Ascot/Artie stops Posey from shooting West. She decides to get down to business and lays out her plans to her colleagues. Posey intends to devise six regional crime organizations to unite the abilities of the world's most notorious criminal minds. She has developed a super crime cartel and the six present experts, now including Ascot Sam, will fuse the regions.

West is taken to an ice factory for an inventive execution. He is tied up on an ice chute right in the path of a huge block of ice that has been secured by only a single rope, which is slowly being burned by a single candle flame. As West awaits his unusual fate, greed takes over and the criminal experts begin fighting among themselves. Ascot/Artie manages to survive, at least until the real Ascot Sam (Philippe) arrives. West frees himself by cutting his binds with an exposed nail and is able to stand just as the huge block of ice breaks free and slides between his legs.

Artie is tossed into the same ice factory with Jim. Pinto arrives shortly thereafter and shoots at them, but West's makeshift spear, devised from his collar knife and a broom handle, ends the annoyance. As the two agents escape the ice house, they're spotted by Brutus and the shooting starts again as Sergei gets involved. West and Gordon are able to subdue them both and they head back to the funeral parlor to gather up Posey, who is dressed to kill. West tells her that her experts are all dead. She escapes through a sliding door and West finds himself trapped in the room. Giant organ pipes convert into rotating guns and West falls to the floor avoiding death, but stopping him from pursuing Posey. The door opens when the shooting stops and West catches up with Gordon who explains how he has just assisted a pretty woman onto the stagecoach out of town. Realizing the woman was Posey, Gordon immediately leaps on his horse and bolts after the coach.

Having captured the elusive Posey, the ride-weary Artie arrives at the train five hours later. Jim tells him that he might receive a commendation for his work. The telegraph keys tap out an immediate assignment for the agents – one that involves a six-hour ride on horseback. Artie is in pain.

Author's Notes:

Can't Jim and Artie even enjoy their vacation without running into some kind of trouble? Not only do they encounter villains, but they hit the jackpot. They could have vacationed at a Federal Penitentiary and had fewer troubles.

First assistant Mike Moder recalled the stunt that could easily have been Bob Conrad's last. "As Bob was tied up on the ice chute; the stunt involved a block of ice that was to come crashing down on his head at the moment that the rope burned through and snapped. I was to cut the rope when Bob gave the go-ahead. At that *precise* moment, as the block of ice was released, Bob was to cut the rope holding his wrist and jump up. If Bob was a *split second* off the ice would have smashed into his head." Yes, they used real ice.

This episode tests the skills and prowess of our heroes while trying to stay one step ahead of the villains. The storyline for "Posey" may not be as bizarre and unusual as we've come to expect from the "West," but it was impressive. It took the idea of a traditional Western setting and ramped it up just enough to give it that "Wild" feeling. An interesting study of the demented criminal mastermind, "Posey" makes for an entertaining hour.

The Night of the
Watery Death

At the Mermaid Bar, James West inquires about Marquis Philippe and is shot with a blow dart by Dominique (Lane) disguised as a mermaid. When West awakens, he is aboard a ship and meets a mysterious woman with an unusual compact. Suddenly, the ship is attacked by what appears to be a dragon. The ship explodes and West is sent plummeting into the dark water. He awakens clinging onto a drifting board and soon realizes that he has the unusual compact in his hand. West drifts in and out of consciousness as the ship becomes engulfed in flames.

Lieutenant Keighley (Ashley) is aboard the agent's train and is having a difficult time believing West's bizarre story. Everyone is concerned with the situation since the SS Virginia is due into San Francisco in three days with Admiral Farragut on board. As luck would have it, the Virginia will also be carrying a

John Van Dreelen plays an evil seafarer bent on killing Admiral Farragut in "Watery Death."

CBS Photo

CBS # 6609 Shooting Order 40
First Air Date: 11/11/66

Produced by Bruce Lansbury
Directed by Irving J. Moore
Written by Michael Edwards

Marquis Philippe: John Van Dreelen
Dominique: Jocelyn Lane
Lieutenant Keighley: John Ashley
Pratt : Forrest Lewis
Third Officer: James Galante

load of explosives making the possibility of an attack even more imminent.

Artemus had interviewed some of the passengers aboard the attacked ship and no one recalls seeing a dragon. Without thought, Artemus toys with the mysterious compact. Frustrated, he slams the compact onto the desk and notices that it has left an impression on a piece of paper; the image of a dragon. The agents prepare to embark on their rounds, but first Artie gives Jim his newest invention: a magnetized exploding coin. When the coin is exposed to 100 degree heat for five seconds, it explodes.

West and Gordon walk through town searching for clues. They notice The Three Anchors maritime dealer. The proprietor, Captain Pratt (Lewis), a salty old dog, immediately offers the agents $5000 for the compact. West hikes the bid to $15,000 and Pratt accepts. The agents insist that Pratt reveal who really wants the compact. He instructs them to go to The Mermaid Bar at 2:00 a.m. They arrive at the bar, sit down, have a drink and a Neptune look-alike hurls his trident at them. West shoots Neptune and a brawl breaks out. West and Gordon realize they were set up so West returns to Pratt's store only to find the shopkeeper hanging from the rafters.

Suddenly, the floor gives way and West falls into a room where he is attacked. Struck by a blackjack from behind, West finally has the opportunity to meet Marquis Philippe (Van Dreelen). Artie follows West's path to The Three Anchors and finds Pratt hanging but no sign of West. He returns to The Mermaid Bar for some answers and finds it has mysteriously been converted into a dress shop.

West is awakened by Dominique just as the Marquis enters the room. Sensing their desire for the compact, he tells them that he does not have it. The Marquis knows that Artemus has it in his possession. The plan is explained and the reason for the bombings is evident. The Marquis has designs on creating an underwater city named Le Mar in the Pacific Ocean. From there he will be able to control all the nation's shipping.

They leave West, who is held inside the room by an electrical force field that is capable of disintegrating anything that it touches. West uses his sleeve knife to cut the bonds from his arms and legs.

Artie is strolling down an alley looking for clues when he notices two of the Marquis' thugs following him. When he turns the corner, he quickly transforms himself into a drunken Swedish sailor and the thugs pass by him. A watchful Dominique notices the switch and Artie is captured.

A now freed West hurls his knife at the force field, hits the operating mechanism and disengages the field. The guards enter and lunge a him, but he pulls his knife free of the unit, thereby engaging the field and the guards perish into nothingness. West gets to the front door when the Marquis captures him again. The agent is led to their headquarters where West sees the dragons and their torpedo mechanism is explained. The dragons are able to travel great distances to reach their targets but the compact is required as a homing device. Artie is also brought to headquarters and gives the compact to the Marquis. The agents are then bound to posts to await their fates.

Dominique has been allowed to board the SS Virginia by stating that she has a message from James West for the lieutenant. She convinces Keighley to have the ship go through fisherman's point as per West's orders.

Jim and Artie free themselves using Jim's boot knife, but discover they must still contend with another force field. When the guards come calling, the agents get a fight going. This time the guards had to turn off the field to enter and Artie manages to escape. He heads for the SS Virginia to warn Admiral Farragut and to stop Dominique from carrying out their evil plan. Jim is not so lucky and is caught again by the Marquis, who now needs West to negotiate with the U.S. Government when Le Mar comes into existence.

Back at the Virginia, Keighley has recognized the compact that Dominique is carrying and attempts to arrest her. As Gordon enters, she gets the drop on both men. West is with the Marquis as witness to the dragon torpedo being launched. He incites a fight, and when the Marquis charges at him, West hurls him directly into the force field and into nothingness. West crashes through a window into the water and swims after the slow-moving dragon. He catches up to the device and affixes the magnetic coin near the dragon's fire-shooting nostrils, swimming away just as the torpedo explodes against the backdrop of the safe SS Virginia.

The tag finds West reading a newspaper outlining Gordon as the hero for saving Admiral Farragut's life. Artie is suffering terribly from a cold that he caught after diving into the water after Dominique. Gordon reads his acceptance speech to West about how the torpedo will be a deadly weapon in the future. Gordon also suggests another weapon that could combat it, aerial bombs. As West leaves, Gordon continues his speech and uses his cold pills to demonstrate an aerial attack. As pills hit the bucket of steaming water, he is soaking his feet in an unexpected explosion occurs, leaving a baffled and bewildered Gordon.

Author's Notes:
This episode revolves around another one of "West's" crazy devices, this time a torpedo shaped like a dragon. The thought of a torpedo was not so far advanced since the first successful torpedo was actually launched in 1867 by British engineer, Robert Whitehead. Gordon was right on when he suggests that torpedoes will become the deadly war machines of the fu-

ture; but he really gets ahead of himself with the idea of aerial bombs.

An interesting aside to the crux of this tale is that the agents are going to great lengths to protect Admiral Farragut from being torpedoed. Known for his statement, "Damn the torpedoes, full speed ahead," the real Admiral Farragut died in 1870, several years prior to our agents' adventures, and barely one year into the administration of President Ulysses S. Grant.

Other futuristic devices used include: The force field that could incinerate anyone crossing its beam; the underwater spyglass, now more commonly known as a periscope; the homing device in the compact; and Gordon's magnetized coin that explodes at 100 degrees Fahrenheit. "Watery Death" is an entertaining episode with lots of action and more than its share of futuristic inventions.

The Night of the
Green Terror

West and Gordon notice the unusual absence of plant and animal life as they ride through a forest. They encounter a giant knight who hurls a huge boulder in their direction. Suddenly, they are accosted by a band of merry men who encircle the agents and take them prisoner. They are lead to a tent where the lovely Antoinette (Dorin) serenades them. A minute Robin Hood, AKA Dr. Loveless (Dunn), greets them. West instructs Artie to feign no interest in order to compel Loveless to reveal his plan. As expected Loveless tells the agents that the Indian village of Bright Star has been suffering a terrible famine caused by the *Lord of the Forest*. Loveless is the assigned go-between for the Indians and the so-called *Lord* and wants to become known as a great benefactor to the hungry Indians, thereby gaining their loyalty.

The agents start a scuffle and quickly escape on their horses as Loveless emits his signature demonic laugh. The diminutive doctor wanted the escape to occur knowing that the agents will be killed when they reach Bright Star (Caruso).

West and Gordon arrive at Bright Star's village and receive a hostile welcome. West is about to tell the Indians how he can help when Loveless arrives and tells them that the *Lord of the Forest* is angry with them for harboring his enemies, West and Gordon. Artie escapes

Dr. Loveless returns as a would-be Robin Hood with designs on ending all life on the planet in "TNOT Green Terror."

CBS Photos

CBS #6610 Shooting Order 41
First Air Date: 11/18/66

Produced by Bruce Lansbury
Directed by Robert Sparr
Written by John Kneubuhl

Dr. Miguelito Loveless: Michael Dunn
Antoinette: Phoebe Dorin
Bright Star: Anthony Caruso
Old Chief: Paul Fix
Bright Star's Wife: Peggy Rea

Michael Dunn as Dr. Miguelito Loveless

but West is captured and Loveless requests the customary slow and agonizing death for his captive.

Artie returns to the camp disguised as an old Indian woman. Jim is being held in a tepee where Loveless has set up a crossbow aimed at his chest set to release when a candle flame burns through the rope that passes through the candle.

Loveless enters and explains to West the principle behind his special spray that kills all insects, thus plants are no longer pollinated and birds are unable to survive. The tiny doctor plans to use the spray to kill fish, birds, elk and, if necessary, man. Loveless, claiming to be squeamish, cannot stand to watch West be shot by the arrow so he departs. West is about to cut his binds when Artie enters and frees him just in time. As they are about to escape, Bright Star's wife (Rea) greets them and turns around to reveal Dr. Loveless strapped to her back papoose-style, with crossbow aimed at the agents.

The Old Chief (Fix) shows up at Loveless' camp for a powwow with the *Lord of the Forest.* It is revealed, as Loveless climbs into a suit of armor, that he operates it from the inside and pretends to be the powerful Lord.

The *Lord of the Forest* appears and tells the chiefs attending the powwow that his servant, Robin, will show them how they can regain their land. Artemus estimates that, if Loveless succeeds, more than 10,000 Indians will become his servants.

Loveless takes the blindfolded agents inside his hollow tree hideout. Inside there is a scale model of Washington D.C., showing President Grant's house, along with the residences of the vice president and all the cabinet officers. Above the model is a balloon with a cargo of green powder. The balloon bursts and showers the cargo onto all the model homes. They burn instantly. Loveless explains that, anywhere the wind carries the balloons, chaos will follow, and the Indians will take over.

West, to delay his execution, challenges the *Lord of the Forest* to a duel. The old chiefs side with West, wanting the *Lord* to further prove himself. If the

Dunn is in top form as Loveless and Dorin as Antoinette in "Terror." This episode presented the duo with a risky stunt (pg. 81) — all part of a day's work.

Lord wins, the Indians will follow him. If West wins, the Indians will give their loyalty to him. The duel begins with maces as the chosen weapons. West is offered a mace with an exploding tip, but warily chooses the other one. West triumphs over the *Lord* and the Indians attack Loveless and his men.

As they have done before, Loveless and Antoinette slip away, but not before managing to launch a small balloon equipped with the green powder. West shoots down the balloon and it falls to the ground, exploding near Loveless. The doctor and Antoinette climb into a nearby hollow log as the forest burns. After the fire, West and Gordon can only find the remains of Dr. Loveless' horn.

The tag finds the agents back at the train practicing their fighting skills. Jim repeatedly gets the better of Artie when a package arrives from an unknown admirer. Artie demonstrates the skillful way to open a package. He smashes his hand on the box trying to open it via karate chop, nearly breaking his hand in the process. Jim laughs and Artie asks him to do better. West slowly raises his hand, poised to execute a perfect karate chop, breathes in preparation, lifts his hand and gently reaches down to untie the package string. The opened box reveals a small model of a knight accompanied by the singing voices of Loveless and Antoinette, confirming the duos' survival.

Author's Notes:

"Green Terror" was the fifth Loveless episode marking the halfway point for the Loveless series. When West and Gordon last saw Loveless and Antoinette they were making an inventive escape on a raven. Loveless is famous for his use of irony, posing as Robin Hood to cause death and destruction. This is also another feeble attempt by Loveless to become tall; donning a full-sized mechanical suit of armor. Proof, once again, that the little man is capable of great ingenuity.

Writer John Kneubuhl does a nice job conforming to the Loveless tradition of creating elaborate schemes to rule the world. On a Loveless scale of 1-10, "Terror" rates a nine.

The Night of the
Lord of Limbo

The agents face off with Ricardo Montalban as Vautrain, a man who dabbles in alternate dimensions in "TNOT Lord of Limbo."

CBS #6615 Shooting Order 42

CBS Photo

Produced by Bruce Lansbury
Directed by Jesse Hibbs
Written by Henry Sharp

Theater Manager: Harry Harvey Sr.
Levering: Gregory Morton
Colonel Vautrain: Ricardo Montalban
Fairchild: Ed Prentiss
Amanda Vautrain: Dianne Foster
Robber: Will J. White
Captain Scofield: Felice Orlandi
Professor: Howard Wright
Professor: Tyler McVey
Bartender: Davis Roberts

The agents are given tickets to a magician's performance, which is quite bad. They attempt to leave when the magician manifests a sword. West and Gordon are impressed and return to their seats in hopes that the show will improve. The magician instructs his female assistant to select a gentleman from the audience. As she scans the audience, she obviously notices West, but chooses Artie. Feeling privileged, Artie scoffs at West, "Many are called, but only few are chosen."

Artie is brought onstage and placed in a large chair. The magician chants a few magic words and he, his assistant, and Artie suddenly disappear. After a few moments, the emcee announces that the show is over, but Artie has yet to return. West investigates backstage and even the stage manager (Harvey) has no idea what happened since all the floors are solid and no one has left. West continually hears Artie's voice around him but has no idea where he is or what to do. A clue has been left onstage in the form of the magician's sword with NBV, Vicksburg, Mississippi, inscribed upon it.

West travels to Vicksburg and enters an officers club looking for the man with the initials NBV. No one claims to know such a man. One member thinks that West is asking too many questions but West quickly puts him in his place. As West leaves, the bartender slips him a note with the address Live Oak Manor written on it.

When the agent arrives at the rundown mansion, he meets Colonel Vautrain (Montalban), a Confederate officer confined to a wheelchair as a result of injuries during the war. West persists with questions but Vautrain is equally persistent at avoiding answers. Vautrain simply insists that West stay for dinner if he ever wants to see his friend again… alive. West agrees and discovers why Vautrain needs his presence so badly.

The Colonel explains that he was in the Civil War and that West had saved his life, but not before his legs were shattered and rendered useless. Now he wants West to help him travel back through the fourth dimension to help him reclaim the use of his legs. West asks how Vautrain intends to accomplish this feat. Before answering, the Colonel sends West to a door at the top of the stairs telling him that is where he will find Gordon. As West passes through the doorway, he is suddenly transported into another time and place. It is now the 1700s and he meets Artie, who identifies himself as Jack Maitland. Maitland is scheduled to duel with West, claiming that he had insulted him earlier. They must settle the matter with swords. West refuses but Maitland (Artie) insists and the fight begins. West does his best to not hurt his friend, or be hurt until a band of pirates appears and robs everyone. A fight ensues and Maitland (Artie) is shot. With his dying breath, he tells West that he felt as if they have met before. West carries Maitland back through the dimensions and returns to Vautrain's mansion. When they arrive, Artie is no longer the dead Maitland but is the live Gordon.

Vautrain explains that there are warps in space. When an object enters such a warp, it travels through time. A person can travel through time as well if they can prepare themselves and focus their energies.

The Colonel is now ready to return to the incident that claimed his legs. West, Gordon and Vautrain all journey back to relive the Civil War. Suddenly, Vautraine is young again and has the use of his legs. Ulterior motives surface and we discover that Vautrain also wanted to return to change the course of the war to the Confederate's advantage. The mansion is being used as a munitions dump. It is hit by a shell, explodes and is engulfed in flames. The smoke clears revealing Vautrain trapped beneath a heavy post with his legs crushed. The house will surely explode further so Vautrain, convinced of the failure of his scheme, insists the agents return to their own time without him.

At the train, West is writing a report to Washington to explain the bizarre circumstances behind Artie's disappearance. He chooses to tell them I was a case of amnesia, but Gordon wants the truth to be known. West claims they will never believe it. Colonel Falk, their supervisor, enters and awaits the report. West graciously turns the floor over to Artie who tries to explain but the words somehow elude him. As Falk's patience wears thin, so does Artie's conviction to the truth. He claims to have had amnesia.

Author's Notes:

"Lord of Limbo" definitely gets my vote as one of the most bizarre tales of the "West." Time warps, trips in and out of the fourth dimension and the ability to redo history certainly must be seen to be believed. Writer/story consultant Henry Sharp goes all out with this premise and it allows his background as a cartoonist to really shine through. This episode really lives up to the series' title, and Michael Garrison would have been proud of this *wild* story. A bit of trivia, the name for Colonel Falk was derived from Bob Conrad's real name, Conrad Robert Falk.

The Night of the
Skulls

A kangaroo court leaves agent West at the mercy of a gang of cutthroat criminals in "Skulls."

CBS Photos

CBS #6614 Shooting Order 43
First Air Date: 12/16/66

Produced by Bruce Lansbury
Directed by Alan Crosland
Written by Robert C. Dennis and Earl Barret

Monk: Quintin Sondergaard
Axe Lady: Madame Spivy
Senator Fenlow: Donald Woods
Bluebeard: Mike Masters
Colonel Richmond: Douglas Henderson
Samurai: Sebastian Tom
Lorelei: Lisa Gaye
Prisoner: Bill Baghad
Reporter: Lou Straley
Tigo: Robert Herron
Lucinda: Anne Doud
Officer: Kem Dibbs
Charlton:
    Francis De Sales
Ron Hook:
    Calvin Brown

Artie in one of his three disguises in "Skulls."

Agent James T. West escapes after pretending to shoot and kill his fellow agent, Artemus Gordon. At Gordon's funeral, Artemus is disguised as a minister and is giving his own eulogy. As the mourners leave, West appears from behind the bushes to talk to Gordon. West's plan of becoming a wanted man seems to be working. Previously, more than 19 murderers have disappeared into limbo with no clue as to their whereabouts. West hopes to locate their hideout with this ruse. Hopefully, the ploy of killing Gordon will cause the murderers to seek out their fellow killer, West. Detectives suddenly notice West and a chase ensues, but our agent eludes his pursuers by hiding in a hearse. Once inside, the carriage is gassed. The bait has worked.

West awakens in an abandoned monastery and is surrounded by people wearing skull masks and dark, flowing robes. He is lead to a simulated courtroom where he is put on trial for the murder of his friend and colleague. The jury is comprised of the nation's most wanted killers. West is surprised to discover his acceptance into the group when the guilty verdict is passed down.

Meanwhile, Gordon investigates a barn where the horses, carriage and hearse that carried West away are being kept.

Now that West has been initiated as a member of the murderer's clan he dines with them to uncover what will be their next dastardly deed. The ringleader is a masked man who is called Skull. Of the group of expert killers only three will be chosen for the next special assignment. The fun starts with the elimination round – and I do mean elimination. The killers must do in before being done in, in order to be granted the assignment. West is included in the final three and is instructed that the special assignment involves killing the president, the vice president and the secretary of state.

At the barn, Artie has knocked out Tigo (Herron), a hunchbacked bell ringer, and has taken his place at the monastery. Unfortunately, Gordon rings the alarm bell instead of curfew as the real Tigo awakens. West and Skull confront Gordon, but West insists that he thought Gordon was dead. Skull no longer believes West is a killer and both agents are left in an abandoned well in search of an escape route.

Gordon attempts to throw rocks in the bucket overhead so that the weight will lower the rope. It occurs to Artie that it would make a great game — *bucketball*. After West repeatedly misses the bucket, he exclaims, "It'll never catch on." A final throw lands the rock in the bucket and he changes his tune. West attempts to climb the rope but it breaks. The agents concoct a small rocket with the bucket, gunpowder and a fuse and shoot West out of the well.

It is soon discovered that Skull is none other than Senator Fenlow (Woods) who is motivated by presidential aspirations. Gordon goes to warn the president while West goes after Skull. West must fight his way through a few murderers but eventually reaches Skull/Fenlow.

Gordon, disguised as an assistant to the secretary of state, appears and tells Fenlow that the heads of state have all been killed and that he is now the president. Ready to take command, Fenlow is swiftly arrested by West and confesses to the crimes.

Later that night, Artie turns on the charm as he shares champagne with Lorelei (Gaye), Skull's assistant. He is trying desperately to get her to pay attention to him but West enters, along with an armed guard, to take her to prison. Jim tells Artie that, if he keeps stealing his girlfriends, he'll end up dead. Gordon replies, "Oh, come on…" West says that he wouldn't do it. But Lorelei is also known as the Peoria Poisoner. Artie changes his mind about drinking the champagne.

Author's Notes:

"Skulls" is the first "West" for writers Robert C. Dennis and Earl Barret who infuse the episode with a wonderful humor. Barret admitted that he and Dennis wrote all their episodes with an intentionally comic flair. "We saw 'The Wild Wild West' as a comic book type of a show, so we really camped it up.

"Skulls" marked the first appearance of the agent's new supervisor, Colonel Richmond, played, and occasionally overplayed, by Douglas Henderson. His character became popular with audiences so he was added as a semi-regular for the remaining two seasons of the series.

"Skulls" has the usual "West" elements, complete with dungeons, eerie corridors and hooded figures lurking in the dark. This episode really tests Ross Martin's versatility with four different disguises with the old preacher, the bum in the barn, hunchback Tigo and the assistant to the secretary of state.

The Night of the
Tottering Tontine

An unique group of wealthy investors consults a crystal ball for advice in "Tottering Tontine."

CBS Photo

CBS #6616 Shooting Order 44
First Air Date: 01/06/67

Produced by Bruce Lansbury
Directed by Irving J. Moore
Written by Elon Packard and Norman Hudis

Maurice: Henry Darrow
Applegate: Arthur Space
Raven: Harry Townes
Baring: William Wintersole
Grevely: Robert Emhardt
Stimson: Steve Gravers
Amelia: Lisa Pera
Pearse: Wilhelm Von Homburn
Dexter: Michael Road
Bartender: Ted Stanhope

West and Gordon are assigned to protect Dr. Raven (Townes), who is developing a secret weapon. West discovers that he is a member of a wealthy investment group known as the Tontine. The bylaws of the Tontine say that the surviving members of the group stand to inherit all the group's assets. When another member of the group, Martin Dexter (Road), is murdered and an attempt is made on Raven's life, West decides to accompany Raven to the Tontine's annual meeting. Gordon also attends but is disguised as Mr. McGordon, donning a mustache and mutton chops.

During the meeting, West explains to the members that someone intends to murder them. Before the proceeds begin, the room is, as always, sealed off. When the lever is pulled to release the seal, it mysteriously malfunctions and they are all trapped and open targets.

One by one the members are murdered. One is stabbed by a knife hidden in the back of a chair, the second is shot by a backfiring gun, while yet another is electrocuted.

West is captured by a hooded assailant and is tied to a jet propelled car set to fly out of a cave and over a cliff and smash on the rocks below. West escapes using a vial of acid from the heel of his boot to dissolve his binds. He returns to the meeting room. There he questions Grevely (Emhardt), the homeowner, why there are so many hidden surprises in the house. Grevely explains the house was designed by architect Martin Dexter, one of the deceased members.

The agents suspect everyone so Amelia (Pera), the actress, suggests they consult her crystal ball. Trying to break the tension, they all agree. As the séance starts, the ball explodes and Amelia disappears. West searches for her in the wine cellar, but the door slams shut and locks behind him. A panel slides open revealing a spiked wall that closes in on our hero. Using a handy bracing device, West escapes. He discovers that Dexter actually had a twin brother who was substituted for the dead Dexter. It is revealed that Dexter and Amelia are behind the murders. Dexter tries to kill West by placing him in a room equipped with a spinning blade. West jams the blade with his coat and escapes. Dexter, frustrated by his failure, opens a secret panel into the room. West is knocked off balance, the coat is worked loose setting the blade in motion once again and claiming the murderer's life. The Tontine is safe.

Back at the train, our agents are entertaining two lady friends. They introduce the girls to the crystal ball that belonged to Amelia. While they describe its magic, the ball fills with smoke and starts glowing. West waves his hand above the ball and Gordon reminisces on how the ball exploded on Amelia. The frightened women cling to their grinning saviors.

The Night of the
Gypsy Peril

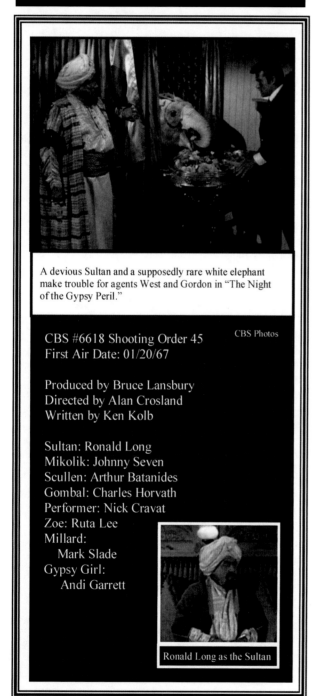

A devious Sultan and a supposedly rare white elephant make trouble for agents West and Gordon in "The Night of the Gypsy Peril."

CBS #6618 Shooting Order 45
First Air Date: 01/20/67

CBS Photos

Produced by Bruce Lansbury
Directed by Alan Crosland
Written by Ken Kolb

Sultan: Ronald Long
Mikolik: Johnny Seven
Scullen: Arthur Batanides
Gombal: Charles Horvath
Performer: Nick Cravat
Zoe: Ruta Lee
Millard:
     Mark Slade
Gypsy Girl:
     Andi Garrett

Ronald Long as the Sultan

Agents West and Gordon are en route to Washington with the Sultan of Ramapur (Long) and his priceless sacred white elephant, Akbar, which is to be presented as a gift to President Grant. Their train is boarded by Scullen (Batanides) and three other bandits. West tries in vain to intervene as they take the Sultan's jewels and lead off Akbar. West goes in pursuit while Gordon stays to attend to the unconscious Sultan. When the Sultan awakens, his first utterance is a demand that the U.S. pay $1 million for the loss of Akbar. Gordon soon joins West in pursuit of the bandits. They discover it was a band of gypsies, headed by the beautiful Queen Zoe (Lee), that spirited Akbar, who is now remarkably gray, away from the robbers.

The irate Sultan, in addition to demanding the money, has decided to end relations with the United States and hold all U.S. citizens currently in Ramapur hostage. West goes to the gypsy camp and joins their circus in an attempt to retrieve Akbar. Gordon shows up as Uncle Moe, a peddler, to tell West that there is something rotten in the state of Ramapur.

During an attempt to sneak Akbar from the gypsy camp, the agents are discovered. West tries to prove that Akbar is really the sacred white elephant and has been painted gray, but the paint won't wash off. It turns out that Akbar really is just a plain old gray beast. West and Gordon realize that the whole fiasco has been a scam perpetrated by the Sultan in order to extort $1 million from the United States. The agents escape the gypsies and go after the Sultan, who is summarily deported. The gypsies get to keep Akbar.

Author's Notes:

In most "West" episodes the agents deal with evil villains, corrupt government officials and/or bizarre weapons. This time around they must contend with an elephant, which actually makes for a fun episode. Our heroes go through a lot to retrieve the priceless pachyderm which turns out to be nothing more than – Dumbo. Writer Ken Kolb said that he originally wrote the script for another project, "... for Hanna Barbera's 'The Thief of Baghdad,' in which an elephant was stolen. I liked the way the elephant was stolen and since the script was never used I suggested the idea to 'The Wild Wild West.'"

The Night of the
Feathered Fury

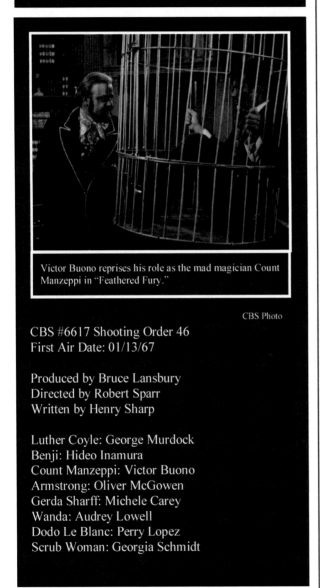

Victor Buono reprises his role as the mad magician Count Manzeppi in "Feathered Fury."

CBS Photo

CBS #6617 Shooting Order 46
First Air Date: 01/13/67

Produced by Bruce Lansbury
Directed by Robert Sparr
Written by Henry Sharp

Luther Coyle: George Murdock
Benji: Hideo Inamura
Count Manzeppi: Victor Buono
Armstrong: Oliver McGowen
Gerda Sharff: Michele Carey
Wanda: Audrey Lowell
Dodo Le Blanc: Perry Lopez
Scrub Woman: Georgia Schmidt

Agents West and Gordon meet with Gerda Sharff (Carey), who has vital information about the agents' old nemesis, Count Manzeppi (Buono). A monkey comes through an open window and everyone thinks it's cute until West, looking out the window, recognizes the organ grinder as the Count himself. The monkey tosses a smoke bomb into the room and when the smoke clears Gerda is gone, leaving behind a toy chicken.

Later, Gerda returns to the railroad car and confronts West with a revolver, demanding the bird. They are joined by Manzeppi and his cohorts, Luther (Murdock) and Dodo (Lopez) who also want the chicken. West knocks Luther out of the car and signals Gordon to get the Count, but the mischievous monkey tosses another smoke bomb and Manzeppi and his cohorts vanish.

West follows clues to the toy maker who originally made the chicken, but finds him dead. West encounters the Count and hides the chicken. When the Count demands the toy be returned, West gives him the bird: a fake, of course. The Count loses his temper and decides that torture will make the agent a little less deceptive and more willing to reveal the whereabouts of the chicken. Manzeppi explains that the toy contains a fabulously mystical Philosopher's Stone. Anything near the stone during the full moon will turn to gold. West is placed in a birdcage.

Gordon disguises himself as an organ grinder with an exact duplicate of the chicken to give to Gerda. He finds out where Manzeppi's hideout is and changes disguises. Now he is the toy maker's Uncle Hanzi and is trying to help West escape. While helping his fellow agent, they manage to recover the real toy. For a while it's a game of "chicken, chicken, who's got the chicken?" Gerda ends up with the bird but, unfortunately, is in direct moonlight. She and the bird are miraculously turned to gold. Manzeppi (alias, Goldfinger) watches as Gerda explodes and transforms into a wispy gold leaf. The Count escapes using a hot air balloon and bids West farewell, "Until another day..."

That night at the train, Gordon is showing the gold leaf to their lady friends and tells of their bizarre adventure. Gordon believes the leaf may reconstitute itself into its original form, given the proper conditions. They leave for the evening and as the moonlight pierces the window shade, the leaf is converted back into the chicken. The cook walks in to clean up after dinner and notices the toy. She places it in her apron pocket.

Author's Notes:

This is the second and final episode featuring the evil Count. CBS didn't feel that the Manzeppi character was popular with the viewing audience. That,

115

coupled with the fact that actor Victor Buono was not readily available because of his outstanding popularity as the flamboyant relic, King Tut of "Batman" fame, likely lead to their decision to discontinue the Count.

Regardless of the opinion of CBS and others, I liked the Manzeppi character. His trickery and flamboyance were truly reminiscent of the essence of the "West."

There's an interesting bit of information regarding the Philosopher's Stone. Legend has it that during alchemy the stone was used to turn inexpensive metals into gold. It could not turn *anything* into gold, most especially young women. It was also believed by some that it was the elixir of eternal life or immortality, and contained the ability to perfect the human soul, cure illness and bring about spiritual revitalization. It supposedly contained a mythic element no longer in existence.

The Night of the
Brain

In a mysterious cave dwelling, an unseen figure moves a doll resembling agent James West across a giant chessboard, predicting and planning each move the agent will make. At the train, Artemus Gordon receives a copy of tomorrow's newspaper reporting the death of a magician friend. At first the agents believe it is a prank, but convinced it's better to be safe than sorry they attend the magician's performance that evening. On his last trick the agents witness the magician being killed by an unexpected part of the act — a not-so-trick bomb.

They return to the train and carefully examine the day early newspaper when it bursts into blames in a timed spontaneous combustion. Another paper arrives via invisible messenger predicting the death of West's old army commander, Colonel Arnett (Warburton). Gordon notices the shop mark on the paper and, while he investigates, West tries to warn Arnett.

At Arnett's home, the Colonel offers West a drink. Just when West is ready to tell the Colonel his life is in danger, West is overcome by a drug that was placed in the drink. At the same time a package arrives for Arnett — a pair of dueling pistols from an unknown admirer. West is frozen by the drug and can only watch

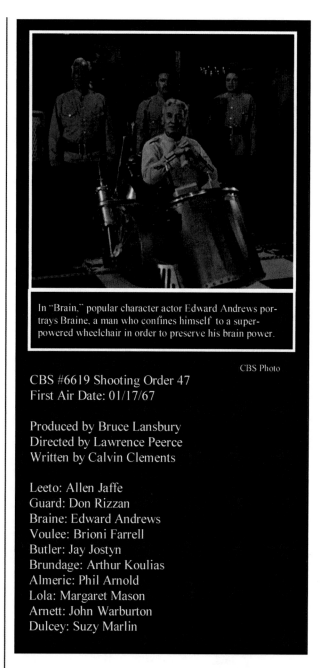

In "Brain," popular character actor Edward Andrews portrays Braine, a man who confines himself to a super-powered wheelchair in order to preserve his brain power.

CBS Photo

CBS #6619 Shooting Order 47
First Air Date: 01/17/67

Produced by Bruce Lansbury
Directed by Lawrence Peerce
Written by Calvin Clements

Leeto: Allen Jaffe
Guard: Don Rizzan
Braine: Edward Andrews
Voulee: Brioni Farrell
Butler: Jay Jostyn
Brundage: Arthur Koulias
Almeric: Phil Arnold
Lola: Margaret Mason
Arnett: John Warburton
Dulcey: Suzy Marlin

helplessly as Arnette is killed by a backfiring pistol. Again, the mysterious hand moves the chess piece.

The agents go to the print shop responsible for the early newspapers and find the shopkeeper dead. Looking further, they run an already prepared press that churns out a poster that reads, "Mysteries of the East, Revealed to the West." It directs the agents to the fortune teller Voulee (Farrell). West follows the lead, leaving Gordon to contend with authorities and the dead shopkeeper.

West arrives at the fortune teller and is greeted by the beautiful Voulee. She tries to subtly warn him, but he perseveres at seeking more information on the murders. He is suddenly catapulted into the bizarre cave dwelling of the prodigious Mr. Braine (Andrews). There are likenesses of both West and Gordon on his chessboard.

Braine wants West as his second in command for his new society. He plans on murdering all the world leaders as they attend a secret peace meeting and replacing them with look-alike men who will be operating under his rule. One of Braine's men has been disguised as Artemus Gordon, an incredible simulation, demonstrating the effectiveness of his techniques. To demonstrate his evil destructive powers Braine kills one of his own henchmen with a rocket fired from his steam-operated wheelchair, a rolling arsenal for which he uses as personal transportation and for conserving his energy for thinking.

Braine's incredible thought processes enable him to know the agents every move before they do, so he undoubtedly expects the appearance of Gordon, who has followed West to the cave. Gordon outsmarts Braine by masking a mask over a mask. This is just enough of a diversion for West to gain control of the situation, giving Braine a terrible headache, and battling the genius' ingenuity until his own inventiveness sends the demented Braine up in smoke.

Later the agents are charming two lady friends at the train. When the girls notice the splendor of their surroundings they ask what Jim and Artie do for the living. The agents toy with the girls and avoid a straight answer. Suddenly, various secret devices sound off and the guys are forced to reveal the truth – they're international jewel thieves. As the girls grasp at their precious stones, they soon realize a good thing when they see it.

Author's Notes:

Veteran actor Edward Andrews is well cast as the all-knowing Mr. Braine in this interesting episode of mind games and mayhem. Although he is always one step ahead of everyone, except West and Gordon, the villain's folly is in the inevitable triumph of good over evil, something the evil Braine never would consider. Andrews played well over 100 roles in film and television before his death in 1985.

This episode shows very effective use of the frequently seen cave set at CBS with excellent art direction and moody cinematography. The second season offers up some of the most amusing moments in "West," this one being one of my favorites: If you look closely in Braine's laboratory, you'll see Ross Martin's actual life mask on one of the tables.

The Night of the
Vicious Valentine

Agnes Moorehead won an Emmy for her performance of Emma Valentine in this memorable "West" tale of love, betrayal and murder.

CBS Photo

CBS # 6620 Shooting Order 48
First Air Date: 02/10/67

Produced by Bruce Lansbury
Directed by Irving J. Moore
Written by Leigh Chapman

P.J. Lambert: Henry Beckman
Itnelav: Shepard Menken
Emma Valentine: Agnes Moorehead
Curtis Dodd: J. Edward McKinley
Elaine Dodd: Diane McBain
Butler: Don Dillaway
Michele: Sherry Jackson
Colonel Armstrong: Walter Sande

Agents West and Gordon go to see wealthy Curtis Dodd (McKinley), who may be the next victim in a series of systematic murders of the nation's wealthiest men in a scheme that has become known as The Alphabet Murders. They are detained by the butler, who won't allow them to see Dodd. West becomes indignant and warns that Dodd's life is in danger. He forces entry and hears music from upstairs. He finds Dodd seated at the piano. While West tries to warn Dodd of the potential danger, he only scoffs. Suddenly, a spear is shot from behind the piano keys, piercing Dodd through the heart and killing him.

West and Gordon discuss the enigma at the train. Wealthy industrialists are being murdered on holidays. In the mail they receive a thank-you card from Mrs. Dodd who is appreciative of their concern. West notices a unique flaw in the printing of the card. They find another thank-you card from the previous victim's widow and notice the same flaw; all of the serifs are broken on the letter M. They quickly trace the print stock to the Friendly Card Company. Following the clues they notice wedding invitations going out for P.J. Lambert (Beckman), another industrialist. Gordon figures that Mrs. Dodd has set up the killings since all of the murdered men had recently married much younger women.

West goes to meet Emma Valentine (Moorehead), the matchmaker who arranged the Lambert wedding to a much younger woman named Michele (Jackson). West suspects that Lambert will be the next intended victim. Gordon makes an unsuccessful attempt to stop the wedding. West is captured by Valentine, strapped to a chair comprised of giant women's hands and held at bay while she describes her plan to the agent. Valentine confesses that she marries off her youthful employees to wealthy men then has their new husbands killed, gaining wealth and power as a result.

Prior to the Lambert wedding, Gordon appears on the scene dressed as a Jewish tailor assigned to *fix* Lambert's dress coat and stall the nuptials. He is discovered by one of Valentine's girls and, with the wedding just moments away, our heroes are left tied to a huge glass dome directly above where Lambert will be standing during his vows. After the services, as the music sounds and a certain chord is struck, the glass will shatter and West and Gordon will fall to their deaths taking the unsuspecting Lambert below with them. West uses his shoe knife to cut Gordon's binds. Gordon comments, "I usually don't cry at weddings,

but this time I'll make an exception." They work their ropes loose and use projected anchors to safely lower themselves to the ground as Lambert evades the falling glass. Valentine and the girls are apprehended.

When the agents return to the train, they discover a package waiting on the table. Not taking any chances West throws the box outside and prepares for an explosion. Hearing no kabooms Artie retrieves the package which turns out to be a slightly mashed box of chocolate cherries with a note from Michelle, who has found her heart really belongs to the older millionaire and their real marriage is taking place.

Author's Notes:

Agnes Moorehead stars as the vicious Emma Valentine, a wicked woman with a more than passing interest in murder. So convincing was her performance that she received the Best Supporting Actress Emmy award for the 1966-67 season from the Academy of Television Arts and Sciences. This also marks the second "West" appearance of actor Henry Beckman, who plays P.J. Lambert. His previous role on the series was that of Governor Bradford in "The Night of the Torture Chamber." The same portrait hanging in the Lambert home graces the offices of his honor the governor in "Torture Chamber."

The Night of the
Tartar

In a prisoner exchange President Grant orders agents West and Gordon to deliver prisoner Rimsky (Philippe) to Valdivostok, Siberia, where he will be traded for the American Vice Consul Millard Boyer (Blaine). During an escape attempt, Rimsky dies in a fall prompting Gordon to assume his identity. When the agents refuse to sail on the same ship with their contact, Kuprin (Throne), they are drugged. When they regain consciousness, they are lead to believe they are in Siberia. En route to meet Sazanov (Astin), who is to arrange the exchange, they escape. West is taken prisoner and is put in a jail cell with Boyer. The vice consul reveals that Rimsky was sent to America by his cousin, Sazanov, to shake down wealthy Russian immigrants. When Rimsky was arrested, Sazanov retaliated by taking Boyer prisoner. To force him to reveal Rim-

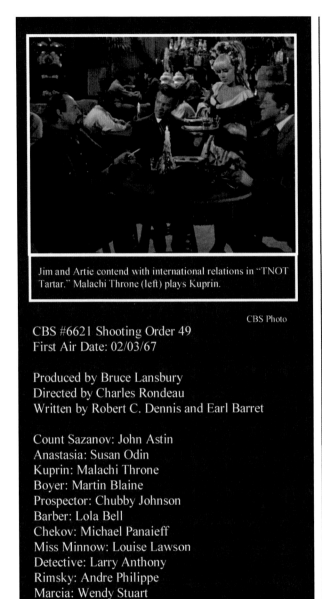
Jim and Artie contend with international relations in "TNOT Tartar." Malachi Throne (left) plays Kuprin.

CBS Photo

CBS #6621 Shooting Order 49
First Air Date: 02/03/67

Produced by Bruce Lansbury
Directed by Charles Rondeau
Written by Robert C. Dennis and Earl Barret

Count Sazanov: John Astin
Anastasia: Susan Odin
Kuprin: Malachi Throne
Boyer: Martin Blaine
Prospector: Chubby Johnson
Barber: Lola Bell
Chekov: Michael Panaieff
Miss Minnow: Louise Lawson
Detective: Larry Anthony
Rimsky: Andre Philippe
Marcia: Wendy Stuart

sky's whereabouts, West is tied to a stake while saber-swinging Cossacks ride closer and closer.

Gordon appears as Rimsky. Sazanov is looking for the $5 million that was supposed to be extorted by Rimsky in America. Sazanov cannot return to St. Petersburg until his debts are paid off. Gordon is exposed as an imposter by Rimsky's wife. She tells Sazanov the truth and Gordon is also thrown into the cell with West and Boyer. Boyer finds out where the money is from the agents and quickly betrays them by telling Sazanov in exchange for an equal partnership. Boyer is promptly killed.

West and Gordon break out of the cell but are again captured. This time Kuprin is about to shoot them so West stalls by suggesting a game of Russian Roulette. Using his sleeve knife to cut himself loose, West knocks out Kuprin. As the agents try to figure out where they are they stumble upon an old prospector (Johnson) who tells them they are in the Russian River settlement near San Francisco. West meets up with Sazanov at the Russian grotto where the money is hidden. Sazanov is deservedly stabbed by West.

The Night of the
Deadly Bubble

Agents West and Gordon meet with Professor McClennon (Welch) to investigate his study on a recent rash of destructive tidal waves. Before he divulges any information, he is shot and killed, leaving behind only one clue: a note to meet a Dr. Pringle (Lang) at the local cantina. West goes to the cantina and is attacked by cutthroats, all of whom he quickly subdues.

Later at the train Gordon is examining the bullet that killed the McClennon. West leaves to seek out Dr. Pringle again. At the hotel, West searches the late professor's room and is confronted by the spectacled Dr. Abigail Pringle, McClennon's associate, who is looking for important papers. While they both search, a shot rings out. Captain Philo (Ryder) demands to know what they're doing. Philo, who is a fanatic about preserving sea life, knew McClennon and had invited him to dinner. Satisfied with the intruders' explanation, he invites West and Pringle to join him for dinner instead. West is suspicious and retrieves the bullet shot by Philo. After comparing bullets, they discover they came from the same gun that killed McClennon.

At dinner, Pringle makes herself a target for trouble by revealing to Philo that she was the ward of all of McClennon's experiments. Philo kidnaps her and brings her to his undersea laboratory located inside a volcano. West discovers a secret entrance to the underwater lab but is captured by Philo. He explains how he

119

Alfred Ryder plays Captain Philo, a sea-life fanatic who controls the oceans in " The Night of the Deadly Bubble."

CBS #6622 Shooting Order 50
First Air Date: 02/24/67

CBS Photo

Produced by Bruce Lansbury
Directed by Irving J. Moore
Written by Michael Edwards

Captain Philo: Alfred Ryder
Dr. Abigail Pringle: Judy Lang
Felix/Blind Beggar: Lou Krugman
Professor McClennon: Nelson Welch
Pepe: Nacho Galindo
Maid: Kai Hernandez

creates the tidal waves by releasing giant underwater bubbles using a huge air compressor. He plans to destroy all the world's coastal towns as punishment for polluting the oceans. He has also designed a delivery tube that would release poison into the population's drinking water supply.

Gordon appears on the scene disguised as a phony blind beggar and rescues West and Pringle. West kills the captain before he can release the deadly bubble.

The agents are back at the train with Dr. Pringle and discover she is engaged to be married. She leaves after a drink and a toast. Artie notices that she left her glasses behind. Jim tells him to take a closer look at them. Artie learns that they are plain glass. Jim explains that is how she kept men away. When Artie removes them, Jim stares into his eyes and says, "Artie, you're beautiful." The remark is summarily disregarded.

The Night of the
Surreal McCoy

Agents West and Gordon are charged with guarding the famous Hertzberg crown jewels that are on display at a museum. In the same room as the jewels, the Ambassador of Hertzberg (Triesault) notices and unusual Western scene painting, a Wellington. Owned by wealthy rancher, Axel Morgan (Doucette), the painting seems strangely out of place. The men leave the room momentarily and, despite our agents best efforts, the jewels are stolen and the guard murdered.

After the theft, Morgan insists on removing his *valuable* painting from the museum even though, Gordon observes, that the painting is a forgery. The agent wrangles a dinner invitation to Morgan's ranch for the agents and ambassador.

At the ranch, Morgan slips through a secret panel revealing Dr. Miguelito Loveless (Dunn) standing at an easel with brush in hand. Loveless explains that he has hired Lightnin' McCoy (Alonzo) to come to the ranch. The agents arrive with the ambassador and West checks the rooms for anything suspicious. In his room, West notices something funny about the decanter of wine. He feigns sleeping and is attacked by four of Morgan's men. West and Gordon dart into the ambassador's room and realize he has disappeared.

As the agents investigate further, Gordon takes closer looks at all of Morgan's *priceless* paintings, making note that most are forgeries. On a particular portrait, he notices a child's thumbprint. He presses on the painting and it moves aside revealing a safe. Easily cracked by Gordon, they find that the safe contains the crown jewels. They're caught in the act by Morgan and elude his men just long enough for Gordon to escape. West is trapped at gunpoint by the demonic doctor.

Loveless offers West dinner and explains his plan in detail. He demonstrates how by using tuning-

Miguelito Loveless (Dunn) is at it again, this time using a sound machine to move in and out of paintings in the bizarre tale "Surreal McCoy."

CBS #6623 Shooting Order 51
First Air Date: 03/03/67

CBS Photo

Produced by Bruce Lansbury
Directed by Alan Crosland Jr.
Written by John Kneubuhl

Dr. Miguelito Loveless: Michael Dunn
Lightnin' McCoy: John Alonzo
Axel Morgan: John Doucette
Ambassador: Ivan Triesault
Museum Director: Noel Drayton
Gunman: Quintin Sondegaard
Barkeep: Jorge Moreno

fork technology he is able to activate a machine that moves living beings in and out of paintings, paintings expertly copied by Loveless himself. He is then able to embed professional killers in the paintings that are to be distributed as gifts to top officials, world leaders and financial institutions worldwide. When the killers emerge from their ethereal bonds and perform their evil deeds of exterminating the rulers, Loveless will graciously step in and take over the world.

Gordon rides into town to find a telegraph machine and wire for help. He is told by the barkeep that the telegraphs are all down. At the bar, he happens to run across Lightnin' McCoy, who asks the agent for directions to Morgan's ranch and a man named Loveless. Artie drugs McCoy and takes his place. He arrives at the ranch and is fed in a private room while Loveless prepares West for his plan.

Downstairs, Morgan, having grown impatient with Loveless, holds both Loveless and West at gunpoint. They get away using one of West's explosive buttons and Loveless, West and Gordon/Lightnin' are quickly zapped into a painting. Loveless tells West he wants to find out how fast the agent really is with a gun. The two agents are sent into the street to face off. Loveless, always prepared, has brought in six of the other *fastest* guns in the West, just in case West should prevail. The agents team up and take out the other hired guns. They set off after Loveless, who has already transported himself through a painting of Morgan's ranch. West explains that it's done with sound and a handy triangle on the wall suffices.

Back at the ranch, Loveless escapes by disappearing into one of the paintings. The camera plays on a painting of carpenters, indicating the likelihood that Loveless is hiding there. The agents crate and load all the paintings onto their train, assuming Loveless will not be able to escape the crated works. With the jewels safely returned to the ambassador they all turn in for the night. In the quiet train car, the sound of sawing erupts from one of the crated paintings.

Author's Notes:

My editor, Jude, thinks that Artie, as Lightnin' McCoy, has a swarthy, dark and dangerous appeal in this episode. While I prefer a more traditional Artie, Jude couldn't take her eyes off his black tailored jacket, unshaven face and steely stare. She said this was a whole new and wildly captivating look for the dapper Mr. Gordon.

The shootout in the Western street was a departure from the "West" essence and contained purely traditional elements, such as the idea of who's the fastest draw. Six-guns, black hats and standoffs actually worked well in the backdrop of miraculous dimensional travel.

An interesting observation about this episode that makes it rare among all the other "West" shows: There is no romantic element whatsoever. There are no female guest stars in it at all. Even the tag, which usually involves some relaxation for the agents with female company, showed only the agents and the ambassador turning in for an early night's rest. I guess even Casanova needs an evening off every so often.

A "Surreal" Love Story

"Surreal McCoy" marks the final Loveless episode penned by John Kneubuhl. "Writing for television had become kind of a drag. I had been doing it for a long time. I had to find another reason for writing scripts.

"Mike Garrison's secretary had fallen in love with a young man who had moved to Australia. They were quite poor, and he said that if she could make her way to Australia they would marry. She told me that she had an idea for a 'West' episode and wanted to write it out and try to sell it. I told her if she wrote it up that I would write the entire treatment and storyline if it was acceptable. I said I'd write the script and give her every cent of the whole thing for her trip as a wedding present.

"What she came up with was a pretty dreadful notion, except for the basic idea that a person could step into pictures and get embroiled in incidents, events, in the picture. So I worked that one out. Paley, who loved 'Terror Stalked the Town,' wanted to give me CBS, but he hated the next Western, 'Surreal McCoy' – absolutely hated it. But he paid me a lot of money for it. It allowed a very sweet girl to go to Australia and marry her young man. I hope they lived happily ever after."

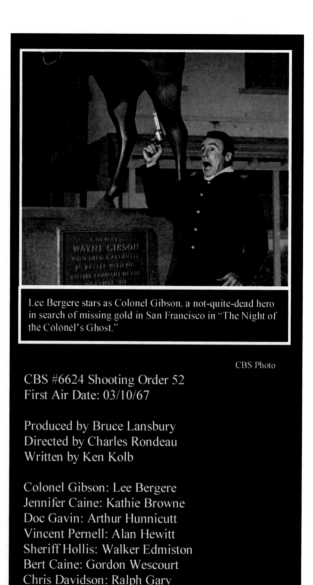

Lee Bergere stars as Colonel Gibson, a not-quite-dead hero in search of missing gold in San Francisco in "The Night of the Colonel's Ghost."

CBS #6624 Shooting Order 52
First Air Date: 03/10/67

Produced by Bruce Lansbury
Directed by Charles Rondeau
Written by Ken Kolb

Colonel Gibson: Lee Bergere
Jennifer Caine: Kathie Browne
Doc Gavin: Arthur Hunnicutt
Vincent Pernell: Alan Hewitt
Sheriff Hollis: Walker Edmiston
Bert Caine: Gordon Wescourt
Chris Davidson: Ralph Gary
Able Caine: Billy Shannon
President Grant: Roy Engel

The Night of the
Colonel's Ghost

West and Gordon escort President Grant to San Francisco to dedicate a statue of the late Colonel Wayne Gibson in Gibsonville. West rides ahead to check out the town and is confronted by a man wielding an axe who claims there is a bundle of gold hidden somewhere. The agent subdues him and moves on. West arrives at a nearly empty town, an eerie aftermath to an epidemic of broken necks. The few remaining citizens are also convinced there is hidden gold.

After the next victim is killed, muffled organ music is heard. The agent meets other townspeople who all claim their right to the hidden gold. Pernell (Hewitt), an attorney, claims a legal right to the money, as do Sheriff Hollis (Edmiston) and Doc Gavin (Hunnicutt). At the sheriff's office, West if told that Joshua Gibson, the Colonel's father, founded the town. When his son was killed, Joshua lost his mind and purposely misguided funds that were to be used for the railroad into a memorial for his son. This left Gibsonville a virtual ghost town.

West sends a message warning the president, who is indignant about the delay. Gordon appears on the scene disguised as an Englishman, Ian Gellico Cooper Fentstone, bearing news of the very few hours allotted West to solve the crimes.

Nearby, West discovers a secret panel in the hotel revealing the no-so-dead Gibson (Bergere) playing the organ. The Gibson *ghost* grabs Jennifer (Browne) and holds her and West at gunpoint. West explains that he was sent by the government to correct the inscription on the statue. Gordon appears disguised as President Grant and tries to get the gun away from Gibson. Gordon tells the colonel how valuable he was in the war, but inadvertently names the wrong battles and is exposed. Gordon throws his cigar, which blows up in Gibson's face and the agents escape. Gibson fires at them and accidentally grazes the commemorative statue revealing that it is made of 100% gold bullion. Gibson is shot and dies dramatically at the foot of the statue.

The Night of the
Deadly Blossom

Agents West and Gordon report to Admiral Agnow's San Francisco headquarters and find him dead along with three other officers. The agents believe the admiral's death ties in with the recent mysterious sinking of the cruiser Youngstown. West and Gordon are assigned to guard the Hawaiian king (Santos) who is due to arrive secretly by ship.

Gordon makes use of a stevedore's permit he found as a clue by going to the docks to investigate. In his search, he discovers a crate of rockets and stows away inside as it is shipped of to a secret launching site.

West visits a wealthy but suspicious Polynesian named Adam Barclay (Persoff), and is drugged. He awakens to relive a moment for Edgar Allen Poe's *The Pit and the Pendulum*. He escapes with the aid of a pretty secretary and is lead the secret launch site to stop Barclay from destroying the Hawaiian king . Gordon has already infiltrated the launch site disguised as one of Barclay's men. Together, the agents efficiently de-

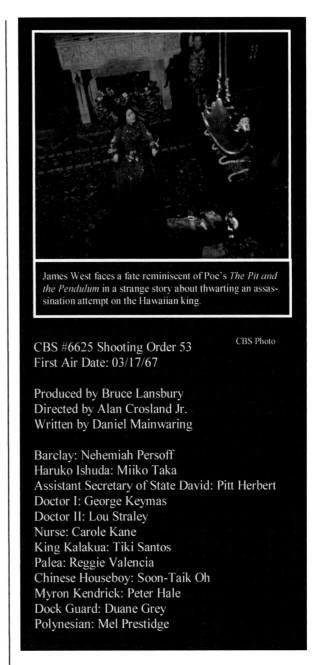

James West faces a fate reminiscent of Poe's *The Pit and the Pendulum* in a strange story about thwarting an assassination attempt on the Hawaiian king.

CBS #6625 Shooting Order 53   CBS Photo
First Air Date: 03/17/67

Produced by Bruce Lansbury
Directed by Alan Crosland Jr.
Written by Daniel Mainwaring

Barclay: Nehemiah Persoff
Haruko Ishuda: Miiko Taka
Assistant Secretary of State David: Pitt Herbert
Doctor I: George Keymas
Doctor II: Lou Straley
Nurse: Carole Kane
King Kalakua: Tiki Santos
Palea: Reggie Valencia
Chinese Houseboy: Soon-Taik Oh
Myron Kendrick: Peter Hale
Dock Guard: Duane Grey
Polynesian: Mel Prestidge

stroy Barclay's evil plan.

Later that night, Gordon has a date and rushes out the door not wanting to keep his lady friend waiting. He plans on leaving West to entertain the Hawaiian king. Gordon asks West to lie a little by saying he was called away by an illness in the family. As the King arrives, he introduces his family that is accompanying

123

him on his journey. A bevy of exotically beautiful cousins and daughters enter the room. Gordon peeks in from outside the train door. He decides to go back into the train, tossing the flowers aside and announcing his Aunt Maude has made a miraculous recovery.

The Night of the
Cadre

Franconium rears its ugly head once again in this episode that deals with controlled behavior and presidential assassination. Vince Howard guest stars as Kleed.

CBS Photo

CBS #6626 Shooting Order 54
First Air Date: 03/24/67

Produced by Bruce Lansbury
Directed by Leon Benson
Written By Digby Wolfe

Sergeant Stryker: Richard Jaeckel
General Trask: Donald Gordon
Josephine: Sheilah Wells
Professor Frimm: Ken Drake
Warden Primwick: Tol Avery
Ralph Kleed: Vince Howard

Agent James West witnesses the release of condemned murder, Ralph Kleed (Howard) by Warden Primwick (Avery). Kleed blows a whistle and the warden attacks West with his cane. West restrains the warden, who dies suddenly from the exertion. West goes after Kleed, who manages to escape, but he leaves behind his unusual whistle that emits a special pitch only heard by dogs and wardens. The warden's autopsy reveals that a *franconium* crystal has been implanted in his brain. Triggered by the whistle, the crystal incites strange and violent behavior.

All of the escaped criminals have one common goal and that is the assassination of President Grant. West poses as Carl Storch, the only convicted murdered to remain behind bars. While transporting West in a guarded wagon a cadre surrounds them and kidnaps West. He is taken to master criminal General Titus Trask (Gordon), who was dishonorably discharged from the army, and harbors the ambition of becoming the dictator of the United States. West's identity is discovered but, instead of killing the agent, Trask intends to implant a *franconium* crystal in his brain and West, in turn, can implant President Grant with a crystal; leaving both men at the mercy of Trask.

Gordon traces West to the cadre's hideout where he appears as Kelton, the peddler. Just as West is being prepared for crystallization, Gordon bursts in and saves his partner. West leads the Cadre straight into a trap and Gordon overpowers them with knock-out gas. Trask pursues West but eventually falls from a cliff to his death.

Gordon works on perfecting his knock-out gas back at the train. He tries to make it odorless and colorless. The mixture spills when the train stops and Gordon falls blissfully asleep.

Author's Notes:
This isn't the first episode where we hear about *franconium*. In "The Night of the Glowing Corpse," the magical fictitious substance has radiant properties that lead our heroes to their quarry.

The Night of the
Wolf

Joseph Campanella sports an iron claw as he vies for the throne of his country and threatens women in "TNOT Wolf."

CBS Photo

CBS #6627 Shooting Order 55
First Air Date: 03/31/67

Produced by Bruce Lansbury
Directed by Charles Rondeau
Written by Robert C. Dennis and Earl Barret

Talamantes: Joseph Campanella
Leandra: Lorri Scot
King Stefan: John Marley
Captain Dushan: Jonathan Lippe
Dr. Hanska: Michael Shillo
Sheriff Twilley: Eddie Fontaine
The Priest: Charles Radilac
Stage Driver: Jimmie Booth

Assigned to protect King Stefan (Marley), who is to become ruler in place of his late brother, West and Gordon must contend with the sinister Mr. Talamantes (Campanella), who wants Stefan to renounce the throne. The coronation is to take place in the United States in a town called Lukas. To force Stefan to comply with his wishes, Talamantes kidnaps his daughter, Leandra (Scot) and injects her with a serum that will force her to do his bidding whenever she hears the word *vrkalak*. While tracking down Talamantes and Leandra, West is attacked by a wolf at every turn. When he does find the duo, Talamantes croaks, "vrkalak" and Leandra dutifully knocks West unconscious.

Stefan has a stroke when he hears that his daughter has been abducted so Gordon must bring the town to the prince, who is crowned king and then dies. Now Leandra is officially the queen.

West manages to escape from Talamantes and Leandra is also freed, though still under Talamantes' spell. The press has gathered at the train and Leandra reads a letter renouncing the throne, hoping the ruse will coax the infiltrator to reveal his identity. Gordon slips out unnoticed. Leandra is given a note by Captian Dushan (Lippe), an attendee at the conference. The note simply reads: VRKALAK: Kill West at once. She attempts to kill the agent. After shots are heard Dushan and Talamantes enter the train car and find West laying on the floor. Gordon, however, appears from the next room disguised as Stefan. Dushan shoots and wounds Gordon and West quickly springs into action. Talamantes battles West and dies by falling on his own claw. Leandra, having seen the image of her dead father, is shocked free of the spell and can now assume the role as leader of her country.

The Night of the
Bogus Bandits

Rehearsing his men for bigger things, the evil genius Dr. Miguelito Loveless leads his gang of cohorts in a small bank robbery then burns the stolen *pittance*. One of his men hides two charred $100 bills and spends them, providing West and Gordon with a much needed clue that leads them to Loveless. Gordon, impersonating an artist named Lindsay, investigates the boarding house from where the bill was traced. West goes to the saloon where the other bill was passed and questions largely unreceptive employees. Loveless enters and asks for the return of the charred bill.

Dr. Loveless gets even more creative and demonic "The Night of the Bogus Bandits," a tale of disguises, deception and creative transportation.

CBS Photos

CBS #6628 Shooting Order 56
First Air Date: 04/07/67

Produced by Bruce Lansbury
Directed by Irving J. Moore
Written by Henry Sharp

Dr. Miguelito Loveless:
          Michael Dunn
Joe Kirby: Roland LaStarza
Vance Rawlinson:
          Charles Wagenheim
Belladonna: Marianna Hill
Mrs. Bancroft: Patsy Kelly
Pearline Hastings:
          Grace Gaynor
Rainey: Donald Barry
Colonel Crockett:
          Walter Sande
Fargo: William Challee
Bartender: Murray Alper
Whaley: Troy Melton

... all he really wants to do is direct.

The doctor proudly shows West his mock prison, an arsenal and the U.S. sub-treasury; all training aids for his men who will soon take over these federal establishments, placing Loveless as America's dictator.

While Gordon inquires at the boarding house, he is shot by Loveless' accomplice Pearline (Gaynor). He awakens to discover that his sketch pad in his pocket has saved his life. He recalls a certain type of spurs, *Senora Stompers*, worn by a man he saw just before being shot.

At the Loveless hide-out, the diminutive genius feels it's time to end West's life. Gordon enters, dressed as Mr. Fargo, the silversmith who made the *Stompers*, claiming he has an order that has yet to be paid. As he turns to leave, he loosens the cap on his canteen, spills highly flammable liquid and lights a line of fire to help West in his escape.

The agents soon discover that all the telegraph lines are down, leading them to Junction City, where they find Loveless at the communications center. He is preparing to signal his gang in various sections of the United States to begin their catastrophic plans. Gordon throws himself into the electrical circuits, thus putting an end to Loveless' evil scheme. Loveless customarily escapes, this time eluding our duo in a baby carriage.

Chapter 7
Makeup: If You Look Real Close – It's Me!

A Ross by Any Other Name

Just as Robert Conrad has his entourage of stuntmen, so did Ross Martin have his own entourage comprised of a kindly old railroad worker, a crusty desert rat, a Chinese coolie, a Russian priest, a Jewish tailor and even President Grant himself, among others. All of these colorful characters were actually one man – the remarkable Ross Martin.

Ross Martin's talents were unquestionable. His ability to grasp the nuances of personalities and mannerisms made each of his characters, regardless of how outrageous, believable and oddly charming. Each week in the role of Secret Service Agent Artemus Gordon, the wildly versatile Martin portrayed an array of characters as vast as any actor could imagine. "The Wild Wild West" afforded Martin the unique opportunity to display his amazing talent. He is quoted from a previous interview as saying, "It's an actor's dream – a show-off's showcase."

Behind every character and disguise was the actor, but behind the actor was the makeup man — in this case the multi-talented Don Schoenfeld. Schoenfeld started his career with the traditional Western television series "Rawhide." When the time came for "West" to hire a makeup artist, Eddie Denault, head of production at CBS, and George Lane, the network's head of makeup, liked what Schoenfeld was doing and asked him if he would like to work on "The Wild Wild West." Schoenfeld saw the opportunity as a fun challenge and accepted the position.

He would soon discover that the show posed a real challenge, for the shooting schedule alone. He re-

called, "We never had time to prepare. We would get the script two or three days before we'd start shooting." Not only was time a major factor, but the materials he had to work with also posed problems. "We had very little time and not a hell of a lot of money for prosthetics. It was the second and third year before I was ready to quit 'cause they couldn't give me noses for Ross. I had to use whatever John Chandler made for 'Planet of the Apes,' or whatever was in stock."

A problem arose with stock noses having been sized for the original actors. It became a nuisance getting the stock noses to fit Martin. Schoenfeld argued his case to CBS and they finally came through with a set of five different types of noses for Martin to wear.

During the first season, Schoenfeld praised the show's producer, Michael Garrison for his freeness toward his job. "Mike was great. He would let me do whatever we wanted, 'cause it wasn't an authentic Western; it was tongue-in-cheek.' He let us do whatever we wanted as long as it was far out and went with the character. Mike was the nicest man in the world and a bright, bright man. He knew the concept of 'The Wild Wild West' and what it should be," he said.

Schoenfeld explained that a plaster cast (life mask) was made of Ross' face, and every time there was a nose or mouth change, they would do a clay model from the plaster face. They'd make a cast of that face, pour it and put them in the oven. The cast could only be used 10 times which proved time consuming and very costly.

As each new script was preparing to be shot, Martin would have a few days to read it over and then

Art Courtesy of CBS

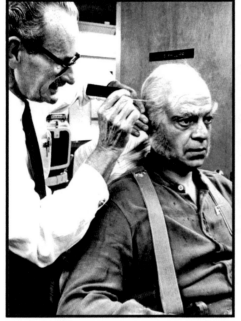

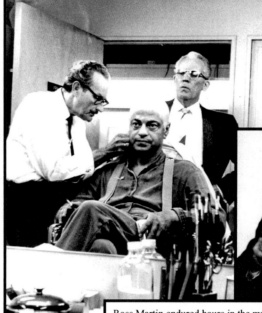

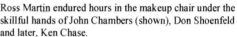

Ross Martin endured hours in the makeup chair under the skillful hands of John Chambers (shown), Don Shoenfeld and later, Ken Chase.

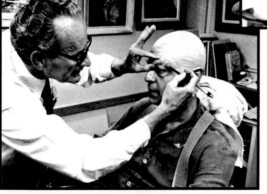

he would sketch on the back pages of the script the way he wanted his character(s) to look and present the ideas to Schoenfeld for review. "It was really a joint venture because Ross had to play the part and I had to do the makeup."

Gold Prospector Sketch

TNOT Underground Terror

Once Schoenfeld and Martin agreed on the look, the makeup process would begin, lasting anywhere from and one to one and a half hours. According to Schoenfeld, the time constraints made changes an absolute impossibility and every disguise remained unaltered once it was agreed upon.

Olavee Martin, Ross' widow, told us that, although Ross liked all of the characters he portrayed on "The Wild Wild West," he did have his favorites. "The English gold prospector in 'Night of the Underground Terror' was one of his favorite roles," she said. Of his other much loved performances — the Jewish tailor in "Vicious Valentine" and the German cook, Herr Osterpolster, in "Night of the Infernal Machine."

TNOT Infernal Machine

TNOT Vicious Valentine

128

Guest stars often found themselves in the makeup chair, some with extremely elaborate characters to portray. The top image shows actor Christopher Carey in "Winged Terror," center, John Dehner in "Steel Assassin," and bottom, Lloyd Bochner in "TNOT Puppeteer."

Guests Stars

In addition to doing Martin's makeup Schoenfeld also created interesting makeup for "West's" many guest stars. In "Night of the Steel Assassin," John Dehner played the vengeful Torres who had survived an explosion only to be fully reconstructed in steel. In the opening scene of the episode, West shoots Torres in the face and you see skin flying off to reveal metal underneath. "We glued the thin aluminum on and then took a scar material, which was plastic, covered that with a light piece of gauze and covered that with a cap sealer. I attached a piece of nylon fishing line to the fake skin and when the line was pulled the skin came off," Schoenfeld explained.

Of all "The Wild Wild West" guest stars Schoenfeld worked on, he recalled the most difficult as being actor Lloyd Bochner in "The Night of the Puppeteer." "That was the hardest thing I'd ever done. It took about two and half hours of makeup, which was a long time, especially for a TV show in those days. And, of course, we had to do the rest of the cast also. The toughest part was that I didn't have a second man assigned permanently. Actors get used to their makeup man and they didn't want a stranger coming in, so it was a hassle. During the scenes of "The Puppeteer," the crew was shooting the whole setup of the puppet master pulling the ropes and strings in the tower," and he noticed a problem.

Schoenfeld complained to director Irving Moore that in that scene, Bochner's bald cap didn't look right. "I told him that when-

TNOT Skulls

The preacher "TNOT Skulls"

Martin would execute detailed sketches, often on the backs of his scripts, and then work with the makeup artist to perfect the look.

TNOT Skulls

TNOT Skulls Tigo Sketch

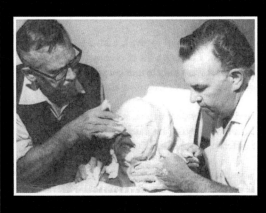

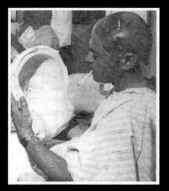

CBS Photos

ever he turned his head around with a bald cap on it would wrinkle; not like skin. For some reason, you can never get them to look good." Moore thought it looked fine and shot the scene regardless of Schoenfeld's concerns. The next day in dailies the wrinkles showed up and Moore said he was unhappy with the results, holding Schoenfeld responsible for the shoddy makeup.

Makeup artist, Don Schoenfeld shows off the final product with Ross Martin.

CBS Photo

Stuntmen in the Makeup Chair

CBS Photo

Stuntmen Whitey Hughes (front) and Chuck O'Brien sport beards and mustaches to disguise the fact that they were series *regulars*.

Not only did Schoenfeld have his hands full every day making up Martin and the many guest stars who appeared on "West," but disguising the stunt *regulars* was a challenging part of his duties. The easily recognizable stuntmen had to look different in every episode and it became standard procedure to come up with ways, show after show, to mix and match combinations of mustaches, beards and other makeup techniques.

Dick Cangey, resident stuntman and catcher, hated to wear a disguise in every show. "I would go to Don and say, 'The director wants a full beard on Red (West) and I get a mustache.' Now these beards were miserable to wear. Everyone hated them. The next week I'd tell Don, 'Red gets a beard and I get sideburns,' or 'Red gets a beard and I get a goatee.' Finally, Red said to me, 'How come I always have to wear a beard?' I said, 'I don't know. I guess that's the way they want it.' So Red went to Don and asked the same question. Don said, 'Don't ask me. Dick keeps telling me what you get each week.'"

The Mirror with Two Faces

During the third season Schoenfeld felt he had proven himself and was growing tired of working on the show. After he left, makeup man Ken Chase joined the series. "I had worked helping on the show during the first year. I was a novice. I was teaching myself at that time and made some noses and took them to George Lane at that time. Shortly after, CBS gave me the job," Chase recalled.

130

TNOT Cutthroats

CBS Photos

Even when there wasn't a lot of makeup needed Martin would sketch out the character, as above in "Cutthroats."

TNOT Pistoleros

Chase's job was the same routine as Schoenfeld's, but not on the creative end. Chase's favorite makeup job on Martin was the Russian Orthodox priest in "The Night of the Cossacks." Another interesting effort was the oversized head for actor Christopher Carey in "The Night of the Winged Terror." John Chambers had originally designed the head for several earlier "Star Trek" episodes.

Chase admitted that he also found the time factor a problem. "Morning would start by making up half a dozen regular stuntmen who were forever being disguised. Those disguises took one to two hours to do; then Ross, then the guest stars. Ross' disguises were primarily false noses and beards. We didn't have much of a budget."

In "The Night of the Avaricious Actuary," Martin was in full makeup as an old gas inspector, complete with wig, goatee and a latex face and nose. The scene called for Martin to shoot a gun and throw it to the side, but the gun hit the wall and bounced back. Martin tripped over the gun and broke his leg. "I can remember peeling off the appliqués on Ross as they dragged him off to the hospital. I needed the appliqués to makeup another actor that replaced him in that scene," Chase recalled.

During the fourth season after recovering from his broken leg, Martin suffered a major heart attack. Actor Charles Aidman stepped in as Secret Service agent Jeremy

From "TNOT Firebrand" Martin perfects two, quite opposite, disguises, another example of his versatility as a performer. Martin never shied away from a challenge when it came to makeup as is evident in the behind-the-scene images on the following pages — when he gets in touch with his *feminine* side.

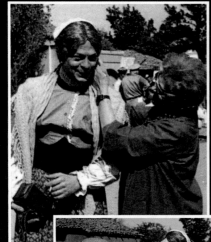

Ross appears as a Mexican lady in order to create an effective diversion in "TNOT Freebooters." Below, Schoenfeld preps Martin as Ted Voightlander looks on. Right, Keenan Wynn teases the demure Martin on the set.

Charles Aidman as Jeremy Pike dons his share of makeup while filling in for the recovering Martin.

Pike. Aidman recalled how similar his role was to that of Artemus Gordon. "Most of the makeup jobs were extremely simple, but the longest job was as a Chinese in "Night of the Pelican." After Aidman left, noted character actor William Schallert stepped in as a slightly more demure guest partner for James West. For the final three episodes of the fourth season, and the series, Martin returned.

After "The Wild Wild West" was cancelled, Chase went on to become one of Hollywood's most sought after makeup artists, going on to win three Emmy Awards in 1977, 1979 and 1990. He also worked on such well-known films as "Jeremiah Johnson," "The Color Purple," "Back to the Future," "When Harry Met Sally," "Who Framed Roger Rabbit" and "City Slickers," to name only a few.

Don Schoenfeld continued working in the business until his death in 1980.

In a behind-the-scenes shot Martin takes a moment to relax.

Ross Martin Alias Artemus Gordon

Cast of Characters — In Order of Air Date

Season 1
Episode: **The Night of the Inferno**
Character(s): a drunken soldier; a poor Mexican beggar

Episode: **The Night of the Deadly Bed**
Character(s): a Mexican peon

Episode: **The Night of the Sudden Death**
Character(s): a clown

Episode: **The Night of the Casual Killer**
Character(s): an actor, as hammy Artemus Gordon

Episode: **The Night of a Thousand Eyes**
Character(s): a dapper gentleman, with top hat, cape, cane and mustache

Episode: **The Night of the Glowing Corpse**
Character(s): an Irish freight man

Episode: **The Night of the Dancing Death**
Character(s): the Grand Elector of Saxony, British

Episode: **The Night of the Double-Edged Knife**
Character(s): a tame Indian; a gentle old railroad worker; a dead Indian (2 shown)

Episode: **The Night of the Red-Eyed Madman**
Character(s): German military expert, Colonel Cross

Episode: **The Night of the Human Trigger**
Character(s): Professor Neinkindorf of Austria

Episode: **The Night of the Torture Chamber**
Character(s): art critic Messr. Gaston LaRusse of Sorbonne

Episode: **The Night of the Fatal Trap**
Character(s): crusty desert rat Mojave Mike

All Photos Courtesy CBS   **133**

Episode: **The Night of the
Steel Assassin**
Character(s): President Grant

Episode: **The Night the
Dragon Screamed**
Character(s): a coolie on
the docks;
General Sumatra, an armaments
expert

Episode: **The Night of the
Flaming Ghost**
Character(s): drunken whiskey
salesman R.P.McGuffy; a cavalry
soldier

Episode: **The Night of the
Grand Emir**
Character(s): the minister to the
Emir, Sultan Sheik Hokar

Episode: **The Night of the
Whirring Death**
Character(s): opera singer
Caruso del Artemo

Episode: **The Night of the
Bars of Hell**
Character(s):
Jeremiah P. Threadneedle,
dealer in ladies' corsets;
aged prison executioner;
a street preacher

Episode: **The Night of the
Two-Legged Buffalo**
Character(s): a Hawaiian prince

Episode: **The Night of the
Freebooters**
Character(s): Colonel Hernandez
Del Valle Santiago y Sandoval;
old lady running the cantina

Episode: **The Night of the
Burning Diamond**
Character(s): Count Baron Felix
von Schlesweig und Holtzbergen

Season 2
Episode: **The Night of the Eccentrics**
Character(s): an aide to
President Juarez

Episode: **The Night of the
Golden Cobra**
Character(s): an East Indian magician

Episode: **The Night of the Big Blast**
Character(s): no disguise,
but a robot version of Artie

Episode: **The Night of
the Flying Pie Plate**
Character(s): gem expert
Dirk DeJohn;
A temporary alien

Episode: **The Night of the Poisonous Posey**
Character(s): villain Ascot Sam

Episode: **The Night of the Bottomless Pit**
Character(s): former legionnaire Pierre Gaspard

Episode: **The Night of the Watery Death**
Character(s): a Swedish sailor

Episode: **The Night of the Green Terror**
Character(s): an Indian woman

Episode: **The Night of the Ready-Made Corpse**
Character(s): a bespectacled man who is the criminal Thomas Link

Episode: **The Night of the Skulls**
Character(s): funeral officiator at his own funeral;
a bum;
Tigo, the hunchback;
a pompous senator

Episode: **The Night of the Infernal Machine**
Character(s): pastry chef Herr Ostropolyer

Episode: **The Night of the Lord of Limbo**
Character(s): duelist Jack Maitland (with no makeup)

Episode: **The Night of the Tottering Tontine**
Character(s): Angus MacGordon, blond secretary to Dr. Raven

Episode: **The Night of the Feathered Fury**
Character(s): bald Uncle Hansi; an organ grinder

Episode: **The Night of the Gypsy Peril**
Character(s): peddler Uncle Moe

Episode: **The Night of the Tartar**
Character(s): Russian immigrant Theodore Rimsky

Episode: **The Night of the Vicious Valentine**
Character(s): excellent as the Jewish tailor

Episode: **The Night of the Brain**
Character(s): villain's #1 henchman Leeto, with an Artemus Gordon mask over Leeto's face

Episode: **The Night of the Deadly Bubble**
Character(s): an old blind beggar; drunken sailor

Episode: **The Night of the Surreal McCoy**
Character(s): gunfighter Lightnin' McCoy

Episode: **The Night of the Colonel's Ghost**
Character(s): big game hunter Ian Gellico Cooper-Featherstone; President Grant

Episode: **The Night of the Deadly Blossom**
Character(s): a stevedore (no makeup); a red-suited villain

Episode: **The Night of the Cadre**
Character(s): Kelton the traveling salesman; prison guard

Episode: **The Night of the Wolf**
Character(s): King Stefan

Episode: **The Night of the Bogus Bandits**
Character(s): southern artist Mr. Lindsay; old-timer blacksmith Mr. Fargo

Season 3
Episode: **The Night of the Bubbling Death**
Character(s): a one-eyed snake-in-the-grass; a greenhorn liquor salesman

Episode: **The Night of the Firebrand**
Character(s): trapper Bluebeard; Canadian patriot Claude Beaumont

Episode: **The Night of
the Assassin**
Character(s):
a Mexican soldier;
a priest;
fat, old Texan Halverson

Episode: **The Night
Dr. Loveless Died**
Character(s): Dr. Roman De Pe-
tritier

Episode: **The Night of the
Jack O'Diamonds**
Character(s): bandit Pancho,
complete with sombrero and han-
dlebar mustache

Episode: **The Night of
the Samurai**
Character(s): Portuguese sea
skipper Paolo Martinez

Episode: **The Night of
the Hangman**
Character(s): a jewelry salesman;
A preacher

Episode: **The Night of
Montezuma's Hordes**
Character(s): an aged desert guide;
a Swedish waiter

Episode: **The Night of
the Circus of Death**
Character(s): Southerner
Emerson P. Gentry;
old cleaning man; quick-change in
heart of the Bronx

Episode: **The Night of the Falcon**
Character(s): Spanish syndicate chief,
Felice Munez

Episode: **The Night of the
Cutthroats**
Character(s): Joe the piano player

Episode: **The Night of
the Legion of Death**
Character(s): the short-lived
Aaron Addison;
a Moroccan

Episode: **The Night of the Turncoat**
Character(s): a mail carrier; a longshoreman; a waiter

Episode: **The Night of the Iron Fist**
Character(s): the elegant Count Draja

Episode: **The Night of the Running Death**
Character(s): actor Jonathan Ashley Kingston; Italian waiter

Episode: **The Night of the Arrow**
Character(s): cavalry officer Jonathan Greeley; a drunk, scruffy jailbird; a dead Indian

Episode: **The Night of the Headless Woman**
Character(s): old sea dog

Episode: **The Night of the Vipers**
Character(s): Ned Buntline, personal friend to Wyatt Earp

Episode: **The Night of the Underground Terror**
Character(s): Englishman with a douser rod; Colonel Mosley

Episode: **The Night of the Death Masks**
Character(s): the villain Emmett Stark

Episode: **The Night of the Undead**
Character(s): conventioneer Beldon Scoville Jr.; Major Brainard of the Corps of Engineers

Episode: **The Night of the Amnesiac**
Character(s): magician Dr. Zorbi

Episode: **The Night of the Simian Terror**
Character(s): scientist Dr. Marvin Gentry of St. Louis

Episode: **The Night of the Death Maker**
Character(s): French wine expert Claude Assir Renard; President Grant

Season 4
Episode: **The Night of the Big Blackmail**
Character(s): a German cook; President Grant on kinetoscope

Episode: **The Night of the Doomsday Formula**
Character(s): briefly as Dr. Crane; not so briefly, Arab weapons dealer Mr. Ortuglo

Episode: **The Night of the Juggernaut**
Character(s): wealthy Texas gentleman Ellsworth Caldwell

Episode: **The Night of the Sedgewick Curse**
Character(s): an Englishman; a Frenchman

Episode: **The Night of the Gruesome Games**
Character(s): Dr. Raker; saddle bum; Rufus Kraus (a nasty old coot)

Episode: **The Night of the Kraken**
Character(s): a Portuguese fisherman; a workman; a Swedish repairman

Episode: **The Night of the Fugitives**
Character(s): preacher Hallelujah Harry

Episode: **The Night of the Egyptian Queen**
Character(s): Captain Hull of Her Majesty's frigate the Northumberland

Episode: **The Night of the Fire and Brimstone**
Character(s): the aged Dr. Crane; the yellow-sashed General Lee

Episode: **The Night of the Avaricious Actuary**
Character(s): Salvatore, the waiter in an exclusive epicurean club; an old gas man (effectively played by Martin's temporary replacement)

Ross Martin's unidentified temporary replacement who finished out the scene in "Actuary" when the actor broke his leg.

Episode: **The Night of the Spanish Curse**
Character(s): a young Mexican; an old Mexican

Episode: **The Night of the Pistoleros**
Character(s): General Rondell

Episode: **The Night of the Diva**
Character(s): Count Vladislav De Raja, the Duke of Korba, that is, Hungary's finest

Episode: **The Night of the Cossacks**
Character(s): briefly as a Russian priest

Episode: **The Night of the Plague**
Character(s): actor Kevin Kemball

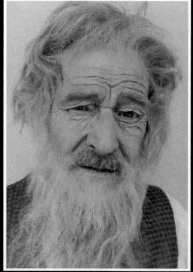

In "The Night of the Sedgewick Curse" the skills of the "West" makeup artists are evident as actor Arthur Space was not only made up as his character, but was made to age exponentially during the course of the episode.

Chapter 8
Third Season: The Calm Before the Storm

Daily Variety, *Thursday, January 19, 1967*
TV Now Spy-Shy; Once Torrid 007 Trend May Wind up Almost 000

TV's once torrid spy trend is cooling off. None of the networks have a single spy series among its pilots for next season, proof of the sentiment among network execs that the James Bond cycle has just about run its course. This is not to say all spy series are dead, but it does mean networkers – and most production companies – feel the peak of the cloak-and-dagger set has passed. Network execs contacted seemed to feel that the trend is kaput, that the few good ones still on will survive, but the saturation point has been reached. Perry Lafferty commented: "I think the (spy) trend is going downhill from the James Bond era. It's downward with rare exceptions." Lafferty said gimmick shows are also fading, that there is a trend back to reality.

In early 1967, this was the consensus of many of the network chiefs, and the statistically agreed preference of audiences. But there was a remaining exception to the fizzling Bond intrigue in "The Wild Wild West." The third season found the popular series adopting a more Western theme and shying away from the bizarre fantasy for which it had become known, as its villains shifted into becoming more political and considerably less outrageous.

A problem ensued when toward the end of the second season Bob Conrad was present during a violent argument at The Backstage Bar, the stunt crew's after-hours hangout. The altercation left one man near death and incited another crew shakeup on the set. In a second attempt by the network to let Conrad know "who's the boss," and to protect their substantial investment, CBS fired an array of regulars. Sources said a shift in personnel took place because there were crew members who were simply too close to Conrad, they socialized after hours and they "were his buddies." It was suggested that the fight incident gave the network just the excuse they needed to break up the team.

Another major change in the third season was with West's familiar nemesis, Dr. Miguelito Loveless. Michael Dunn's health had been deteriorating rapidly resulting from an ongoing bout with achondroplasia, a progressive form of dwarfism. His condition was aggravated by personal problems and his inordinate drive for success. "The more successful he became, the more driven he was to be more successful; to prove that this little guy wasn't just a little guy," Phoebe Dorin said. Dunn slowly began to lose friends in the industry, and instead of dealing with his problems, they were allowed to progress. When he returned to work on "The Wild Wild West" set for the third season, it was the first time that his personal life was allowed to interfere with his professional one. He suffered falls and in one incident injured his leg, disrupting the shooting schedule. As a result, "The Night Dr. Loveless Died," was the only third season episode to feature the devious doctor.

Aside from these changes, "The Wild Wild West" experienced a smooth third season as compared to previous seasons. Having already worked out production problems and character development issues, Robert Conrad and Ross Martin were now poised to become even more popular with the television viewing audience. Martin even received Mexico's top honor as the most popular TV actor of the year. According to Olavee Martin, Ross was also notably popular in Europe, especially with Italian, French and English audiences.

But the last part of the third season was anything but smooth, and it spilled over into the fourth season, with Bob Conrad's serious stunt accident in "The Night of the Fugitives," and the ensuing lengthy break in the shooting schedule. Slated as one of the last three episodes of the season it had to be completed a full 12 weeks later and was placed fourth in the following season. The accident abruptly ended the series' third successful year on the air.

The Night of the
Jack O'Diamonds

James West contends with a valuable stallion in this very Western "West." Although the episode has no bizarre villainy, director Irving Moore gives it a special touch reminiscent of far more grand productions.

CBS Photo

CBS #6706 Shooting Order 57
First Air Date: 10/06/67

Produced by Bruce Lansbury
Directed by Irving J. Moore
Written by Denne Bart Petiticlerc

Antonio : Ref Sanchez
Captain Fortuna: Mario Alcalde
El Sordo: Frank Silvera
Isabel: Marie Gomez
Enrique: David Renard
Chico: Rico Alaniz
Gregorio: James Almanzar
Juan: Louis Massad

Agents West and Gordon are delivering Jack O'Diamonds, a prize Arabian stallion, to President Juarez of Mexico as a gift from President Grant. They are met by Gregorio (Almanzar), an Imperialista, who is posing as Captain Fortuna, their escort to Mexico City. Later the real Fortuna (Alcalde) saves their lives by shooting a hidden assassin. When the bandit El Sordo (Silvera) steals the stallion, his lieutenant Enrique (Renard) offers to lead West to Sordo for a price. The next day West finds Enrique dying, but is able to retrieve a map to Sordo's hideout. The Imperialistas attack but after West shoots two of them, Gregorio falls back only to follow the agent, hoping he will lead him to the valuable horse. West's life is threatened at Sordo's camp but he creates a diversion and gallops away on the stallion with El Sordo in hot pursuit.

Gordon and the army are trying to follow West, but they soon lose the trail. Gordon decides that it's time to go undercover to find Sordo. Disguised as Poncho, a bandito, Gordon goes to the cantina that Sordo is known to frequent. After asking a few questions, he discovers where Sordo was headed. The real Poncho's men unexpectedly enter the cantina and recognize Gordon as an imposter. The agent escapes by throwing a wine bottle containing an explosive concoction. The room fills with smoke and Gordon slips away.

Sordo and West have a back-and-forth confrontation until the Imperialistas catch up. Gordon also appears with the help of the army and Sordo gives back the horse. After the confusion clears, one of the Imperialistas shoots and kills Sordo. As West and Gordon turn their backs, they note that he wasn't really a bad guy after all. Suddenly, Sordo springs to his feet and holds the agents at gunpoint. As he escapes, he waves at the agents and they look at each other a little ashamed for having fallen for the oldest trick in the book.

Author's Notes:
"Jack O'Diamonds" is the first episode in shooting order for the third season and is very different from what "West" used to be: No bizarre villains, no crazy devices, just a very straight, run-of-the-mill Western. Though it may have all the earmarks of a Western, it far surpasses certain black and white episodes from the first season. "Jack O'Diamonds" had the distinct advantage of being directed by Irving Moore, and had the foundation of the previous "Wests," familiar and popular characters with whom to work.

Director Moore enjoyed directing this episode because of its grandiose look. "'Jack O'Diamonds' is one of the biggest Westerns that I've ever done. I think it compares to 'How the West Was Won.' It was a marvelous show," he said. The director remembered that the role of El Sordo was originally cast with veteran actor Keenan Wynn. "On the first day of shooting I asked Keenan if he would have any trouble riding a horse. He said he'd have no trouble. When Keenan tried to get up on a horse, I turned around for just a second and heard a thud. I turned back around and Keenan was flat on his back on the ground. He got up and got back on the horse. Again, the horse threw him back onto the ground. This time the actor ended up with five broken ribs. Then he was out and his replacement was Frank Silvera."

This episode proves to be a nice change of pace for "West" although it does drag in some places... but, they can't all be gems.

The Night of the
Firebrand

President Grant sends James West to Fort Savage to meet with major Jason (Wayland). His mission (should he decide to accept it) is to help the major prevent a revolution in Canada incited by the outlaw Shawn O'Reilley (Roberts). At the fort, West read the description of O'Reilley to Major Jason. Amazingly, West notices that the major bears a striking resemblance to O'Reilley. West is apparently too late as O'Reilley explains that he is now in control of Fort Savage and is holding the real Major and his men prisoner. West holds O'Reilley at gunpoint until the lovely "Vixen" (Wood) hits the agent over the head.

Held captive with his hands tied overhead, West is left hanging from a large stake on the fort grounds with crates of dynamite situated beneath him. The dynamite is lit and Major Jason and his men watch anxiously through the prison bars. O'Reilley and his men ride away to their hidden campsite and await the explosion. West swings over and kicks open the side of some conveniently placed water barrels that douse the fuse. He uses his familiar boot knife to aid in the rest of his escape.

Popular Western performer, Pernell Roberts, of "Bonanza" fame, stars a Sean O'Reilley, an outlaw trying to incite a Canadian revolution.

CBS Photo

CBS #6702 Shooting Order 58
First Air Date: 09/15/67

Produced by Bruce Lansbury
Directed by Michael Caffey
Written by Edward J. Lakso

Sean O'Reilley: Pernell Roberts
Sheila "Vixen" O'Shaugnessy: Lana Wood
Andre Durain: Paul Lambert
Major Jason: Len Wayland
Clint Hoxie: Paul Prokop
Briscoe: Ross McCubbin
Pierre: Zack Banks

O'Reilley makes his way to Canada to meet with Andre Durain (Lambert) who will help facilitate his plans for the revolution. In a bar, two of O'Reilley's men meet up with a disguised Artemus Gordon. Acting bored and very tough, Gordon starts a bar fight. O'Reilley's men are impressed by his boisterous attitude and take him into their confidence, sharing with him their revolutionary plans.

West has managed to catch up to O'Reilley at his campsite. The agent overpowers the guards, blows up the explosives (while saving a few for his personal use) and escapes in the wagon with Vixen. O'Reilley catches up with West just as Gordon arrives disguised as Jacque Beaumont, a Canadian revolutionary. Gordon saves his partner from execution but, once again, West is held captive until Gordon slips him a device to cut himself free. He escapes again with Vixen with O'Reilley still hot on their trail. West gathers his supply of dynamite and jumps from the wagon, confronting O'Reilley and his men. Gordon heads to the next fort as West tosses a stick of dynamite at O'Reilley, stopping him in his tracks. A hand-to-hand battle ensues and the agent sends the troublesome Irishman over a cliff and to his death.

The Night of the
Assassin

United States and Mexican relations have been strained by border issues when agents West and Gordon foil an assassination attempt on Mexican President Juarez. The would-be killer is disguised as a padre and believed to be an American. He manages to elude the agents when pursued, and is later identified as notorious American gunman Halvorsen (Carter). West is able to catch up with him and persuade him to return to Texas.

En route, West and Halvorsen are fired upon by Mexican soldiers working for the ruthless Colonel "Arsenic" Barbossa (Loggia). Halvorsen is wounded and taken prisoner. Gordon disguises himself as Halvorsen's father and is allowed to visit the prisoner, but the gunslinger refuses to give any details about the assassination plot until the agents are able to get him safely to Texas. Gordon gives Halvorsen a pill that will put him to sleep believing that even Barbossa cannot torture a sleeping man.

In a pottery shop, a woman asks Gordon what Halvorsen has told him but the agent refuses to divulge anything. A fight breaks out and after what Gordon refers to as a "smashing victory," West discovers a hidden letter that tells of the midnight meeting, better known as the lynching, of Juarez' attempted assassin. The agents think it's time to help Halvorsen escape. Gordon, disguised as a priest, rides a wagon near the prison and drops West off outside the prison walls.

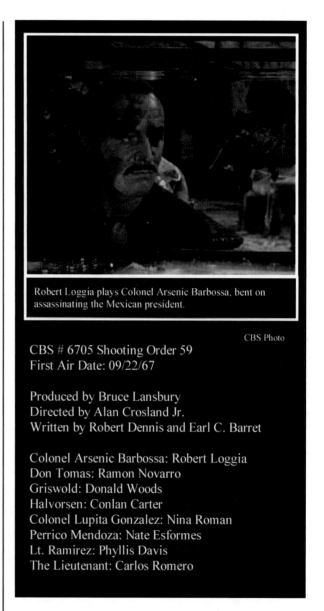

Robert Loggia plays Colonel Arsenic Barbossa, bent on assassinating the Mexican president.

CBS # 6705 Shooting Order 59
First Air Date: 09/22/67

Produced by Bruce Lansbury
Directed by Alan Crosland Jr.
Written by Robert Dennis and Earl C. Barret

Colonel Arsenic Barbossa: Robert Loggia
Don Tomas: Ramon Novarro
Griswold: Donald Woods
Halvorsen: Conlan Carter
Colonel Lupita Gonzalez: Nina Roman
Perrico Mendoza: Nate Esformes
Lt. Ramirez: Phyllis Davis
The Lieutenant: Carlos Romero

Gordon tells the guard he is there to pick up a dead prisoner.

West is captured as he attempts to help Halvorsen escape, but the agent refuses to cooperate with the ruthless colonel. West and the colonel fight, leaving Barbossa unconscious. Gordon enters and they place Halvorsen in a coffin to eliminate suspicion. The agents split up but later West finds Gordon in the same coffin that earlier contained Halvorsen.

A female bushwhacker (Roman) now has

Halvorsen and interrogates the assassin. He tells her the
he doesn't know who hired him to kill Juarez. West
appears and the woman identifies herself as being from
the Mexican Secret Service. The agents find out that
Colonel Barbossa is behind the assassination plot in
order to discredit the United States and strip Juarez of
his power. West and Barbossa battle it out, leading the
wicked colonel to an appropriately fatal end.

Author's Notes:

Silent film star Ramon Novarro appears in this
episode as Don Thomas. Novarro started in films in
1917 and was well-known for his dashing and debonair
persona. He was brutally murdered in his North Hollywood home in 1968, just one year after his "West" appearance. His final television appearance was on "The
High Chaparral."

The Night of the
Bubbling Death

The government sends agents West and Gordon
to a small section of the then Panhandle Strip of
Texas to try to recover the U.S. Constitution,
which has been stolen by crazed revolutionary Victor
Freemantle (Gould). West and Silas Grigsby
(Schallert), a curator for the U.S. Archives, go to a secret underground installation that is reportedly holding
the valuable document. After locating the document
and verifying its authenticity, Freemantle explains that
certain conditions are required before the document
will be safely returned. He demands that the United
States cease negotiations with Mexico; the U.S. is to
recognize the Panhandle Strip as a sovereign enclave
between the borders; and a ransom of $1 million in
gold must be paid. Freemantle holds Grigsby hostage
until West returns.

At the train, West and Gordon decide to ignore
the demands and retrieve the Constitution themselves.
They use Gordon's scale model of Freemantle's castle
to help devise a plan. The agents return to town,
Gordon disguised as a whiskey salesman and West hidden under the wagon. While Gordon distracts the
townspeople, West slips into the castle with his partner
soon following behind. Freemantle's accomplice, Car-

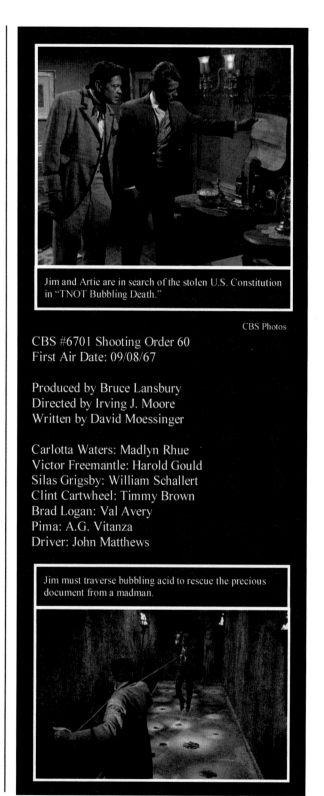

Jim and Artie are in search of the stolen U.S. Constitution
in "TNOT Bubbling Death."

CBS Photos

CBS #6701 Shooting Order 60
First Air Date: 09/08/67

Produced by Bruce Lansbury
Directed by Irving J. Moore
Written by David Moessinger

Carlotta Waters: Madlyn Rhue
Victor Freemantle: Harold Gould
Silas Grigsby: William Schallert
Clint Cartwheel: Timmy Brown
Brad Logan: Val Avery
Pima: A.G. Vitanza
Driver: John Matthews

Jim must traverse bubbling acid to rescue the precious
document from a madman.

lotta (Rhue), spots West and pretends to be on the agent's side. She tries to warn Freemantle, but Gordon stifles her by putting a handkerchief in her mouth. West gives her a pressure point pinch and she goes quietly to sleep.

As the agents inch their way toward where the Constitution is supposedly hidden, they encounter an array of obstacles, including a pool of acid specifically designed to halt such intrusions. They are finally able to retrieve the document only to discover that it is a forgery. Freemantle catches them in the act and poses a riddle to the agents. The real document is somewhere, "where his lady fair can stare at it for hours." After a brief fight, West and Gordon defeat Freemantle, who falls into the pool of acid. The agents begin their search for the document using Freemantle's final clue as a guide. They work their way to Carlotta's room and discover the Constitution hidden behind her vanity mirror.

Back at the train, Grigsby is revealed as the real brains behind the crime when he appears with Carlotta and demands the precious document. Grigsby doesn't stand a chance on the agent's turf and they quickly get the better of him with their vast selection of gadgets. The Constitution is safely returned to Washington.

Author's Notes:

"Bubbling Death" was chosen as the third season opener and for good reason. This is an action-packed, thoroughly entertaining story. Nearly every device that West and Gordon are famous for is used in this episode, including a ring that cuts glass, a powder that burns through floors and the famous sleeve gun that shoots an anchor into a wall and traverses West over the pool of bubbling acid. This is definitely an interesting and suspenseful episode with a surprising twist in the end as actor William Schallert reveals that he is behind the entire devious scheme. We'll be seeing him again in later episodes as a guest star and as Frank Harper, one of the short-term replacements for the recovering Ross Martin.

We also see some fun disguises for Artie as the one-eyed saddle bum and the timid whiskey salesman. This is another one of my personal favorites done in a more traditional Western style.

The Night of the
Cutthroats

Bradford Dillman stars as ex-con Trayne who leads an army of "Cutthroats" trying to take over a town.

CBS #6712 Shooting Order 61   CBS Photo
First Air Date: 11/17/67

Produced by Bruce Lansbury
Directed by Alan Crosland Jr.
Written by Edward H. Lasko

Sheriff Koster: Jackie Coogan
Mike Trayne: Bradford Dillman
Sally Yarnell: Beverly Garland
John Cassidy: Walter Burke
Jeremiah: Shug Fisher
Hogan: Eddie Quillan
Bartender: Harry Swoger
Clerk: Lou Straley
Man: Quintin Sondergaard
Waiting Lady: Sharon Cintron

While traveling by stage with dapper ex-con Mike Trayne (Dillman), secret agent James T. West helps him fight off four would-be robbers. Arriving in New Athens, West finds all of the townspeople hastily departing. The cowardly Sheriff

Koster (Coogan) explains that they all fear an army of cutthroats camped outside of town. West contacts his fellow agent Artemus Gordon at Sally Yarnell's (Garland) saloon. Gordon is disguised as Joe the piano player, where he is futilely investigating the disappearing of another agent named Mason.

West has an altercation with two of Trayne's men. His ensuing investigation leads him to a ranch where he is attacked by two more men. In town, Mayor Cassidy (Burke) reveals that Trayne is seeking revenge on the town for having been imprisoned for murdering a man with his cane. He plans on destroying the town with his cutthroat army. It is revealed that agent Mason was murdered when he learned of the plan. Now West and Gordon must mount a defense for the defenseless townspeople.

West immediately tries to send a telegraph to Fort Savage and request reinforcements, but the lines have been cut. As more people leave town, Sally wants to join them. Gordon takes Sally with him as he rides to the fort to get help. Gordon is bushwhacked along the way and discovers that Sally is part of the plan. Gordon is held hostage but manages to escape and return to town. Cassidy sneaks off to the bank and hides all the money in a booby-trapped wall safe.

When Trayne's men arrive, the battle begins. Cassidy and Trayne meet and it turns out that Cassidy is involved in the heist. With the entire town, including the bank, doomed to be incinerated, no one would suspect that the bank had been robbed. But Trayne brutally beats Cassidy with his cane, a signature behavior of the wicked criminal, and leaves him for dead. As Trayne goes to the mirror to retrieve the money, he suspects something isn't quite right, and he carefully triggers the booby trap. He realizes that Sally failed to warn him of the trap and she must also want him dead. West tries to stop Trayne before he gets away, and the murderer falls over the balcony and is killed.

The tag finds West and Gordon at the train discussing the case. West tells Gordon that he had it figured out that Sally was involved because anyone who would hire Artie as a piano player *must* have a mean streak in them.

Author's Notes:

"Cutthroats" is a mediocre episode with a sluggish storyline. Veteran actor Jackie Coogan, appearing as the town sheriff, lacks excitement and depth. Bradford Dillman is good as the matter-of-fact Trayne, but is a dull villain by comparison. Trayne seems like

he would be just small potatoes for our resourceful and versatile agents. The ladies will undoubtedly enjoy watching Ross Martin as he dons a dapper mustache to become the dashing piano player, Joe.

The Night of the
Hangman

Harry Dean Stanton (right) plays Brand, a man unjustly accused of murder in "The Night of the Hangman."

CBS Photo

CBS #6708 Shooting Order 62
First Air Date: 10/20/67

Produced by Bruce Lansbury
Directed by James B. Clark
Written by Peter G. Robinson and Ron Silver

Lucius Brand: Harry Dean Stanton
Judge Blake: Paul Fix
Mrs. Peacock: Jesslyn Fax
Franklin Poore: Martin Brooks
Abigail Moss: Anna Capri
Eugenia Rawlins: Sarah Marshall
Roger Creed: Charles Lane
Mrs. Brand: Carolan Daniels
Amos Rawlins: John Pickard
Sheriff Jonas Bolt: Gregg Palmer

Agents West and Gordon stop off for a brief stay in a Kansas town that is celebrating the success of the Rolling Ranch and the agents decide to join in on the fun. Suddenly, rich Kansas rancher Amos Rawlins (Pickard) is shot. When Abigail Moss (Capri) points out the fleeing killer, the agents give chase. They apprehend the dazed Lucius Brand (Stanton) as he sits in his apartment holding a gun.

At the trial, Brand insists that he did not fire the weapon, but testimony from Abigail, West and banker Roger Creed (Lane) results in a hanging verdict. Later, in his cell, the convicted man tells West and Gordon about being awakened the day of the murder by a nightmare of a train bearing down on him. In Brand's apartment, the agents find a tube above the bed connected to a train whistle sound effects device. The apartment suddenly bursts into flames and the agents escape.

West goes to Judge Blake (Fix) to explain the strange occurrence while Gordon goes back to the train to examine a picture plate of the proceedings where Rawlins was shot. The photograph shows that a balloon was released one second after the shot was fired. This signaled the man in the attic to get Brand prepared to take the blame.

Gordon, disguised as a preacher, searches for Abigail, but learns that she is leaving town on the next stage. West is led to the Ace Novelty Company and finds himself trapped in a room quickly filling with poisonous gas. He escapes with the usual West style and a handy device. Gordon catches up with the stage now disguised as a German jeweler. He convinces Abigail that the jewel she is wearing is a fake and she turns and heads back into town.

Gordon informs West via carrier pigeon that Abigail will be returning. West sees her and follows her to a building, but is captured. Gordon visits the sheriff and shows him the picture of a man on horseback who was directly in Brand's line of fire. This is proof positive that, from that angle, Brand could not have shot Rawlins. Gordon is held by the sheriff, who is in on the scheme. Both agents escape and find that Mrs. Rawlings (Marshall), motivated by greed, murdered her husband with the help of the bank manager.

Later at the train, Gordon sees West holding a picture of a woman named Jennifer Colt. Gordon is very interested and asks how to get a hold of her. West tells him that he can see her the first Sunday of every month at the State Prison for Women: Jennifer Colt's alias is Abigail Moss. Gordon looks at West and asks him, "Why do you have to spoil *everything*?"

The Night of the
Montezuma's Hordes

Ray Walston is our *favorite* duplicitous criminal in "TNOT Montezuma's Hordes."

CBS Photo

CBS #6709 Shooting Order 63
First Air Date: 10/27/67

Produced by Bruce Lansbury
Directed by Irving J. Moore
Written by Max Ehrlich

Professor Henry Johnson: Ray Walston
Zack Slade: Jack Elam
Colonel Pedro Sanchez: Edmund Hashim
Jake: Roland La Starza
Indian Guide: Hal Jon Norman
Dr. John Mallory: Roy Monsell
Aztec Chief: Eddie Little Sky
Sun Goddess: Carla Borelli
Handmaiden: Ludmila Alixanova

Secret agent James T. West goes to a museum to discuss plans for an upcoming expedition to seek the lost treasure of Montezuma. There he meets Henry Johnson (Walston) pretending to be noted archaeologist Dr. John Mallory (Monsell). West is nearly crushed by a mummy case and Zack Slade (Elam) blames Johnson for bungling the murder.

West meets Colonel Pedro Sanchez (Hashim), who is assigned to escort the expedition to the treasure site. Gordon, disguised as a desert rat, is hired as a digger. They go in search of the treasure and find themselves among the Aztecs. They find their way to an Aztec temple and are suddenly surrounded by warriors. One of Slade's men gets nervous and shoots two of the warriors. This angers the Aztec Chief and he tells Colonel Sanchez that in retaliation they are to give up the lives of two of his men. Everyone is thrown into a cell and forced to choose among themselves which two will die. Slade and his men select West and Gordon as the sacrificial lambs, and they call to the guards to take them away.

The agents escape from their impending doom and make their way through a secret passageway that leads to the opening of the Aztec's sacred dragon. As they appear through its fiery mouth, the Aztec's all bow in awe. Gordon replies, "Jim, they think we're gods. I guess no one has ever lived through Montezuma's Revenge before." West walks over and kisses the Sun Goddess (Borelli) and the Aztecs instantly trust the two agents.

Slade and his men escape from their cell and locate the treasure. West stops Slade from stealing the treasure and West, Gordon and Sanchez leave the Aztec nation with a gift from the grateful people: a golden mask.

At the train, West and Gordon propose a toast to the Sun Goddess and her vision miraculously appears on the golden mask: West smiles.

The Night of the
Amnesiac

West is carrying by stage the state's only supply of a crucial smallpox vaccine. A gang of men led by Silas Crotty (Hagen) attack the stage and Crotty steals the serum. West tries to retrieve the precious liquid but is shot in the head and left for dead.

West's disappearance is of growing concern until Crotty's brother, Furman (Asner), a prisoner serving time at Leavenworth, tries to bargain for a pardon in exchange for the vaccine.

Ed Asner is Crotty doing time in Leavenworth prison and holding a vital vaccine hostage in "TNOT Amnesiac."

CBS Photo

CBS #6721 Shooting Order 64
First Air Date: 02/09/67

Produced by Bruce Lansbury
Directed by Lawrence Dobkin
Written by Leigh Chapman and Robert Bloomfield

Furman Crotty: Ed Asner
Silas Crotty: Kevin Hagen
Claude Peepers: Gil Lamb
Cloris Colton: Sharon Farrell
Colonel Petrie: George Petrie
Rusty: John Kellogg
The Boy: Johnny Jensen
The Warden: Jim Nolan
Bartender: Jack Rigney
Brute: Don Howarth
Irish: Jerry Laveroni
Masseur: Sebastian Tom

West awakens in a field and realizes that he has lost his memory and his identity. He wanders into the town of Cactus Flowers, where he instinctually defends the honor of Cloris Colton (Farrell), a local dancehall girl. After the excitement, the agent passes out and later awakens with Cloris, who has taken him to her home.

Furman Crotty is released from prison and

reneges on his promise to return the serum. He demands to be paid $1 million in gold or promises to destroy the vital liquid. Crotty also knows that West is in town. The agent still has not regained his memory.

Artemus Gordon is on Crotty's trail and is led to the Cactus Flowers. He notices West's gun belt in a pawn shop and traces it to his partner. Crotty's men get West and challenge him to a gunfight. West doesn't know why anyone would want to kill him. Cloris and West escape and hide out in a theater. Gordon sees West and goes after him, but West doesn't recognize him either and assumes that he, too, is trying to kill him. Crotty's men appear soon after and they sneak up behind Gordon. When West witnesses his partner in deep trouble, his memory miraculously comes flooding back.

The agents are captured and placed on a wagon scale with explosives underneath. If they move off the scale they will be blown to bits. They compensate their weight with barrels that they carefully roll onto the scale. Just as they go after Crotty, Cloris develops smallpox. Gordon must tend to her while West pursues the criminal. West defeats Crotty and his gang and is able to get the vaccine safely to Cloris to save her life and the lives of many others.

Back at the train, West and Gordon are preparing to go out on the town just when a telegraph comes through requesting that they attend a recital given by the senator's wife, with no excuses except for sickness. West plays up, "Who am I? Who are you?" Gordon cries out, "You've lost your memory. I prescribe dinner and a little medicinal dancing."

Author's Notes:

Ed Asner has a fair turn as Furman Crotty. Later known as Lou Grant from the popular "Mary Tyler Moore Show," Asner has appeared in more than 250 roles in his long career. He continues to perform regularly, doing voiceovers as well as appearing in front of the camera. And, if anyone's counting, Asner has won seven Emmys out of 16 nominations and won five Golden Globes out of 11 nominations over his long and apparently successful career.

The Night
Dr. Loveless Died

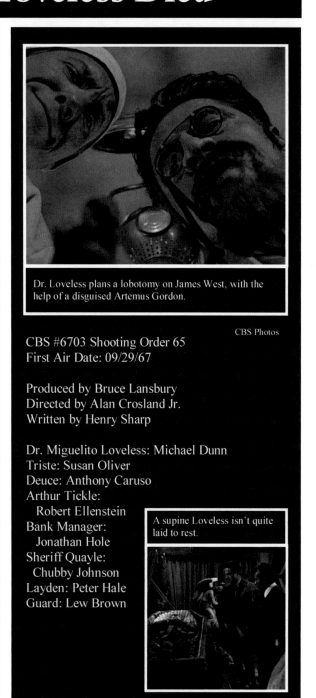

Dr. Loveless plans a lobotomy on James West, with the help of a disguised Artemus Gordon.

CBS Photos

CBS #6703 Shooting Order 65
First Air Date: 09/29/67

Produced by Bruce Lansbury
Directed by Alan Crosland Jr.
Written by Henry Sharp

Dr. Miguelito Loveless: Michael Dunn
Triste: Susan Oliver
Deuce: Anthony Caruso
Arthur Tickle:
　Robert Ellenstein
Bank Manager:
　Jonathan Hole
Sheriff Quayle:
　Chubby Johnson
Layden: Peter Hale
Guard: Lew Brown

A supine Loveless isn't quite laid to rest.

West and Gordon go to the mortuary in the town of Hayes City in order to identify the corpse of their old nemesis, Dr. Miguelito Loveless (Dunn). Gordon does the *mirror test* and the agents are relatively satisfied that it is not a hoax. A woman named Triste (Oliver) enters as a mourner and surreptitiously slips a key from the wrist of the deceased doctor. A group of men enter and are looking for the key. West takes the key from Triste and a shooting spree begins. Triste escapes and West is left with the key, which is to a safety deposit box. The agents go to the bank listed on the key and find instructions to contact an attorney named Arthur Tickle (Ellenstein).

While West seeks out Tickle, Triste visits the train and tries to kill Gordon. Instead, he stops her and finds out what she knows about the key. West arrives at the house and finds Tickle and Loveless' supposed next of kin, a Swiss neurologist, Dr. Liebknict, who bears an eerie resemblance to his late nephew. The same men who appeared at the mortuary are at the house demanding money that Dr. Loveless owed them before his death. West and Leibknict escape and head to the doctor's sanatorium. Once West is there, Leibknict reveals that he is really Dr. Loveless, whose death was a ruse to lure the agents into his evil clutches.

Triste takes Gordon to the supposed hideout, but she gets his gun, shoots him and leaves. He reveals that he was wearing a bullet-proof vest and is able to follow her.

West is now at the mercy of the mad doctor, who intends to put the agent permanently out of commission with a lobotomy. Gordon finds the real hideout and disguises himself as one of the visiting doctors who are expected to arrive to observe the operation. Just as Loveless is about to operate, Gordon interferes and helps his colleague escape. They chase Loveless into his office, but he sneaks away through a secret panel in the wall. The room suddenly goes up in smoke and, once again, Loveless has escaped.

A package arrives for the agents as they relax at the train. When they open it a loud whistle sounds and they quickly take cover. It turns out to be a relatively harmless practical joke from the agents' favorite nemesis, the very much alive Dr. Loveless.

Author's Notes:

This is the only third season Loveless episode because of Michael Dunn's escalating personal and health problems. This is a reasonably interesting episode, and is far better than the upcoming final Loveless show,

"The Night of Miguelito's Revenge." The good doctor does lose some of his childlike charm in this double role as both Miguelito and Dr. Liebknicht. Perhaps his edge has gotten just a little sharper because of Dunn's health issues inevitably seeping into his performance.

The Night of the
Samurai

Paul Stevens (left) as Gideon Falconer faces off against his old friend James West in "TNOT Samurai."

CBS #6707 Shooting Order 66
First Air Date: 10/13/67

CBS Photo

Produced by Bruce Lansbury
Directed by Gunnar Hellstrom
Written by Shimon Wincelberg

Gideon Falconer: Paul Stevens
Hannibal Egloff: Thayer David
Reiko O'Hara: Irene Tsu
Baron Saigo: Khigh Dhiegh
Clive Finsbury: John Hubbard
Prince Shinosuke: Jerry Fujikawa
Madame Moustache: Jane Betts
Japanese Maiden: Helen Funai
Soapy: Anders Andelius

Agents West and Gordon attend a dinner in San Francisco celebrating the return of a historical weapon, the Sword of Kuniyoshi, from the United States to Japan. They discover all the guests have been drugged and they lose a fight to keep the sword from being stolen. The missing sword means shame to America in the eyes of Japan. Japan's Prince Shinosuke (Fujikawa), through is interpreter, Baron Saigo (Dhiegh), avows that his hari-kari would be inevitable if the sword is not recovered.

West's investigation leads him to an old friend, fencing master Gideon Falconer (Stevens), where West spies the sword and gives chase. The agent meets a mysterious man named Hannibal (David) who says he can put West in contact with the sword thief through a man called the Dutchman.

Gordon disguises himself as a Portuguese sea captain and is contacted by Saigo, who becomes a suspect when he offers the incognito agent $25,000 if he can have the weapon for just 15 minutes. He tells him it is to be used in a ritual. West meets the Dutchman and strikes a deal for a money exchange, but a double-cross is pulled and he loses the case of money and doesn't get the sword. A glowing substance has been placed on the case making it easy to follow. The man leads West back to Hannibal, who had been masquerading as the Dutchman. Before the agents are able to discover the true identity of the Dutchman, Hannibal is killed by a knife and the sword is gone.

West returns to the martial arts academy and meets his friend, Gideon, who turns out to be the real Dutchman. West and Gideon face off in a duel with swords with West triumphant and the Sword of Kuniyoshi is safely returned to the Prince.

At the train, the Prince and Saigo reveal why the sword is so valuable. It contains precious jewels hidden within its shaft. Saigo wanted the sword for 15 minutes just to retrieve the jewels and keep them for himself. He will inevitably face punishment in his homeland and is promptly arrested.

The Night of the
Arrow

James West protects Aimee (Jeannine Riley) against hostile Indians in "TNOT Arrow."

CBS Photo

CBS #6716 Shooting Order 67
First Air Date: 12/29/67

Produced by Bruce Lansbury
Directed by Alex Nicol
Written by Leigh Chapman

General Titus Baldwin: Robert J. Wilke
Colonel Theodore M. Rath: Frank Marth
Aimee Baldwin: Jeannine Riley
Oconee: Robert Phillips
Sergeant: Logan Field
Major Lock: Paul Sorensen
President Grant: Roy Engel

Several hostile Indians sneak into the Fort commanded by General Titus Baldwin (Wilke) just as he expresses his dislike for Indians to secret agent James West. West helps Baldwin fight off the interlopers.

Later, President Grant (Engel) pays a surprise visit to the agent's railroad car and expresses his fear that Baldwin, who has gained a morbid popularity through his bloody massacres of Indians, may run for president. West and his fellow agent, Artemus Gordon, tell Grant that they suspect the Indian attack on the fort was staged by Baldwin in a deliberate attempt to make it appear the Indians were breaking a peace treaty. Massacring the Indians in retaliation for this attack would give Baldwin a boost toward his candidacy.

Gordon goes undercover as a cavalry officer and finds Indian clothing in Colonel Rath's (Marth) office. Meanwhile, West arranges a meeting with Strong Bear, the head Indian chief, at an abandoned mine. When he arrives, he finds the chief murdered with the blame for the killing placed squarely on the agent.

During Strong Bear's funeral at the sacred burial ground the Indian liaison, Oconee (Phillips), tries to convince the other chiefs that West is obviously to blame for Strong Bear's death and that all the Indian nations should join together and revolt against their common adversaries. As usual, Gordon appears in disguise, this time as Strong Bear himself, rising from the dead and telling his fellow chiefs to return to their tepees and live in peace. The chiefs are frightened by the apparition and leave as commanded. Oconee knows that it is Gordon in disguise but is unable to convince the superstitious Indians of the ruse.

A frustrated Oconee battles West and is killed. Colonel Rath is arrested for being responsible for inciting an Indian uprising, along with Aimee Baldwin (Riley), the General's daughter, who was motivated by wanting to see her daddy in the White House. General Baldwin had no idea of the deception but, disappointed by his daughter's involvement in such a devious scheme, chooses to retire and spend more time with his family.

Author's Notes:

An interesting anecdote comes from actor Bob Phillips, who co-stars as the wild Indian liaison Oconee in this very, very Western tale of cowboys and Indians. He remembered that the script called for him to speak with an authentic Sioux dialect. "During the scene where I speak to the chiefs, I just talked gibberish. Director Alex Nicol asked me where I learned to speak Sioux. I told him it was just double-talk. When it came time to loop some of my lines, Bruce (Lansbury) wanted me to dub over my speech with authentic Sioux. I did, and we ended up with two versions; but Bruce wasn't happy with how the real Sioux sounded and we decided to keep my original with the double-talk. Bruce said that the authentic Sioux dialect didn't sound real."

The Night of the
Circus of Death

Circus performers and petticoats come into play in an elaborate counterfeiting scheme in "Circus of Death."

CBS Photo

CBS #6710 Shooting Order 68
First Air Date: 11/03/67

Produced by Bruce Lansbury
Directed by Irving J. Moore
Written by Arthur Weingarten

Abner Lennox: Philip Bruns
Mary Lennox: Joan Huntington
Erika: Arlene Martel
Bert Farnsworth: Paul Comi
Doc Keyno: Arthur Malet
Mrs. Moore: Florence Sundstrom
Colonel Housley: Dort Clark
Harry Holmes: Morgan Farley
Priscilla Goodbody: Judi Sherven
Lola: Barbara Hemmingway

Agent West drives off a man with a flame-thrower who is trying to steal a valise filled with counterfeit money. The man leaves circus performer Bronzini dead. Upon investigation, West learns from director of the Denver Mint Abner Lennox (Bruns) that there has been a recent flood of near-perfect bogus money circulating. He says that only engraver Harry Holmes (Farley) could produce such perfect plates, the problem being that Holmes is dead.

West visits the circus and learns that the late Bronzini occasionally presented petticoats to female acquaintances. Simultaneously, fellow agent Gordon hears that Mrs. Moore (Sundstrom), proprietor of Moore's Emporium, had forwarded the phony money to Bronzini, hiding it in the lingerie he ordered. Bronzini was the bill passer and Mrs. Moore apparently had him killed for bungling his duties.

It is now obvious that the traveling circus is used to distribute the bogus bills. Gordon returns to the Mint and finds the assistant to the Mint director is helping Mrs. Lennox (Huntington) steal the paper and the ink, which is then taken to her father, the very much alive Harry Holmes, to make the plates. All this is unbeknownst to Abner Lennox (Bruns). West and Gordon unravel the scheme and close up the counterfeiting shop.

Later at the train, the agents are preparing to entertain two young ladies with a night on the town. Unfortunately, they realize that the only money they have is the Harry Holmes money and they cannot go out to eat.

Author's Notes:

The term *hot dog*, as mentioned by West while he eats at the circus, actually wasn't commonly used until the early 1920s.

The Night of the
Falcon

After helping to vacate the town of Tonka Flats, agents West and Gordon witness its total destruction by a single cannon shell. A man calling himself The Falcon, then threatens to obliterate all of Denver unless the U.S. government pays him $1 million. En route to negotiate with The Falcon are a syndicate of leaders from Turkey, Spain, Prussia and England.

Agent Gordon is threatened by the whip-wielding Spaniard Munez (Ruskin), who believes he knows the weapon's secret. West disarms Munez, who is quickly killed by an explosive meant for the agents. West and Gordon find an invitation from The Falcon on Munez' body, so Gordon disguises himself as the Span-

A huge and deadly falcon cannon threatens Denver in "The Night of the Falcon."

CBS #6711   Shooting Order 69   CBS Photo
First Air Date: 11/10/67

Produced by Bruce Lansbury
Directed by Marvin Chomsky
Written by Robert E. Kent

Dr. Humphries: Robert Duvall
Lana Benson: Lisa Gaye
Alex Heindorf : Kurt Kreuger
Clive Marchmount : John Alderson
Felice Munez: Joseph Ruskin
Colonel James Richmond: Douglas Henderson
General Lassiter: Edward Knight
Silvio Balya: George Keymas
Felton: Gene Tyburn

iard and goes to attend the meeting while West attempts to crack the stronghold where the cannon is hidden.

The invitation says to go to see Dr. Horace Humphries (Duvall) and request a cold remedy. When Gordon locates the doctor he is drugged and later awakens in the room with the other foreign powers. West followed Gordon to the underground hideout and awaits a signal from Gordon to find the super-destructive Falcon cannon. The powers are all bidding for the powerful weapon. After Gordon discovers where the cannon is hidden, he signals West, who infiltrates the location and destroys the cannon. The shell intended for Denver is set off course and the city is saved.

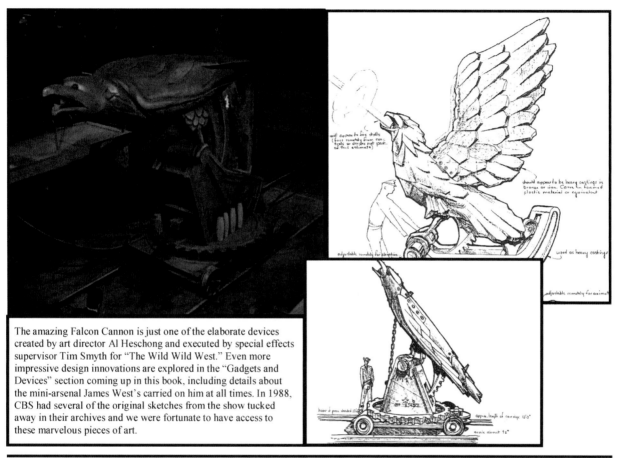

The amazing Falcon Cannon is just one of the elaborate devices created by art director Al Heschong and executed by special effects supervisor Tim Smyth for "The Wild Wild West." Even more impressive design innovations are explored in the "Gadgets and Devices" section coming up in this book, including details about the mini-arsenal James West's carried on him at all times. In 1988, CBS had several of the original sketches from the show tucked away in their archives and we were fortunate to have access to these marvelous pieces of art.

Author's Notes:

"Falcon" was director Marvin Chomsky's first attempt at an adventure show. Chomsky's prior experience was that of an art director and then director of the 1960s series "Maya," starring Jay North. Chomsky's break came when another director for "Falcon" became ill and producer Bruce Lansbury put Chomsky in his place. CBS was very pleased at Chomsky's direction and he was kept on as a regular director.

Chomsky felt that the show went smoothly, despite the numerous late nights. "We worked very hard and there were late nights so often that I was known as Captain Midnight." He remembered the effect for blowing up the town in the opening scene. "We took the lagoon ('Gilligan's') at the back lot of CBS, drained it and put a camera at a low angle to a backdrop of the town. We used an explosive, filmed the explosion, and then shot a high angle of the lagoon painted black filled with prima cord. After the black smoke cleared, a big hole appeared in the ground as if the town blew up."

Fans will notice the excellent performance by actor Robert Duvall. Duvall went on to have an exceptional film career having appeared in such notable movies as "Apocalypse Now," "The Godfather," "The Apostle" and "Tender Mercies."

If you watch closely during the scene where the real Munez is killed in the explosion, West and Gordon are talking about the situation and Bob Conrad is trying hard not to laugh, while Martin manages to keep a straight face. Whatever the joke was, it must've been good. The Falcon cannon itself was the biggest prop ever constructed for the "West." Overall, this makes for a fun episode with the only truly bizarre device of the entire third season.

During the production of "Falcon," on September 10, 1967, Ross Martin married fashion model Olavee Parsons.

The Night of the
Legion of Death

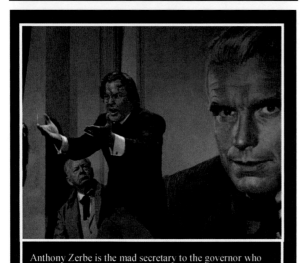

Anthony Zerbe is the mad secretary to the governor who promotes dictatorial practices in "TNOT Legion of Death."

CBS Photo

CBS #6704 Shooting Order 70
First Air Date: 11/24/67

Produced by Bruce Lansbury
Directed by Alex Nicol
Written by Robert C. Dennis and Earl Barret

Zeke Montgomery: Anthony Zerbe
Governor Brubaker: Kent Smith
Captain Dansby: Donnelly Rhodes
Catherine Kittridge: Karen Jensen
Henriette Fauer: Tioan Matchinga
Prosecutor: Walter Brooke
Judge: Alex Gerry
Reeves: James Nusser
Warden: Eli Behar
Dan Kittridge: Robert Terry

Posing as a man named Addison, secret agent Artemus Gordon is about to be hanged for investigating the dictatorial activities of Territorial Governor Brubaker (Smith). He is suddenly *shot* (with an immobilizing drug) by fellow agent James West. West subdues several members of Brubaker's pursuing *Black Legion* and eludes others by slipping into a secret tunnel. Then West heads to the morgue where he hides until Addison/Gordon's *body* arrives. He injects Gordon with a serum to counteract the drug.

West is later arrested by Brubaker for Addison/Gordon's murder. West is surprisingly awarded a "not guilty" verdict at trial, but soon finds himself, along with a completely recovered Gordon, in an explosives-filled tunnel. It is revealed that Zeke Montgomery (Zerbe), Brubaker's secretary, is apparently responsible for their dilemma and the two agents deduce that he is to blame for the region's dictatorial governmental practices.

It is discovered that Montgomery is behind the *Legion* and that Brubaker is merely a puppet. Should the governor become President of the United States then Montgomery will run the nation. West and Gordon arrest the governor and, at a later rally for President, the governor doesn't show. Montgomery tries to lead the rally, but no one will listen to him and the crowd disburses. Montgomery is a defeated man without the people's support. A new governor is elected and the Legion is disbanded.

Author's Notes:
"Legion of Death" takes a serious look at power-crazed men who manipulate others to gain control. The only problem is that writers Robert C. Dennis and Earl Barret take a relatively lighthearted approach with the script. West and Gordon act as if they're having a grand old time with their jobs. I felt that the West character is very cutesy, and a real departure from the traditional James West we know and love. Not to say that this is not a good story, just, different.

The Night of the
Running Death

As agent James West attempts to meet with Mr. Markham (Rizzan), he hears a strange voice coming from Markham's hotel room. He breaks down the door and is attacked by a masked assailant with powerful hands. The attacker flees, leaving Markham dying on his hotel room floor. With his final breath, Markham utters two words to West: Enzo and Silver.

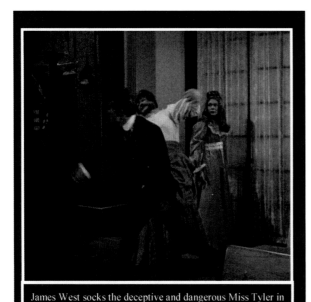

James West socks the deceptive and dangerous Miss Tyler in "The Night of the Running Death."

CBS #6715 Shooting Order 71   CBS Photo
First Air Date: 12/15/67

Produced by Bruce Lansbury
Directed by Gunnar Hellstrom
Written by Edward J. Lakso

Christopher Kohner: Jason Evers
Gerta: Karen Arthur
Enzo/Miss Tyler: T.C. Jones
Dierdre: Maggie Thrett
Alice: Laurie Burton
Joan : Britt Nilsson
Colonel Dieboldt : Oscar Beregi Jr.
Pete: Dub Taylor
Sloan: Ken Swofford
Governor Ireland: John Pickard
Ed Bardhoom: Jerry Laveroni
Markham: Don Rizzan
Silva: Sherry Mitchell

A wagon train headed by casino operator Christopher Kohner (Evers) is traveling through Apache country to Denver. Transporting a group of entertainers, the troupe has welcomed Artemus Gordon, who is posing as Shakespearean actor Jonathan Ashley Kingston. West meets up with the group as he serves as rescuer from an Apache attack. Gordon has learned that a hired killer called Enzo (Jones) and his girlfriend, Topaz, are traveling with the troupe under assumed names. The agents are puzzled as to the target of such a notorious killer. The first girl to die is Joan, who stumbles from behind a wagon after being knifed in the back. The very helpful and powerfully built Miss Tyler (also Jones) offers to help with the burial. Dancer Gerta (Arthur) tries to flirt with West, but a jealous Kohner interrupts. He leaves the huge weightlifter El Bardhoom (Laveroni) and West to fight it out. West prevails.

During his watch, Artemus describes a strange voice he heard coming from one of the wagons. West believes it is the voice of Markham's masked slayer. Dierdre asks to meet West at midnight by the river but she, too, is killed by an unseen assailant. Again, Miss Tyler accommodates and prepares the girl for burial.

The wagon train arrives in Denver and Miss Tyler leaves the group. Still baffled about he clue "silver," West meets a man in a bar wearing the hat that belonged to Smith, one of the travelers. After a fight, the man reveals that he found Smith's body and that he had been brutally strangled — Enzo's signature. The agents are concerned for the governor's life, believing that the prey must be very important for anyone to import such an expert assassin. West goes to the governor and tells him to stay in hiding because of a possible attempt on his life.

At the governor's mansion, West meets Colonel Dieboldt (Beregi) who is assigned to take his country's Princess Silva (Mitchell) back to her homeland. The agent realizes the connection. West asks where the princess is and Dieboldt explains that she has been attending Miss Gentry's Private School in Denver, and is now ready to graduate and rule her country. West figures out that it is the princess who is in danger and he rushes to the school. There he is greeted by Miss Tyler, who reveals her/himself as Enzo, the killer. West defeats Enzo in a fierce battle and takes the princess to safety.

While at the governor's party, Gordon, undercover as an old Mexican waiter, realizes that Dierdre is still alive after an order of her favorite dessert, an unusual cherries jubilee with molasses concoction, is being brought to her room. Gordon follows Dierdre to the school and intervenes when she holds the escaping West and princess at gunpoint. It is discovered that Dierdre was Topaz after all.

Back at the train, Gordon is anxious to try the cherries jubilee concoction with unpleasant results. Definitely not as good as it sounds.

Author's Notes:

"Running Death" is a classic *whodunnit* a la wagon train. The story holds your attention and has an interesting twist ending, with Miss Tyler as the murderous Enzo. Stuntman Red West recalled a "Running Death" stunt that did not go as smoothly as planned. In the scene where West gets information from a drifter, he jogs his memory using a classic West persuasion technique — by throwing him into a piano. "It was a mistake because the piano was a breakaway prop that didn't breakaway. The only thing that was breakaway was my head. I was knocked unconscious and split my head wide open. No one knew and the scene continued until Ross looked down and started to panic. He yelled, 'Cut! Cut! Red is hurt! Stop shooting!'"

In the tag of this episode, when Gordon is trying the cherries jubilee, they had a difficult time getting the brandy to light. Wanting to go on without it, first assistant director Mike Moder said they didn't have time. But Martin, always looking for true authenticity, insisted and the crew waited for 15 minutes while the prop man ran to the liquor store to get anything that would make it work.

There is a strange second tag after the cherries jubilee, showing the two agents in a *friendly* game of poker. West received a deck of cards from a card shark on the wagon train and shows a definite advantage over his partner as his chips are piled significantly higher.

The Night of the
Turncoat

A series of strange events occur aimed to discredit Agent James West. Without proper investigation, Colonel Richmond (Henderson) discharges the agent from the Secret Service. Pretending to drink heavily as a result of his discharge, West follows Crystal (Dusay), who claimed that he beat her after breaking off their engagement. A Chinese girl in a tattoo parlor shoots West with a dart, knocking the former agent unconscious.

West awakens to find he is in the residence of a man named Elisha Calamander (McGiver), who explains that his profession is stealing priceless art objects for high-paying clientele. He admits that he had plotted West's dishonorable discharge hoping a $50,000 offer

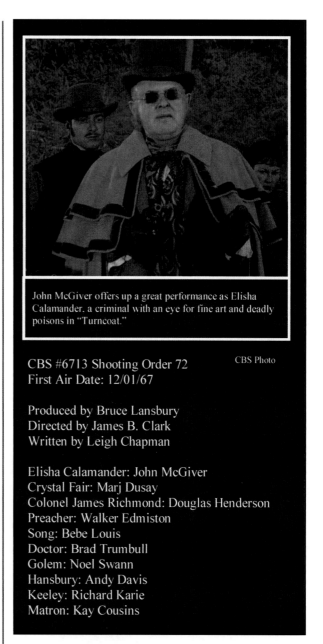

John McGiver offers up a great performance as Elisha Calamander, a criminal with an eye for fine art and deadly poisons in "Turncoat."

CBS #6713 Shooting Order 72   CBS Photo
First Air Date: 12/01/67

Produced by Bruce Lansbury
Directed by James B. Clark
Written by Leigh Chapman

Elisha Calamander: John McGiver
Crystal Fair: Marj Dusay
Colonel James Richmond: Douglas Henderson
Preacher: Walker Edmiston
Song: Bebe Louis
Doctor: Brad Trumbull
Golem: Noel Swann
Hansbury: Andy Davis
Keeley: Richard Karie
Matron: Kay Cousins

for him to join him for an assignment would be enticing to the desperate West. West feigns accepting the offer and celebrates his new job by taking Crystal out to dinner. West gets her drunk and she gives him enough hints for him to figure out exactly what his mysterious assignment will be. As she talks, West leaves symbols written on the menu. When they leave, Gordon, dressed as a waiter, picks up the menu, but one of Calamander's men takes it away. Fortunately, Gordon put a piece of carbon paper underneath and gets the information anyway.

Calamander questions West about the symbols believing it is a code to the agent's former partner. But Crystal claims that it was merely a game that she had taught West over dinner.

Gordon breaks the code and finds out that Calamander wants to use West for his physical prowess. He also learns that the ring that Crystal threw at Jim was actually a priceless gem and that a vial of deadly calcium is going to be stolen. The substance is highly unstable and must be kept at a steady 70 degrees and stored in sea water or it transforms into a deadly gas.

West still doesn't know that his assignment is to retrieve the calcium, but believes that it's an art object that is hidden in a 30-foot deep tank of water. As West goes after the treasure Crystal warns him that Calamander intends to kill him when his assignment is completed. West, closely guarded by another criminal, retrieves the metal box containing the calcium.

Gordon discovers the whereabouts of the hideout and shows up disguised as a postal worker. The agents get the calcium and Gordon explains to West that it is actually a deadly gas. West drops the box and they quickly exit before the substance transforms. With the guarding villain close behind, West and Gordon leave the hideout and run into Calamander, who goes back in to retrieve the vial. As the two villains meet in the passageway, the vial explodes into a cloud of gas and kills them both. The passage is sealed off and the gas locked safely inside as West returns to the service of his country.

The Night of the
Iron Fist

Agent James West takes Bosnian nobleman Count Draja (Lenard) into custody for extradition. The count, who has a mechanical iron hand that he uses as a deadly club, has stolen $500,000 from his country and hidden it somewhere in Arizona. When West learns of a plan to capture his prisoner, he has his fellow agent, Artemus Gordon, disguise himself as Draja and board a train with the sheriff and his deputies; while West and the authentic

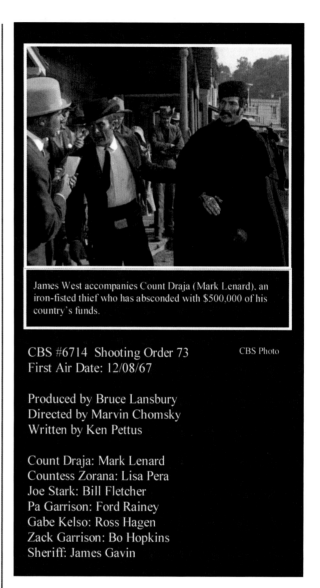

James West accompanies Count Draja (Mark Lenard), an iron-fisted thief who has absconded with $500,000 of his country's funds.

CBS #6714 Shooting Order 73   CBS Photo
First Air Date: 12/08/67

Produced by Bruce Lansbury
Directed by Marvin Chomsky
Written by Ken Pettus

Count Draja: Mark Lenard
Countess Zorana: Lisa Pera
Joe Stark: Bill Fletcher
Pa Garrison: Ford Rainey
Gabe Kelso: Ross Hagen
Zack Garrison: Bo Hopkins
Sheriff: James Gavin

Draja proceed on horseback.

On the train, two outlaws try to free the fake Draja. In the desert with West, the real Draja attempts to free himself. When the Countess Zorana (Pera) boards the train, she recognizes that Gordon is not the real count, but doesn't reveal him to the gunmen. Gordon tricks the hired guns to fight amongst themselves until only one, the ringleader, is left standing. Gordon is able to easily subdue him just in time for West to arrive and capture the wanted Zorana. With everyone captured the count is shipped back to his homeland to face his fate.

Author's Notes:
Author's Notes:

This is a flat story that leaves our heroes with the relatively humdrum task of extradition. West does encounter some interesting characters that are pursuing the count, but the only redeeming factor in "Fist" is Count Draja's fascinating iron hand: perhaps a pun on his ruling methods, but that's even stretching it a bit.

The Night of the
Headless Woman

Secret agent James West and a U.S. marshal stop a stagecoach and are unexpectedly fired upon. In the ensuing exchange of gunfire, the marshal and a passenger are wounded. Another *passenger* proves to be a female mannequin stuffed with boll weevils. West forces the coach driver to admit that Tim Cass of the Department of Harbors in San Francisco has hired him.

West's fellow agent, Gordon, questions the harbor commissioner, Jeffers (Anderson), when Cass turns up missing. Meanwhile, West finds the Egyptian Hassan (Marcuse) lolling in plush quarters at an isolated ranch. Hassan candidly divulges to West a scheme of using hybrid boll weevils that will devour foodstuffs as well as cotton to destroy massive amounts of crops. His syndicate would then handle all of the world's food and cotton supplies and control the prices. West is determined to put a stop to the evil Egyptian's nefarious plan.

Gordon is captured. West, seeking his partner, is also captured and both are held in a warehouse. Jeffers is revealed as the head of the operation and he must eliminate the agents. He decides to burn down the warehouse with the agents inside. West escapes using his trusty and universally handy shoe knife, and the agents quickly defeat Jeffers and confiscate all the renegade boll weevils.

Later at the train, Gordon is dining with a lady friend when West enters with another woman. Gordon tries to usher his partner out, but he has brought with him two mating boll weevils. West shows the fascinated girls the pesky critters and they completely forget about their dates. Artie is chagrined.

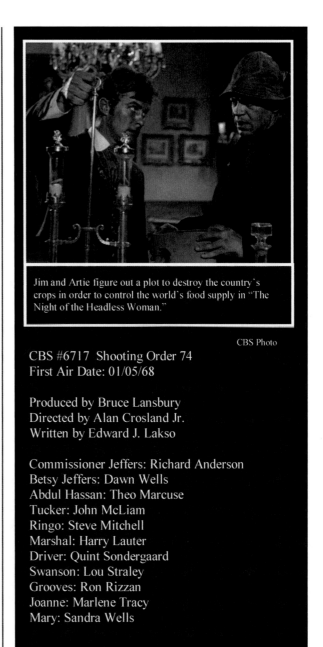

Jim and Artie figure out a plot to destroy the country's crops in order to control the world's food supply in "The Night of the Headless Woman."

CBS Photo

CBS #6717 Shooting Order 74
First Air Date: 01/05/68

Produced by Bruce Lansbury
Directed by Alan Crosland Jr.
Written by Edward J. Lakso

Commissioner Jeffers: Richard Anderson
Betsy Jeffers: Dawn Wells
Abdul Hassan: Theo Marcuse
Tucker: John McLiam
Ringo: Steve Mitchell
Marshal: Harry Lauter
Driver: Quint Sondergaard
Swanson: Lou Straley
Grooves: Ron Rizzan
Joanne: Marlene Tracy
Mary: Sandra Wells

Author's Notes:

This is a much more intriguing title than storyline. An alumnus of "Gilligan's Island," Dawn Wells appears in this unremarkable episode. In the Fourth Season's "TNOT Sabatini Death," "West" welcomes Alan Hale and Jim Backus, both island mates of Wells' Mary Ann Summers.

The Night of the
Underground Terror

Nehemiah Persoff (center) makes his third "West" appearance, this time as a sadistic Civil War major with an eye for gold in "The Night of the Underground Terror."

CBS #6719 Shooting Order 75   CBS Photo
First Air Date: 01/19/68

Produced by Bruce Lansbury
Directed by James B. Clark
Written by Max Hodge

Major Hazard: Nehemiah Persoff
Colonel Tacitus Mosely: Jeff Corey
Colonel Richmond: Douglas Henderson
China Hazard: Sabrina Scharf
Madame Pompadour: Kenya Coburn
Cajun: Gregg Martell
Slave Girl: Louise Lawson

West and Gordon find themselves in New Orleans during Mardi Gras as the agents seek out Colonel Mosely (Corey), a sadistic ex-commandant of a Civil War prison who has eluded capture for years after committing atrocities at the camp. West is contacted by a young girl named China (Scharf) and taken to her father, Major Hazard (Persoff), the legless leader of a group of men allegedly maimed while in Mosely's prison. Hazard resents West's intervention because his group is seeking their own vengeance against the cruel colonel. Hazard awards West just two days to arrest Mosely.

West finds Mosely entrenched as a squire of a plantation but, before West can make his move, both men are captured by Hazard and his cohorts. Hazard's legs seem to have miraculously returned. West and Mosely are taken to a long-deserted prison camp where Hazard plans to try Mosely for his war crimes, with the agent as Mosely's defense counsel.

At the train, Gordon finds a code from West signifying that he as been taken to the prison camp. While at the camp, West figures out that Mosely was not the actual perpetrator of the crimes, but it was Hazard who was the ringleader. West suspected Hazard when he entered the camp and saw eight gallery seats. The agent had read in the file that the commandant had seven helpers, all conveniently disappearing after the war. It is revealed that $1 million in gold was scheduled for delivery, but never made it to its destination. It was Mosely who hid the gold, and now Hazard plans to torture him until its whereabouts is revealed.

Gordon appears disguised as an English gold prospector and distracts Hazard and his men into thinking he's located the gold. West breaks loose and battles with Hazard's men. Hazard quickly tries to escape by climbing up a water tower. Quick-draw West shoots him and he falls from the tower, knocks the water spout loose and releases a stream of gold. The agents wrap up another exciting day on the job.

Author's Notes:
"Underground Terror" is a good, action-packed adventure with another twist ending, something for which the "West" was becoming known. This marks the third "West" appearance for character actor Nehemiah Persoff, as the not-so-legless Major Hazard. A familiar face during TV's heyday, Persoff has appeared in more than 200 roles on film and television.

The Night of the
Vipers

"Vipers" is a trite story of bank robbery and power- hungry politicians. This was one of the episodes slightly modified to comply with government violence edicts.

CBS #6718 Shooting Order 76
First Air Date: 01/12/68

Produced by Bruce Lansbury
Directed by Marvin Chomsky
Written by Robert E. Kent

Sheriff Dave Cord: Nick Adams
Mayor Beaumont: Donald Davis
Nadine Conover: Sandra Smith
Sheriff Tenny: Richard O'Brien
Aloyisius Moriarity: Johnny Haymer

Using a cannon hidden inside a wagon, the hooded Viper gang shoots its way into a Kansas bank. In the ensuing gun battle, one of the gang members is killed. A locker key found in his clothing leads secret agents West and Gordon to Moriarity's Gymnasium in Freedom, Kansas. There they meet a boxer named Klaxton who is taking on all challengers. West becomes the next challenger and knocks Klaxton into the street, leaving Gordon with the opportunity to use the mysterious locker key. All the locker contains is a slug, which it is later discovered is used to open a secret passage to where the cannon-laden wagon is hidden.

West observes dynamite being loaded onto the wagon and spots Sheriff Cord (Adams), with the Viper gang. The gang captures West and sends him down the river in a coffin. The ever-resourceful agent escapes using one of his secret devices. He quickly contacts Gordon who has since discovered a document locked in Mayor Beaumont's cabinet that links him, too, to the Viper gang. The mayor's plan was to become governor by capturing the Vipers in a cooperative effort. The agents place Beaumont (Davis) under arrest. West has an inevitable showdown with Sheriff Cord with the agent is triumphant once again.

Author's Notes:

"Vipers" is another simple story of power-hungry men with agents West and Gordon doing their righteous best to thwart their evil deeds. Actor Nick Adams as the corrupt sheriff does very little to propel this story. There's nothing even a little weird here with the exception of the Vipers' costumes.

Director Marvin Chomsky recalled how the *violence factor* interfered with one of the scenes. "We were shooting the scene where the bank is being robbed by the Viper gang and gunfire was going off with people getting killed. The bodies were starting to pile up, like 25 dead. Someone at CBS panicked and complained. So to get around having so many dead bodies we modified the script – having someone say, 'Hey, give me a hand with these wounded men.'"

The Night of the
Death Masks

Escaped murderer Emmett Stark (Selzer), who was imprisoned years earlier by James West, conceives a bizarre plan to harass and then kill the agent. After being engaged in a fight, West is locked inside a stagecoach and rendered unconscious by gas. He awakens in the apparently deserted town of

Milton Selzer plays Stark, a criminal out for revenge against James West in "Death Masks." Patty McCormack plays Stark's daughter.

CBS Photo

CBS #6720 Shooting Order 77
First Air Date: 01/26/68

Produced by Bruce Lansbury
Directed by Mike Moder
Written by Ken Pettus

Emmet Stark: Milton Selzer
Betsy: Patty McCormack
Colonel Richmond: Douglas Henderson
Mr. Goff: Louis Quinn
Dr. Prior: Bill Quinn
Fleur Fogarty: Bobbi Jordan
Amanda: Judy McConnell
Velia: Kristi Kimble

Paradox, where he is fired upon and wounded in the leg. West returns fire, but his assailants prove to be mannequins wearing masks of Stark's likeness. Then West must fight three men wearing Stark masks. When he's knocked out again, he awakens only to find more adversaries and more mannequins.

A woman named Betsy (McCormack) appears and tells West she is lost. She cares for the wounded agent, but when she goes into a store, she is shot and killed by Stark. West investigates and discovers her body has mysteriously disappeared. Suddenly, a stage-coach with a broken axel enters town with three people on board. One traveler is a doctor who attends to West and gives him an injection for the pain. When the stage is repaired and ready to leave, the drugged West is unable to go with them.

Gordon, who has been concerned about his missing partner, leaves a lady friend in a restaurant and goes to the station. He encounters the three stage passengers who he hears were with his partner. They agree to take Gordon to West, but he is unsuspectingly drugged by a cup of coffee.

West awakens still in the deserted town. He goes into the saloon and faints. The stage rides into town and drops off the dazed Gordon, who doesn't realize that he, too, has been disguised as Stark. Another man, dressed as West, exits the saloon and shoots at Gordon. West awakens and runs outside. Gordon, mistaking West for the gunman, opens fire. Both keep shooting until Gordon runs out of bullets and throws his gun at West. He makes a run for it but West shoots him in the leg. West checks the assailant's gun and sees the initials AG on it. Artie has since found another gun. He shoots West, who falls to the ground. When Gordon gets closer, he realizes he has just shot his best friend. West, however, is pretending to be shot, as he starts to figure out this bizarre scheme.

Gordon approaches and West whispers to him to keep the show going. The real Stark appears and West springs to his feet, holding the adversary at gunpoint. Betsy, who turns out to be Stark's daughter and very much alive, gets the better of both agents while Stark makes his getaway. Stark's men try to kill the agents but our dynamic team will out and the evil Stark is captured.

The two agents are laid up with their respective leg injuries when a package arrives for Gordon from the woman he abandoned in the restaurant. When he opens it he winces, "Oh! Something died!" as the week-old escargot percolates its distinctive aroma from the box. Both agents hobble into another room.

Author's Notes:

"Death Masks" marks the directorial debut for Mike Moder, who came to "West" from his post as unit production manager on "The Big Valley," then moved up to first assistant director on every other show. "Toward the end of the year, Lenny Katzman and Bruce Lansbury asked me if I could do the UPM job next year. I said alright, if I can direct an episode. They agreed and near the end of the third season they gave me 'Death Masks.'"

Moder's first attempt came off quite well, crediting a good script and crew cooperation. The director remembered that he expressly asked for help from Conrad. "I asked Bob to read the script because he would only read most of them. We shot the scene with Patty McCormack (Betsy) when we discovered her connection with Stark. Bob said, 'James West wouldn't act like this.' I asked him if he'd read the script and if not, just do what I tell you to do, I said. Overall, he was very cooperative."

As a first-time director. Moder also had a slight confrontation with Ross Martin. "During the tag, where West and Gordon are sitting on the couch, Ross had it in his mind that he didn't want to sit there. His perception of the scene has him sitting across the room. Ross finally agreed to do the scene my way."

"Masks" gets four stars from me for an original story with a strange and bizarre undercurrent running throughout the episode; again, with what was becoming the customary twist in the end. Moder's direction is excellent and really captures the "West" essence.

The Night of the
Undead

Agent West thinks he is witnessing a voodoo sacrificial ritual. He tries to stop the killing by firing warning shots in the air but the people seem to be in a trance and leave the area. A large man named Tiny John (Grier) pursues West and the agent is forced to shoot him in the heart. The man doesn't die instantly and he heads to the swamp. West goes to the altar and discovers the sacrificial figure is made of wax. Later, Tiny John's body is brought to the morgue and as West and Gordon examine him they notice his hands glow in the dark.

West is looking for Dr. Armbruster and goes to see Dr. Eddington (Zaremba). He finds that the wax figure at the ritual was in the likeness of Eddington. West also meets Eddington's daughter, Mariah (Delaney). Eddington tells the agent that a Dr. Articulous (Hatfield) had been working with Dr. Armbruster on experiments with the glowing process. Articulous started to use the process on humans and that was when he and the doctor broke off their partnership. Mariah leaves the house with West following. She goes to see

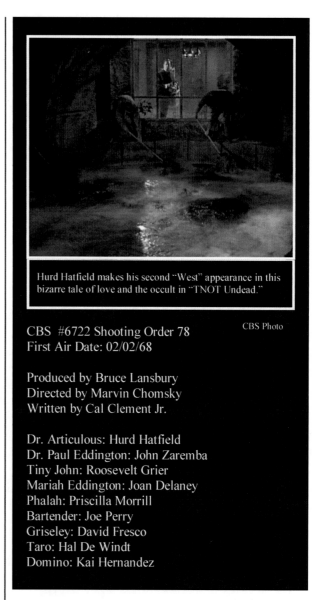

Hurd Hatfield makes his second "West" appearance in this bizarre tale of love and the occult in "TNOT Undead."

CBS Photo

CBS #6722 Shooting Order 78
First Air Date: 02/02/68

Produced by Bruce Lansbury
Directed by Marvin Chomsky
Written by Cal Clement Jr.

Dr. Articulous: Hurd Hatfield
Dr. Paul Eddington: John Zaremba
Tiny John: Roosevelt Grier
Mariah Eddington: Joan Delaney
Phalah: Priscilla Morrill
Bartender: Joe Perry
Griseley: David Fresco
Taro: Hal De Windt
Domino: Kai Hernandez

Articulous. West find an underground swamp and notices Dr. Armbruster.

Gordon finds a medallion worn by Tiny John that leads him to Phalah (Morrill). Disguised as Beldon Scoville Jr., the agent asks her where to find another medallion like it so that he may buy it for his Great Aunt Maude. Gordon is led to the home of Articulous, this time disguised as Major Samuel P. Brainard, a civil engineer who wants to tear down the house and build a canal. Phalah recognizes Gordon from his other disguise and he is captured. He finds out that Articulous is getting married and that Phalah is jealous. He escapes, finds West and the two go back into the house.

The agents come across a wedding setting that was supposed to take place years ago. Articulous was planning to marry, but the malpractice charge forced him into hiding and the woman he loved instead married Dr. Eddington. With revenge in mind, Articulous plans on marrying Eddington's daughter, Mariah, who is under a trance and obeys his every command.

Just before the wedding, Phalah, consumed by jealousy, shoots Articulous. After a fight, a fierce fire rages through the house as the agents and Mariah escape.

Author's Notes:

"Undead" is a wonderfully bizarre tale of voodoo and the world of the occult. Director Marvin Chomsky interestingly combines fantasy and reality and does a fair job of depicting this unusual world.

Chomsky tells how he made the fantasy element work. "It all comes down to the ability of Bob Conrad. A character like West is thrown into a situation with a bizarre atmosphere – he is a solid and secure character. In other words, wherever West trod, reality would come back to any situation that was too far out to be believed."

Football star Rosie Grier appears as Tiny John. An ordained minister, Grier was one of the earliest sports stars to make the tough transition into acting, and does a nice job. He even went on to briefly have his own variety show in 1969, but his acting career never reached significant heights.

The Night of the
Simian Terror

Agents West and Gordon show up at the home of Senator Buckley (Greer) and West finds the plantation foreman badly crushed. West investigates, but one of the senator's sons discourages the agent from pursuing the assailant. Before the foreman dies, he tells Gordon that he was attacked by a giant beast. Dr. Sigmund Von Leibig (Abbott) arrives to pronounce the man dead. Gordon recognizes the doctor's name, but can't seem to place it. When West and Gordon want to see the senator, they are told by his daughter Naomi (Gaynor) that he is in a family meet-

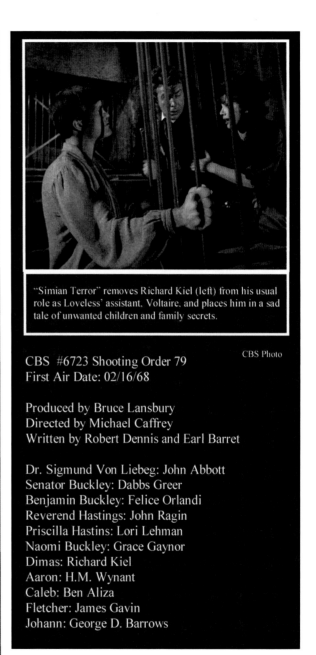

"Simian Terror" removes Richard Kiel (left) from his usual role as Loveless' assistant, Voltaire, and places him in a sad tale of unwanted children and family secrets.

CBS Photo

CBS #6723 Shooting Order 79
First Air Date: 02/16/68

Produced by Bruce Lansbury
Directed by Michael Caffrey
Written by Robert Dennis and Earl Barret

Dr. Sigmund Von Liebeg: John Abbott
Senator Buckley: Dabbs Greer
Benjamin Buckley: Felice Orlandi
Reverend Hastings: John Ragin
Priscilla Hastins: Lori Lehman
Naomi Buckley: Grace Gaynor
Dimas: Richard Kiel
Aaron: H.M. Wynant
Caleb: Ben Aliza
Fletcher: James Gavin
Johann: George D. Barrows

ing. As she takes them to their rooms Gordon notices a door and asks where it leads. Naomi warns them that it was a nursery and no one is allowed to enter that room.

West has dinner with Naomi while Gordon goes off to the forbidden nursery. He overhears the conversation between the senator and his sons and discovers that the sons want *it* killed and to finally be rid of the *Buckley secret*. When the senator leaves, he

165

walks into the room where Gordon is and clubs him with his cane. One of the brothers goes to the family church and destroys the family records just as the dazed Gordon stumbles down the stairs and tries to tell West what he has heard. The church bell rings and Gordon remembers that the meeting had something to do with the family records. West races down to the church and finds one of the brothers dead. The preacher claims to have seen an ape.

At the plantation, Gordon finally remembers where he'd heard of Dr. Leibig before – he was famous for his experiments with apes. The agent pays him a visit disguised as Dr. Marvin Gentry. Leibig does not wish to talk to the visitor and leaves for the day. Gordon/Gentry snoops around and happens upon a huge man named Dimas (Kiel). When he tries to grab the agent, Gordon locks himself in a cage for protection. Dimas leaves to investigate the chiming church bell. Gordon escapes and asks the senator about his *other* son. When the senator refuses to offer any information, Gordon tells him that he found the family bible that has listed not a set of triplets, but quadruplets, born unto him.

Meanwhile, West is told that a big ape has taken Naomi away. West goes to Dr. Leibig's lab and runs into Dimas and the ape. Dimas tells West that he is going to kill all the Buckleys for having deprived him of his birthright. West and Naomi are held captive by the ape as Demas goes to perform his wicked deed.

The senator confesses to Gordon that he had given his son, Dimas, to Dr. Leibig for experiments because he was so different from the others. Dimas comes to the house and kills another brother. West escapes and runs into Dimas while the ape crashes through the house. West hits Dimas, who falls over the staircase and dies. The ape runs to Dimas and then, heartbroken, runs from the house and into a hail of gunfire. The senator feels abject remorse over Dimas and can't believe he shut out his son all those years.

Author's Notes:

While most people may recognize actor Richard Kiel as Jaws, the indestructible nemesis in the 1977 Roger Moore Bond film "The Spy Who Loved Me," he can also be remembered as the peckish and duplicitous alien Kanamit, in "The Twilight Zone's" unsettling episode "To Serve Man."

The Night of the
Death Maker

James West disguises as a monk in order to infiltrate a plot to kill President Grant in "TNOT Death Maker."

CBS Photo

CBS #6724 Shooting Order 80
First Air Date: 02/23/68

Produced by Bruce Lansbury
Directed by Irving J. Moore
Written by Robert Kent

Cullen Dane: Wendell Corey
Marcia Dennison: Angel Tompkins
President Grant: Roy Engle
Sergeant: Arthur Betanides
Brother Angelo: J. Pat O'Malley
Monk: Nicky Blair
Gillespie: Michael Fox
Secret Service man: Joe Lansden

An organ grinder with a Gatling gun makes an attempt President Grant's (Engle) life. The attempt is thwarted by agent Artemus Gordon, disguised as the president, and his partner, James West. They tell Grant that he will have to wait to go to Denver. He allows the agents only 36 hours to find his would-be assassins, so that he can continue his journey. The Gatling gun offers an unusual clue in the form of a raisin found in one of the barrels. It is a certain type of grape only grown in one place – Jubalee, California.

West and Gordon travel to Jubalee and pass a monk that is delivering wine to the hotel. Gordon impersonates French wine expert Claude Assir Renard to find out more information. He discovers that the wine is made in a monastery, but when Gordon tastes it, he realizes it is terrible. This leads West to believe that there is something wrong at the monastery. West also noticed that the monk that delivered the wine was wearing a ring and monks are not allowed to adorn themselves with jewelry. Gordon diverts the monk's attention long enough for West to sneak into the wagon. Once in the monastery, West finds out that President Grant broke Cullen Dane (Corey) of command and the vengeful Dane now wants Grant dead. He also intends to take over the state of California in the process.

The real monks are being held prisoner in a pit at the monastery. West gets captured and is also put in the pit. Gordon/Renard comes to the monastery and meets Dane, who is dressed as a monk. Gordon tells him he has an appointment to help fix the wine problem. When the monks announce that one of their brothers has died, West escapes by taking the place of the dead monk in the casket supplied to them by their captors. While snooping around Cullen's office Gordon finds the map of the planned ambush of the president's train – and the agents are quickly off to stop it. Once again, the president's life and California are saved by our favorite duo.

Author's Notes:
Here we have another villain seeking vengeance against the apparently unpopular President Grant and West and Gordon must step in to save him. "Death Maker" is an entertaining, though not entirely original, story. Only two stuntmen, Red West and Dick Cangey, were available for scenes — so a quick change of hats, beards and clothing placed the same two stuntmen at different cannons to be blown up again and again. I wonder if that qualifies them for hazard pay.

CBS Photo

Charles Aidman served as pinch hitter for Martin during his recuperation from his heart attack. Aidman originally planned a career as an attorney, but was sidetracked during World War II attending naval officer training at DePaul University.

During a speech class, the instructor, who also headed the drama department, saw Aidman as ideal for a role in an upcoming play. "I did the play and enjoyed it. It was the first play I was in in my life. One of the gals in the play; her mother came down from Chicago. Chicago, to me, was big stuff. Her mother said to me, 'You should go on the stage. You are a born actor.' I was so impressed only because she was from Chicago. If she was from Indianapolis I couldn't have cared less. While overseas, I thought about it all the time. I didn't want to be a lawyer. I wanted to be an actor. So when I got back to the university, I got into the drama department, got my degree and went to New York. I've been acting ever since," Aidman said.

Aidman believed CBS wanted a good, solid, putty-nose actor who liked to do character portrayals as Ross' temporary replacement. Previously, he had adapted a book of poetry for the stage called, "Spoon River." Aidman believed that the many characters he portrayed in the play had a great deal to do with being chosen for the "West" role.

"CBS didn't want to bring in guest peddlers, although it was discussed. They wanted a solid actor who would come in and do it and not be a threat to Ross. That was the other thing. We didn't want to have to say to Ross, 'We're replacing you,'" Aidman added.

167

Chapter 9
Gadgets and Devices: The Element of Surprise

The fascination with "The Wild Wild West" wasn't only with the great stunts, the amazing makeup or the unusual storylines. Audiences were intrigued and amazed by the weekly array of anachronistic gadgetry and devices designed and used by West, Gordon and "The Wild Wild West" villains. In the pilot, "The Night of the Inferno" many of James West's secret gadgets were from the imagination of writer Gil Ralston. West's sleeve gun, a derringer that would immediately spring into action via an automated device attached to his arm, was one of the most popular surprises from the pilot. The nifty device not only expels a gun, but knives, a vial of acid and whatever else West happens to have up his sleeve. The device got James West out of countless sticky situations.

West also carried a breakaway derringer neatly tucked into the removable heel of one of his boots. His belt buckle usually supplied the ammunition for his secret weapons. As time went on, any number of exploding balls, smoke bombs and incendiary buttons burst onto the scene, and the show became famous for its inventive escapes.

Making these fantastically futuristic gadgets become reality involved a great deal of planning in very little time. A team of uniquely skilled designers and art directors helped to bring the idea from fantasy to reality – usually in one week or less. Adding these devices to the script was only the first step in leading our heroes to victory against their equally as inventive adversaries.

After a writer came up with a new gadget, then the concept was developed in a story conference. During the show's first season, "West" story editors took the writers' words and, along with the art director, would create a workable piece. During the second season, new story consultant Henry Sharp, who had previously been a designer and illustrator, had the advantage of being able to visualize what a device might look like even before the design stage.

Usually a writer would dream up an unusual device but Sharp would reverse the roles. He would come up with the ideas and the writer would build a script around the concept. Once the preliminary sketch was completed, Sharp teamed with the art director to bring it to fruition. For the first season through the first

James West's sleeve gun was entirely unique to the show. The device was completely undetectable, but always present when needed.

Explosive putty was just one of the items West would hide in the heels of his boots. His signature derringer (see following page) was also stored there.

Photos Courtesy of CBS

half of the second season, Al Heschong was the art director. Once the idea was presented to Heschong, he would come up with the best way to create the piece and then turn in a cost estimate. If the ideas would cost more money than was allotted in the budget, Heschong would have to modify it accordingly. When Sharp came in as story editor, the two men worked closely together.

"The challenge came from the scripts and Henry Sharp's sketches. He would do little doodles that had a cartoon-like look. Then we would take the cartoon and say, 'Yes, we can do that,' or 'No, we can't do that.' But the ideas came from all directions, really," Heschong recalled. Heschong said that the most challenging of all the episodes was the pilot. "The pilot was almost a feature in its scope, but we had plenty of time to prepare it. We had two months, which was a long time."

Aside from any problems that arose, Heschong worked out some very fun sets. "My favorite was the clock in 'The Night the Wizard Shook the Earth,' when Loveless jumped down onto the pendulum and swung back and forth. He was about to set off a bomb." Another of the art director's favorites was "The Night of the Raven," another Loveless episode. "We used some blue screen, which was pretty new to some people at the time, and used large scale sets."

Once the art director set a price on a certain device, the next step in completing the task involved the special effects man. Tim Smyth was the effects man at CBS and he was assigned to the pilot episode. He continued throughout the following four seasons of "West." Smyth was responsible for the actual devices that come from the original concepts and detailed illustrations. Many of James West's weapons were a direct result of Smyth's creative acumen. "All the props were made at CBS's prop shop. They all had their own degree of difficulty. Very seldom did we know from one show to the next what we were going to do. It always had to be done in a week," Smyth said.

West's sleeve gun was an original concept never before used in any other television series. The sleeve gun was made out of a traverse rod with a carrier attached made of nylon rollers. A frame was built into the gun grip and bolted

Above, James West shows off his full regalia in this promotional shot from CBS. Below we see a detail of the derringer safely hidden in the heel of his shoe. Inserts show coat knife (top), gun belt (center) and ring.

169

into the mechanism. When the gun was pushed up the rollers, it locked into place and remained hidden from the eyes of unsuspecting captors. It was released when the inside of the wearer's elbow was struck against the body. At times, with West's arm fully extended, the gun was shown to release as the camera filmed the only the lower part of his arm. The problem was, there would have had to have been an unseen finger pressing the release button. This method of focused filming was called an insert, that is, inserted clips of a script detail. Inserts are usually filmed at an optical house after regular filming was completed.

Another completely original device created especially for "The Wild Wild West" was a metal spike that was designed to shoot from the end of West's derringer to aid in the agent's escape over various acid pits, smoke screens, bell towers, snake pits and the like. Tim Smyth said that when West shot the spike and it embedded into a wall, they would actually stick the spike into the wall first, tighten it up and then yank it out. "Then we reversed the action so it would appear to be going into the wall," he added.

An amusing anecdote involves the actual speed of the spike being expelled from

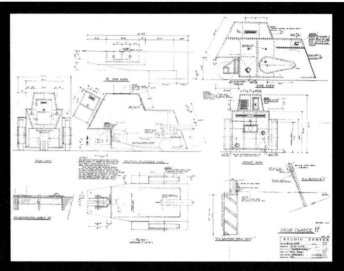

The attention to detail, as is evident in the sketch of the tank used in "TNOT Freebooters" (above), is remarkable. Designers had to create not just visually fascinating inventions, but functional ones as well.
Visual effects supervisor, Tim Smyth, stands on the final product (left).

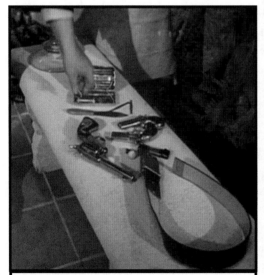

In "TNOT Two-Legged Buffalo" West's gear is put on full display.

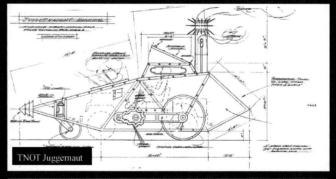

TNOT Juggernaut

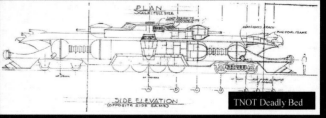

TNOT Deadly Bed

170

Photos and Sketches Courtesy CBS

the gun. There was always backstage laughter when the gun would shoot the spike and it would go no more than three feet, at best, and fall, unceremoniously to the ground — a rather anticlimactic and embarrassing ejection. But when the scene was aired, it created the illusion that the high-speed projectile would piece a concrete wall and the "West" fantasy would continue unscathed.

West's shoe knife was used frequently in the 104 "West" episodes to get the agent out of sticky situations. The diagram at right was created by Art Director Al Heschong as part of the personal arsenal West would carry on him at all times.

This inventive method of escape impressed even James Bond himself, so much so that it was used in the popular Bond film "Diamonds Are Forever." "Bond was in Las Vegas up in an outside elevator. He took out a gun, stuck in a spike, shot it overhead and swung out to safety. We did it first on 'The Wild Wild West,'" Smyth said.

Smyth explained that the sleeve gun mechanism was also used during West's inventive escapes with and aid of an invisible wire that suspended the actor. "We hooked Bob (Conrad) onto a wire so he would not come off and sailed him across anything we wanted to," Smyth recalled.

Most of "The Wild Wild West's" fantastic devices were made from a very basic design. The giant sized octopus in "The Night of the Kraken" was made out of simple rubber and foam. Many of Dr. Loveless' murderous machines were made of no more than flashing lights and a lot of intimidating switches. "We probably used more colored smoke than anything else," Smyth remembered. "We used it when West needed to escape from something; the color made a nice effect."

Through the series' four seasons audiences had the pleasure of witnessing devices from the bizarre to the futuristic, to even the intergalactic. All culminating in the most fantastic gadgetry every devised for a

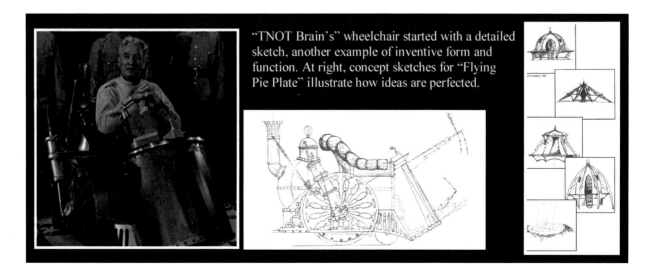

"TNOT Brain's" wheelchair started with a detailed sketch, another example of inventive form and function. At right, concept sketches for "Flying Pie Plate" illustrate how ideas are perfected.

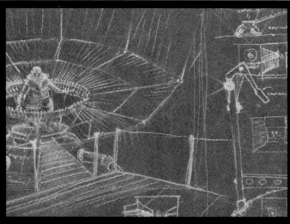

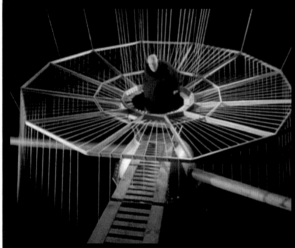

The concept sketch for the "Puppeteer" shows how beautifully executed the idea was in the episode.

television show at the time. This, coupled with the fact that the show was set in the early 1870s, made for a creative challenge that entertained and amazed audiences. No matter how outrageous or sophisticated the devices may have appeared, they still maintained the essence of the period.

Each of the many producers in the first season had a favorite slant for devices made available to the characters. The pilot, of course, introduced many of James West's staple gadgets that were to become his trademarks. Collier Young episodes used West's devices, but used more villainous ingenuity than gadgetry for his adversaries. Fred Freiberger introduced the inimitable genius of Dr. Miguelito Loveless along with weapons such as a trombone shaped pea shooter (complete with scope) for projecting explosive pellets. Loveless' creativity leaned more toward poisonous powders and powerful, world-ending explosives. When West combats Loveless in "The Night the Wizard Shook the Earth," he is equipped with a Bond-like carriage rigged with an ejector seat and surprising restraints to hold unwanted guests at bay. In Freiberger's "The Night of the Human Trigger," West is rigged to a balance device on which the slightest move would send several kegs of dynamite, and our hero, into an explosive memory.

Like West, Artemus Gordon had his own array of gadgets and formulas, only these would spring from his own brilliant imagination, as did many of West's handy devices. Spending hours concocting, Artie's motivation was to equip his partner with whatever would get him out of even the most hopeless of

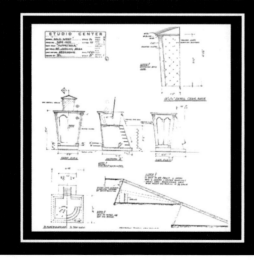

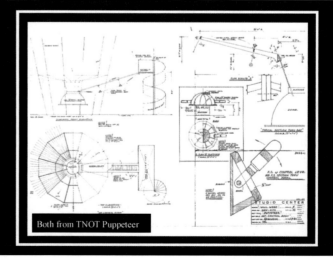

Both from TNOT Puppeteer

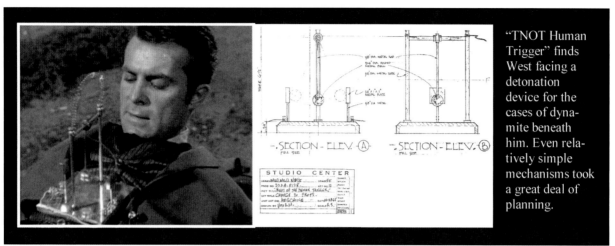

"TNOT Human Trigger" finds West facing a detonation device for the cases of dynamite beneath him. Even relatively simple mechanisms took a great deal of planning.

situations. In "The Night of the Glowing Corpse," another Freiberger episode, Gordon invents an artificial lung that is the equivalent of a modern oxygen mask. He also creates a chemical leech that could hold a man's weight for 10 seconds. Both items served to save our agents' lives. Over the four seasons, a great many of our modern devices are dubiously credited to the genius inventor Artemus Gordon.

Producer John Mantley used the bizarre and the phenomenal when developing his villains. Many of his adversaries were bent on vengeance and utilized highly unusual methods of exacting revenge. In "The Night of the Puppeteer," Mantley created an amazingly complex circuit of string puppets to trap and try West for a marionette's murder. The contraption was run by the grossly deformed genius Zachariah Skull, skillfully portrayed by actor Lloyd Bochner. This was distinctly similar to the criminal genius in John Dehner's portrayal of the vengeful Colonel Torres in "The Night of the Steel Assassin." Torres' body is reconstructed in steel that created a type of superhuman villain to battle our agents and their super gadgets. In Torres' case, his reinforced stature not only aided in his villainy, but also expedited his demise.

During Gene Coon's producing days, Michael Garrison had returned as executive producer and his influence showed, as the stories ranged from those of total fantasy, such as "The Night of the Burning Diamond's" accelerated villainy, to "The Night of the Freebooters" futuristic tank. The first electric chair, which might be considered more cruel and unusual than bizarre, appeared in "The Night of the Bars of Hell"; although the actual electric chair was first used nearly 20 years after the West and Gordon period, around 1890.

When Garrison returned as producer, the theme of the show leaned even more toward the world of fantasy – as did the gadgets used. "The Night of the Big Blast" was essentially a Frankenstein story complete with mad scientist Ida Lupino as Dr. Faustina, perfectly duplicating our heroes. "The Night of the Man-Eating House" found West and Gordon battling poltergeists with supernatural and dream-like imagery, similar to "The Night of

One lady West couldn't tame was Amorous Amanda from "TNOT Eccentrics." Her clutches were designed to hang onto her man... permanently.

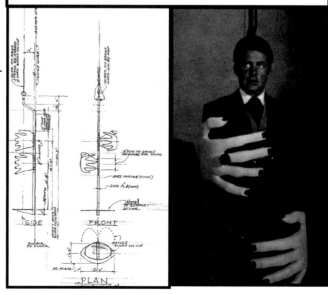

173

Special effects supervisor Tim Smyth (left) and Art Director Al Heschong made the perfect "West" team, successfully combining the wildly bizarre and futuristic with the old West.

the Eccentrics," which introduced the mysterious character of Count Manzeppi, played by Victor Buono, a magician with a passionate penchant for power.

After Garrison's death in August of 1966, Bruce Lansbury took over as producer. He and story consultant Henry Sharp joined forces to create a more comic book image for the show complete with a new array of villainous devices and occasionally a few old, familiar adversaries.

In "The Night of the Flying Pie Plate," a huge flying saucer, equipped with pale green pilots, fooled the townspeople of Morning Glory, Arizona. "The Night of the Watery Death" used a prototype of a modern torpedo, but with the added feature of a fierce dragon to disguise and enhance the invention. "The Night of the Brain" placed actor Edward Andrews as a villain voluntarily confined to an automatic steam-powered wheelchair, making him able to focus all his energies on his mental abilities. This becomes even more evident when the wheelchair transforms into an arsenal during the climax of the show. In "The Night of the Eccentrics," West finds himself in the clutches of Amorous Amanda, a mechanism whose powerful grip suspends its victim over an electric force field. Dr. Loveless returns in "The Night of the Green Terror" with a diabolical scheme for trouble and robotic suit of armor. "The Night of the Surreal McCoy" finds Loveless dabbling in dimensions with a device that emits a high-pitched sound and is capable of transmitting people in and out of paintings.

The fourth season gave a few more villains the advantage of gadgetry such as "The Night of the Avaricious Actuary," with a giant tuning fork used to destroy buildings and raise havoc in a small Western town. Again, a futuristic tank appeared in "The Night of the Juggernaut," when an evil land baron attempts to take over the territory. Actor Ted Knight appeared as Daniel in "The Night of the Kraken," where a mechanical Kraken, a giant octopus, was devised for guarding an underwater installation as well as sending fear into the seaside township. Dr. Loveless' final appearance was in "The Night of Miguelito's Revenge" where the clever doctor has designed a steam-driven man with super powers.

Though more than 100 gadgets and devices throughout the show's four seasons may have posed considerable risk to the cast and crew members, remarkably, no gadget-related accidents occurred. According to Tim Smyth, the mechanical success rate of the devices was better than 99%.

No other television show, past or present, can match the imaginations of the creative team behind "The Wild Wild West." Every week, they were able to make fantasy a reality for millions of viewers, where the surreal became real, the phenomenal believable and the magical a matter of fact.

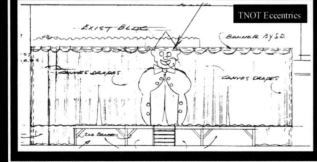

Turncoat concept of West, retrieving a deadly vial.

TNOT Turncoat

TNOT Eccentrics

EXIST BLDG

Sketches Courtesy CBS

174

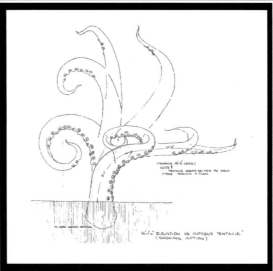

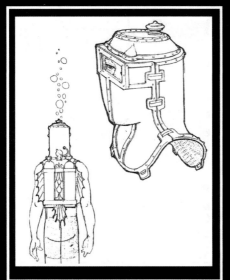

In "TNOT Kraken" Artie devises a deep sea helmet to help Jim investigate a deadly giant octopus that had been terrorizing the town. In reality the Kraken was one of the simpler devices ever built, made primarily of rubber and foam.

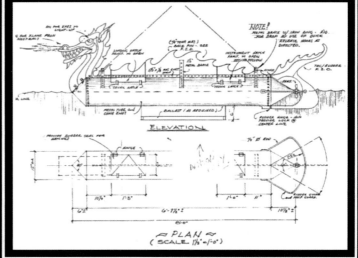

Another demon from the sea was the torpedo-bearing dragon from "TNOT Watery Death." Of course, torpedoes had not yet made their way into common usage in warfare, but "West" made it so with the elaboration of a fierce dragon for added panache.

The Best Laid Plans of ...

CBS Photo

During the 1968-1969 season, "The Wild Wild West" experienced a few changes. After Robert Conrad's accident at the end of the third season, his stunt participation was given strict limitations. No longer was he permitted to do high falls or anything that the studio deemed chancy and he was only able to take part in close-up fights.

While the third season had more Western-style stories, the fourth season was primed for change and, once again, tended to lean toward the bizarre, shedding the comic-book look so evident in the second season.

The Wild Wild Whoops!

The first seven episodes shot were from very solid scripts; complete with a significant amount of action and adventure. "The Night of the Avaricious Actuary" became Ross Martin's turn to have an on-stage mishap that resulted in a broken leg, and several weeks' worth of modified scripts. Director Irving Moore recalled the incident.

"Ross was at a shooting gallery with an old-

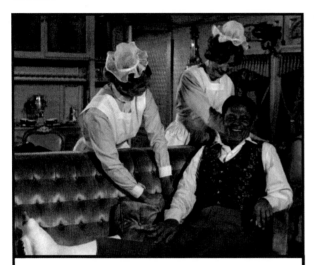

Ross Martin didn't seem to have too many complaints as the writers cleverly worked his cast into the scripts.

time rifle. He was supposed to fire the rifle, throw it down and run under the table because the building was going to collapse around him. We got the setup ready, but Bob was not in the scene. So Bob came to me and said, 'How long are we going to stay around here? I've got to get out of here. I've got to get going.' I told him that we just had this one scene left to shoot. I told Ross to aim the rifle, fire, throw it, run and jump under the table – and that would be the scene. Ross wanted to rehearse it but I told him we didn't have time to rehearse it and that Bob was going to leave. 'I don't care what Bob's going to do,' Ross said. So Bob was threatening to leave and Ross kept saying he wanted to rehearse.

"I said to shoot it and told Ross to just throw the gun down. I rolled the cameras; he fired the gun, ran across, threw the gun in front of himself and ran into it with his shins. It knocked him down, he crawled under the table and the entire set collapsed. Then I could hear him under the table moaning. I ran over and called to him – asked him what was the matter. As Ross struggled to get up, he looked at me in pain and said, 'While I'm down here, you want to get my close up?'

"He got a hairline fracture in his shin. He couldn't get up so several men helped him up and took him to the doctor. They put a cast on him up to his hip and we couldn't shoot for a couple of days. He returned after a few days, still in a cast. We dressed him and hid everything, except the tip of the white cast sticking out

of the end of his brown pants. I told one of the set painters to get some brown paint and paint the cast."

Martin was back in front of the cameras with the following show, "The Night of the Juggernaut." Writer Cal Clements Jr. rewrote Ross into the script with a leg injury. Olavee Martin remembered, "Ross didn't want to hold anybody up, and certainly not the stories. He was a very dedicated performer and he believed that the show must go on, even though it was painful for him." In the next two episodes, "The Night of the Kraken" and "The Night of the Sedgewick Curse," although he was fitted with a walking cast, writers usually had Martin disguised as characters either on crutches or using a cane.

A Rough Trail Ahead

Ross and his beautiful new bride, Olavee, celebrated their first wedding anniversary in his hospital room. Ross says Olavee's love and courage gave him the will to live.

Problems didn't end with the removal of the cast, as was soon discovered just one week prior to a long-awaited hiatus for the cast and crew. During the week of August 8, 1968, "The Night of Fire and Brimstone" was in production and everyone seemed anxious for the well-deserved time off. According to guest star

177

Bob Phillips, Ross Martin appeared noticeable tired.

Phillips recalled a particular incident that lead to his concern. "On our last day of shooting, the scene took place in a saloon and we wanted to wrap. Ross was upset because he wanted a rehearsal. One of the guys on the catwalk said something, I guess derogatory, and Ross came *unglued*. Ross fired the guy. Then a supervisor said, 'No one is going to fire one of my guys.' I even went to Conrad and told him it was my fault; that I was talking to the guy on the catwalk and provoked the comment. Later, things got straightened out, but Ross looked like something was bothering him and it wasn't like him to act that way. He must have felt something coming on. The next day Ross has a massive heart attack."

On Saturday, August 17, 1968, Ross Martin was sailing in Marina del Rey, California, with his daughter, who was visiting from New York, and a group of friends. Martin developed what they thought was seasickness. After quickly returning to shore, two waiting doctors found no serious symptoms. Martin and his wife returned home, but when the pains increased, he was rushed to UCLA Medical Center in Westwood, California. It was there that the doctors confirmed a cardiac infarction, better known as a heart attack.

Martin was immediately placed in intensive care with what was then known as an inoperable condition. Doctors speculated a 50% chance of survival. Olavee Martin said that fans and industry members were lead to believe his condition was far less serious than it actually was. She recalled that her husband was considered a prime candidate for the attack. Both his father and mother died from heart conditions. "He drank anywhere between 20-30 cups of black coffee on the set each day. He smoked three to four packs of cigarettes a day and he loved red meat. This, along with very little exercise..." Olavee said, greatly contributed to his condition.

Mr. Gordon Goes to Washington

Back on the set, producer Bruce Lansbury was facing the start of production in just five weeks and was faced with the inevitability of locating a hopefully temporary replacement for Ross' character. Actor Charles Aidman was quickly cast in the role of fellow Secret Service agent Jeremy Pike. Aidman was preparing for a Steve McQueen film called "The Reivers" when he got the call from CBS. "I was within a week of leaving for Mississippi. I had a chance to do 'The Wild Wild West.' The idea initially was that Ross would never be able to work again. That's what the doctor had told

Ross Martin substitutes included (top) Charles Aidman as Jeremy Pike and (center) William Schallert as Frank Harper. Pike appeared in four episodes, Harper in the two-parter, "Winged Terror." In "TNOT Camera," comedian Pat Paulsen made a guest appearance as Bosley Cranston, an agent with surprising talents.

them. They hoped he would recover, but it was a tremendous heart attack. At the same time, they only wanted to book me for four episodes. CBS told me that they could get me out of the movie because CBS produced the movie. It really wasn't an incredibly important part. The job was given to Lonny Chapman. It was a long job. Something that should have taken three or four weeks went on for four months."

Two scripts had been written with Artemus Gordon in mind. CBS didn't want to create another character and didn't want to change the show because they were optimistic that Ross would return. "By that time Bruce (Lansbury) had things fairly organized and the scripts had been decided upon, so they just found an actor who could play what Ross played. Besides, having a 'guest peddler' was hard to write for. This way they didn't have to change any scripts," Aidman said.

In the beginning, the actor admitted that he had reservations about doing the part. "In the first place, you're taking a job and replacing somebody who's almost dead. There was something not right about that to me. In the second place, how can you really do it, unless the part becomes very different and you're not that part; you're something different, no matter what they call you. I presented all this to Bruce Lansbury and others involved. They said not to worry about it. They said that if I'd do it, they would rewrite everything. There was only one thing they rewrote and it was only on the first script. That was the character's name. That was it. I didn't realize it because I saw the script come to me – the changes came to me; it all had Jeremy Pike by the time I got the second script. You're to be called Jeremy Pike, but it is Artemus Gordon, so it has already been written. They didn't change anything."

Charles Aidman continued with the series for four episodes: "The Night of Miguelito's Revenge," "The Night of the Camera," "The Night of the Pelican" and "The Night of the Janus." The actor admitted that he enjoyed working on the show, but approached his role with a definitely different style than Martin.

"I'm pretty good at characters. Not in the way that Ross was, but I approached them a little more seriously than he did. Except for a couple of them that were so obviously campy. But Ross, I noted watching the show, approached them with a much more campy kind of flavor. He was always looking for the comedy and I think he was right. I don't think I caught on to that – I guess it really wasn't my style."

The positive impression Aidman had on the audience was evident with the notable amount of fan mail that was received. Aidman recalled his final episode of "The Wild Wild West." "I was very happy at what I did and I think CBS was, too. I remember talking to Bruce Lansbury who said, 'You know we're not going to use you anymore on this show, but I want you to know we are totally happy with what you did. It's just that CBS is so nervous about the ratings on the show right now that they're thinking about canceling it. Their

179

idea is that they're going to use a lot of big guest stars for that role until Ross gets back.' Overall, if was four very nice jobs in a row. It was a very good experience. I enjoyed the makeup and I enjoyed doing the accents – the kind of things actors are very rarely given the opportunity to do, even if they're capable to doing it."

Aidman said that as a result of his appearances on "West" and on CBS' "Twilight Zone" many people recognized him. At the first printing of this book, Aidman became better known for his voice than his appearances, having done numerous voiceovers for film trailers and commercials. He died of cancer in 1993 at the age of 68 after having appeared in more than 160 roles on TV and film.

More Replacements

For the three remaining episodes, James West was teamed with guest partners to help him perform his crime fighting duties. Actor William Schallert guest starred as Frank Harper in the series' first two-part episode, "The Night of the Winged Terror Part I & II," which also starred Jackie Coogan, better known for his role as Uncle Fester on "The Addams Family," which ran from 1964-1966. Schallert is still performing in films and on TV and has, to date, more than 300 roles to his credit. Guest star, Pat Paulsen appeared as Bosley Cranston in "The Night of the Camera." He is sent to help West and Agent Pike with a special assignment. In "The Night of the Sabatini Death," actor Alan Hale, Jr. guest starred as Secret Service agent Swanson. Of Hale's 200+ roles, he is best known as the loveable and bungling Skipper on "Gilligan's Island." Hale died in 1990 of respiratory failure.

The Return of Artemus Gordon

By September of 1968, Ross Martin was out of the intensive care unit and spent the next two months at home recuperating. In December, he returned to work on the set of "The Wild Wild West" in an episode originally entitled, "The Return of Artemus Gordon." Later re-titled, "The Night of the Diva," Ross appeared trim and in good spirits and had adopted a slightly new look and hairstyle.

Season 4 – Episode Listing

The Night of the
Fugitives

In "TNOT Fugitives" a powerful mining syndicate and a photographic memory make for a relatively tame "West."

CBS Photo

CBS # 6807 Shooting Order 81
First Air Date: 11/08/68

Produced by Bruce Lansbury
Directed by Mike Moder
Written by Ken Pettus

Rhoda: Susan Hart
Colonel James Richmond: Douglas Henderson
Norbet Plank: J.S. Johnson
Sheriff Baggs: Charles McGraw
Diamond Dave Desmond: Simon Oakland
Tod Warner: Sid McCoy
Hallelujah Harry: Bill Baldwin
Grady: A.G. Vitanza
Shopkeeper: Gabriel Walsh

In Epitaph, a company owned by Epitaph Mines, agents West and Gordon arrest Norbet Plank (Johnson), the chief bookkeeper for a powerful syndicate that owns the mining company. They hope to get their hands on the syndicate's records and build a case. Soon the whole town turns out to free Plank from the agents.

West hides Plank in the bell tower of a nearby church and Gordon masquerades as Hallelujah Harry, a larcenous lay-preacher. The latter hopes he can get to Diamond Dave Desmond (Oakland), who heads the syndicate and may abscond with the vital ledgers. The agents find that Desmond's girlfriend, Rhoda (Hart), has a yen for the same books with blackmail on her mind.

West is caught and refuses to reveal the whereabouts of Plank. He does let Gordon know by using secret hand signals. West gets away from Desmond and Gordon goes to the hotel and discovers a secret panel that has the books, all of which Plank has left blank.

Gordon goes downstairs and encounters the real Hallelujah Harry (Baldwin). Desmond forces West to come out of hiding by threatening to kill Gordon. As a diversion, Gordon lights a fuse to an explosive wagon. The explosion allows West, Gordon and Plank to escape.

At the train, the agents learn that Plank had memorized everything and did not keep any written records. Gordon did find a book that sparks West's interests, however. It is a list of girls Plank knows. West takes the book, but Gordon wants it back claiming he'll never see it again. West promises that he won't and tells Gordon, "That's what I like about you, Artie. You're always thinking about our future."

Author's Notes:

"Fugitives" was the last show shot from the third season, but aired during the middle of the fourth season. This is the infamous episode that shows Bob Conrad's near-fatal fall from the chandelier (detailed in Chapter 5). The first part of the episode was directed by Gunner Hellstrom, but because of the 12-week shutdown after the accident the rest of the episode was directed by Mike Moder, who got full credit.

After the accident, due to insurance restrictions, Conrad was no longer allowed to do risky stunts.

Because of his likeness to the actor, wardrobe man James George was brought in to do many of the major falls and crash stunts for Conrad. Mike Moder remembered George's first stunt and how, when the rookie stuntman was supposed to crash through a window the crew sort of lent him a hand. "Bob really hated to have the stunts done for him, but he cooperated. We built a ramp for Jimmy (George), and everyone on the crew signed this board that said, 'Go this way... No detour.'"

The Night of the
Doomsday Formula

Kevin McCarthy (left) and E.J. Endre star in "Doomsday Formula," about an earth-shattering explosive and international powers.

CBS Photo

CBS # 6802 Shooting Order 82
First Air Date: 10/04/68
Produced by Bruce Lansbury
Directed by Irving J. Moore
Written by Samuel Newman

Major General Walter Kroll: Kevin McCarthy
Dr. Crane: E.J. Andre
Lorna Crane: Melinda Plowman
Verna Scott : Gail Billings
Bartender : Vince Howard

West goes to meet Dr. Crane (Andre) at his home and is told by his daughter, Lorna (Plowman), that her father is already meeting with James West. West doesn't want to alarm the daughter, so he leaves quickly. After he exits a group of men break into the house and she screams. West returns to offer aid but is hit hard by a cane with a distinctive fist-shaped handle, which he sees just before he blacks out. Lorna is missing.

West and Gordon check out Crane's house in search of clues. In an out-of-place pot belly stove they find Crane's new secret formula known as the *Doomsday Formula*. Tests prove it is a very powerful and deadly explosive. West learns that the Doctor went to meet the fake West at The Union Bar, a favorite hangout. Gordon tags along, disguised as Dr. Crane to help garner information. The proprietor tells them that Crane was drinking a *Shenandoah*, along with another gentleman. This is a drink only partaken by members of the Seventh Calvary's elite squad known as The Improbables. Gordon leaves to search for more clues. West spots the fist-shaped cane in the bar and follows its owners, stowing away in a wagon headed for The Doubletree Farm.

Gordon finds out that only three survivors are left of the Seventh Calvary, with only one of them a viable suspect: General Kroll (McCarthy), who now runs The Doubletree Farm for guests and the occasional foreign visitor. Gordon disguises himself as Hassan Tamir Ortuglo and arranges to meet Kroll at the swanky Hadrian's Club. He tells the General he is interested in purchasing Crane's new formula with a $500,000 down payment.

West locates Dr. Crane at the farm. He is being forced to reveal his secret doomsday formula or Lorna will die. West sees the daughter perched in the center of a ring of fire. West asks the Doctor to give him one hour to save his daughter before giving up the formula to Kroll. Crane agrees.

Gordon and West meet outside and make plans. Gordon sets off his usual style of diversion in the house, causing enough confusion for West to rescue Crane's daughter. She is safe, but Dr. Crane suddenly dies of a heart attack. West goes after Kroll and becomes trapped by Gatling gunfire in an internal training facility. West throws a small explosive and Kroll is blown up. The agent sets off a fuse that blows up the barn and the arsenal. Crane's daughter and the formula are saved, as is the world.

Author's Notes:

A solid enough episode, there is some evident effort to assuage violence to comply with the looming government standards. Some of the fight scenes are noticeably more acrobatic, and even as West is fired upon by a room full of Gatling guns, he is easily able to avoid injury. The army of henchmen can't seem to hit the side of a barn and their efforts to maintain control of this fortress are practically comical. Kroll is defeated by a swift, well-placed explosive, and Crane's daughter's rescue is flamboyant, but hardly a serious challenge for the imperishable James West.

Robert Prince's music in this episode is clearly misplaced. The very jazzy score that accompanies the fight scenes shatters the idea of the 1870s and places the viewers squarely in a mid-60s beach movie.

The Night of the
Egyptian Queen

Agent Artemus Gordon and the curator (Farley) of the San Francisco Museum of Art are set upon in the Egyptian exhibit by three masked men. Agent West and Mr. Heisel (Brooke), the Egyptian government's representative, are also attacked when they enter the room. When the men regain consciousness, they realize that a priceless ruby has been stolen from the eye of the statue of the Sun God Ra. West and Gordon are then commissioned by Miasmin (Hunter), the Egyptian princess, to recover the jewel.

A ransom note leads the agents to a waterfront bar where Gordon poses as a sea captain. West recognizes one of the museum assailants, a man who calls himself Jason (Troupe). He indicates that the beautiful Rosie (Gaston), who is dancing on their table, is wearing the precious gem on her toe. She dancer disappears before West can get the stone. Gordon chases after her but she eludes him. A fight breaks out and, when the dust settles, West removes a dagger from one of Jason's men. Gordon tracks down the origins of the dagger while West looks for Rosie.

Gordon goes to a waterfront bar waving the dagger. When the proprietor, Amalek (Marshall), wishes to buy it, Gordon says it isn't for sale. Amalek tries to take the knife, but Gordon tells him that the knife comes with a large ruby. Amalek offers $50,000

A mysterious Egyptian statue and a priceless ruby cause trouble for the agents in "Egyptian Queen." co-starring William Marshall (center) and Morgan Farley (right).

CBS # 6808 Shooting Order 83
First Air Date: 11/15/68

Produced by Bruce Lansbury
Directed by Marvin Chomsky
Written by Paul Playdon

Jason Starr: Tom Troupe
Heisel: Sorrell Brooke
Rosie: Penny Gaston
Finley: Walter Brooke
Amalek: William Marshall
Curator: Morgan Farley
Gambler: Gene Tyburn
Miasmin: Cindy Hunter
Guard: Rush Williams
Waiter: Kana Awni
Ferret: Hal K. Dawson

if he can bring him the ruby within three hours.

Jason finds Rosie, but the ruby has slipped off her foot. Jason doesn't believe her story and moves in to hurt the dancer until West intervenes, causing a Mexican standoff. West manages to escape with Rosie and they go to his train. She still claims to have lost the ruby. She pretends to need rest and goes to lay down, slipping away when the agent's back is turned. West

follows her to an ice house where the gem has been frozen in a block of ice. Jason enters and battles West, knocking out the agent and grabbing the ruby. West is left with Rosie to die in the freezer. As Jason takes the ruby, Amalek appears and kills him, absconding with the gem. When Gordon meets Amalek with a fake ruby, he is discovered.

West escapes using an explosive from the heel of his boot and saves Gordon. The agents head to the museum and find Heisel and Amalek placing the ruby back onto its rightful place on the statue. West and Gordon discover that when the ruby is placed onto the statue and the moonlight hits it a certain way, the angle of the beam points to hidden treasure. The beam indicates the spot, but the greedy Heisel acts too quickly and is killed by a booby-trap device. The gold is revealed and the ruby is returned to the Egyptian government.

At the train, the princess gives west and Gordon a beautiful diamond, but they cannot accept gifts so they give it to Rosie so that she may buy a dress shop. Rosie is so happy that she guiltily returns the stolen items she took from the train.

Author's Notes:

A really action packed adventure with the best fight in the whole series. Director Marvin Chomsky recalled setting up the fight. "The script said to destroy the bar, so I got about 25 of the best stunt guys and I let them do their best stunts. What we had was a wild and rowdy bar fight. We worked our way around for each stuntman to do their best."

The Night of the
Pistolaros

West and Gordon investigate a report from Charlie Tobin (O'Brien), an old army buddy, that a plot is afoot to start a war on the Mexican border. They are waylaid at a ranch by a group of Mexicans calling themselves The Pistoleros. The agents fight their way out with the aid of a grenade shot from West's gun. After finding Gordon's photo on one of the wounded Pistoleros, they decide West will take the prisoner to Fort Challenge while Gordon looks for the source of the photo.

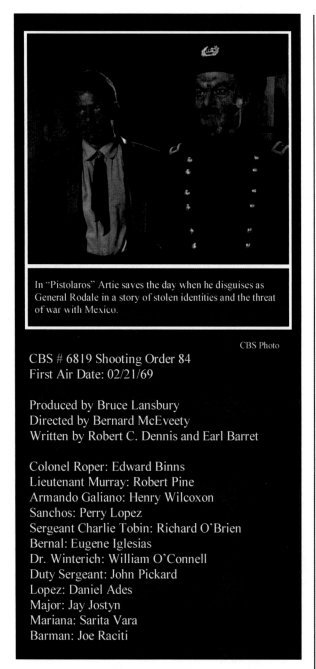

In "Pistolaros" Artie saves the day when he disguises as General Rodale in a story of stolen identities and the threat of war with Mexico.

CBS # 6819 Shooting Order 84
First Air Date: 02/21/69

Produced by Bruce Lansbury
Directed by Bernard McEveety
Written by Robert C. Dennis and Earl Barret

Colonel Roper: Edward Binns
Lieutenant Murray: Robert Pine
Armando Galiano: Henry Wilcoxon
Sanchos: Perry Lopez
Sergeant Charlie Tobin: Richard O'Brien
Bernal: Eugene Iglesias
Dr. Winterich: William O'Connell
Duty Sergeant: John Pickard
Lopez: Daniel Ades
Major: Jay Jostyn
Mariana: Sarita Vara
Barman: Joe Raciti

At the fort, Tobin is locked up and inaccessible when West arrives. West picks the guardhouse lock and Tobin doubts West is who he claims to be until the two share a memory. Tobin believes *ringers* have replaced army men so that a war may be incited. Tobin escapes during a scuffle when the guard returns, but is later shot by a *ringer*.

In nearby Tohachi, Gordon confronts Bernal (Iglesias), the photographer, and learns that many copies were made of his photo. When Bernal takes him into the studio to look for the name of the person who brought in the negative, Gordon is knocked out by a poisoned dart and wakes up in the custody of Armando Galiano (Wilcoxon).

West arrives in Tohachi to find Bernal dead. The supposed Gordon hails West in the street and tells him he'd been shanghaied. Lieutenant Murray (Pine) summons them to see Colonel Roper (Binns), the commander of the fort, who is waiting at the hotel. Gordon vouches for the identity of Lieutenant Murray, the man who killed Tobin and who Tobin had accused of being a *ringer*.

The agents are ambushed when they arrive at the hotel and Gordon is killed. After the funeral, West heads to Mexico and finds the pistolero who killed Gordon. The man stabs himself during a struggle with West. Before dying, he reveals that Gordon was assassinated to get Colonel Roper to Mexico, where he will be killed the moment he crosses the border, thus inciting a war between the United States and Mexico.

As he crosses the boarder, Colonel Roper is injured by an explosion and taken to the home of Galiano under the guise of receiving medical attention. At Galiano's home, Roper is held captive with the real Artemus Gordon. The Colonel's *ringer* is sent to meet West in his place. West meets with Roper's *ringer* at the fort. Roper has brought with him a telegram from the president with orders for the army to march on Mexico. Realizing this means war, West protests that the telegram must be verified and is locked up as a traitor. The army will march at dawn.

West tricks the pistolero incarcerated in the guardhouse into revealing that Galiano is the head of the renegades. West escapes and rides to confront Galiano. When he arrives, shooting breaks out and just when Galiano is about to shoot West in the back, a shot from Gordon saves his partner's life, abruptly ending Galiano's plan to take over Mexico in the confusion of a fabricated war. West is stunned and pleased to see his partner alive. In order to safely diffuse the troops at the border, Gordon impersonates General Rodale, exposes Roper and Murray as impersonators and orders the troops to return to the fort.

The trial for the *ringers* is on a rainy day. Gordon reports to West that the *ringers* and the ring leaders are all convicted. He is ready to go out to dinner to cheer himself up on this miserable day. Instead, West rings a dinner bell and two lovely ladies bring in a prepared feast for the agents.

Author's Notes:

"Pistoleros" is a very, very Western "West," but also is very well done. It may not have the outrageous disguises or the craziest villains, but it does have a good story. If you look closely in the last fight scene, Conrad goes all out in his actions, enough to rip the back of his pants: Quite a sight and a treat for the ladies. Watch closely and you'll see he's not the only one with a wardrobe malfunction.

While this script is entertaining, it is full of holes. The nagging question for me was why did they need a *ringer* for Artemus Gordon? If the death of the agent would help incite a war then why not kill the real agent? And why was the real Roper spared, but not the real Lieutenant Murray? My guess is it had something to do with softening the violence factor. We never actually see the young Lieutenant die, it is only assumed. With all the guns going off, there's very little actual bloodshed. Even when West confronts Artemus' supposed killer, the pistolero accidentally falls on his own knife rather than West overtaking him. This all seems a little tame for a very Western "West."

You'll notice a few changes in West and Gordon in the tag, with a different hairstyle for both and much trimmer looking Gordon. The tag was shot after Martin returned to the set after his heart attack. Since the episode itself was shot in May of 1968, three months prior to his attack, but aired in February of 1969, it could be that they found they needed the tag at the time of scheduling.

The Night of the
Spanish Curse

Just as agent James West is meeting with the terrified townspeople of Soledad, New Mexico, Cortez (David) and his Conquistadors, a mysterious outlaw gang, fire a cannon shot into the wall of the building where the meeting is taking place. Artemus Gordon learns that the gang always flees through Vasquez Pass,

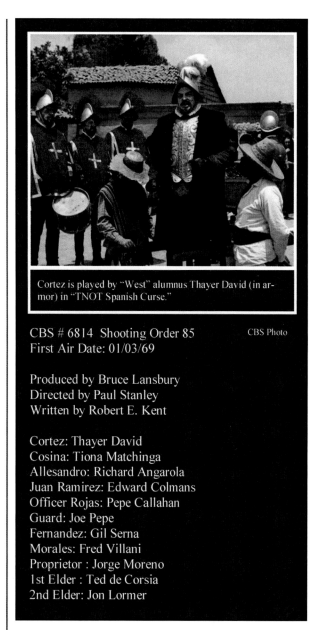

Cortez is played by "West" alumnus Thayer David (in armor) in "TNOT Spanish Curse."

CBS # 6814 Shooting Order 85   CBS Photo
First Air Date: 01/03/69

Produced by Bruce Lansbury
Directed by Paul Stanley
Written by Robert E. Kent

Cortez: Thayer David
Cosina: Tiona Matchinga
Allesandro: Richard Angarola
Juan Ramirez: Edward Colmans
Officer Rojas: Pepe Callahan
Guard: Joe Pepe
Fernandez: Gil Serna
Morales: Fred Villani
Proprietor : Jorge Moreno
1st Elder : Ted de Corsia
2nd Elder: Jon Lormer

from where superstitious natives believe no one ever returns. Many of the townsmen have been lured there, with the same results.

West follows the Conquistadores across the border and enlists the aid of a Mexican resident, Juan Ramirez (Colmans), and his beautiful daughter, Cosina (Matchinga), to track Cortez to his cavernous headquarters deep inside an extinct volcano. There he forces the enslaved villagers to work in a mercury mine. Cortez kidnaps Cosina and says he will be lenient on the workers and her father if she will marry him.

Gordon poses as Cosina's father and infiltrates the volcano. When Cosnia sees that her *father* is safe, she goes along with the charade and tells Cortez that she will be his bride. West discovers that the loud thundering sound they hear is a giant drum that is amplified to sound like the volcano is preparing to erupt. West doesn't get far with the discovery before he is captured.

Gordon is cooking for the men and brings food to those guarding West. They are knocked out by his meal and Gordon gives West a putty explosive to free him of his chains. Gordon sets off timed explosive devices and the agents make their way out of the volcano. The explosives are charged and it brings the volcano to life, trapping Cortez and killing him. The workers are returned to their village, which is now freed from the curse of Cortez.

The Night of the
Big Blackmail

While President Grant (Engel) attends a fencing competition at the German consulate, Baron Hinterstoisser (Korman) tells him that he has something to show him at a special reception and would appreciate his attendance. West, always looking out for President Grant's best interests, sneaks away to recover the mysterious box about which the Baron refers. West intercepts the dumbwaiter and replaces the contents of the box with a heavy book, as not to arouse suspicion. What was so carefully guarded is a kinetoscope of a bogus depiction of President Grant signing a secret agreement with an unsavory nation. If the film is shown to international powers, Grant will suffer horrible indignation and cause distrust and strained relationships with the rest of the world. If the film is not returned, however, the Baron will accuse the United States of stealing on embassy soil, a far greater crime.

Gordon decides that the only option is to create a duplicate kinetoscope, with a few modifications, and return it to the embassy before it is discovered missing. West must locate the blueprints of the em-

Harvey Korman (left) does an outstanding job as Baron Hinterstoisser, a duplicitous German trying to discredit President Grant.

CBS # 6801 Shooting Order 86   CBS Photos
First Air Date: 09/27/68

Produced by Bruce Lansbury
Directed by Irving J. Moore
Written by David Mossinger

Baron Hinterstoisser: Harvey Korman
Dick January: Ron Rich
Count Hackmar: Martin Kosleck
President Grant: Roy Engel
Hilda: Alice Nunn
Herr Hess: Wilhelm von Homburg
Gruber: Gil Stuart
Ziegler: Jerry Laveroni

Artie's comic talents get the chance to shine.

bassy and devise an alternate entrance option.

The agents go back to the embassy and get past several guards and a very sophisticated safe. The safe is locked by a pressure system that West must keep open with one hand while fighting with the other one. Gordon quickly places the film back in its box and replaces the seal. West and Gordon finish just in time to meet up with the president upon his arrival.

The Baron announces that he has proof of President Grant's intimate connection to the unsavory nation. As the film is run before an attentive crowd, it quickly transforms into a comedy, with Gordon ably impersonating the president. This proves to be a great embarrassment to the Germans and now the Baron must answer to his superiors.

Later, West congratulates Gordon on a great performance on screen. This gives Gordon an idea. He imagines a show, much like the one at the embassy, only longer and with charged admission. West just shakes his head and tells Gordon, "It'll never catch on."

Author's Notes:

CBS knew they had a winner with "Big Blackmail," which is why they slotted it for the fourth season's premiere episode. It is an excellent script, accented by elaborate sets and studded with some great mechanical gimmicks. It is a fast paced, suspenseful hour well spent for any fan. Critics seemed to enjoy reviewing the episode, giving it high marks across the board.

Guest star Harvey Korman is a very good Baron Hinterstoisser. Director Irving Moore remembered trying to get through a scene with Korman. "In the scene where Harvey meets all the dignitaries, he came to me and said, 'You've got to be careful because every time I speak I start to think of the "Carol Burnett Show,"' So he came in, his mouth opened, and I started to laugh and he started to laugh."

The flip card system referred to as the kinetoscope wasn't invented until 1888 by George Eastman (of Eastman Kodak fame). The kinetoscope actually was more like a short piece of film, less than 50 feet, that ran for about 13 seconds. The Mutoscope — a development by Herman Casler in 1894 — was made with pictures on flip cards printed from large format Mutograph/Biograph camera negatives. It soon superseded the kinetoscope. The movie screen wasn't invented until 1895.

The Night of the
Gruesome Games

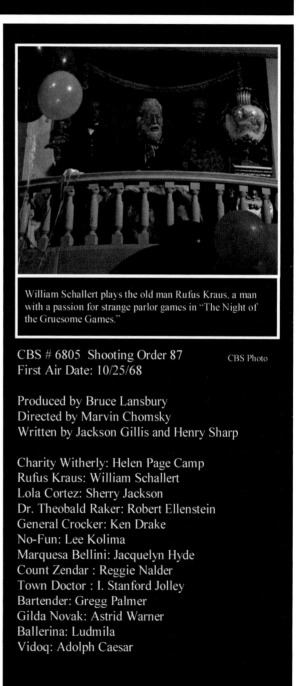

William Schallert plays the old man Rufus Kraus, a man with a passion for strange parlor games in "The Night of the Gruesome Games."

CBS # 6805 Shooting Order 87   CBS Photo
First Air Date: 10/25/68

Produced by Bruce Lansbury
Directed by Marvin Chomsky
Written by Jackson Gillis and Henry Sharp

Charity Witherly: Helen Page Camp
Rufus Kraus: William Schallert
Lola Cortez: Sherry Jackson
Dr. Theobald Raker: Robert Ellenstein
General Crocker: Ken Drake
No-Fun: Lee Kolima
Marquesa Bellini: Jacquelyn Hyde
Count Zendar : Reggie Nalder
Town Doctor : I. Stanford Jolley
Bartender: Gregg Palmer
Gilda Novak: Astrid Warner
Ballerina: Ludmila
Vidoq: Adolph Caesar

Agent West is on the trail of Dr. Theobald Raker (Ellenstein), who has recently stolen a vial containing a deadly germ. After a chase, West finds the doctor dead. Before dying, he had managed to hide the vial. Highly unstable, the germ, when exposed to room temperature, will burst and rampantly spread the deadly culture, creating a plague the likes of which the world has never known. The agent estimates that the vial will burst around midnight – making time of the essence.

The agents discover that Dr. Raker was one of the invited guests at a party thrown by the eccentric millionaire Rufus Kraus (Schallert), who is known for parties with added surprises. Knowing Raker has hidden the deadly culture in the luggage of one of the guests, West and Gordon are left with only three hours to locate the vial. The agents attend the party with Gordon posing as Dr. Raker.

Once at the party, Kraus announces that everyone there will be remembered generously in his will, but only those who are alive at the hour of his death will receive any inheritance. Kraus puts his guests through a series of childish party games, with certain consequences. Many of the guests are murdered in the process. Knowing that Kraus is not responsible for the murders, and to flush out the actual killer, Gordon disguises himself as Kraus and announces that the games have ceased and the authorities have been notified to claim the killer.

Dr. Raker, who it turns out is very much alive, attempts to kill Kraus/Gordon and the agents step in and force him to reveal the location of the deadly vial. The party hostess gets the drop on the agents, revealing that she is Raker's accomplice. Soon the agents regain the upper hand, locate the vial and toss it into the furnace just before it explodes. The world is safe again.

At the train, West and Gordon receive a package that contains the book *The Encyclopedia of Parlor Games*, graciously sent by Rufus Kraus. Gordon opens the door and West tosses out the book.

Author's Notes:

William Schallert plays, or rather overplays, Kraus, a unlikable codger with a penchant for games. Schallert will return later in the fourth season as agent Frank Harper filling in for Artemus Gordon, (the recuperating Ross Martin), who has been called to Washington on urgent business.

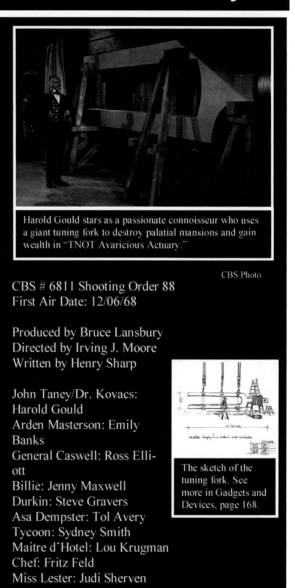

The Night of the
Avaricious Actuary

Harold Gould stars as a passionate connoisseur who uses a giant tuning fork to destroy palatial mansions and gain wealth in "TNOT Avaricious Actuary."

CBS Photo

CBS # 6811 Shooting Order 88
First Air Date: 12/06/68

Produced by Bruce Lansbury
Directed by Irving J. Moore
Written by Henry Sharp

John Taney/Dr. Kovacs: Harold Gould
Arden Masterson: Emily Banks
General Caswell: Ross Elliott
Billie: Jenny Maxwell
Durkin: Steve Gravers
Asa Dempster: Tol Avery
Tycoon: Sydney Smith
Maitre d'Hotel: Lou Krugman
Chef: Fritz Feld
Miss Lester: Judi Sherven

The sketch of the tuning fork. See more in Gadgets and Devices, page 168.

Investigating strange events that have demolished several palatial homes, secret agents West and Gordon burst into the residence of the wealthy Mr. Taney (Gould) when they suddenly hear a high, whining sound. As plaster falls and wine glasses crash to the floor, they escape the building just in time. A wagon parked at the front of the house contains a gigantic tuning fork that emits powerful sound waves. West disposes of three burly guards around the wagon, but when the sound energy is directed toward him, he fall unconscious.

The agents get deeper into the case when they find a letter in the rubble of Mr. Taney's house from the Cyclops Insurance Company, urging him to take out a policy against destruction of his home. When West investigates the company, he finds a false front office, a few thugs and some declining weight cards of an unusual shape. West checks out the weight cards and they lead him to a penny arcade supply house. West is soon captured when he is caught snooping around.

Meanwhile, Artie goes to The Midas Club, a group of wealthy men who have all received notices from Cyclops Insurance, and tries to convince them to refuse to do business with the extortionists. The men refuse to listen, believing it's easier to just pay the protection money and keep their homes intact.

Knowing that the giant tuning fork is the cause of the destruction, the agents believe that a Dr. Kovacs, who had just spent several years in prison for selling classified information, must be involved because of his previous experiments with tuning forks. Gordon follows a possible lead to Kovacs through the menu from a prestigious club of food connoisseurs known as The Epicurean Society. Gordon disguises himself as an Italian waiter to see if Dr. Kovacs shows. Instead, a very crude man comes in his place.

At the arcade, West learns that Mr. Taney is actually Dr. Kovacs, whose prison stay prompted him to lose a tremendous amount of weight, hence the weight cards. A devout epicurean by nature, the doctor's prison stay left him bitter and vindictive. Kovacs' plan is to continue his path of destruction with bigger tuning forks to even bigger targets.

West is tied up at a shooting gallery and, just as he thinks he's a sitting duck, Gordon appears disguised as a slightly deaf, incredibly nearsighted gas man in search of a reported leak. Kovacs finds it rather amusing that a gas man thinks that West is a large dummy target and tells Gordon to shoot the eyes off the dummy. Gordon pretends to lose control of the gun, allowing West time to cut his bonds.

Gordon activates the tuning fork and it rattles the warehouse just enough to help West overtake Kovacs.

At the train, the agents are trying to impress their dates by showing them how to use a small tuning fork. After several attempts to make it work, to no avail, Artie's date picks up the fork, strikes it and everything in the lab explodes and shatters.

Author's Notes:

This episode marks another "West" casualty, when Ross Martin earns his badge of honor as a performer injured during a stunt. Martin broke his leg in this shooting gallery scene. After a quick change, a stand-in was made up as the gas meter reader to complete the scene. It's a fairly evident switch-off, though, that serves to break the pacing of the climax. Production on the series was halted for just a few days. Martin returned, bearing a cast that had to be hidden beneath costuming or cleverly written into the scripts.

The Night of the
Juggernaut

Another "West" device, a deadly and colorful tank, wreaks havoc on homesteaders in "Juggernaut."

After they find a homesteader dead, agents West and Gordon are attacked by a steam-driven *Juggernaut*. They learn that someone is using the massive machine to drive the homesteaders off their land. The county clerk (Foulger), backed by two gunmen, remains silent when West inquires as to who

Boxer Floyd Patterson plays Lyle Dixon, one of the homesteaders. Bob Conrad recruited notable boxers as guest stars because of his passion for the sport. Below Conrad chats with Patterson in a behind-the-scenes shot.

CBS # 6803 Shooting Order 89   CBS Photos
First Air Date: 10/11/68

Produced by Bruce Lansbury
Directed by Irving J. Moore
Written by Calvin Clements Jr.

Lyle Dixon: Floyd Patterson
Theodore Beck: Simon Scott
Lonie Millard: Gloria Calomee
Tom Harwood: Peter Hale
Maddox: Bart La Rue
County Clerk: Byron Foulger
1st Farmer: Stuart Nisbet
2nd Farmer: Irvin Mosley
Old Geezer: Wild Bill Reynolds
Nurse: Evelyn Dutton

wants the land. The owner of the general store is equally reluctant to offer information and announces he will no longer sell goods to the homesteaders.

Lyle Dixon (Patterson), a rebellious homesteader, invites West to a secret meeting of the homesteaders, only to have it disrupted by the arrival of the destructive *Juggernaut*. The intimidated homesteaders agree to sell Gordon, disguised as a wealthy Texan, their land on a temporary basis. Gordon believes that the *Juggernaut* owner/landgrabber will reveal himself to a single landowner.

In a local saloon, Gordon is approached by the owner of the D & F Land Company, Theodore Beck (Scott). Beck offers to buy the land but Gordon refuses and is promptly drugged. West finds the *Juggernaut* at Beck's home, which confirms his involvement. After investigating a little further, West climbs into the machine and is off and running.

Beck brings Gordon to his home to force him to sign over his land. West tries to rescue Gordon and is also captured. The agents discover that Beck wants the land for its oil. The agents manage to escape and seize control of the powerful machine, quickly overtaking Beck and his men.

Author's Notes:

"Juggernaut" was the first episode shot after Ross Martin's mishap. The role was rewritten to include an opening scene in which Gordon is injured by a falling building, explaining his leg cast. The remaining scenes with Martin were shot with the actor either seated or using a double when walking or running.

The Night of the
Kraken

Just as Navy Lieutenant Bartlett (Davis) is about to explain to agents West and Gordon why fishing has been prohibited in local waters, they are attacked by four rough and tough sailors. As the agents subdue the foursome, they hear a scream and find Bartlett dead on the dock, the apparent victim of a giant sea monster: The Kraken. Daniel (Knight), a crazed preacher, espouses warnings that San Francisco is doomed.

Admiral Hammond (Rainey) tells the agents

Ted Knight gets the chance to show his acting chops as he plays the mad preacher, Daniel, and the brains behind a giant fake sea monster in "TNOT Kraken."

CBS Photo

CBS # 6806 Shooting Order 90
First Air Date: 11/01/68

Produced by Bruce Lansbury
Directed by Michael Caffey
Written by Stephen Kandel

Commander Beech: Jason Evers
Admiral Charles Hammond: Ford Rainey
Daniel: Ted Knight
Jose Aguila: Anthony Caruso
Dolores Hammond: Marj Dusay
Lieutenant Dave Bartlett: Brent Davis
1ˢᵗ Bartender: Gregg Martel
2ⁿᵈ Bartender: Claudio Miranda
Workman: Bill Baldwin
Aide: Larry Grant

that Bartlett was going to tell them that fishing has been halted due to a giant squid that has been terrorizing the harbor. West accompanies Jose Aguila (Caruso), an obstinate fisherman, who declares he is going fishing, squid or no squid. In the harbor, Aguila's boat is attacked by the monster, which pulls the fisherman overboard. As West fights free of the creature, he manages

to break off a portion of one of its tentacles – which is made of vulcanized rubber. This convinces everyone that the monster is much more than just a natural phenomenon. The Kraken is apparently a mechanical device operated by someone.

At Admiral Hammond's office, the Admiral shows West and Gordon a note indicating that Admiral Farragut is scheduled to be on the U.S.S. Missouri, which could be the Kraken's next target. Just as Hammond is about to reveal the key to the entire scheme, an explosion kills him. West and Gordon find a model of an underwater installation in his office and devise an infiltration plan. West decides to take Bartlett's experimental diving helmet for its first run.

At the installation, it is revealed that Hammond's wife, Dolores (Dusay), is involved, along with preacher Daniel, in the plan to destroy the Missouri. West infiltrates the installation, but is quickly captured and tied up. Gordon sneaks in using one of his disguises. West is set free by Gordon, but the bomb is released. West swims out after the bomb before it reaches the ship and reprograms the device to return to explode the installation. With the installation destroyed, Admiral Farragut is now safe.

At the train, Gordon is looking through the many books left by Bartlett. West, too, is looking through a book – his from playboy millionaire Irving Moore. Gordon wants to see West's book because of all the women once known to the playboy. West hesitates as Gordon persuades him with a collection of volumes on underwater diving equipment. West still declines, until Gordon offers him the book entitled, *How You'll Live to Regret It If You Don't Give Me That Book.* West smiles and hands it over.

Author's Notes:

The diving helmet used in "Kraken" is a from scuba gear or an aqualung. The first one ever developed was by British designer H.A. Fleuss in 1877. Martin is still in his cast in this episode. Note the clever name of the playboy millionaire. As mentioned in second season's "Watery Death," Admiral Farragut died in 1870, but the writers seemed to lean on saving the deceased admiral from, perhaps, a fate worse than death.

Actor Ted Knight appears as the demented preacher-turned-criminal Daniel. Knight is best known for his role as Ted Baxter on the long-running "Mary Tyler Moore Show." He appeared in nearly 90 roles on film and television before his death in 1986.

The Night of the
Sedgewick Curse

West finds Redmond (Arthur Space), a once younger man, held captive by the strange Sedgewick family in "The Night of the Sedgewick Curse."

CBS # 6804 Shooting Order 91
First Air Date: 10/18/68

CBS Photo

Produced by Bruce Lansbury
Directed by Marvin Chomsky
Written by Paul Playdon

Lavinia Sedgewick: Sharon Acker
Dr. Maitland: Jay Robinson
Philip Sedgewick: Richard Hale
Jessica: Maria Lennard
Fingers: Frank Campanella
A.T. Redmond: Arthur Space
Old Lady/Aged Lavinia: Kathryn Minner
1st Prisoner: William Challee
2nd Prisoner: Anthony Jochim
1st Desk Clerk: Arthur Adams
2nd Desk Clerk: Lee Weaver
Boy: Brian Nash
Felix: Gene LeBell

Agent James West is getting papers signed by Mr. Redmond (Space) at the Sedgewick Hotel. The agent leaves for just a moment and, when he returns, Redmond has disappeared without a trace, with everyone denying ever having seen him. The suspicious Gordon returns to the hotel disguised as an old Englishman and asks too many questions. The agent is nearly parboiled, but discovers that Redmond was taken away because of a rare blood disorder known as Lubbock's Distemper.

In town, West rescues lovely and wealthy Lavinia Sedgewick (Acker) in her runaway carriage, the perfect mode of introduction. The grateful woman invites West to dinner at the Sedgewick mansion. He quickly accepts, recognizing the Sedgewick crest is similar to a symbol drawn in blood by a murder victim.

West arrives for dinner and the housekeeper tries to warn him to go away. She says there is evil in the Sedgewick House.

Gordon returns to the hotel disguised as a Frenchman suffering from Lubbock's Distemper. He makes sure the hotel clerk knows of his disorder. He checks in and fakes being drugged and awaits his fate.

Back at the Sedgewick house, West is introduced to Dr. Maitland (Robinson), the family physician, and to the Sedgewick's grandfather. After the agent is shown to his room, he is almost killed. He searches the rest of the house, following strange sounds emanating from a strange, secluded area. Voices of old people resonate throughout the corridor. West discovers a room full of very aged people, one of whom he recognizes as Redmond, now 40 years older than when he saw him at the hotel.

Gordon, still disguised as the ailing Frenchman, is brought to the house and is prepared by Dr. Maitland for injection of a mysterious serum. It is discovered that the doctor has been conducting experiments that have had adverse effects on his guinea pigs. In an effort to save the Sedgewick family from inherited rapid aging, Maitland has prematurely aged several innocent people with the unique blood disorder Lubbock's Distemper, which is eerily similar to the Sedgewick genetic disorder. Maitland is motivated by Lavinia, who is terrified of growing old before her time and is bent on inheriting the family fortune. Gordon is prepared for the injection, but he has switched the serum with pure distilled water while everyone was turned away.

After Maitland injects Gordon, West bursts in

192

and a fight ensues. Lavinia notices the unconscious Gordon has not aged like all the others and excitedly believes that the serum has been perfected. She quickly injects herself with the drug. Gordon awakens, but is too late to tell her he substituted the serum for water. Maitland, knowing what the result will be, stops fighting the agents.

As the authorities take away Maitland, he expresses concern to the agents over what's to become of Lavinia. West simply says, "She will be cared for." A frighteningly shriveled, trembling woman is taken out of the house in a wheelchair.

Author's Notes:

"Sedgewick" is a very bizarre tale that fits nicely into the "West" format. During the fourth season the violence issue prompted considerable changes on the set. The limit on fights and the restrictions imposed on pointing guns definitely let a little air out of the show's excitement factor.

In the scene where Maitland's men point a gun at West everyone was reminded of the *new rules*. So when West says, "You'll never get away with this," Maitland responds, "You're right, give him your gun."

The Night of the
Fire and Brimstone

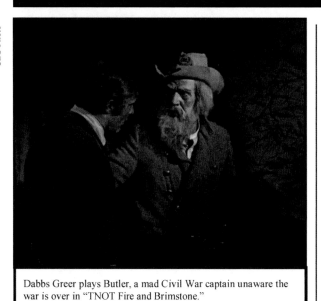

Dabbs Greer plays Butler, a mad Civil War captain unaware the war is over in "TNOT Fire and Brimstone."

CBS # 6809 Shooting Order 92
First Air Date: 11/22/68

Produced by Bruce Lansbury
Directed by Bernard McEveety
Written by Joel Kane and Milton Smith

Frank Roach: Robert Phillips
Dooley Sloan: Leslie Charleson
Professor Philip Colecrest: John Crawford
Zack Morton: Charles McCauley
Captain Lyman Butler: Dabbs Greer
Hannon: Ken Mayer
Lefty: Fred Stromsoe
Dr. Emmett Sloan: Bill Quinn

Professor Philip Colecrest (Crawford) is being held for ransom in the abandoned mining town, Brimstone. West and Gordon receive a note from the professor telling them to come to the town because of a great discovery. When the agents arrive, they meet Zack Morton (McCauley), who tells them that he is the professor and the discovery was not really that important. The suspicious agents think otherwise and a gunfight ensues.

West and Gordon escape into a barn and find a trap door that leads to a tunnel. West finds the real Professor Colecrest, who has been injured in a fall. Gordon sneaks out of the tunnel to seek a doctor while West watches over the professor.

Hiding in another part of the tunnel is former Confederate officer Captain Lyman Butler (Greer). The severely unbalanced Butler had been the commander of a southern supply train in the final days of the war. After being attacked by bandits, the captain stashed his supplies in the abandoned tunnel and has since guarded it with the help of his sergeant, a skeleton of a man.

The captain orders West to inform General Lee that his shipment is intact. The agents pretend to go along with the deranged man, knowing that the supplies also contain gold and other valuables.

Morton's gang intends to steal everything the captain is guarding. Gordon returns to the tunnel with the doctor, whose daughter goes to find him and is captured and held hostage by Morton's men until the professor's whereabouts is revealed. Gordon disguises himself as the doctor and with West's help, they defeat

CBS Photo

the Morton gang. Now they are faced with convincing the captain to give up his charge. Gordon again dons a disguise, this time as General Lee, who demands the captain relinquish command.

Author's Notes:
"Fire and Brimstone" was the last show before the crew's break on hiatus. This is also the episode before Ross Martin's near fatal heart attack. This "West" episode had the highest audience response in all of the series' four seasons.

The Night of
Miguelito's Revenge

CBS Photo

This is the last time we get to see the agents battle the likes of Loveless. This is more a story of vengeance than the usual world domination for the doctor, who executes a dramatic escape and is sadly never to be heard from again.

Agent West is called to the local barbershop by a note from fellow agent Gordon. West decides to get a shave while waiting for his partner and is anesthetized by a hot towel. When the agent awakens, he is in a carnival funhouse where he sees the dazed justice Alonzo Fairlie (Morrow). West subdues a quartet of gunmen, but Fairlie disappears leaving only a mysterious note, which reads: Thursday's child has far to go.

A confused West finds himself back at the barbershop. At the train, West is greeted by another fellow agent, Jeremy Pike (Aidman), Gordon's temporary replacement while he's away on a business in Washington. Together the agents figure out that Judge Fairlie was kidnapped and the children's rhyme probably has involved others. They look into the Monday disappearance of actress Lynn Carstairs (Chandler).

Pike finds a brandy snifter and deduces that the head criminal drank a specific kind of brandy. Pike poses as a brandy salesman and investigates further. He is told to deliver the unique brandy to the Wells Fargo office in Denver. Considering the next part of the rhyme, Pike figures the next victim will be millionaire Cyrus Pylo (Batanides).

West goes to Fiddlers Bend to follow the circus and discovers another unexplained disappearance. When he passes by a saloon, he hears the familiar voice of Dr. Miguelito Loveless (Dunn). West finds Loveless in a room along with his newest invention: a powerful, steam-driven man. West is no match for the machine and is knocked uncon-

CBS # 6812 Shooting Order 93
First Air Date: 12/13/68

Produced by Bruce Lansbury
Directed by James B. Clark
Written by Jerry Thomas

Dr. Miguelito Loveless: Michael Dunn
Jeremy Pike: Charles Aidman
Delilah: Susan Seaforth
Colonel James Richmond: Douglas Henderson
Pylo: Arthur Batanides
Tiny: Jim Shane
Abbie Carter: Don Pedro Colley
Judge Alonzo Fairlie: Byron Morrow
Ivan Kalinkovitch: Peter Bruni
Cyrus Barlow: Walter Coy
Biff Trout: Johnny S. Luer
Proprietor: Percy Helton
Lynn Carstairs: Linda Chandler
Sheriff: Roy Barcroft
Biff Trout: Johnny Silver
Theater Manager: Dort Clark

scious. The agent is placed in a coffin and sent to the bottom of the river. West, using West ingenuity, quickly escapes.

Pike poses as Pylo and is kidnapped. West returns to the circus and learns that Loveless is behind all the kidnappings. The Doctor plans a mock trial for each victim with the inevitable verdict of guilty and therefore sentenced to death. The agents discover that each person had, in some way, wronged the diminutive demon. West is to be included as Sunday's Child.

Pike as Pylo is brought to Loveless and creates a handy diversion. West is busy fighting an array of henchmen when Loveless climbs into a nearby cannon and shoots himself out of the tent. The agent cannot stop his escape. West and Pike give chase but find only a strange dummy, equipped with Loveless' familiar voice saying, "There will be another time."

At the train, Pike reads that the Loveless gang has been rounded up and justice is served. West says that he feels sorry for Artie, being stuck in Washington. They pour a drink for themselves and one for Gordon (an absent colleague). As they toast, Gordon's drink mysteriously disappears, leaving two bewildered agents.

Author's Notes:

With the onset of Martin's heart attack, actor Charles Aidman was quickly cast as a replacement. The script called for Artie to be sent on special assignment to Washington, where he was much needed. CBS decided to alternate episodes with Gordon and Pike so that audiences wouldn't be so jarred by the absence of the beloved Artie character.

Aidman remembered the first day on the set. "Bob (Conrad) told me the very first day I worked on the show, 'You gotta remember one thing about me. I don't learn my lines until they are ready to shoot the shot.' I knew the first three or four takes I'd do with him I couldn't possibly get the timing. At least he told me upfront. That helped a lot. I think if he hadn't told me that, I would've gone crazy."

Unfortunately, there wouldn't be *another time* for Dr. Loveless, as he predicts at the end of this episode. "Miguelito's Revenge" turned out to be an anti-climactic swan song for Dunn and an end to Loveless' complex and ambivalent relationship with James West.

The Night of the
Camera

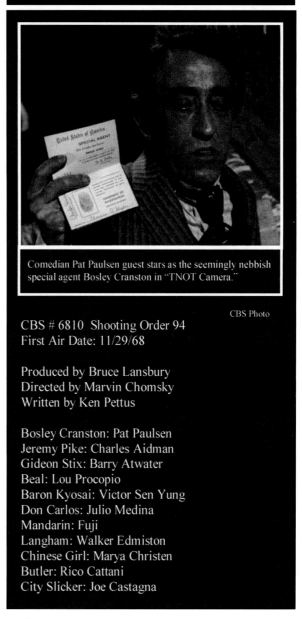

Comedian Pat Paulsen guest stars as the seemingly nebbish special agent Bosley Cranston in "TNOT Camera."

CBS Photo

CBS # 6810 Shooting Order 94
First Air Date: 11/29/68

Produced by Bruce Lansbury
Directed by Marvin Chomsky
Written by Ken Pettus

Bosley Cranston: Pat Paulsen
Jeremy Pike: Charles Aidman
Gideon Stix: Barry Atwater
Beal: Lou Procopio
Baron Kyosai: Victor Sen Yung
Don Carlos: Julio Medina
Mandarin: Fuji
Langham: Walker Edmiston
Chinese Girl: Marya Christen
Butler: Rico Cattani
City Slicker: Joe Castagna

Agent James West trails a suspected member of an opium ring into a warehouse. As West and the suspect fight, meek Bosley Cranston (Paulsen) rushes in intent on helping West. Instead

Cranston accidentally releases a suspended piano crate, which falls and kills West's only lead to the crime ring. Cranston turns out to be a new secret agent sent out by the department to gain some field experience. West and his associate Jeremy Pike (Aidman) at first feel that Cranston will be a detriment to their efforts to crack the opium smuggling ring. To keep him out of trouble, the agents assign the novice to catching up on paperwork.

West and Pike are in search of a code book that contains the names of the members of the ring. They get one of the two volumes and use a ruse of selling it to uncover the head of the ring, a wealthy businessman named Gideon Stix (Atwater). They are also able to uncover the whereabouts of the second volume. The agents learn that Cranston is gifted with a photographic memory, a handy talent when they break into Stix's home and must duplicated the contents of both books.

Pike disguises as a bogus Brit Cecil Smythe Allen and goes to Stix's home pretending to sell him a phony jewel. Stix, an avid collector, is distracted long enough for West and Cranston to break into the upstairs office and duplicate the books. A fight ensues and West and Pike defeat Stix's henchmen while Cranston goes after the exiting Stix. Pike and West are astonished to see that Cranston is a Karate expert, and in a showdown with the villain, overcomes Stix in a matter of moments.

Back at the train, Cranston tries to convince his fellow agents to join him for an evening with three *very intelligent* sisters. West and Pike devise a story to gracefully decline the invitation, assuming that any female friend of Cranston's would be equally as demure and unassuming. They are, again, surprised by Bosley's versatility as he climbs into a carriage with three ravishing women and makes polite excuses for his partners.

Author's Notes:

Marvin Chomsky directed "Camera" and, since this episode did not include Ross Martin, he opted to take a completely different approach to West's partner. "During the episodes that Ross was not in, if a Secret Service agent came in, I would not have that character do the same things that Ross did. I would try to do something that gave a unique quality to that character. I would call Ross' Gordon an intelligent bumbler, a much better bumbler than Charles Aidman or William Schallert. Aidman played Pike much more straight [sic] than Ross played Gordon, who added a touch of humor to every scene."

The Night of the
Pelican

A bizarre puppet show is the backdrop for this strange tale about Chang, a madman who has taken over Alcatraz prison in "The Night of the Pelican."

CBS # 6813 Shooting Order 95   CBS Photo
First Air Date: 12/27/68

Produced by Bruce Lansbury
Directed by Alex Nicol
Written by Richard Landau

Jeremy Pike: Charles Aidman
Din Chang: Khigh Dhiegh
Corporal Simon: Vincent Beck
Major Frederick Frey: Lou Cutell
Dr. Sara Gibson: Francine York
Jean-Paul: Andre Philippe
Kuei : Debbie Wong
Amy : Ella Edwards
Lieutenant Bengston: Buck Kartalian
Colonel Kelton Morse: John Creamer
Quen Yung: James Shen
Molly: Holly Mascott
Jeanne: Lorna Denels
Chinese Girl #1: Linda Ho

Agents West and Pike are waiting for a contact to arrive at a Chinese restaurant with information to lead to a criminal named Chang (Dheigh). A fortune cookie directs them to a young Asian girl. The agents witness the girl being suddenly attacked and killed by two men. Before she dies, she tells the agents one word: pelican. After giving chase, West captures one of the men and immediately recognizes him as a prisoner who should still be serving his time in Alcatraz. West wires the authorities to see if the prisoner has escaped, but is told that the man is still in prison. West investigates further.

The dead girl left two clues: a ring and a marionette stick. Pike checks out the marionettes by visiting a local puppet show. He finds out that the dead girl was the sister of the owner of the show. She tells Pike abut a Frenchman named Jean-Paul (Philippe) who is a friend of Chang's. She informs him of his whereabouts at the docks.

West poses as a prisoner in Alcatraz and comes under the supervision of a guard named Corporal Simon (Beck). Simon eventually reveals that the underworld figure, Chang, has taken over the island.

Pike, disguised as a stevedore, sneaks onto the docks and stows away in one of the crates of rockets heading for Alcatraz. West has an audience with Chang, who tells the agent about his plan to control the San Francisco Bay with rockets fired from Alcatraz at the U.S. fleet. Pike arrives and helps West escape. West races to the rocket launch area as one rocket scores a hit on a ship. West blows up the room and stops Chang and Jean-Paul from escaping.

At the train, West and Pike are entertaining two young ladies, but West can't help but think of poor Artie all alone at a desk in Washington. Pike tells West he received a new talking record from Gordon. As they play it, a woman's voice comes on and tells them that Mr. Gordon is working so hard in Washington. As she continues, she commences laughing and giggling. West and Pike now know that Artie is not so lonely.

Author's Notes:
        This is the third episode without Ross Martin and with the capable Charles Aidman continuing his role as Jeremy Pike. Aidman proved to be popular with the audiences but the team of Jim and Artie could not be challenged. Again, CBS shuffled the Gordon episodes with the Pike episodes to take the sting out of the actor's absence. During the series of Aidman/Gordon

switch offs, I remember, as a young viewer, being confused about why Gordon was popping back and forth to Washington.

The Night of the
Janus

James West returns to his training academy and into the middle of a counterfeiting ring in "TNOT Janus." Pike steps in disguised and ready to help.

CBS # 6818 Shooting Order 96   CBS Photo
First Air Date: 02/14/69

Produced by Bruce Lansbury
Directed by Irving J. Moore
Teleplay by Leonard Katzman
Story by Paul Playdon

Jeremy Pike: Charles Aidman
Alan Thorpe: Jack Carter
Warren Blessing: Anthony Eisley
Torrey Elder: Jackie de Shannon
Professor Montague: Arthur Malet
Thompson: Nicky Blair
Janus: Benny Rubin
Swanson: Vince Barnett
Instructor: Mark Allen

West investigates the death of trusted Secret Service agent Fred Doorman. A woman who knew him has sheet music he left behind. While the piano man plays, she sings a song and is interrupted by a gunshot. In the subsequent melee, the sheet music is destroyed except for its title: *Two Faced Stranger in the Garden.*

On the train, agent Jeremy Pike checks the music notes for clues. He and West know that Doorman was investigating a traitor in the service. The telegraph brings a response to an earlier inquiry: One of the outlets for the paper the music was printed on is named Janus. West points out that Janus is the name of the ancient two-faced god.

Pike goes to the Janus Music Company in Eden, Colorado, while West goes to the Secret Service Academy in Denver to have Professor Montague (Malet) determine if the musical notes represent some kind of code.

When West arrives he finds himself challenged by Professor Blessing (Eisley), who has set up a series of obstacles to conquer, teaching students how it should be done. This surprise welcome was an amiable demonstration except that one of the bullets fired was not a blank and nicked Alan Thorpe (Carter), Blessing's assistant. West locates Professor Montague and he tries to decipher the supposed code.

At the Janus Music Company, the proprietor gives Pike a legacy left by Doorman, a music box designed by Doorman that plays a tubular disk, which is another clue the dead agent recorded. The disk is partially destroyed when four men attempt to steal it from Pike.

At the Academy, Professor Blessing has received notice that a Baron Klaus Esterhouser of the Estavian Army will be arriving and will require diplomatic courtesy. West receives a fake summons from Blessing that lures him into the *dying room* – where West faces very real attempts on his life with explosions, a plunging spear and gunshots. He escapes over the balcony.

Pike arrives at the academy posing as the Baron. He insists he be allowed in the currency section on the opposite side from the academy quarters. West enters at the same time, but through the sewer, and finds all the legitimate workers unconscious on the floor. By the time he reaches the printing room the Baron, too, is slumped on the floor while Alan's men print currency, reusing the serial numbers already printed on legitimate bills. Alan is revealed as the traitor and he faked the earlier shooting accident.

Pike, who had takes the precaution of a rubber glove, was not affected by the drug put in the facility hand stamp, and is not really unconscious. He provides the needed distraction to allow West to get the upper hand. As the criminals are led out, West and Pike realize that the duplicate bills must be destroyed. When West lights their cigars with the bogus bills, Pike says, "You've got real style."

Author's Notes:

This is the third episode sans the many charms of Ross Martin. In "Janus" we see West and Pike in an attempt to stop a counterfeiting ring that operates from the inside out. Aidman dons a disguise in order to infiltrate the Academy and rescue his temporary partner, not unlike something Artie would do.

Director Irving Moore commented on how he felt Aidman was put into an awkward position playing the same type of character as Martin. "Charles was trying in every way to change the Pike character so not to be in the shadow of the Gordon character. All in all, he handled it very well."

The Night of the
Winged Terror
Parts 1 & 2

Agent West attempts to warn a mayor dedicating a new railroad in their town of a pending disaster. Suddenly, a large raven rides into town on a rail car and the mayor seems to go into a trance. Mesmerized, he puts on a pair of amber-colored glasses, goes to a hidden explosive device and blows up the railroad. After another suspicious occurrence involving the raven, West and his new temporary partner, Frank Harper (Schallert), pursue the elusive bird. They hear of another incident, this one involving a sheriff who is letting dangerous criminals out of his jail. West arrives just in time to stop the escaping cons. In a scuffle, the raven is locked inside one of the cells.

West and Harper find out that an eye doctor named Occularis (Ellenstein) had stopped by to fit the sheriff for new glasses. While doing so, the doctor

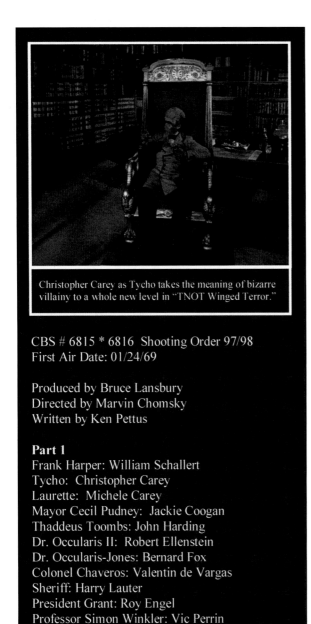
Christopher Carey as Tycho takes the meaning of bizarre villainy to a whole new level in "TNOT Winged Terror."

CBS # 6815 * 6816 Shooting Order 97/98
First Air Date: 01/24/69

Produced by Bruce Lansbury
Directed by Marvin Chomsky
Written by Ken Pettus

Part 1
Frank Harper: William Schallert
Tycho: Christopher Carey
Laurette: Michele Carey
Mayor Cecil Pudney: Jackie Coogan
Thaddeus Toombs: John Harding
Dr. Occularis II: Robert Ellenstein
Dr. Occularis-Jones: Bernard Fox
Colonel Chaveros: Valentin de Vargas
Sheriff: Harry Lauter
President Grant: Roy Engel
Professor Simon Winkler: Vic Perrin
Hiram Sneed: Norman Leavitt
Deputy: Ron Pinkard
Judd Bass: James George   CBS Photo

placed eye drops in his eyes and had him gaze into a machine with swirling images. He then asks the entranced victims about other high officials. Harper discovers that Occularis is scheduled to visit another nearby mayor. West releases the bird and follows it to

Occularis' wagon. West brings the doctor back to town but Occularis is killed by a backfiring gun given to him by Laurette (Carey), a stowaway on the doctor's wagon. Laurette disappears.

Another Occularis visits Mayor Sneed, who is actually Frank Harper in disguise. He offers the same treatment as the previous Occularis. That night West asks Harper what happened with the doctor and suddenly, when the raven appears, Harper tries to kill West.

West goes to the cantina, sees Laurette, and is drugged. He awakens in a room with a group of men belonging to an organization called The Raven. Their leader is Thaddeus Toombs (Harding). Toombs is under the command of an unusual, extremely intelligent, man with an oversized head called Tycho (Chris Carey). The group has plans to disrupt U.S.-Mexican relations by murdering the Mexican ambassador and taking over the world by using scientific means.

West blacks out and wakes up in the cantina. He tells Harper that he was put through the same conditioning as the others, but then thinks he may not have been because he has not been equipped with the signature amber spectacles. (To Be Continued...)

Part 2

At the conference with Ambassador Ramirez (Sorello), Harper is concerned that West hasn't shown up yet. Ramirez makes his appearance just as West manifests. A Mexican man approaches West with a box and a raven on his shoulder. West goes into a trance and shoots the ambassador. Harper, suspecting that West might be under the same trance as he was, had taken the precaution of disguising himself as the ambassador, but is wearing a bullet-proof vest.

When West recovers from his hypnotic state, he finds himself at The Raven headquarters. He is told he shot the ambassador, and they show him photos of the slain dignitary as proof. West notices the ring on Ramirez's hand and recognizes that it is Harper that has been shot. He feigns agreement to joining the organization. West toys with them and then sneaks out to confront Tycho, but his attempt to subdue him is futile.

Harper finds out more information on Toombs and learns that he studied under a Professor Krowler in Germany. Toombs and Krowler experimented on certain types of conditioning similar to those used by The Raven organization. Harper disguises himself as Krowler and goes in search of

James West is under the spell of amber-colored glasses forcing him to perform deadly deeds in "Winged Terror."

Part 2

Frank Harper: William Schallert
Tycho: Christopher Carey
Laurette: Michele Carey
Mayor Cecil Pudney: Jackie Coogan
Thaddeus Toombs: John Harding
Dr. Occularis II: Robert Ellenstein
President Grant: Roy Engel
Colonel Chaveros: Valentin de Vargas
Professor Simon Winkler: Vic Perrin
Ambassador Ramirez: Frank Sorello
Mexican Agent: Rico Alaniz
Townsman: Julio Medina
Agent #2: James McEachin
Peon: Jerado deCordovier

Toombs. Being obvious in town, Harper/Krowler is quickly kidnapped by Toombs. The agent tells his captor that he has perfected his conditioning serum and wants to test it on someone. Toombs says that someone should be James West. Harper/Krowler prepares West and injects him with a fake serum. The ensuing tests on West prove to Tycho and Toombs that the serum is the breakthrough they've been waiting for that will lead them to guaranteed victory.

Harper asks to talk to Tycho alone and every-

one obliges. The agents manage to seize Tycho but don't get very far. West and Harper are left to die, tied up in the exposed hideout. Toombs plans to destroy the building with explosives. When left alone, West uses his shoe knife to cut his and Harper's bonds. Tycho and Toombs make their getaway, but West quickly overtakes them. Everyone is caught except for Tycho, who escapes through a trap door to an awaiting wagon.

At the train, West and Harper are entertaining two lovely women. Harper tells West that one of the experiments used on him was from Gordon's junior chemist set. He shows the girls a sample of how the harmless concoction works. Harper uses the same amount was used on West and puts it in the ice bucket. They wait for a small, but effective, puff of smoke, but instead the bucket is blown to bits. West tells Harper not to do him anymore favors.

Author's Notes:

CBS decided not to use Charles Aidman and to move on to guest agents. The first was agent Frank Harper, played by popular character actor William Schallert. He could previously be seen on "West" in "Deadly Bubble," and "Gruesome Games."

Schallert recalled, "Aidman and myself were called in to fill in for Ross as he recovered. The reason Chuck (Aidman) and I were chosen is that we were capable of doing a versatile range of characters; versatile in our ability to create other characters convincingly. That was the key to the Gordon role; the fact that he was a man of many faces. However, when the writer wrote the Frank Harper role, he made him a bit of a dandy. I wasn't thinking so much of Ross' character as much as creating a character who was only like Artemus Gordon in the sense that he did other characters. My approach was a little more farcical. I would play the character more outrageously."

Schallert admitted that he got as much response from "West" as he did from his appearance on the wildly popular "Star Trek" episode "The Trouble with Tribbles." When one can say that, one is saying a good deal because the *Trekkies* are a huge following.

The Night of the
Sabatini Death

Alan Hale Jr. (left of Conrad) is guest agent Ned Brown in this story of inheritance and misfortune. Below, Hale's "Gilligan's Island" co-star Jim Backus appears as funeral director Swanson.

CBS Photos

CBS # 6817 Shooting Order 99
First Air Date: 02/07/69

Produced by Bruce Lansbury
Directed by Charles Rondeau
Written by Shirl Hendryx

Sylvia Nolan: Jill Townsend
Melanie Nolan: Bethel Leslie
Ned Brown: Alan Hale Jr.
Fabian Swanson: Jim Backus
Colonel James Richmond:
Douglas Henderson
Farnsworth: Donald Barry
Sheriff Chayne: Tom Geas
Johnny Sabatini:
Ted deCorsia
Clarence: Ben Wright
Snidley: Eddie Quillan

West is summoned to meet crime *tsar* Sabatini (deCorsia). The *tsar* is dying and needs someone trustworthy to protect the life of a lady who will be in great danger upon his death. He tells West to travel to Calliope, Missouri, and give a man named Swanson (Backus) a key. He warns the agent that a Mr. Boorman will try to stop him. He also explains that the mysterious lady-in-danger only knows him by the name of Mr. Caroline. Before he is able to give any more details, Sabatini, with his dying breath, says the words "Madonna statue."

Ned Brown (Hale), the department chemist, and Colonel Richmond (Henderson), discuss Sabatini's request with West. The agents recall that Calliope is where the finance officer of the army, Captain Nolan, was murdered after cheating on the gang who stole one of the army's $500,000 payrolls.

West heads for Calliope and finds Swanson, who is a funeral director, napping in one of his caskets. Their conversation is interrupted, but they agree to meet later. The few remaining occupants of Calliope dine together at the boarding house, including Melanie Nolan (Leslie), the sister of the murdered captain. West follows Swanson when he leaves, but the agent is delayed at Melanie's request. By the time West returns to the mortuary, Swanson is dead. West is attacked but Brown arrives and helps him with the fight.

Brown brings West up to date about Sylvia (Townsend), a blind girl whose memories were stirred by the death of her benefactor, Mr. Caroline. She has decided to return to Calliope with the assistance of her manservant, Clarence (Wright).

West finds Sylvia and Clarence at the Nolan mansion. The room stirs even more of Sylvia's frightening memories. When West insists she return to St. Louis for her own safety, Clarence disagrees and rushes at West. Clarence flies over the balcony as the agent outsmarts his attacker.

Brown has gone to the cemetery to search for a Madonna statue, following Sabatini's final clue. There is no Madonna in the Nolan mausoleum, but Brown discovers that Sabatini and Captain Nolan were the same man, as evidenced by the scar on the image on Nolan's crypt.

Brown escapes an attack by several thugs and joins West back at the house. Sylvia is recalling the night of the fire that killed her mother. Melanie, who had fainted earlier when she recognized Sylvia at the mansion, is encouraging Sylvia to tell about an angry man – Boorman – who followed her and her mother as they ran to the church. The man had a distinct walk such that he dragged a lame foot. He had demanded that Sylvia's mother tell him where the money was hidden. Sylvia suddenly springs a concealed lever and escapes from the room through a secret passage behind the mantel. She hears the distinctive footsteps again and Boorman has entered the room while West and Brown confer downstairs.

West and Melanie pursue Sylvia into the yard. West catches up with Sylvia and pulls her into the mausoleum. When he asks her about the Madonna statue, she turns the statue's pedestal and Nolan's crypt slides open. They are suddenly confronted by Boorman and Melanie, but Sylvia creates a diversion and West is able to grab the rifle. Brown joins them and reads the contents of an envelope; the only thing found in Nolan's crypt. Sabatini, alias Captain Nolan, alias Mr. Caroline has left all his property to Sylvia.

Back at the train, Brown tells West he's had enough Secret Service work and is planning a long vacation. When West asks if he's going to London, Paris or Rome, Brown states he just wants to be alone on a desert island. He exits to the "Gilligan's Island" theme song.

Author's Notes:

With the temporary sidelining of Martin, CBS tried different ways to keep the show interesting with-out West's better half to back him up. This week's guest agent was none other than the Skipper from "Gilligan's Island," Alan Hale Jr., with a special guest appearance from his co-star Jim Backus. Hale stars as an agent whose expertise is science. Unlike Gordon, Harper and Pike, his character does not go undercover in disguise. For a while there, I was beginning to think that it was a prerequisite to be a disguise artist if assigned to work with James West.

This is a good episode, fun and complex without being overly complicated. The tag is memorable and follows the tongue-in-cheek theme of original "West" episodes.

The Night of the
Bleak Island

West takes a boat journey through a raging storm to Bleak Island in order to attend the reading of Bleak's will and guard the bequest left to the National Museum. Gathered relatives and associates are spooked by a hound that won't stop howling. When it howls with a particularly discordant sound, the butler falls over dead and the lights flicker out. The door blows open and West follows a figure in black to the greenhouse on the island. There he fights two men until Sir Nigel Scott (Williams) comes to his aid. Nigel has been invited to the island by Celia (Garland) to pursue the mysterious hound. He and West worked together years ago in London pursing Calendar, a master criminal presumed dead. Sir Nigel tells West that certain crimes committed over the past year bear the modus operandi of Calendar and he is certain Calendar is on the island.

After the usual bequests and snubs during the reading of the will, it is revealed that the more than 1,000 carat Moon Diamond has been left to the National Museum. West and Nigel are in Bleak's treasure room when the lights go out and the window is broken. The diamond is missing and West discovers the glass has been broken from the inside. He and Nigel also discover another exit from the room, this one to the wine cellar, where the diamond turns up in an empty wine keg.

When Bleak's nephew Mark (Tyburn) and his

Noted British actor John Williams plays the two-faced investigator Sir Nigel Scott in "The Night of the Bleak Island."

CBS Photo

CBS # 6821   Shooting Order 100
First Air Date: 03/14/69

Produced by Bruce Lansbury
Directed by Marvin Chomsky
Written by Robert E. Kent

Sir Nigel Scott: John Williams
Mordecai Krone: Richard Erdman
Celia Rydell: Beverly Garland
Steven Rydell: Robert H. Harris
Helen Merritt: Lorna Lewis
Boatman: Jon Lormer
Jarvis: Pat O'Hara
Girl: Yvonne Shubert
Alicia Crane: Jana Taylor
Mark Chambers: Gene Tyburn
Ronald McAvity: James Westerfield
Servant #2: Christian Anderson

ward Alicia (Taylor) meet for a tryst, they are nearly attacked. West consults with them and gives them his gun to go back into the house safely. Having discovered that Alicia and the butler knew about the wine kegs, West proceeds to the caretaker's cottage and confronts Nigel, accusing him of imitating Calendar. Nigel admits he found life dull after the death of the real Cal-

endar and has made a new career out of duplicating the actions of the deceased criminal.

Nigel has West knocked out and placed in a well. The hound howls and Nigel admits that the dog hates him. It was Nigel who originally trained and placed the hound in order to assure that Celia would call upon him for assistance before the diamond, now in his possession, had been removed. Nigel leaves for a boat awaiting him on the other side of the island. West straps on his handy claws and climbs up the sheer well wall. He quickly pursues Nigel, who is also being pursued by the demented hound. The dog chases the wayward Londoner to the edge of a cliff, lunges at him and Nigel drops the diamond before falling to his death.

Back on the train, West informs his companion, Nancy Conrad, that the diamond has been safely delivered to the National Museum. They are interrupted by a visit from Mark and Alicia, who report they met Artemus Gordon on their recent honeymoon in Washington. They depart promptly but leave behind a gift from Artie — his photo. As West leans in to kiss Nancy he turns the photo away.

Author's Notes:

CBS decided to give "West" a little foreign flair in this episode that teams Jim with an agent from Scotland Yard, Sir Nigel Scott, appropriately played by veteran actor John Williams. Scott is the duplicitous mastermind behind all the troubles on "Bleak Island" and meets with a vicious end in this story replete with shades of Sir Arthur Conan Doyle's classic Sherlock Holmes tale, *The Hound of the Baskervilles*. It seems that West could exercise a little more discretion when choosing partners.

Williams is a recognizable face to many 1960s TV fans, having appeared in "Alfred Hitchcock Presents," "Twilight Zone" and "Night Gallery," among many others. He was memorable stepping in as Nigel French, brother to the ailing Giles French, on "Family Affair," before turning the role back over to Sebastian Cabot. Williams died in 1983.

Once in a while an inside joke sneaks into the episodes. This one comes in the form of Nancy Conrad, the woman West shares a romantic drink with in the tag. The name Nancy came from Bob Conrad's daughter.

The Night of the
Tycoons

Fake mannequins add to the mystery of a corporation's dying board members in "Tycoons."

CBS Photo

CBS # 6823 Shooting Order 101
First Air Date: 03/28/69

Produced by Bruce Lansbury
Directed by Mike Moder
Teleplay by Louis Vittes
Story by Barney Slater

Amelia Bronston: Jo Van Fleet
Lionel Bronston: Steve Carlson
Krya Vanders: Joanie Sommers
Mr. Gorhan: Tol Avery
O'Brien : E.A. Sirianni
Melanie : Michelle Breeze
Mr. Van Cleve: Richard O'Brien
Kessel: Milton Parsons
Businessman: Cal Currens
Bartender: Lee Duncan
Honey: María García
Head Guard: Mike Mahoney
Matron: Virginia Peters
Butler: Buff Brady

West crashes a board meeting of the Jupiter Corporation, and so does an organ grinder's monkey, who climbs in a second story window and drops a rolling white ball that explodes. Saved by West's warning, the board is inclined to agree that they need his protection while he investigates the untimely deaths of two board members.

Amelia Bronston (Van Fleet), the acting chair since the death of her brother, vetoes their vote. West attempts to visit her and discuss the issue at her home, but is barred by her servants. He climbs in through a second story window and encounters Amelia's secretary, Kyra Vanders (Sommers). Amelia enters and decides to listen to West when he informs her that yet another, board member was murdered that very day. The murdered board member had met with West to tell him of a plot to dump stock and create a panic, thus making a killing when the stock is driven down. Amelia still refuses to allow West to offer the board protection. She explains that she believes that her brother, Simon, died of heart disease brought on by dealing with the other members. West meets Lionel (Carlson), who is Simon's son. Amelia dismisses West but, as he departs, he baits them by stating that Simon did not die of a heart attack, but was also murdered.

Amelia and Lionel pay a call to West at the train. Lionel calls a truce, saying he'll work with West for now. Amelia announces at the next meeting that if West is to protect them, then he should have the commensurate position of acting chair. They concur since otherwise she would veto his offer of protection.

West orders Lionel to search stock certificates for different companies that use the same address. Lionel finds a common address and heads there himself. He is followed by West to a weird saloon that features circus entertainment. The bartender claims not have seen Lionel, but West finds a cigar butt of the recognizably cheap variety that Lionel smokes. The bartender agrees to check the back and asks West to be seated. West enjoys the seal act until the seal bounces a ball directly to his table. The agent escapes the ensuing explosion just in time. West fights off several attackers and makes it to the storeroom where he frees the captive Lionel. The men find a duplicate boardroom, complete with a replica machine gun mounted on a display and mannequins representing the board members.

Both men are knocked unconscious by the mannequins, who turn out to be live people. They are tied back to back with an arrow rigged to shoot them

204

when a candle burns through a rope. They rock their chairs back and forth and manage to tip over in time to escape and rush back to the real boardroom. West shouts to the members to duck just as the machine gun starts shooting. He tells them all to remain down on the floor and stay quiet. Amelia is disappointed to see them all alive when she enters the room.

Now exposed, Amelia pulls a gun on Kyra and holds her hostage. She admits that she killed her brother Simon when he refused to go along with her plan to incite the stock panic. The other board members were killed when they each tried to stop her plan.

Kyra accidentally hits the elevator button when Amelia knocks her aside. The door closes and the elevator leaves while Amelia explains that the members will die courtesy of a new device the company has developed. Ignoring West's attempt to warn her, she steps backward and falls to her death down the open elevator shaft.

Lionel pays West a visit at the train, West thinks the feisty young man has come to box, but it turns out he just wanted to announce his marriage to Kyra.

Author's Notes:

This time around, there is no guest agent. West goes it alone, except for the help of a strong-minded youth who thinks with his fists rather than his brains. Look for a flub as West rides into town. He is dressed in his road outfit with the blue corduroy jacket and chaps. A quick cut and back to West shows him walking to a house in an entirely new outfit. That was the quickest change since "Superman." This is the last episode shot without Gordon, who returns in episode number 102, "The Night of the Diva."

The Night of the
Diva

Gordon brings the train to New Orleans to meet up with his partner, James West. Gordon's traveling companion is the famous Italian diva Rosa Montebello (Munsel). Montebello is the niece of the Italian ambassador, and Gordon was gracious enough to provide her with transportation to her next appearance. In return, she gave him nothing but

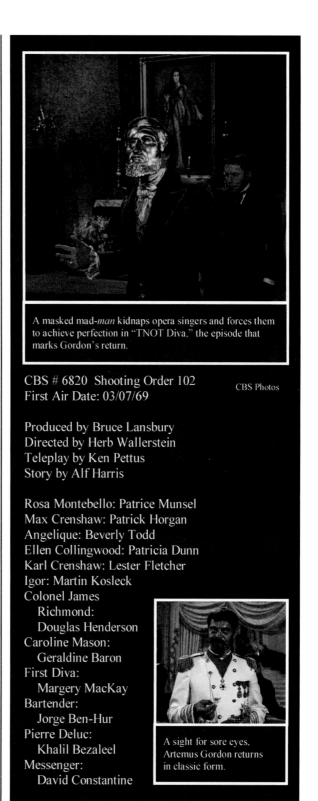

A masked mad-*man* kidnaps opera singers and forces them to achieve perfection in "TNOT Diva," the episode that marks Gordon's return.

CBS # 6820 Shooting Order 102
First Air Date: 03/07/69

CBS Photos

Produced by Bruce Lansbury
Directed by Herb Wallerstein
Teleplay by Ken Pettus
Story by Alf Harris

Rosa Montebello: Patrice Munsel
Max Crenshaw: Patrick Horgan
Angelique: Beverly Todd
Ellen Collingwood: Patricia Dunn
Karl Crenshaw: Lester Fletcher
Igor: Martin Kosleck
Colonel James
  Richmond:
  Douglas Henderson
Caroline Mason:
  Geraldine Baron
First Diva:
  Margery MacKay
Bartender:
  Jorge Ben-Hur
Pierre Deluc:
  Khalil Bezaleel
Messenger:
  David Constantine

A sight for sore eyes. Artemus Gordon returns in classic form.

grief during the entire trip. Now he must escort her to several affairs by order of the president.

West agrees to substitute for Gordon at the opera "Lucia di L'Amour." The opera is interrupted when the curtain falls mid-performance. West wastes no time as he dives through the wall, lands on the stage and fights off Montebello's would-be kidnappers. In the melee, Pierre Deluc (Bezaleel), a minor character in the opera, is killed. West notices that he is wearing the ring of the Order of Lucia. Two other divas who had performed the role in New Orleans have both mysteriously disappeared.

Gordon must guard Miss Montebello at the next affair, an event in her honor given by Max Crenshaw (Horgan). Gordon solves the problem of inciting Montebello's potential wrath by disguising himself as the Duke of Colba, a titled European. Rosa is easily smitten by the debonair duke. While at the Crenshaw home, Gordon makes it a point to spy on Karl (Fletcher), the strange brother to the host, Max. He follows him to a room that is designed as a shrine to Caroline Mason, a great opera star who tragically died in a fire years earlier while in town to perform in "Lucia."

West finds Deluc's niece, who confirms the strange goings on with her uncle and the opera that all began after Mason's death. Thugs interrupt their meeting at the opera house.

Gordon enlists the aid of an agency secretary, Miss Collingwood (Dunn), to impersonate Rosa, shrouded by a veil, at her next public appearance. Their carriage is suddenly diverted from its destination. West discovers the Deluc's strange ring opens a locker door in the dressing room of the opera house. Behind the door is a small chamber that doubles as an elevator. West and Gordon end up with Miss Collingwood in the basement chamber, Gordon unconscious and West in hiding.

The two missing divas are in cages and made to sing "Lucia," but Karl is enraged at their inability to match the magnificent Caroline Mason's performance. He orders Igor (Kosleck), his manservant, to get rid of them. Karl now turns to Collingwood. When he lifts her veil he is enraged to see it is not Rosa Montebello. In the ensuing battle Karl is killed. With the charade over, the agents realize that Karl was really the very much alive Caroline Mason, and it was a maid's body discov-

ered in the fire. Mason's beautiful voice was destroyed by the smoke, and the vain diva kept it a secret, spending the rest of her life trying to find a substitute so that Max, her love, could again hear "Lucia" sung as only Caroline Mason could.

Rosa Montebello never realized how well protected she had been. At the next reception in her honor, she is nice to West and Collingwood, imploring them not to worry about being so provincial in an otherwise sophisticated crowd. She frets that the dreadful Mr. Gordon might show up. When West assures her that he was unable to attend, she rushes to share the good news with her escort the Duke of Colba, alias Artemus Gordon.

Author's Notes:

Gordon's back and is a sight for sore eyes for James West and the viewing audience. Martin's return came with a whole new look to his Gordon character, complete with a new hairstyle and less at least 10 pounds.

In this episode, which some say is the best "Phantom of the Opera" story since the original, the story offers a fun twist and a surprise ending. There is a rare opportunity to hear Conrad sing when he vocalizes "Buffalo Gals" as a minor distraction for his would-be assassins. Overall, this is one of the more worthy episodes of the "West's" inconsistent fourth season.

The Night of the
Plague

Snobbish Averi Trent (Wood) is put out when the crowded stagecoach she is on takes on another passenger: James West. At the next small town, the stage is taken out of service. Averi must get to Fort Cordovan, but her offer to pay extra is summarily refused. She decides to sneak aboard and is surprised to find her co-passengers are all mannequins. Unaware of her presence, West and the driver proceed as planned; splitting up.

Outside of town, the stage comes upon an unlawful hanging. The driver stops, arms himself with a rifle and orders the crowd to disburse. All the parties

Lana Wood stars as the snobbish Averi Trent, a troublesome woman who ends up in the middle of a toxic situation in "TNOT Plague."

CBS # 6824 Shooting Order 103   CBS Photo
First Air Date: 04/04/69

Produced by Bruce Lansbury
Directed by Irving J. Moore
Teleplay by Frank Moss
Story by Edward Adamson

Averi Trent: Lana Wood
Drummer: Cliff Norton
Duncan Lansing: William Bryant
Guild: John Hoyt
Colonel James Richmond: Douglas Henderson
Malcolm Lansing: James Lanphier
Stillis: Eddie Firestone
Mexican Matron: Pilar del Rey
Stacey: Wayne Cochran
Ben: Steve Raines
Sheriff: Bill Zuckert
Olin: Dan Cass
Stagehand: Doug Pence

involved, including the condemned man, turn on the driver and demand the stagecoach strongbox. West suddenly steps out from behind some bushes and orders them all to drop their weapons. Averi picks this time to emerge from the stage and is grabbed by the band of crooks and held as a hostage. They escape, with the exception of one man who is ill. The driver takes him to town to see a doctor while West pursues the outlaws and Averi.

Averi explains she is the governor's daughter and tries to buy her freedom. She offers to pay them if they will take her to Fort Cordovan and release her. The crooks appear to agree but actually write a ransom note. West intercepts the messenger and realizes that the life of the governor's daughter is at stake. When he attempts to rescue her from the crooks' campsite, she alerts her captors and they tie West up.

In town, Artemus Gordon is being inoculated by a doctor. The sick criminal, after oddly spouting Shakespeare from his deathbed, succumbs to a highly contagious disease, fatal to those not protected by inoculation. Artemus must reach West within three days to inoculate him in time. Gordon contrives, through disguise, to be hired as a last-minute replacement to portray Falstaff in a traveling group of actors whose troupe has appeared in towns that have recently suffered various crimes. He manages to rifle through the possessions of the troupe leader and discovers that he is the brother of the leader of the band of criminals. They are planning to meet at a prearranged date at Red Rock Cave.

Gordon forges a letter requesting a change of plans and to please come immediately. Gordon can then follow him and hopefully find West. By showing her the ransom note, West convinces Averi to cooperate. Once she is safely in his custody they are able to escape. West remains in the area to stalk the band of men and find a way to arrest them. As they battle at the entrance to Red Rock Cave, Gordon arrives right behind the actor/brother and locates West and Averi. He inoculates them both. The agents convince the criminals that they, too, must all be inoculated. Since they are experiencing the early symptoms of the plague, they easily surrender and receive treatment.

Later, Averi brings her fiancé, Donald, to meet the agents at the train. Given Averi's instant dislike when she first met West, they are amazed to see that Donald is the spitting image of the dashing agent.

Author's Notes:
Too bad "The Wild Wild West" had to go off the air by airing this episode. This is a very basic story with nothing exciting going on for the entire hour. "Plague" was a sickly farewell to a wonderful series.

The Night of the
Cossacks

Guy Stockwell (seated), Nina Foch (left) and Jennifer Douglas star in "The Night of the Cossacks," a "West" with a Russian flair and a rather disappointing ending to a great series.

CBS # 6822 Shooting Order 104   CBS Photo
First Air Date: 03/21/69

Produced by Bruce Lansbury
Directed by Mike Moder
Written by Oliver Crawford

Prince Gregor: Guy Stockwell
Duchess Sophia: Nina Foch
Princess Lina: Jennifer Douglas
Count Balkovitch: John Van Dreelen
Petrovsky: Oscar Beregi Jr.
Captain Zaboff: Donnelly Rhodes
Sheriff Corby: Norman Leavitt
Bishop Kucharyk: Ivan Triesault
Cossack #1: Tim Burns
Priest: Luis de Córdova
Maria: Alizia Gur
Sorkhev: Sonny Klein
Grobe: Nikita Knatz
Cossack #2: Michael Kriss

West joins up with a band of Karovnians making their way to a Russian settlement in America: New Petersburg. The Captain of the Guard, Zaboff (Rhodes), resents the implication that his manpower cannot sufficiently guard Duchess Sophia (Foch), her nephew Prince Gregor (Stockwell), and her niece Princess Lina (Douglas). They are being pursued by the evil Count Balkovitch (Van Dreelen), who has recently murdered the rightful leader of Karovnia, Sophia's late husband.

In order for Prince Gregor to take up the throne with full cooperation of the Karovnian people, he must retrieve a sacred icon from New Petersburg. Whoever possesses the icon will unite the people. Balkovich trails after them in hopes of taking the icon from the prince, who is the only one who knows where the precious item is kept.

Gordon is in New Petersburg and finds the townsfolk fleeing because they are aware of the warring factions that will soon be descending upon them. The sheriff (Leavitt) refuses to do anything since the problem is not really a local matter. When the royal Karovnians make camp for the night, Princess Lina is kidnapped. She leaves behind a note she had received, but it is in Russian. Lina is in Balkovitch's custody and he is threatening to marry her and thus unite the two opposing factions.

Sheltered inside a mining cave, Balkovitch is about to torture Lina for refusing to tell him where the icon is located. West intervenes but is overcome and dropped into a bottomless pit. He manages to climb out just before the ledge he landed on breaks away. By now Gregor is willing to trade the icon for his sister, but the agents refuse, knowing the Balkovich intends to kill her anyway.

Arriving in New Petersburg, West accompanies Gregor while he claims the icon from the Russian priests. Balkovitch is held up across the street and taunts them with an offer to trade Lina for the icon. He gives them until morning to decide.

West and Gordon devise a con game. West brings one of Balkovitch's men, unconscious, into the building the royals are using and announces he is the one who will tell them which of the royal party is a traitor. He and Gordon make a big show out of locking him in the cellar. Later, Gordon apprehends Duchess Sophia as she plunges a knife into what she believed was the sleeping Balkovitch guard. Lina must still be rescued. Working as a team, West frees her by sneaking upstairs to untie her bonds while Gordon distracts attention by coming through the front door disguised as a priest bearing the icon.

When the icon is opened it squirts ink onto Balkovitch's face. There is a prolonged fight and the sheriff finally arrives to take the attempted usurpers into custody. West and Gordon explain to the Prince and the Captain of the Guard that they suspected Sophia after Gordon had the Russian note translated. It contained a term that was a familiar endearment from an older to a younger person. Apparently, Sophia couldn't accept that she would have no power once Gregor ascended the throne.

Gordon appears briefly as a Russian priest with a surprising icon. This really makes the episode.

Prince Gregor invites the agents to his coronation and his impending marriage. He is now reconciled to his choice of their servant Maria (Gur), the blushing bride to be. The agents want to indoctrinate the Russians to a local tradition, namely, kissing the bride. Gregor insists they wait until after the ceremony.

Author's Notes:

"Cossacks" was the final show for "The Wild Wild West" in shooting order, but not in air date. Many changes prevented the show from being the way it was intended to be when originally conceptualized by the brilliant Michael Garrison. The Acts of Violence issue seemed to target "West" and restricted the use of guns and fighting, the kiss of death to a show of this type.

Director Mike Moder recalled, "Because of the big fight on horseback, I wanted to go on location. Back then you made do on a stage or with the back lot, so CBS said no to the location. We ended up shooting the scene with tight camera angles, so the audience couldn't see we were by the Los Angeles County Wash, right next to CBS."

"Cossacks features no fancy gadgets or devices. Overall, it was a completely unexciting way to finish the final season and show.

Cancelled: And So the Sun Sinks Slowly on the "West"

Shortly after Ross Martin's return, another problem descended upon the set of "The Wild Wild West." In the front offices at CBS the possibility of cancellation came with an influx of governmental and administrative concerns about the level of violence portrayed on television. Earlier in the season, a crackdown on excessive violence came as a result of the close assassinations of Rev. Martin Luther King Jr. and Sen. Robert Kennedy. Washington created The National Commission on Causes and Prevention of Violence, which indirectly linked video/television violence to real-life actions. The Commission felt that, in the absence of family, peer and school relationships, television became a most compatible substitute for real-life experiences. The Commission also recommended a self-policing policy in networks with Commission-supplied guidelines. A notable reduction in programs that contained violence was encouraged, along with the total elimination of

These promo shots of Robert Conrad as James West were from archived contact prints stored at the CBS New York offices. Above, Red West and Bob duke it out during a scene from "TNOT Vipers."

CBS Photos

violence from children's programming, along with the rescheduling of crime and adventure series in the evening hours, long after children's bedtime.

NBC, CBS and ABC network staffs claimed that the violence was a result of civil disorders and the Vietnam War, both widely covered in graphic detail during news broadcasts. The network executives claimed that they were only portraying the reality of the modern world. But the pressure increased and soon proved to be too much for the networks to withstand.

As a result of government influence, the 1969-1970 television season schedule was comprised almost completely of nonviolent programs. The likes of "The Brady Bunch" and "The Partridge Family" found their way to the airwaves, bringing the focus back to the more traditional family unit (with a slight twist) that had previously faded away with "Ozzie and Harriet," "The Donna Reed Show" and "Father Knows Best," having made room for action/adventure programming. Even Norman Lear's controversial "All in the Family" debuted in 1971, where violence wasn't even a possibility, even though each script was replete with social statements and inter-family arguing, the governmental violence limits were astutely respected.

To demonstrate good standing, Frank Stanton, the CBS network president, called for an overall reduction of violence. The first show to truly feel the iron fist of governmental intervention was "The Wild Wild West." The network imposed tight restrictions for the fourth season with a set of rules for every director and every script. Guidelines set forth included not using chairs, guns or kicks in fight scenes. Bob Conrad and his team of stuntmen were restricted to doing nothing short of physical acrobatics.

In an interview with *Daily Variety*, Conrad explained, "I didn't wear a gun at all. I was an unarmed secret agent. If I caught the bad guys, I would first say, 'Would you negotiate this fellows?'" "West" stunts were allowed fisticuffs, but many of the punches were edited. "They scored the pictures so that, instead of hearing a punch land, you would hear music instead. I would flip a stuntman with Judo; it was a ballet," Conrad said. " Through most episodes in the fourth season, the quelled violence was painfully evident.

After Ross Martin's return, there were only three more episodes shot. In March of 1969, while on hiatus, the word from the network came to producer Bruce Lansbury: "The Wild Wild West" had been canceled due to excessive violence. For much of the cast and crew, the cancellation was a complete surprise, but Lansbury had been forewarned by the network's upper echelons that the axe was about to fall.

TNOT Golden Cobra

TNOT Doomsday Formula

TNOT Raven

TNOT Falcon

Director Irving Moore found the circumstances questionable. "To this day I don't know why it was cancelled. When you look at 'The Wild Wild West,' you can't consider it violent. Yes, there were shootings, but things were done tongue-in-cheek. Nowadays, I call TV violent. I'd get Bob in a situation where he was surrounded by 12 men and he does them all in. Everybody knows that can't be done," Moore said.

Former producer John Mantley felt that the series did not demonstrate true violence. "The show was the first victim of the anti-violence crusade. 'Gunsmoke' also felt the crunch by re-editing the main title where the shooting occurred."

Ethel Winant said that CBS could have made "The Wild Wild West" less violent, but it would be difficult to do the show without a certain degree of violence. It was, after all, a spy show dressed as a Western. Both elements constitute a certain amount of reasonable violence in order to effectively depict a time and place, albeit somewhat fictional, where villains confront the heroes – the classic good against evil quest. How does one prevail without the element of violence? By comparison, television today barely considers the violence factor. The FCC will get a performer in far deeper trouble for espousing expletives than for espousing blood.

When the cast was informed of the show's demise, Robert Conrad was out doing a rodeo benefit for crippled children. Conrad had been warned of the impending cancellation so it came as no real surprise to the actor. "I had mixed emotions. I thought, it's too bad they're canceling the show because of politics. But on the other hand, they may have canceled the show at the appropriate time. Maybe someone was going to get seriously hurt. We got real close to that on more occasions than I care to remember."

Conrad realized the show was becoming increasingly dangerous with another close call during the filming of "The Night of the Cossacks," the final episode shot. "I realized that you can't look danger in the face and thumb your nose too many times," Conrad said. "In the last show, I was hurt again. I wasn't hurt seriously, I was just damaged. I wasn't carted out on a stretcher to an ambulance, like I had been in the past, but I thought, 'Geez, this is no way to make a living.'" Conrad's damage was a knee injury.

Ross Martin was not upset at the cancellation, but rather looked at it from a pragmatic standpoint. Olavee Martin recalled her husband's feelings at the time of the cancellation. "He felt the network was making a major mistake, financially. He saw the potential of 'The Wild Wild West' going on and on and on.

"He was tired and he didn't have to work, so he wasn't disappointed, economically. He felt the network had been pressured into dropping the show because of the investigation going on in Washington on violence. To make a point about violence, they had people write down how many were killed, hit, how many fights, and it upset Ross to think that someone wasn't bright enough to understand the 'The Wild Wild West' wasn't violent. It was a comic strip, tongue-in-cheek; it was James Bond in the 1800s. He thought it was a misjudgment on their part to cancel it because it could have run for a few more years."

In a strange and fitting swan song for the show, Ross Martin was nominated by The Academy of Television Arts and Sciences for an Emmy Award for outstanding continuing performance by an actor in a leading role in a dramatic series. The role of Artemus Gordon, with all its pains and pleasures, finally paid off for Martin.

Olavee recalled, "Ross was extremely flattered by the nomination, but he also felt it was appropriate." The other nominees were Carl Betz for "Judd for the Defense," Raymond Burr for "Ironside," Peter Graves for "Mission: Impossible and Martin Landau for "Mission: Impossible. Carl Betz took the award that year and Martin was very happy for the winner. He was, naturally, disappointed, but he loved the idea of finally being recognized with the nomination.

According to various sources, the violence issue was only part of the reason for "West's" demise. It was the consensus that CBS considered Robert Conrad too hot to handle because of earlier experiences with the actor. The network needed to protect their investment, and, as was proven with previous production costs, a hearty investment it was. They likely felt the element of risk was too great to continue filming. Considering the risks taken by stunt performers every week, the risk was even greater than with most programs.

"The Wild Wild West" could be considered a scapegoat or example, showing the government watchdogs that CBS was fully cooperating by eliminating programs that were considered violent, but then pushing the show immediately into syndication,

TNOT Doomsday Formula

TNOT Amnesiac

TNOT Undead

TNOT Camera

TNOT Big Blackmail

fetching substantial financial returns for the network and minimizing costs. If the show had been cancelled exclusively for the violence factor, then the reruns would have been of equal concern to the network and the watchdog agencies. Instead, the rights to the show were purchased by Viacom International in 1970, creating nationwide distribution that made the show successful even 20 (now 40) years later.

During the series' final season, Robert Conrad was drawing a healthy $5,000 per episode with 100% residuals for four years. Conrad went on with a very successful career, later creating his own film company, the A. Shane Company, named for his son. He produced several successful television series and TV movies. He was later seen in "Assignment Vienna" and "Baa Baa Black Sheep" (AKA "Black Sheep Squadron") among several guest appearances. His turn at self-parody on "Saturday Night Live" was truly memorable.

Ross Martin's career also progressed, but in a different direction than Conrad's. As a result of his heart condition, he had a difficult time landing a series of his own. It was obvious that networks wouldn't take the chance on the possibility of another attack mid-production. While not seeing Martin on a regular basis was definitely a tragic loss for fans, he did become the darling of guest appearances through the mid-1970s. He also appeared on numerous talk shows and game shows.

James West and Artemus Gordon, the likes of which television audiences will never again see. The team was TV genius, the concept, unlike anything before or since. It was truly a remarkable program.

Editor's Note: At the time this book was originally published in 1988, "The Wild Wild West" had only rested in the archives of television history for a mere 20 years. Now, for the second printing of this book, another 20 years have passed and "The Wild Wild West" continues to charm and intrigue audiences through reruns and DVD releases.

"He really did that to keep busy," Olavee said. "Sometimes he would accept roles that were quite small and insignificant to the story, but he liked the role. I would ask him, 'Why do this?' Ross would say, 'I kind of like the flavor of this guy,' and he'd just do it for fun." Ross Martin died of a massive heart attack in July of 1981. His performances will forever keep his legacy alive.

One hundred four episodes were syndicated. One hundred four episodes became a memorable part of television history. From black and white to color; through change upon change upon change; through trials, pitfalls, pratfalls, broken legs, broken skulls, costly sets, ingenious gadgets and equally as ingenious disguises, hues of yesterday perfectly mixed with glimpses of the future; all this was "The Wild Wild West." All this was silently slipping into the memory of tens of thousands of baby-boomers. Gone, but never forgotten: James T. West and Artemus Gordon, secret agents extraordinaire.

213

TNOT Lord of Limbo

Chapter 11
Goofs, Gaffs and Guffaws ...

Put that back on!

James West in hot pursuit... in a golf cart.

Paulsen's bid for the White House

You want me to go to *whose* island?!?

214

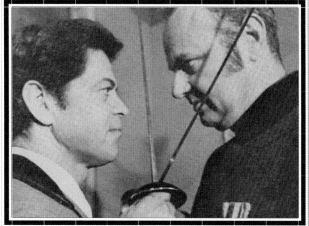

It's a duel to the death between Gordon and the Baron.

Well… maybe not.

Hold it right there!

They went that-a-way. Or maybe it was this-a-way.

Chapter 12
A Day on the Set

A typical day on "The Wild Wild West" set started at 6:00 am. when the crew arrived and the sets prepared. Stunts were blocked out and scenes rehearsed. Stars Robert Conrad and Ross Martin began their day with a trip to makeup and wardrobe – ready to roll by call time.

The location of the scheduled scenes and the difficulty of the shots would determine how the day would fare. Lunch was called from 12:00-1:00, then shooting would resume. The afternoon brought with it more scenes to shoot, a train sequence, a stunt gag, or a new gadgets from the props department. Conrad or Martin, or both, would appear and the script determined how long they would stay on camera and how long the day would last.

The show was always on a tight schedule, suffering constant changes and pick-up shots (re-shooting). Fridays always turned into 16-hour days. One episode shot for seven straight days, leaving little time for the preparation of the following episode.

After a long day, many of the cast and crew retired to their favorite watering hole, The Backstage Bar, directly across the street from the CBS lot. Despite the often grueling schedule, everyone enjoyed working on the set and fondly remembered their team effort and the exciting series that resulted. Here is the backstage look at a day on the set of "The Wild Wild West."

A perfectly timed explosion (above), and raging gunfire (top right) were all part of the daily routine during "West" shooting.

Script supervisor Harry Harvey runs over some details with Sammy Davis Jr. during the filming of "TNOT Returning Dead."

Welcome to behind-the-scenes on "The Wild Wild West," where shooting could last for hours, sometimes days, on end. Many of the crew members in these photographs unfortunately remain unidentified, but their talents are eternally evident in the quality of the production.

Fourth image from top left, shows director of photography Ted Voightlander (red shirt) and his crew.

Bottom left, Jimmy George (then in the wardrobe department), Bob Conrad, script supervisor Harry Harvey and effects man Tim Smyth take a break for a photograph.

Whitey Hughes and Bob Herron in "Returning Dead"

Ross and Bob Herron chat during break.

Bob and Bob take a breather.

Ross and Bob Herron relax on a camera car.

Camera bug Ross

On location during "Returning Dead"

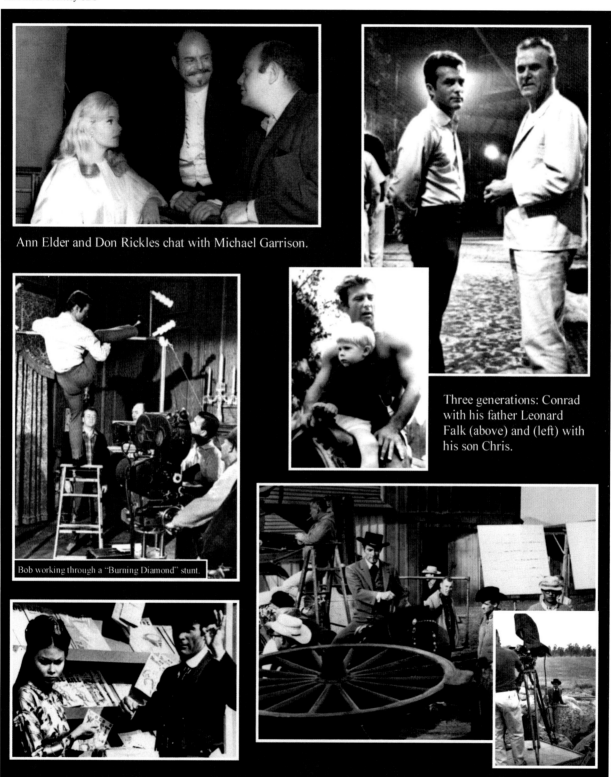

Ann Elder and Don Rickles chat with Michael Garrison.

Bob working through a "Burning Diamond" stunt.

Three generations: Conrad with his father Leonard Falk (above) and (left) with his son Chris.

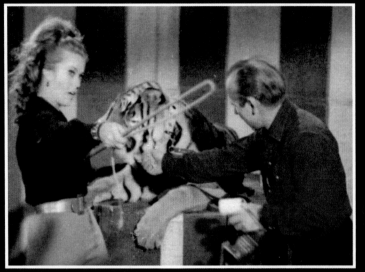

Above left, a kitty moment during "Sudden Death;" right, Conrad and Loggia take a break; left, Conrad tests the "Freebooters" tank with a cool treat; below left, Jimmy George flirts with lady Ross; below, Susanne Pleshette cools down Conrad with champagne after "Inferno"

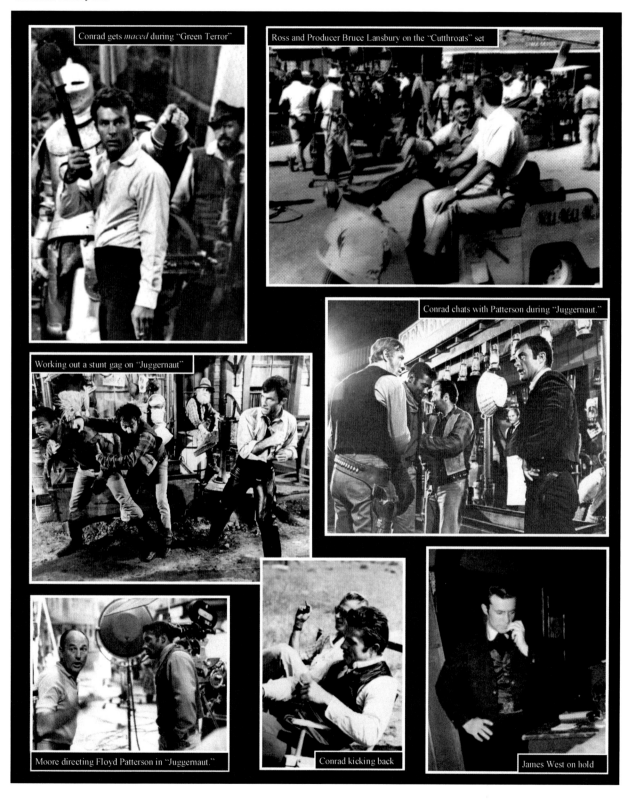

Conrad gets *maced* during "Green Terror"

Ross and Producer Bruce Lansbury on the "Cutthroats" set

Conrad chats with Patterson during "Juggernaut."

Working out a stunt gag on "Juggernaut"

Moore directing Floyd Patterson in "Juggernaut."

Conrad kicking back

James West on hold

Chapter 13
TV Movies — Old and Wiser

The year of 1977 brought a wave of Reunion Specials to television. Audiences were already pining away for their favorite shows of the '50s and '60s, so the networks saw a golden opportunity to rehash proven material and satisfy the viewers, all with a minimal amount of expenditure. Plus, casting was a cinch. People were anxious to see what had happened to their favorite performers, and loved seeing the familiar characters brought to life once again. The new specials were comprised of old television programs revived as a TV movie. The popular 1950's series "Father Knows Best" was the first in the reunion craze. The show proved very successful and it started a resurgence of nostalgia — a trend that lasted more than 10 years. TV producers jumped on the bandwagon and developed plots for a plethora of postmortem revivals. Among the revived series were such programs as "Gilligan's Island," "Dobie Gillis," "Gunsmoke" and, of course, "The Wild Wild West."

Jay Bernstein, Bob Conrad's publicist at the time, came up with the idea to do a "Wild Wild West" reunion show and promptly went to his client and Ross Martin to see if they would be willing to do a special. Conrad and Martin thought it would be great fun and it would incite a welcome sense of déjà vu in reliving the old days. Bernstein sold CBS on the idea and came in as executive producer on "The Wild Wild West, Revisited."

> Former "Wild Wild West" director Irving Moore said he was surprised that he was overlooked for the two TV movies.

Conrad's prior commitments delayed production of the movie for one year. Shooting began on February 5, 1979, in Tucson, Arizona. Veteran Western director Burt Kennedy was chosen to direct even though the consensus among fans was that one of the series' previous directors should have gotten the job. Kennedy was a former radio and TV writer and moved into the director's chair in 1960. He is known for such films as "The War Wagon," "Support Your Local Sheriff" and "Return of the Seven."

Former "Wild Wild West" director Irving Moore said he was surprised that he was overlooked for the two TV movies. "I think I should have done the first one. There would have been more stunts, because the TV movies had to be more like the series. It was make like they were poking fun at the old series, which was done straight. It didn't work. Also, Bob got older and it showed. He didn't have the crispness, the sharpness, the fun; and he could have. If he had someone standing there swatting at his fanny to make him do it."

Jay Bernstein saw it another way. "When you do an episode it's a different type of director," he pointed out. "Burt (Kennedy) was someone that had done a lot of Western movies and CBS wanted someone who did Western TV movies and not episodes."

Some of the series original crew returned to work on the show. Al Heschong, the first and second season art director responsible for many of the gadgets and set designs familiar to the series, joined the crew. He was still working with the CBS art department and he said he was delighted to do the "Revisited" movie. Another alumni of the series was film editor Michael McCroskey, who had been an assistant editor on the series.

"The Wild Wild West Revisited" was shot at the CBS studio center at the series' original location as well as on location in Tucson. CBS still has many of the vintage sets and train interiors from the late 1960s , but the exterior train sequences were shot in Old Tucson, where an actual 1880s train still operated.

The script was written by William Bowers, who had worked extensively with Kennedy in the past. Bowers had written dozens of screenplays starting his career in 1942. The writer depicted our heroes, James T. West and Artemus Gordon, 10 years after their prime. Their heyday with the Secret Service was over. They're noticeably older and years of retirement have taken a certain toll on both agents. West is found living the good life in Mexico with several wives and a passel of children. Artemus had been traveling the United States with a troupe of performers, having returned to his original love — the stage.

A threat to the U.S. and the world becomes evident and West and Gordon are snatched from retirement to match wits

At right: behind-the-scenes shots of "The Wild Wild West, Revisited." Bottom shot shows director Burt Kennedy overseeing the crew. Both TV movies were shot on location in Arizona.

All TV movie behind-the-scenes photos are courtesy of an anonymous contributor.

223

On location in Old Tucson, Arizona, the crew sets up a shot of an actual running locomotive from the 1800s.

with a cunning, not-quite-new adversary: Miguelito Loveless Jr. Singer, songwriter, Paul Williams played the heir apparent to the duo's arch enemy. Audiences saw the same type of wild and wacky devices, mysterious women and evil villains that made the series popular.

 The movie was based on a fantastic and, frankly, implausible story, similar to the series' original run. West and Gordon played it straight, resulting in a nice balance and a thread of believability to hold it all together.

 "The Wild Wild West Revisited" may have had the same qualities as the series, but the main characters had experienced considerable changes. Olavee Martin commented on the revival of West and Gordon. "They weren't kids when they made 'The Wild Wild West' in the first place. So you add another 10 years on top of that. They would have looked ridiculous playing the same two characters as before. No way did Ross want to pick up like it was the week before. No one would have believed it."

 What resulted was a limited amount of stunts, disguises, enthusiasm and adventure. West and Gordon were not so gung-ho over leaving the comforts of their retirement and appear to find it more of a bother than an honor to save their country from another Loveless. A significant plot twist allowed Gordon get the girl for a change, while another lady dumps West, which may have left

diehard fans a little deflated. Many "Wild Wild West" fans were not receptive toward "Revisited," stating that it lacked the overall quality that made the series popular. The pacing was considerably slower and it moved from being tongue-in-cheek to campy. It was an evident marketing move to cast popular *robot* performers Shields and Yarnell as Loveless' $600 bionic couple, drawing in the younger crowd and an alternate fan base. Nevertheless, fans were grateful to see their favorite characters back in action.

 Airing May 12, 1979, "The Wild Wild West Revisited" was viewed by a sizeable audience and became one of CBS' highest rated specials of the year. It was so successful that CBS immediately ordered another special: "More Wild Wild West." The script for "More" called for the Loveless revival, but Paul Williams was unavailable. The Loveless character was quickly transformed into Albert Paradine II, affectionately referred to as AP-2. The casting search began and Ross Martin suggested using multi-talented comedian Jonathan Winters. Harry Morgan, of "MASH" fame, reprised his "Revisited" role as Director of the Secret Service, Robert T. "Skinny" Malone.

 "More Wild Wild West" proved to be aptly titled since it leaned even further toward the unusual and comedy. Along with Conrad and Martin, "More" starred another "West" alumni, Victor Buono. Oddly, Buono did not revive his role as the devoutly evil

Jim and Artie reluctantly ride back from the sunset.

Count Manzeppi, but instead portrayed a good-guy as the Secretary of State.

On location once again in Tucson, Arizona, audiences followed West and Gordon to AP-2's circus tent in the middle of the desert. Art director Al Heschong decided to use a matte painting for the circus tent. "I found a road that circled to a rise in the road. West and Gordon's point of view of the big circus tent was a matte painting. For the actual shot, the wagons and horsemen coming to the big event were coming along this path and as they drive into the tent we gave them a stake, where to stop, so they all bunched up within this space. Then that all got wiped out with a matte (of the tent) so that they seemed to be actually driving into the tented area," Heschong explained.

CBS was not as fortunate in their ratings the second time around. Jay Bernstein recalled, "At the time 'More Wild Wild West' was scheduled to air the film industry was suffering a writers' strike and, since there were no scripts, the network split the movie in half. One hour was aired on Monday, October 7, and the second hour was aired on Tuesday, October 8, both at 8:00 in the evening. Also, it ran opposite "The World Series." The network decided to try running it again earlier the following year. Our ratings were horrible since no one saw it the first time. Then President Ronald Reagan was shot and the network moved "The Academy Awards" up one day. CBS had schedule a movie called 'Stand by Your Man,' but pulled it and put 'More Wild Wild West' in the timeslot. It wasn't even logged in the daily log, so we got killed twice."

It sounded as though the jinx of the "West" had reared its ugly head once more. This time it didn't involve physical injury, but more a slaughter of the ratings. Circumstances kept viewers away in droves, after all, who could compete with "The World Series" and a real presidential assassination attempt? The end result was a very poor audience response and no more "Wests" were to be ordered by the network.

After "More Wild Wild West," Robert Conrad and Ross Martin parted ways, each pursuing their respective careers. Conrad's popularity increased as he continued to star in a number of television series and movies. Ross Martin's career diversified into stage acting and directing.

The Wild Wild West
Revisited

A tired Artie is rudely awakened by James West as the agents reluctantly spring, sort of, back into action in the first TV movie based on the series.

(From a CBS Synopsis)   CBS Photo
Air Date: May 9, 1979

Produced by Robert L. Jacks
Executive Produced by Jay Bernstein
Directed by Burt Kennedy
Written by William Bowers

Miguelito Loveless, Jr.: Paul Williams
Robert T. Malone: Harry Morgan
Captain Sir David Edney: Rene Auberjonois
Carmelita: Jo Ann Harris
Penelope: Trisha Noble
Hugo Kaufman: Jeff MacKay
Gabrielle: Susan Blu
Nadia: Pavla Ustinov
Alan: Robert Shields
Sonya: Lorene Yarnell
President Cleveland: Wilford Brimley
Russian Tsar: Ted Hartley
Queen Victoria: Jacquelyn Hyde
Spanish King: Alberto Morin

Robert Conrad and Ross Martin are reunited as the intrepid team of 19th Century government agents, James West and Artemus Gordon, in a highly imaginative and incredible romp through the old West, featuring a not-so-new nemesis, Miguelito Loveless Jr. In this far-out adventure, West and Gordon are brought out of retirement after 10 years by Robert T. (Skinny) Malone, now the director of the Secret Service under President Grover Cleveland. Malone has received guarded information that clone-like impostors may have been substituted for the crowned heads of Britain, Spain and Russia. They fear that President Cleveland has also been substituted with a bogus president. The retired agents spring, sort of, into action.

West is recruited from his happy, indolent life with a bevy of wives and children. Gordon is found practicing his stage talents in a rundown traveling wagon show. The dynamic 1880s duo respond to the summons and, aboard their old luxurious railcar are preparing for the task. Gordon puts West through a series of rigorous exercises to get him back into fighting condition.

The agents set out on the trail of the son of their familiar adversary, Dr. Miguelito Loveless. They soon find they must contend with the Secret Service

Bob and Ross prepare for a shot in "More WWW."

arms of Britain, Spain and Imperial Russia as they go about their investigation. They discover that Miguelito Loveless Jr. is no less ruthless than his genius father, from whom he has also inherited a driving compulsion to rule the world.

Loveless has not only captured heads of state, but cloned his own copies to rule in their stead. He has also created the world's first $600 people (Shields and Yarnell in their robotic best and spoofing "The Six-Million Dollar Man"), who are capable of prodigious feats of strength and are intensely loyal to the good Doctor.

Throughout their investigation, West and Gordon meet the usual fare of beautiful women including Miguelito's sister, Carmelita; Penelope, a cool-eyed English beauty and member of British Intelligence (with eyes for Artemus); Nadia, a member of the Russian Intelligence Service, and Gabrielle, a gorgeous saloon dancer who also works for Loveless.

Loveless' intent is to locate the two agents who are responsible for his father's death. (Loveless senior died of ulcers – complications from too many encounters with the indestructible agents.) This is coupled with his larger plot of replacing all the heads of Europe with clones and taking over the world. The real heads are in his hidden cave and are forced to write to their respec-

Jonathan Winters chats with Bob and Ross during a break.

Lights play on Conrad as he takes a break on the train.

tive countries, telling them to surrender. He has also placed various atomic-type bombs all over the world and threatens to blow up the world if they do not comply with his demands.

West and Gordon are to deliver a message to their government. When their superiors find their message difficult to believe, they must take matters into their own hands. Gordon goes undercover as a dance-hall girl to uncover more information in the town. In the meantime, West meets up with Carmelita, who tells him that she has no part of her brother's evil plan and wants to help stop him from blowing up the world.

With the information supplied by Carmelita, West returns to the hideout and finds Loveless accompanied by other concerned counties' agents. Loveless captures everyone and attempts to carry out his plan to blow up his captors. West escapes and overpowers the guard, leaving everyone else free to locate the bomb that is planted somewhere in the cave. The bomb is found and disarmed. West and Gordon must now pursue Loveless.

They meet the demonic seed and tell him they're taking the bomb with them. As they exit, Carmelita asks to go along and advises them that they should leave the bomb behind because Loveless could activate it and blow them up as they carry it. Everyone gets miles away and a large explosion comes from the hideout. The assumption is that Junior is destroyed.

But is he? Carmelita explains that her brother has cloned himself and planted his look-alikes all over the world. West and Gordon decide that they only signed on for one Loveless and choose to go their separate ways, confident that they will have to deal with Loveless again another time.

More
Wild Wild West

Jonathan Winters (left) stars as Paradine and Victor Buono as the Secretary of State in the second TV movie about the series.

Air Date: October 7 & 8, 1980

Produced by Robert L. Jacks
Executive Produced by Jay Bernstein
Directed by Burt Kennedy
Written by William Bowers

Albert Paradine II: Jonathan Winters
Robert T. Malone: Harry Morgan
Dr. Henry Messenger, Secretary of State:
        Victor Buono
Colonel Sir David Edney: Rene Auberjonois

When mad scientist Albert Paradine II kills all his brothers by blowing them up, Secret Service agents James West and Artemus Gordon are requested to come out of retirement once again. Gordon has, once again, returned to the stage and is sought out by a youthful agent who is trying to

A behind-the-scenes shot of "More" shows the lighting setup as Jonathan Winters performs onstage.

persuade the veteran agent to return to action. Gordon says he is willing IF James West is willing. He is confident that his partner will refuse.

In Mexico, West is being shot at by a band of Mexican banditos led by a madwoman. The youthful agent appears on the scene and makes the former agent an offer he can't refuse.

Supervisor Malone briefs the two retirees on the situation with Paradine, more affectionately referred at as AP-2. An extremely dangerous man with plans to destroy the world, Paradine plans on pitting one major international power against the other.

The faithful private railcar is dragged out of mothballs and whipped back into shape, as are our favorite agents. The train arrives in Parson's Ridge, Nevada, where they are greeted by the infamous AP-2. He knew of their arrival and invites them for a dink at the local saloon. He elaborates on his plan and quickly disappears using an unusual invention.

AP-2 invites all of the agents to his desert hideout. The agents are surprised by the Las Vegas atmosphere, with gambling, circus performers and merriment surrounding them.

They attempt to stop AP-2, but he always seems to be one step ahead of them. They are captured and held in a pit of hungry tigers. AP-2 explains his plans to go to Washington and attend a peace conference. There he will incite a war between the powers. The agents manage to escape and head to Washington to warn the Secretary of State of AP-2's plan.

It turns out that AP-2 has planted bombs in all the capital cities and West has just 24-hours to locate and diffuse each one. The agents try to vex AP-2's female companions as to where the bombs are located. After charming them with their slightly more mature charm, they discover that the bomb is in the conference room in Washington.

They quickly return to the room and announce there is a bomb nearby. It is found in Dr. Messenger's briefcase. AP-2 suddenly appears and tells everyone in the room they are about to be blown up. Just as he attempts to disappear, his device malfunctions and he is unable to exit. Gordon quickly disarms the bomb and AP-2 is arrested and cuffed to Dr. Messenger. The two men suddenly disappear. Gordon locates the disappearing machine and throws it into the lake. The invisible Messenger and AP-2 start to search the lake as West and Gordon sail away in AP-2's hot air balloon with their two helpful lady friends.

Well-known actor Harry Morgan (right) plays opposite Winters in "More."

Author's Notes:

The two "Wild Wild West" TV movies are proof positive that you can't go home again. Even when taking the approach of intentional camp, they just can't recapture or even approach the magic and mystique of the original episodes. Writer William Bowers had a flair for the ridiculous and put it to full use for both the TV movies.

All TV movie behind-the-scenes photos are courtesy of an anonymous contributor.

The Final Curtain
for a Beloved Performer

CBS Photo

From the time that Martin had his first heart attack, Olavee Martin was keenly aware that there would be another. The couple felt that they had to live with this looming possibility, so the actor was determined to have quality rather than quantity in his life. On July 3, 1981 Ross Martin succumbed to his second heart attack, dying at the age of 61.

Olavee Martin remembered that fateful day. "It happened so suddenly. The doctor sitting next to him said it was over in less than a minute. It was rough on all of us that were left. But it was beautiful for him. If he had a choice, that would have been it: Playing his favorite game, tennis; wearing his favorite tennis outfit; playing doubles with three others he admired and he was in a place he loved. A great day. He had his sister; everything was perfect. His career was going well. How much better to have said good-bye at that point in time. He had a smile on his face at the time he died. He had a good life. It wasn't long enough, but a good life."

At the time of Ross Martin's death, Bob Conrad commented to the press, "I wept when I heard the news. Ross Martin was, to all of us who knew him, full of loving qualities throughout his life. That will never be challenged. We will all miss him."

More than 300 mourners attended the funeral. The love and support of friends and fans demonstrated just how much Ross Martin would be forever missed.

THE WILD WILD WEST

230

Chapter 14 — Collectibles

A Hidden Fortune in a Nostalgic Journey

Along with any popular television show comes a marketing plan to manufacture items pertaining to the show's originality. "The Wild Wild West" was no different. Since the first printing of this book in 1988, the collectible market has taken off in a way that could never have been imagined. Simple items, such as tiny props from the sets of popular series, turn up on eBay for hundreds of dollars. With the increase in disposable income, and the increase in value placed on nostalgia, price is no object for almost any object.

Early on, shows like "The Man from U.N.C.L.E." and "Batman" manufactured everything from bubble gum cards to t-shirts to plastic crime-fighting toys. "The Wild Wild West" marketed relatively few items compared to other series. If you check out eBay, you may get lucky and find the occasional "West" lunchbox or game. But the rarity of these items makes them not only valuable, but difficult to locate. Here is a list of some of the items available from "The Wild Wild West." Be careful when you're searching for authentic "West" collectibles, as many new items were marketed when the highly forgettable 1999 film version was released. A typical promotional deal with Burger King flooded the market with "West" collectibles, including cheap plastic toys, paper cups and other disposables. Before buying, make sure your Jim and Artie are the right ones.

Lunch Box:

1969 by Aladden Industries –This very colorful lunchbox has action scenes on the front and back with various Artemus Gordon disguises around the edge. The thermos is black and white (must've been from the first season), with sketches of Jim and Artie and main title art. Last checked on eBay this item goes for between $225-$450, if you can find it.

Board Game:

1966 by Transogram Company –This interesting game is played with cardboard figures and a marble shooter. A very colorful cover design makes the cost run high. Check with game collectors for this one. Almost impossible to find, this item would go for anywhere between $200-$500.

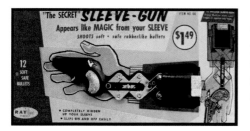

"The Secret" Sleeve Gun:

1966 by Ray Plastics – This device operates by spring action and was designed for younger children. It shoots rubber bullets and was not marketed with "The Wild Wild West' name, but "West" was the only show that featured this type of device. A very, very rare find.

Paperbacks:
1966 by Signet Books – Written by Richard Wormser
A short-lived effort to bring "West" to the paperback audience, this book contains the same story as "The Night of the Double Edged Knife." It is the only early paperback done on the series but, because of a high original production run, is not that rare.

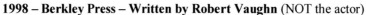

1998 – Berkley Press – Written by Robert Vaughn (NOT the actor)
The Wild Wild West—the Novel
The Wild Wild West – The Night of the Assassin
The Wild Wild West – The Night of the Death Train
These turned up on Amazon, an apparent effort to jump on the assumed coattails of the 1999 film. I found just the three issues; all are credited to the same author and indicate they are based on the popular TV show. Vaughn is apparently a prolific Western writer, but the overall reviews on each volume are unremarkable at best.

Trading Cards:
1999 — Rittenhouse Archives
First season is available, but no longer through the parent site. Local dealers may still carry them.

TV Guide covers:
"West" was featured on two different issues of TV Guide:
1. May 21-27 1966 (Vol. 14 No. 21) features a behind-the-scene shots of Robert Conrad and Ross Martin
2. January 6-12 1968 (Vol. 16 No. 1) features a solo of Conrad in James West costume.

The Book:
1988 by Arnett Press – Written by Susan E. Kesler
The original version of this book is now considered a collectible. It can be found on eBay or on Amazon for anywhere from $75-$450 in varying conditions. Diehard fans have referred to it as "the bible of the show" and found it to be the first comprehensive look at their favorite 1960s drama.

Notepads:
Top Flight Paper Company
Colorful pictures of Conrad and Martin from the "West" series adorn the covers of the 8x10 notepads. The Conrad pad is more rare than the Martin.

DVDs

CBS and Paramount International have released all four seasons of "The Wild Wild West" on DVD. These are crisp, colorful and worth every penny. Although only Season 1 has bonus material, what a treat it is to be able to pause and rewind, play scene by scene and relive the visual splendor of some of "West's" more creative episodes. Available almost anywhere, but Amazon.com seems to have the best prices around.

Cigarette Cards

A selection of cigarette collector cards were made in England and available in the late 1960s. These are difficult to find, especially the entire collection of 14 cards.

Photos:

The search for photo stills has gotten progressively easier with the onset of computers and the Internet. Most of the cinema collectible stores listed in the first version of this book have moved, closed, or can now be easily accessed online. A global search will bring you lots of choices.

Gold Key Comics:
1966-1969 by Western Publishing Company

There are two versions of "West" comics out there. One set is very nicely done, vintage and difficult to find. This series of seven colorful books are filled with action-packed adventure stories. The art captures the likenesses of West and Gordon in issues 1-5. Issues 6 & 7 contain nice renditions also, but more cartoon-like. Condition is a key factor with these collectibles.

In 1990, Millennium Publications came out with a second version of a comic "West." This highly-stylized edition only produced four issues.

Other Items:

If you're lucky you may occasionally run across a 45 rpm recording of Bob Conrad's "Love You," or one of his other releases. These items are definitely a hit or miss and have a greater value to the individual fan more than the *collector*. The "Best of the West" doll was produced in 1999 by Exclusive Toy Products, Inc., and is a very poor likeness of the agent. The plate is from the TV Classics series produced by Hamilton Collections in 1990.

Product shots by Susan Kesler

Chapter 15
The Street Full of Dreams

The Western street and Mexican town square at CBS Studio City that once had James West and Artemus Gordon riding through Anytown, U.S.A., is long gone, torn down to make way for more sound stages, making the lot more conducive to contemporary trends like space adventures or computerized filmmaking. The eerie cave dwelling where our two favorite heroes encountered numerous villains with wild imaginations, and dangerous ingenuity, has long since deteriorated and is no longer standing. The private railroad car that housed Jim and Artie during the many adventures across the country is gone, but not forgotten.

Throughout the world, television audiences have kept "The Wild Wild West" alive in syndication. Reruns introduced generation after generation to the wonders of the "West" and now DVDs bring James West and Artemus Gordon into living rooms, to widescreen television sets or computer monitors not dreamt of in the days of West and Gordon, or even in the 1960s. I find it amazing how so many of the devices concocted by the remarkable imaginations of the talented writers of "West" are now so commonplace, or even obsolete, much like the Western streets on the CBS lot.

I was there, camera in hand, as the buildings tumbled down. Crumbling before my eyes were thousands of memories, and I could almost hear the echoes of a distant train as it slowly chugged its way toward the beckoning sunset. The world of the 'West' had seen its heyday. The richness of the crimson velvets, shimmering satins and gold tassels has faded away. If those walls could speak what tales they would tell. Those walls are now left as piles of broken wood, chips of familiar paint, a silenced church bell tower and shattered saloon windows. A million pre-

The buildings of the old Western town are long gone. But the memories linger on and on.

234

cious moments are cradled on film and only live there now. But there is enough to entertain forever. The voices of James West and Artemus Gordon will always be heard. Robert Conrad's sparkling green eyes and striking physique will grace the screen, while Ross Martin's amazing talent and inimitable smile will continue to entertain and delight future audiences. The wonders of film: It breathes life into a memory, gives voice to the long silent, awakens the magical and ties it to reality for just a few moments in time.

Fan Following

The fans are the blood of shows past. Never is this more true than with "The Wild Wild West" following. Once introduced to the show, aficionados thirst for more. It started in the 1970s with the remarkable interest in the defunct "Star Trek," and it wasn't long before avid fans grew in acceptance. The idea of being an *active* fan in the expanding world of fandom grew into an unrestrained forum where ideas are shared and enthusiasm runs rampant. The market potential was evident to the networks, as they recognized the overall ancillary value of their older properties. It was a slow start, but once fans became acknowledged as a strong buying force, entire divisions were created within the entertainment industry to cater to them. Older properties took on new life as fans flocked to conventions and brought along their wallets ready to shell out whatever it took to recapture that little piece of the past.

With the onset of the Internet, fans connected like never before. Promoting fan events became easier than ever, and attendance skyrocketed. Blogs, discussion boards and chat rooms took hold and kept fans proactive as they would discuss the tiniest details of their favorite shows and speculate on all the possible scenarios that their beloved characters could possibly encounter. Imagination is the key factor, limitlessness the only rule. Some "West" fan sites found visitors fantasizing about Jim and Artie as characters in romance novels. Some took it even further. Others let fans speculate on what new devices may come to pass, while still others might start a conversation about whatever became of our favorite agents, even beyond the TV movies.

It was obvious that early on most of the "West" fans were female. Women seemed to be intrigued by the unique friendship between the two men and combined they made the ideal man: tough and cavalier, yet charming and witty, the cowboy and the connoisseur. Women wondered about their back story, what drew them together, what made them tick? And they wondered who would be the perfect woman that could win the heart of either gentleman.

For the male fan, the focus is very different. They tend to be interested in the gadgetry and the stunts.

There was a gloom to the day when the buildings came down. It was as if a million precious memories were lining up to be forgotten.

Could the falcon cannon really work? Just how did they design the dragon torpedo? All fodder for future blogs as the show is analyzed and discussed over and over again.

The most popular current "West" fan site is **wildwildwest.org** where you'll find discussions going on almost any time of day.

The popularity of "West" comes in many forms. The writers, art director, guest stars, the entire crew were all factors in the show's enormous success. Writer Ken Kolb recalled the wonderful response and recognition he has received over the years as a result of his involvement with the show. "Well, I notice that when people say, 'So, you're a television writer, huh? What have you done?' They won't stop me at 'Wagon Train' or 'Dr. Kildare' or 'Ben Casey,' or anything else. But when I say, 'The Wild Wild West,' they say, 'Really? That was my favorite show.' That seems to always be the response."

Twenty years ago, Olavee Martin spoke of Ross' popularity overseas. She attested that the three European countries that recognized his talent were France, Italy and England. "Ross couldn't walk down the street in any of those countries

The Paradox Hotel, a fitting name for any "West" episode, had long since seen better days. The structures served multiple purposes during the heyday of the Western.

Continued on page 238

A Brief Biography of Agent Artemus Gordon
By Barrie Creedon (Official Secret Service Biographer 1890– 1934)

Artemus Gordon was born to Douglass Gordon and Castalia Eatros Gordon on 5 October 1831, in Baltimore. The elder Gordon, an actor famed for his role as Henry V, wed the Athens-born Eatros, of the Paris Opera, during a Continental tour of Julius Caesar in 1825. Shortly after Artemus's birth, Mrs. Gordon succumbed, at age 25.

Douglass Gordon abandoned the stage upon his wife's death, and opened a rooming house in Baltimore, popular with members of the acting profession. His son grew up in the company of many famous names, including Edwin Forrest and members of the Booth, Kemble, and Kean families, who visited the Gordon establishment during their American tours. The younger Gordon's first stage appearance was in 1843 as Puck in "A Midsummer Night's Dream."

During this period, Artemus also began earning his own living as a translator and tutor. His wife's fondest wish, remembered Douglass Gordon, was that her children be multi-lingual, as she had been. To honor her memory, the rooming house was staffed with immigrants from Europe, the states of the Ottoman Empire and the Orient. By the time he left school, Artemus was fluent in French, German, Italian, Spanish, Russian, Mandarin, Latin and classical Greek, and had a working knowledge of nearly 10 other languages. His facility with languages also served his passion for science. From earliest childhood, the younger Gordon was a subscriber to dozens of European scientific journals and had established a lively correspondence with a number of well-known innovators from all over Europe, including Armedeo Avogadro and Friesrich Wöhler (chemistry); Lord Kelvin and John Tyndall (physics); Ignaz Semmelweis and Charles Darwin (biology), and engineering (Isambard Kingdom Brunel). He spent the summer of 1847 in England as a guest of Michael Faraday, and assisted Faraday and James Prescott Joule in experiments with electro-magnetism.

From 1848 through 1860, Artemus was in great demand as an actor, as well as a teacher of stage combat; he was a formidable fencer and a master Graeco-Roman wrestler. A great success upon the American stage, he also made numerous visits to the Continent, performing for the crowned heads of Great Britain, Austria and Russia, among others.

In May of 1860, Douglass Gordon died and Artemus returned to Baltimore, where he made the acquaintance of a recent West Point graduate, James West. Assigned to the Department of War, West was working on the creation of a new agency to be called the Secret Service. Tired of touring, Gordon was pleased to learn the agency was looking for candidates fluent in foreign languages, and he soon found employment as a consultant. The position was short-lived, however, as plans for the agency were shelved at the beginning of the War Between the States.

Gordon fought bravely for the Northern cause with the 2nd Regiment Cavalry of Baltimore, achieving the rank of captain. After the war, he returned to the stage until 1869, when he was again lured by the Secret Service, which had been officially established in July of 1865. James West had been with the service since its formal inception and was instrumental in securing Gordon's appointment as an agent.

Gordon retired from government service in 1890, and wrote several books about his experiences on the stage and as a government agent. The most memorable of these are *Polonius in Potsdam*, which Mark Twain wryly praised as nearly as fine a read as *Innocents Abroad; The Scientist*, a memoir of the years-long fight to bring Miguelito Loveless to justice; and *Is Spying in Your Future?*, a humorous tome aimed at youth, describing a career option offering, not only fun and profit, but also the opportunity to be shot at on a regular basis.

Artemus Gordon died on February 12, 1900. He was survived by a son, James Douglass Gordon. His wife, Lily Fortune Gordon, predeceased him in 1889.

The Street Full of Dreams
(continued from page 236)

without being recognized. They loved 'The Wild Wild West.'"

Martin was also an easy catch when it came to accommodating autograph-seeking fans. "In our 15 years together he must have been photographed with strangers thousand of times. He was a loveable, warm person and everybody knew if they asked him he would say yes. He was just that kind of person." She also recalled how Ross would always credit his fans for his popularity.

Shortly before his death, Ross Martin reflected on the popularity of "The Wild Wild West." "First of all, there was something special we had in the 'West.' We've rapped about it for years; analyzing it, dissecting it, exploring it. And I've come to the conclusion: I don't understand it. But truly, it must have been a remarkable combination of factors. There was something special about 'West' and the team of Artie and Jim. At the time we were doing it I was so deeply involved with 'West' I wasn't aware of the real magic that was happening on screen. We were just trying to survive; survive and give the show the best we had. Bob (Conrad) liked to call it his *both knees performing*. And that's just what we were doing. Just performing the best we knew how."

238

A Brief Biography of Agent James T. West
By Becky Ratliff
(Official Secret Service Biographer 1935-1948)

On July 2,1842, Gerald West and Laura West of Springfield, Illinois, welcomed their first child, James Thompson West. James was named for his Uncle James, who had died years before, and his mother's maiden name of Thompson. Two more children were to follow, William Gerald, then Julia Grace.

Just weeks after the birth of Julia, the family packed up and moved to Chicago. Chicago had more to offer than Springfield ever had to Jim. And that's when Jim's troubles began.

When Jim entered his teens, he began a rebellious stage: not going to school, getting into fights when he did go to school. After Jim disappeared for two days on what he told his parents was an Indian Survival course, Gerald West had no other choice but to send his son to military school.

To everyone's amazement, Jim adapted well to military school. His academics improved greatly. He also enrolled in all the school's athletic programs. Two programs he seemed to excel at were boxing and swimming.

During his first semester break at home, his parents noticed the change in Jim. They knew that they'd made the right decision.

When Jim graduated from military school in the spring of 1860, he decided to join the Union Army. Jim had already made it to the rank of captain by the time the Civil War broke out. His ability of leadership as well as his military school training caught the eye of General Ulysses Grant.

After the war ended, President Andrew Johnson offered him a job as head of the Washington D.C. security team. By the time Ulysses Grant was elected to office, he had another job in mind for Jim: working for the Secret Service of the United States. It was there he was assigned his first and only partner, Artemus Gordon.

Agents West and Gordon hit it off right from the start. The best team of the Secret Service was born. For more than 10 years, they managed to keep the country from economic and military collapse and were considered undefeatable.

In 1881, at the age of 39, Jim met the love of his life, Leila Brady, daughter of Supreme Court Justice, John R Brady. It was Leila's father who married them in May 1882. Neither Jim nor Leila had a taste for the Washington, D.C. social life, so they decided to settle at a ranch near the Texas-Mexico border. Within the next 10 years, Leila gave birth to five children, three boys and two girls.

It was there at the same cattle ranch, James Thompson West died in his sleep on June 29, 1933, a few days before his 91th birthday. On what would have been his birthday, July 2, 1933, James West was laid to rest in Arlington cemetery with highest military honors.

The Big Event –
The Wild Wild West, the Series Book Launch — August, 1988

In August of 1988, The Wild Wild West, The Series debuted at the San Diego ComicCon at the Omni Hotel in San Diego. According to Wikipedia, attendance that year was a mere 8,000 (compared to 2007 where an excess of 125,000 attendees filled the convention floor). I can say, without modesty, that one of the most popular features at the 1988 convention was "The Wild Wild West" table, where the notable, and notorious, team of stuntmen, along with the gracious Olavee Martin, Ross Martin's widow, and the forever-charming Bruce Lansbury, all gathered to sign books, book covers and meet with the fans. Hundreds lined up to get autographs from Red West, Whitey Hughes, Jimmy George, Bob Herron, Dick Cangey and, of course, Olavee and Bruce.

Arnett Press sold an excess of 500 books during that convention and, more importantly, had the pleasure of reuniting this group of uniquely talented people to reminisce on one of the most fascinating and fantastic programs ever to air. After spending time with this great team I was able to see why "The Wild Wild West" became such a permanent part of classic television history. Even after 20 years, these guys embraced their memories with fervency and joy, and exhibited a special camaraderie rarely seen then and now. It will always be one of my fondest memories to have been a part of this wonderful event and to have had, if only for just the weekend, the opportunity to relive that little piece of history, and revisit that magical and exciting world from my childhood known as "The Wild Wild West."

At right is a copy of the ad we placed in *Variety*, thanking the stunt crew, Bruce and Olavee, for their help with this book and for their participation in the event. We'd like to, again, take this opportunity to thank everyone who was there, and the few who were unable to attend, for their time, their enthusiasm and their undying affection for one another and the "The Wild Wild West." I hope they know what a wonderful part of so many childhoods they will always be, and what a great impact they all had on those wonderful early days of television.

239

1. Whitey Hughes chats it up with Olavee Martin. 2. Red West shares memories with a young fan as he signs books. 3. Bob Herron signs autographs as Bruce Lansbury looks on. 4. Author Susan Kesler with Olavee Martin. 5. The "Wild Wild West" gang (from l-r) — Jimmy George, Whitey Hughes, Bruce Lansbury, Red West, Dick Cangey, Bob Herron. 6. Bob Herron, Bruce Lansbury, Red West and Dick Cangey charm fans with their stories. 7. Bruce greets Red West. 8. Bruce Lansbury signs a fan's book. 9. Bruce and Olavee take a moment to admire the book. 10. Jimmy George (seated) and Whitey Hughes show off their name plates.

Photos by Robert Terborg

Connie Martinson Talks Books
With Sue Kesler and "The Wild Wild West" Stunt Team

On October 6, 1988, Connie Martinson, who hosted a cable series on new book releases, scheduled a shoot with Susan Kesler and the entire stunt team from "The Wild Wild West." It made for a great day of reminiscing, as well as gave the guys a chance to relive their some of their stunt gags as the show was shot out at the Western street at Malibu Ranch, complete with authentic costumes and horse wranglers. These are just a few shots of that great day with the *team* and Olavee Martin.

Photos by Robert Terborg

241

Bob Conrad's Rodeo Days

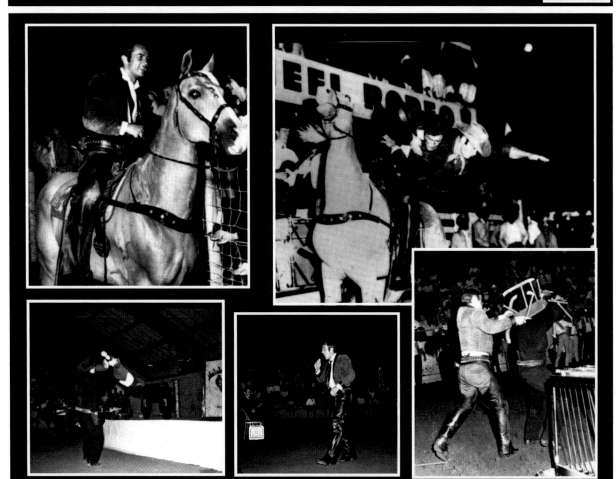

Bob Conrad was well known for his various rodeo appearances during the "West" heyday. He, along with stuntman Dick Cangey, would thrill crowds by performing familiar tackles, leaps, falls and fights for an often unsuspecting audience. Conrad would also give fans the opportunity to hear him sing at these events. All photos above are courtesy of Dick Cangey.

They Can't All Be Gems — The "West" Movie

In 1999, Warner Bros. produced the film version of "West" entitled simply, "Wild Wild West," (sans the "The"). The film starred Will Smith, horribly miscast as James West, Kevin Kline, who was lost as Artemus Gordon, and the woefully misdirected Kenneth Branagh as Dr. Arliss Loveless. This was an unfortunate attempt at reviving (and revising) a classic program, attempting to update it for a younger audience and completely missing the mark. Any fan viewing this offering was likely hoping for a few amusing bits of what made the series so popular. As reviews attested, this didn't happen. At best, one could see a cinematic smidgen of the elements that made the series into a cult classic. At worst, you ended up with a "Wild Wild West" movie in name only. The film fell flat as the myriad special effects attempted to disguise the fact that it completely lacked substance.

About the Author...

Susan Elaine Kesler was born in 1959 in Lynwood, California. In addition to being an author and publisher, Sue is a seasoned assistant editor who has been in the film business for nearly 30 years. Her fascination with "The Wild Wild West" television series prompted her to pursue a career in the film industry. In 1981, she graduated from California State University, Long Beach, with a Bachelor's Degree in Cinema, and has since worked on several feature films and television series including, "'night, Mother," "The Sicilian," "Satisfaction," "CaddyShack II," "The X Files," "Crossing Jordan," and "Heroes." Sue also produced several classic DVD series, including "Get Smart — The Complete Series" and "The Wild Wild West 40th Anniversary Edition."

"Get Smart" was another television program that captivated Sue since her childhood. She was the proud owner of a vintage Sunbeam sports car, a replica of the red Sunbeam Tiger Maxwell Smart drove in the series and has a large collection of "Get Smart" memorabilia, including original scripts.

Author Susan E. Kesler in 1987, still early in her film editing career. Sue wanted to see a comprehensive book on her favorite television heroes, James West and Artemus Gordon, so she wrote one.

Just as Sue's fascination with "The Wild Wild West" led her into a career in the film industry, so did the film industry lead her to becoming an author. Utilizing her industry contacts, she was able to compile an enormous amount of information about her favorite television show, "The Wild Wild West," in order to produce the only complete and painstakingly detailed documentation of the series, fondly dubbed the *bible* of the show by its many devoted fans. Sue worked on the original print edition of *The Wild Wild West, the Series* for nearly two years in order to present to other "Wild Wild West" fans the most in-depth account of the making of the series. As with the original, this updated electronic edition is comprised of exclusive interviews with producers, directors, cast and crew, and contains unique sketches and blueprints never before published.

The Wild Wild West
Shooting Order

First Season	Air Date
1. The Night of the Inferno (Pilot/Garrison)	9/17/65
2. The Night of the Double-Edged Knife (AKA Greatest Train Robbery)	11/12/65
3. The Night of the Casual Killer (AKA Tug-O-War)	10/15/65
4. The Night of the Fatal Trap (AKA Oh, What a Tangled Web We Weave)	12/24/65
5. The Night of the Deadly Bed (AKA Lethal Bed)	9/24/65
6. The Night the Wizard Shook the Earth (Loveless)	10/1/65
7. The Night of the Sudden Death (AKA Circus)	10/8/65
8. The Night of the Thousand Eyes	10/22/65
9. The Night of the Glowing Corpse	10/29/65
10. The Night of the Dancing Death	11/05/65
11. The Night the Terror Stalked the Town (Loveless)	11/19/65
12. The Night of the Red-Eyed Madman	11/26/65
13. The Night of the Human Trigger	12/3/65
14. The Night of the Torture Chamber	12/10/65
15. The Night of the Howling Light	12/17/65
15. The Night of the Steel Assassin	1/7/66
17. The Night the Dragon Screamed	1/14/66
18. The Night of the Flaming Ghost (AKA The Ghost Who Would Not Die)	1/21/66
19. The Night of the Grand Emir	1/28/66
20. The Night of the Whirring Death (Loveless)	2/18/66
21. The Night of the Puppeteer	2/25/66
22. The Night of the Bars of Hell	3/4/66
23. The Night of the Two-Legged Buffalo	3/11/66
24. The Night of the Druids Blood	3/25/66
25. The Night of the Freebooters	4/1/66
26. The Night of the Burning Diamond	4/8/66
27. The Night of the Murderous Spring (Loveless)	4/15/66
28. The Night of the Sudden Plague	4/22/66

Second Season	Air Date
29. The Night of the Golden Cobra	9/23/66
30. The Night of the Big Blast	10/7/66
31. The Night of the Infernal Machine	12/23/66
32. The Night of the Raven (Loveless)	9/30/66
33. The Night of the Man-Eating House	12/12/66
34. The Night of the Eccentrics (Manzeppi) (Season Opener)	9/16/66
35. The Night of the Returning Dead	10/14/66
36. The Night of the Bottomless Pit	11/4/66
37. The Night of the Ready-Made Corpse	11/25/66
38. The Night of the Flying Pie Plate	10/21/66
39. The Night of the Poisonous Posey (AKA Situation Normal)	10/28/66
40. The Night of the Watery Death	11/11/66
41. The Night of the Green Terror (Loveless)	11/18/66
42. The Night of the Lord of Limbo	12/20/66
43. The Night of the Skulls	12/16/66
44. The Night of the Tottering Tontine	1/16/67
45. The Night of the Gypsy Peril	1/20/67
46. The Night of the Feathered Fury (Manzeppi)	1/13/67
47. The Night of the Brain	2/17/67
48. The Night of the Vicious Valentine	2/10/67
49. The Night of the Tartar	2/3/67
50. The Night of the Deadly Bubble (AKA Death Tide)	2/24/67
51. The Night of the Surreal McCoy (Loveless)	3/3/67
52. The Night of the Colonel's Ghost	3/10/67
53. The Night of the Deadly Blossom	3/17/67
54. The Night of the Cadre	3/24/67
55. The Night of the Wolf	3/31/67
56. The Night of the Bogus Bandits (Loveless)	4/7/67

Third Season	Air Date
57. The Night of the Jack O'Diamonds	10/6/67
58. The Night of the Firebrand	9/15/67
59. The Night of the Assassin	9/22/67
60. The Night of the Bubbling Death	9/8/67
61. The Night of the Cutthroats	11/17/67
62. The Night of the Hangman	10/20/67
63. The Night of the Montezuma's Hordes (AKA Montezuma's Revenge)	10/27/67
64. The Night of the Amnesiac	2/9/68
65. The Night Dr. Loveless Died (Loveless)	9/29/67
66. The Night of the Samurai	10/13/67
67. The Night of the Arrow	12/29/67
68. The Night of the Circus of Death	11/3/67
69. The Night of the Falcon	11/10/67
70. The Night of the Legion of Death (AKA Black Legion)	11/24/67
71. The Night of the Running Death	12/15/67
72. The Night of the Turncoat	12/1/67
73. The Night of the Iron Fist	12/8/67
74. The Night of the Headless Woman	1/5/68
75. The Night of the Underground Terror (AKA Brotherhood of Hell)	1/19/68
76. The Night of the Vipers	1/12/68
77. The Night of the Death Masks	1/26/68
78. The Night of the Undead	2/2/68
79. The Night of the Simian Terror (AKA Beast)	2/16/68
80. The Night of the Death Maker	2/23/68

Fourth Season	Air Date
81. The Night of the Fugitives	11/8/68
82. The Night of the Doomsday Formula	10/4/68
83. The Night of the Egyptian Queen (AKA Killing Eye)	11/15/68
84. The Night of the Pistoleros	2/21/69
85. The Night of the Spanish Curse	1/3/69
86. The Night of the Big Blackmail (AKA Deadly Blades)	9/27/68
87. The Night of the Gruesome Games	10/25/68
88. The Night of the Avaricious Actuary	12/6/68
89. The Night of the Juggernaut	10/11/68
90. The Night of the Kraken	11/1/68
91. The Night of the Sedgewick Curse	10/18/68
92. The Night of the Fire and Brimstone	11/2268
93. The Night of the Miguelito's Revenge (Loveless)	12/13/68
94. The Night of the Camera	11/29/68
95. The Night of the Pelican	12/27/68
96. The Night of the Janus	2/14/69
97. The Night of the Winged Terror (Part 1)	1/17/69
98. The Night of the Winged Terror (Part 2)	1/24/69
99. The Night of the Sabatini Death	2/7/69
100. The Night of the Bleak Island	3/14/69
101. The Night of the Tycoons	3/28/69
102. The Night of the Diva (AKA The Return of Artemus Gordon)	3/7/69
103. The Night of the Plague (AKA Long Chase)	4/4/69
104. The Night of the Cossacks (AKA Russian Revenge)	3/21/69

"The Wild Wild West" statistics: James West was in a total of 393 fights with 940 opponents. Artemus Gordon dons a total of 132 disguises.

CBS Photos

Acknowledgments

My first thanks and sincere gratitude goes to my editor and marketing agent formerly known as Judith F. Donner, now the much older and wiser Jude Bradley. Jude took a special interest in this project and, with her vast knowledge and experience in publishing, helped create a book of which I am very proud. When I started this book, Jude came to my "rescue" and guided me thorough an incredible amount of information. Thanks, Jude, I could never have done it without you!

Another very special thanks goes to my production assistant, Tracy Castle for helping put the original printed version of this book together. Together, Jude and Tracy spent countless hours and many sleepless nights with Jim, Artie and myself.

A most gracious thank you to Mr. Robert Conrad for a great interview and for the many years of joy in watching him as James West. Also, a debt of gratitude goes to the late Mrs. Olavee Martin for sharing her memories of Ross. Also, to Mr. Bruce Lansbury for writing a wonderful Foreword and for sharing his memories of producing the show. Their help and support has been instrumental in completing this book.

To the cast and crew of "The Wild Wild West," thank you for being so willing to share your memories and comments with us:

Fred Freiberger, John Mantley, Albert Heschong, Irving Moore, Andy Gilmore, Don Schoenfeld, Ken Chase, Ken Kolb, John Kneubuhl, Ethel Winant, Dick Cangey, Red West, James George, Bob Herron, Whitey Hughes, Charles Aidman, William Schallert, Phoebe Dorin, Tim Smyth, Richard Markowitz, Mike Moder, Richard Rawlings, Ted Voigtlander, Richard Donner, Richard Sarafian, Gil Ralston, Alan Jaggs, Bob Blake, Charles Rondeau, Marvin Chomsky, Cal Clements Jr., Earl Barrett, William Koenig, Bob Phillips, George Anderson, Walker Edmiston, Don Mullally, Jackson Gillis, Sandy Dvore, Jack Muhs, Rowe Wallerstein, Doug Mathias and Joe Ruskin.

And to the following people who have helped make this book possible:

Viacom Contacts: Howard Berke, Terry McKeowan

CBS Contacts: A very special thanks to Regina Berry. This woman really knocked herself out to help us; and to Marty Garcia.

Also to Kathy Green, Pam Barclay, Cap Hartman, Prestige Foil and Patrick Tierney for all their help. For their help with the synopses contained in this book, our sincere gratitude goes to Lori Beatty, Cathy Schlein, Ned Comstock, Mark Sies, Wendy Carter, Bill Kunz, Gilmer Bell, Scott Elisha, Ann Gomez, Debbie (Kid) Bailey, John Weaver, Republic Printing, Duane Greeley, Charles Reed, Dean Gasciogne, Great Aunt Maude, Mil Poos, Pat Martin, Bruce Schwartz, Ann Fourt, Larry Tarpley, Scott Shopshire, Robert Terborg, Terry and Mary Lou Hendry and Frank & Jean Kuhlman. A special thanks goes to Joe Lomonaco who was an enormous help. For the 2008 edition of this book, I'd like to thank Ken Katz, Tim Smyth (our Puppeteer), Todd Smith, Terry Flores, Glenda Tamblyn, John Burlingame, The Film Music Society, Robin Jennings, Corky Quakenbush, Phil Anderson, Bill Wilson, Kris Sabo, Becky Ratliff, Barrie Creedon and Tan Nguyen. I'd also like to thank the "Wild Wild West" discussion board for their fan input on this book.

A very, very special thanks goes to my mom and dad, Jim and Jeanne Kesler, for letting their seven -year-old watch her favorite heroes every Friday night, and for giving so much support when the time came to write this book. To any of those individuals I may have inadvertently overlooked, a sincere and heartfelt Thank You!

This book was created with deep appreciation to the late Michael Garrison, whose creative, bizarre and fantastic imagination made "The Wild Wild West" the classic it is today.

A Poem

by Ross Martin

In that sweet moment
When day
Holds its breath
Waiting
For night to start
Its long slow-motion fall
And shadows stretch
Their full length on the ground
That soft
Suspended
Time
When all the world slows
For some distant sound
I think of you
Of your eyes
So soft with love
Half fearful
In the unspoken knowledge
That beauty
So painful
Cannot be held too long
Suddenly
Sure of death
In that golden hour
I think of you
I think of you

In Memoriam

Olavee Martin

November 2, 1924 – February 3, 2002

Richard (Dick) Cangey

July 9, 1933 – October 29, 2003

Tommy Huff

January 29, 1943 – April 8, 2006

Whitey Hughes

November 9, 1920 – July 7, 2009

Bruce Lansbury

January 12, 1930 – February 13, 2017

Red West

March 8, 1936 – July 18, 2017